IN THE NAME OF

ALLAH

THE ALL-COMPASSIONATE, ALL-MERCIFUL

MAN-MADE LAWS

VS.

SHARI'AH

- Title: MAN-MADE LAWS VS. SHARI'AH
- Author: Dr. Abdur-Rahmaan ibn Salih al-Mahmood
- Arabic Edition 1 (1999)
- Translated from Arabic edition 2 (1999)
- English Edition 1 (2003)
- Translator: Nasiruddin al-Khattab
- Editor: Huda Khattab
- Layout: IIPH, Riyadh, Saudi Arabia
- Cover Designer: *StEyel*, Riyadh, Saudi Arabia

MAN-MADE LAWS VS. SHARI'AH

Ruling by Laws other than what Allah Revealed

Dr. Abdur-Rahmaan ibn Salih al-Mahmood

Translated by:
Nasiruddin al-Khattab

INTERNATIONAL ISLAMIC PUBLISHING HOUSE

King Fahd National Library Cataloging-in-Publication Data

Al-Mahmood, Abdur-Rahman ibn Salih
Man-made-laws vs. shari'ah / Abdur-Rahman al-Mahmood ;
translated by Nasiruddin al-Khattab - Riyadh , 2003

...p ; 22 cm

ISBN: 9960-850-18-8

1- Islamic law I-Nasiruddin al-Khattab (trans.)
II-Title

240 dc 1423/5953

Legal Deposit no. **1423/5953**
ISBN Hard Cover : 9960-850-18-8
ISBN Soft Cover : 9960-850-45-5

International Islamic Publishing House (IIPH)
P.O.Box 55195 Riyadh 11534, Saudi Arabia
Tel: 966 1 4650818 - 4647213 - Fax: 4633489
E-Mail: iiph@iiph.com.sa . www.iiph.com.sa

Please take part in this noble work by conveying your comments to ***IIPH*** *through e-mail, fax or postal-mail address.*

LIST OF CONTENTS

PUBLISHER'S NOTE **09**

TRANSLATOR'S FOREWORD **11**

INTRODUCTION **13**

CHAPTER ONE

RULING ACCORDING TO SHARI'AH AND ITS STATUS IN *'AQEEDAH* **23**

Its connection to *Tawḥeed al-'Ibaadah* 24

Its connection to *Tawḥeed ar-Ruboobiyah* 25

Its connection to *Tawḥeed al-Asmaa' waṣ-Ṣifaat* 26

Its connection to *Eemaan* (Faith) 27

Its connection to Islam 30

Its connection to the *Shahaadatayn* 32

There is evidence to indicate that obedience to anyone other than Allah and turning away from His rulings is *kufr* and *shirk* 33

CHAPTER TWO

THE TEXTS WHICH PROVE THAT IT IS OBLIGATORY TO REFER TO THE LAWS OF ALLAH **59**

The general *aayaat* which prove that it is obligatory to refer for judgement to the laws of Allah 60

Contemplating the meanings of some of the *aayaat* 79

CHAPTER THREE

THE VERSES FROM *SOORAH AL-MAA'IDAH* CONCERNING RULING BY ANYTHING OTHER THAN THAT WHICH ALLAH HAS REVEALED 119

The verses from *Soorah al-Maa'idah* 119

The reasons for revelation 123

Who is referred to in these verses, and are they general or specific in meaning? 129

When does ruling by something other than that which Allah has revealed constitute major *kufr* (*kufr akbar)*? 152

Cases of major *kufr* 158

Ideological (denial and regarding forbidden things as permissible) 158

Man-made legislation that goes against the laws of Allah 171

Obeying those who change the laws of Allah knowing that they are going against the shari'ah and rulings of Allah 203

When does it constitute minor *kufr* (a lesser form of *kufr*)? 208

Ibn 'Abbaas and his comment "*kufr doona kufr* (a lesser form of *kufr*)" 211

The story of Abu Majlaz and the *'Ibaaḍiyah* and analysis of what happened 212

Ibn 'Abbaas and the *Khawaarij* 220

CHAPTER FOUR

EXAMPLES OF THE SCHOLARS' VIEWS ON THOSE WHO ALTER THE LAWS OF ALLAH 231

The *Riddah* (apostasy) movement 231

The *Yaasiq* of the Tartars and Ibn Taymiyah 243

The theoretical angle 251

The practical angle 255

Other examples 257

CHAPTER FIVE

SPECIOUS ARGUMENTS AND RESPONSES TO THEM 263

The first specious argument 264

The reports from Ibn 'Abbaas that he said concerning the *aayah* ﴿A lesser form of *kufr*﴾ 264

The second specious argument

The claim that the *aayaat* refer exclusively to the people of the book, and that the Muslims are not included in the rulings of these *aayaat* 265

The third specious argument 265

That ruling by something other than that which Allah has revealed is *kufr* of action, and *kufr* of action does not put one beyond the pale of Islam 265

The fourth specious argument 273

A person does not become a *kaafir* unless he regards it to be permissible to rule by something other than that which Allah has revealed and rejects that which Allah has revealed 273

The fifth specious argument 302

Comparing ruling by something other than that which Allah has revealed to *bid'ah* 302

The sixth specious argument 315

The narration of consensus that the one who rules by something other than that which Allah has revealed is not a *kaafir*, except in the case of one who denies and rejects (that which Allah has revealed) 315

The seventh specious argument 329

Extending the judgement of *kufr* to include minor incidents 329

CHAPTER SIX

RELATED TOPICS AND ISSUES 339

Differentiating between the *shara'i* system and the administrative system 339

The method of the *salaf* in classifying people as *kaafir* 342

CONCLUSION 353

REFERENCES 357

SYMBOLS' DIRECTORY 370

GLOSSARY 371

INDEX OF THE QUR'AN 379

INDEX OF HADITH 381

TRANSLITERATION CHART 383

PUBLISHER'S NOTE

We worship none but Allah, the One, the First and the Last alone, the only worthy of all praise and thanks, the Creator of the universe, the Lord, the Sustainer, the All-Merciful. Blessings and Peace of Allah be upon the last of the Messengers and Prophets, Muhammad, his family, his Companions and all those who follow in his footprints till the last Day on this universe.

Man turned into men leading to the formation of society. Man and society are thus inseparable and inter-dependent. Sociologists today say that man evolved in centuries, norms, attitudes, rules etc. to demarcate rights and duties for individuals and society to run the society for mutual benefit and harmonious growth. Islam, on the other hand, teaches us that Allah created man and provided him with the "dos and don'ts" to be followed by him and his progeny. This is termed as revelation. Revelation of the "dos and don'ts" from the Lord continued at every stage of history up to the last Prophet Muhammad (Blessings and Peace be upon him) and culminated in the form of the Qur'an.

A Muslim is a person who surrenders to the Laws of God as revealed to the last Prophet Muhammad (Blessings and Peace be upon him), sans any reservation. Anyone who prefers any other set of laws — manmade laws, ceases to be a Muslim. The Muslim societies today are confronted with a number of problems governing their affairs in their respective arena. In the past, too, such situations occured and the scholars of the day discussed the issue.

The research work of Dr. Abdur-Raḥmaan al-Maḥmood discusses the issue from various angles drawing heavily from the original sources — the Qur'an and the Sunnah. Quotations from the writings of well-reputed Muslim scholars — past and present — are scattered through the pages to make the issue crystal clear.

Brother Naṣiruddin al-Khaṭṭab rendered the research work into English for the wider readership.

May Allah bless with acceptance the labour of all those associated with the publication of the book.

Muhammad ibn 'Abdul-Muḥsin Al Tuwaijri

General Manager
International Islamic Publishing House
Riyadh, Saudi Arabia
1424 AH / 2003 CE

TRANSLATOR'S FOREWORD

Ruling by something other than that which Allah (ﷻ) (the Exalted) has revealed is the most obvious deviation from the way of Islam which the ummah is experiencing on a very wide scale.

As the Islamic ruling on ruling by something other than that which Allah (ﷻ) has revealed is not clear in the minds of the majority of Muslims, most Muslims do not realize the seriousness of this deviation and its nature, because the views of the *Murji'ah* are so widespread among the masses. These views say that Islam or faith is simply the matter of what is in the heart, and if a person believes in his heart then nothing can put him beyond the pale of Islam, no matter what he does. This is contrary to the view of the *salaf* and the scholars who followed in their footsteps, who affirmed that there are certain actions which may constitute major *kufr* (disbelief) and thus put a person beyond the pale of Islam. One of these actions, the focus of this book, is the promulgation of laws and legislative systems other than shari'ah, making them binding upon the people and forcing them to refer to these man-made laws for judgement.

It is essential to clarify this serious issue for the ordinary Muslim, so that he may learn to judge any man-made law or system as a system of *kufr*, so that he may know that the action of promulgating these legal systems constitutes major *kufr*, and accepting these systems and thinking that they are as good as, or better than, shari'ah, or that it is permissible to refer to them for judgement, constitutes major *kufr* which puts a person beyond the pale of Islam.

Once this idea is clear in the minds of ordinary Muslims, then the Muslim ummah will not accept anything from their governments and rulers except shari'ah, to rule their lives, and they will realize that any other system or law is nothing more or less than *kufr* and a deviation from Islam.

The author has produced this book at a time when many other books and ideas are being propagated to justify the status quo of the ummah and the position of those who are not ruling by that which Allah has revealed, and to detract from the seriousness of the situation.

This book is a detailed discussion of the extreme views of both the *Murji'ah* and *Khawaarij*, views which are clouding the ummah's vision as they have for far too long. The view of the *Murji'ah* is that faith is simply the matter of belief in the heart, with no link to action, whilst the view of the *Khawaarij* is that any sin constitutes major *kufr* which puts a person beyond the pale of Islam. The author highlights these distorted views, then explains the middle way of *Ahl as-Sunnah wal-Jamaa'ah*, that the faith is composed of both belief and action, and that it may increase and decrease; sin does not necessarily constitute major *kufr*, but there are some sins which in and of themselves do constitute major *kufr* and put a person beyond the pale of Islam, such as ruling by something other than that which Allah (ﷻ) has revealed.

The author quotes the views of scholars both classical and modern, and he also refers to the views of those who hold opposing views, and refutes them with arguments that are based on the Qur'an and Sunnah and which highlight the influence of *Murji'ah* on those misguided views.

We hope that this book will settle the matter for those who are seeking the truth and whose desire is to follow the path of the Prophet (ﷺ) (Blessings and Peace be upon him) and his Companions.

May Allah reward the author for his efforts to describe the path of truth. May He guide us all, leaders, scholars and ordinary Muslims alike, to the way which is pleasing to Him.

Naṣiruddin al-Khaṭṭab

INTRODUCTION

Praise be to Allah, we praise Him and seek His help and forgiveness. We seek refuge in Allah from the evil of our own selves and from our evil deeds. Whomsoever Allah guides, none can lead him astray, and whomsoever Allah sends astray, none can guide him. I bear witness that there is no god except Allah, the Alone, with no partner or associate, and I bear witness that Muhammad (ﷺ) is His slave and Messenger.

﴿ يَـٰٓأَيُّهَا ٱلَّذِينَ ءَامَنُوا۟ ٱتَّقُوا۟ ٱللَّهَ حَقَّ تُقَاتِهِۦ وَلَا تَمُوتُنَّ إِلَّا وَأَنتُم مُّسْلِمُونَ ﴿١٠٢﴾ ﴾

﴾O' you who believe! Fear Allah [by doing all that He has ordered and by abstaining from all that He has forbidden] as He should be feared. [Obey Him, be thankful to Him, and remember Him always] and die not except in a state of Islam [as Muslims (with complete submission to Allah)].﴿ *(Qur'an 3: 102)*

﴿ يَـٰٓأَيُّهَا ٱلنَّاسُ ٱتَّقُوا۟ رَبَّكُمُ ٱلَّذِى خَلَقَكُم مِّن نَّفْسٍ وَٰحِدَةٍ وَخَلَقَ مِنْهَا زَوْجَهَا وَبَثَّ مِنْهُمَا رِجَالًا كَثِيرًا وَنِسَآءً ۚ وَٱتَّقُوا۟ ٱللَّهَ ٱلَّذِى تَسَآءَلُونَ بِهِۦ وَٱلْأَرْحَامَ ۚ إِنَّ ٱللَّهَ كَانَ عَلَيْكُمْ رَقِيبًا ﴿١﴾ ﴾

﴾O' mankind! Be dutiful to your Lord, Who created you from a single person [Adam], and from him [Adam] He created his wife [Ḥawwa (Eve)], and from them both He created many men and women; and fear Allah through Whom you demand [your mutual rights], and [do not cut the relations of] the wombs [kinship]. Surely, Allah is Ever an All-Watcher over you.﴿ *(Qur'an 4: 1)*

﴿ يَٰٓأَيُّهَا ٱلَّذِينَ ءَامَنُوا۟ ٱتَّقُوا۟ ٱللَّهَ وَقُولُوا۟ قَوْلًا سَدِيدًا ﴿٧٠﴾ يُصْلِحْ لَكُمْ أَعْمَٰلَكُمْ وَيَغْفِرْ لَكُمْ ذُنُوبَكُمْ ۗ وَمَن يُطِعِ ٱللَّهَ وَرَسُولَهُۥ فَقَدْ فَازَ فَوْزًا عَظِيمًا ﴿٧١﴾ ﴾

﴿O' you who believe! Keep your duty to Allah and fear Him, and speak [always] the truth. He will direct you to do righteous good deeds and will forgive you your sins. And whosoever obeys Allah and His Messenger, he has indeed achieved a great achievement [i.e. he will be saved from the Hell-fire and will be admitted to Paradise].﴾ *(Qur'an 33: 70-71)*

The most truthful of speech is the book of Allah, and the best of guidance is the guidance of Muhammad (ﷺ). The most evil of things are those which are new-inventions; every new-invention (in religion) is an innovation (*bid'ah*) and every innovation is a going-astray.

Tribulations (*fitan*) have increased tremendously and are of many different kinds. Among the innovations that have been introduced into this ummah in recent times is: ruling according to something other than that which Allah has revealed, and referring to something other than the shari'ah of Allah for judgement. This has become the main characteristic of many Muslim countries and is now a basic principle of their constitutions.

When I was studying the Commentary on *Aṭ-Ṭaḥaawiyah* by Ibn Abil-'Izz al-Ḥanafi (may Allah have mercy on him), in the Faculty of Shari'ah and in the College of Uṣool ad-Deen in Riyadh, I often used to examine what the commentator on *Aṭ-Ṭaḥaawiyah* said about issues connected to *'aqeedah*.

One of those matters was the deviation into which both the *Murji'ah* and the *Wa'eediyah* (the *Khawaarij* and the *Mu'tazilah*) fell concerning the one who commits major sin - what is the ruling on him in the Hereafter and how is he to be classified in this world? Because the *salaf* — the pious predecessors — (may Allah have mercy on them) took a moderate approach to that, it was essential to discuss and examine the view of the two groups who went astray concerning this matter, so that the truth and the correct view might become clear.

The *Khawaarij* — and those among the *Mu'tazilah* and others, of the *Wa'eediyah*, who followed them — believed that *eemaan* (faith) included words, beliefs and the actions of the physical faculties, but they went astray when they made actions as the sole criteria to judge the validity of faith. As a result of this view, they said that those who committed major sins — such as adultery, theft, drinking alcohol, etc., without believing that these things are permissible — were beyond the pale of Islam. Some of them, such as the *Khawaarij*, regarded those who commit major sins as *kaafir*, and others, such as the *Mu'tazilah*, regarded them as being in a state between faith and *kufr*. With regard to the verdict in the Hereafter, they agreed that the person who commits major sin would abide forever in the Fire. This view is based on their corrupt principles.

In contrast to the view of the *Khawaarij* is the view of the *Murji'ah*, who regarded faith as mere knowledge, unconnected to any deeds, whether those deeds were actions of the heart or the body. This was also the view of the extremists among the *Jahamiyah* and others. Or they said that *eemaan* (faith) meant only believing, and that physical actions had nothing to do with it. This is the view of many groups of the *Ahl al-Kalaam* ("Islamic" philosophers) — such as the *Ash'ariyah, Maatureediyah* and others (may Allah forgive them). The belief of these groups is that when there is belief in the heart, there is faith, even if there are other things which may nullify faith. As a result of that, they thought that no one could be a *kaafir* except the one who has disbelief in his heart. They forgot that many of the actions for which the *aimmah* (leading Islamic scholars) of Islam, based on evidence, ruled that a person was an apostate or something else, were merely physical actions, such as the one who insults Allah or His Messenger (ﷺ), or prostrates to an idol, or stamps on the *Muṣ-ḥaf*. They did not stipulate a condition that he should also disbelieve in his heart, etc. Indeed, the scholars discussed many issues where, based on the outward appearance of actions, they ruled a person to be guilty of major *kufr* (*al-kufr al-akbar*), even though he affirmed belief and did not express disbelief, such as deliberately not praying, engaging in *siḥr* (magic or witchcraft), befriending the enemies of Allah, and so on.

With regard to the matter which we are discussing here - the matter of ruling according to something other than that which Allah revealed — we find that those who are inclined towards the view of the *Murji'ah* take the opposite stance and say that no one is a *kaafir* except the one who rejects and disbelieves in that which is revealed by Allah, but with regard to ruling in any way according to something other than that which Allah has revealed, so long as a person does not clearly state that he is rejecting it, then he is guilty "only" of lesser *shirk* (*ash-shirk al-aṣghar*), as with any other major sin.

When Ibn Abil-'Izz wanted to discuss the way in which the *Khawaarij* argued with a number of evidences (*daleel*) as proof, he said, "But there remains an issue which may seem to refute what *Shaykh aṭ-Ṭaḥaawiyah* (may Allah have mercy on him) said, which is that the Lawgiver called some sins *kufr*. Allah (ﷻ) says,

﴿... وَمَن لَّمْ يَحْكُم بِمَآ أَنزَلَ ٱللَّهُ فَأُو۟لَٰٓئِكَ هُمُ ٱلْكَٰفِرُونَ ﴿٤٤﴾﴾

﴾...And whosoever does not judge by what Allah has revealed, such are the *kaafiroon* [i.e. disbelievers - of a lesser degree as they do not act on Allah's Laws].﴿

(Qur'an 5: 44)

And the Prophet (ﷺ) said,

> 'Abusing a Muslim is *fusooq* and fighting him is *kufr...*'[1]"

He quoted a number of other hadiths,[2] then he said: "The response to this is that the *Ahl as-Sunnah* are unanimous that the person who commits a major sin is not a *kaafir* in the sense that he is no longer a Muslim at all, as the *Khawaarij* say; if he were a *kaafir* in the sense that he is no longer a Muslim he would be a *murtadd* (apostate) who would be killed in any case..."[3]

Then he continued to discuss the issue, explaining the *aayah* quoted above and the hadiths which contain warnings, and describe the people who commit these sins as being *kaafir* or hypocrites, or as not having faith. He discussed this matter at length, but in order to avoid misunderstanding, towards the end he said:

"But there is a matter which should not be overlooked, that is, the ruling according to something other than that which Allah has revealed may constitute *kufr* which puts a person beyond the pale of Islam, or it may be a major or minor sin; it may be called *kufr* in a metaphorical sense, or it may be lesser *kufr*, according to the two scholarly opinions mentioned, and depending on the case.

If the judge believes that ruling according to what Allah has revealed is not obligatory and is optional, or he thinks little of it even though he is certain that this is the ruling of Allah, then this is a major *kufr* (*kufr akbar*).

---

[1] Bukhari, *Kitaab al-Eemaan*, hadith no. 48; Muslim, *Kitaab al-Eemaan*, hadith no. 64.

[2] *Sharḥ aṭ-Ṭaḥaawiyah*, Pp. 439, edited by At-Turki and Al-Arna'ooṭ.

[3] Ibid, Pp. 442.

If he believes that ruling according to what Allah has revealed is obligatory, and he knows the correct ruling in this particular case, but he does not judge or rule by it, whilst acknowledging that he deserves to be punished, then he is a sinner and he is described as a *kaafir* in a metaphorical sense, in the sense of lesser *kufr* (*kufr aṣghar*).

If he is unaware of the ruling of Allah in a case, but he does his best to reach the right conclusion, and suffers error, then he has made a mistake. He will be rewarded for his efforts and his mistake will be forgiven."[4]

Here Ibn Abil-'Izz wanted to draw attention to the issue of ruling according to something other than what Allah has revealed. There can be different situation, unlike other major sins which have only two forms — either the person who does it rejects the ruling, even though he is not unaware of it, so he is a *kaafir* in the sense of major *kufr*, or he accepts the ruling but he does it out of disobedience, so he commits a major sin but he is not a *kaafir*.

Think about what Ibn Abil-'Izz said: "He knows the correct ruling in this particular case, but he does not judge or rule by it, whilst he acknowledges that he deserves to be punished." This refers to one of the forms of ruling according to something other than what Allah has revealed, which is a form of lesser *kufr* which does not put a person beyond the pale of Islam. We will discuss this matter in more detail below and quote the comments of the scholars on it.

Hence, as there is confusion concerning this matter, I have written, this book, discussing in detail what has been said about this and have quoted the views of the scholars, both the predecessors and contemporary, dealing this issue.

I have divided this book into six chapters, as follows:

---

[4] *Sharḥ aṭ-Ṭaḥaawiyah*, Pp. 446.

Chapter One: Ruling according to shari'ah and its status in *'aqeedah*.

Here I explained that the matter of obedience to Allah and His Messenger (ﷺ) and connected issues are basic principles of *'aqeedah*, and that they are connected to the pillars of *'aqeedah*, namely the Oneness (*Tawḥeed*) of Divinity (*Uloohiyah*), Lordship (*Ruboobiyah*) and the names and attributes of Allah, and the testimony that Muhammad (ﷺ) is the Messenger of Allah. Here I have quoted the comments of the most prominent *mufassireen* (exegetes - the commentators) and the views of the leading scholars (*aimmah*) of Islam, predecessors and contemporary.

Chapter Two: It deals with the texts which indicate that it is obligatory to refer to the shari'ah of Allah for judgement.

Because these texts are so many — especially in the Qur'an — I have divided them into three sections:

1) The general *aayaat* (verses) which indicate in general terms that it is obligatory to refer to the shari'ah of Allah for judgement and forbid following the laws of anyone else. Because these *aayaat* are so many, I first quoted some of them with the comments of the *mufassireen* and *aimmah* (leading Muslim scholars — Imams), then I quoted the rest of them without comment, for the readers who wish to pursue the commentaries on them.

2) Here I discussed some of the *aayaat* at length, because they contain evidence pertinent to this topic. I limited my discussions to four quotations, with the comments of the *mufassireen* and other Islamic scholars.

3) The *aayaat* (verses) from *Soorah al-Maa'idah* — the fifth chapter — about ruling according to something other than what Allah has revealed. Because this is a lengthy topic, I discussed it separately.

Chapter Three: Under this chapter I quoted the *aayaat* from *Soorah al-Maa'idah* about ruling according to anything other than that which Allah has revealed, and I explained the different forms that it may take: when it is major *kufr* and when it is lesser *kufr*. Because this is a lengthy discussion, I have divided it into five sections, so that the discussion may be clear.

1) The reasons for revelation (*asbaab an-nuzool*) of the *aayaat* in *Soorah al-Maa'idah*; the views of the *mufassireen* and others concerning that, pointing out which is the most correct view.

2) Discussion of who is referred to in this *aayah* - the Jews, the Christians or the Muslims? Are these *aayaat* general or specific? Here I mentioned the various opinions of the scholars and discussed my preference.

3) An explanation of when ruling according to something other than that which Allah has revealed may be major *kufr*, because the verses in *Soorah al-Maa'idah* say that it may be *kufr* or *ẓulm* (wrongdoing) or *fusooq* (rebellion), as Allah says, ﴿Such are the *kaafiroon* [disbelievers]... *ẓaalimoon* [polytheists and wrongdoers]... *faasiqoon* [rebellious, disobedient]﴾ (*Al-Maa'idah* 5: 44, 45, 46). I discussed under this the major *kufr* (*kufr akbar*). It may take three forms:

a) Ideological, i.e., denial and regarding (*ḥaraam*) things as permissible.
b) Legislation that goes against the laws of Allah.
c) Obedience to those who change the laws of Allah knowing that they are going against the shari'ah and rulings of Allah.

I discussed these three types at length, and quoted the evidence (*daleel*) for them, and the views of the *aimmah* — the leading jurists and founders of juristic schools — and scholars of Islam, ancestors and contemporary.

4) When it is considered to be minor or lesser *kufr*. Here I explained the particular case of which the scholars spoke of and explained that the one who does not rule according to that which Allah revealed is not guilty of major *kufr*.

5) This is the conclusion of the previous topic, where I discussed in detail the comment narrated from Ibn 'Abbaas (رضي الله عنه) when he said concerning the *aayah* from *Soorah al-Maa'idah*, "*Kufr doona kufr* (a lesser type of *kufr*)."

Chapter Four: This consists of examples of the stand taken by the scholars and *aimmah* of Islam concerning those who changed the laws of Allah. Here I mention three examples:

1) The movement of the apostates who withheld the zakah and the ruling of the *Ṣaḥaabah* concerning them.

2) The *Yaasiq* of the Tartars, and the stand that *Shaykh al-Islam* Ibn Taymiyah, Ibn Katheer and other scholars took against it. Here I discussed what this *Yaasiq* was and its source, and how the Tartars became Muslim but they still adhered to the *Yaasiq*.

3) Other examples I mentioned in brief, those are important examples.

Chapter Five: This deals with the specious arguments and the responses to them. I have discussed the most important arguments of the people who hold different views, and the response to them.

Chapter Six: This is the conclusion. Here I mentioned other important but related topics:

1) The difference between the *shar'i* system and the administrative system.

2) Denunciation of a person as a *kaafir*, and the methodology of the *salaf* in doing so.

I have tried throughout this book to mention evidence (*daleel*) and to quote the words of the scholars verbatim, even though this may have meant that some of the quotations are relatively long. The importance and seriousness of this research made it imperative that it be based on the evidence of shari'ah and supported by the views of the prominent and leading scholars.

In conclusion, I would like to draw attention to the fact that in this study of this important topic, I have discussed the rulings and cases that apply to it. With regard to its application in real life, that depends on the fulfilment of conditions and the removal of impediments. The purpose of this book is to explain the seriousness of the matter and the danger of turning away from the shari'ah of Allah and referring for judgement to other false laws which go against the laws of Allah.

I have tried my best to deal with this topic. If I have done well, it is by the help of Allah, and if I have made any mistakes, they are from me and from the *Shayṭaan* (Satan).

I ask Allah to show us the truth as truth and to help us to follow it; I ask Him to show us falsehood as falsehood, and to help us to avoid it. And I ask Him to help us to be sincere in word and deed, and to help us to do that which He loves and which pleases Him.

May Allah bless our Prophet Muhammad and his family and Companions, and grant them peace.

Dr. 'Abdur-Raḥmaan ibn Ṣaliḥ al-Maḥmood

CHAPTER ONE

RULING ACCORDING TO SHARI'AH AND ITS STATUS IN *'AQEEDAH*

The connection between ruling according to shari'ah and *'aqeedah* is deep and fundamental. It is not simply a distant relationship that has no effect on *'aqeedah*, rather the matter is more serious as we shall see below. This chapter will discuss two main points, as follows:

1) The importance of this matter, and the principles on which it is based. The scholars' comments which speak of this matter in forceful terms stem from their awareness of this matter.

2) Refutation of some of those who think that the matter of ruling according to the shari'ah of Allah is the matter of visible deeds and actions (as opposed to beliefs), and that any sins that have to do with this matter do not mean that a person is no longer a believer, so long as he does not reject (the shari'ah).

There is a variety of evidence concerning the relationship to *'aqeedah* of obedience, doing that which is commanded, avoiding that which is forbidden, and other issues that are related to ruling according to shari'ah and applying
community level.

— Sometimes it is connected to *'aqeed*
'Ibaadah (the Unity of Worship).

— Sometimes it is connected to *'aqe*
ar-Ruboobiyah (the Unity of Lordsh

— Sometimes it is connected to *'aqee*
Asma' waṣ-Ṣifaat (the Unity of the

— Sometimes it is connected to *'aqeedah* on the basis of *eemaan* (faith, belief).

— Sometimes it is connected to *'aqeedah* on the basis of Islam.

— Sometimes it is connected to *'aqeedah* on the basis of the *Shahaadatayn*.

The *aayaat* which refer to that are very many. We will limit ourselves to quoting just a few examples.

Its Connection to *Tawḥeed al-'Ibaadah*

Allah (سُبْحَانَهُ وَتَعَالَى) says, in the story of Prophet Yoosuf (عَلَيْهِ السَّلَام) (may peace be upon him) and his calling others to Allah in prison:

﴿مَا تَعْبُدُونَ مِن دُونِهِۦٓ إِلَّآ أَسْمَآءً سَمَّيْتُمُوهَآ أَنتُمْ وَءَابَآؤُكُم مَّآ أَنزَلَ
ٱللَّهُ بِهَا مِن سُلْطَـٰنٍ ۚ إِنِ ٱلْحُكْمُ إِلَّا لِلَّهِ ۚ أَمَرَ أَلَّا تَعْبُدُوٓا۟ إِلَّآ إِيَّاهُ ۚ ذَٰلِكَ
ٱلدِّينُ ٱلْقَيِّمُ وَلَـٰكِنَّ أَكْثَرَ ٱلنَّاسِ لَا يَعْلَمُونَ ﴿٤٠﴾﴾

﴿You do not worship besides Him but only names which you have named [forged] - you and your fathers - for which Allah has sent down no authority. The command [or the judgement] is for none but Allah. He has commanded that you worship none but Him [i.e. His Monotheism]; that is the [true] straight religion, but most men know not.﴾ *(Qur'an 12: 40)*

And Allah (سُبْحَانَهُ وَتَعَالَى) says:

﴿لَآ إِكْرَاهَ فِى ٱلدِّينِ ۖ قَد تَّبَيَّنَ ٱلرُّشْدُ مِنَ ٱلْغَىِّ ۚ فَمَن يَكْفُرْ بِٱلطَّـٰغُوتِ
وَيُؤْمِنۢ بِٱللَّهِ فَقَدِ ٱسْتَمْسَكَ بِٱلْعُرْوَةِ ٱلْوُثْقَىٰ لَا ٱنفِصَامَ لَهَا ۗ وَٱللَّهُ سَمِيعٌ
عَلِيمٌ ﴿٢٥٦﴾﴾

is no compulsion in religion. Verily, the Right
ecome distinct from the wrong path. Whoever

disbelieves in *ṭaaghoot* and believes in Allah, then he has grasped the most trustworthy handhold that will never break. And Allah is All-Hearer, All-Knower.》 *(Qur'an 2: 256)*

And Allah (ﷻ) says:

﴿ ٱتَّخَذُوٓاْ أَحْبَارَهُمْ وَرُهْبَٰنَهُمْ أَرْبَابًا مِّن دُونِ ٱللَّهِ وَٱلْمَسِيحَ ٱبْنَ مَرْيَمَ وَمَآ أُمِرُوٓاْ إِلَّا لِيَعْبُدُوٓاْ إِلَٰهًا وَٰحِدًا ۖ لَّآ إِلَٰهَ إِلَّا هُوَ ۚ سُبْحَٰنَهُۥ عَمَّا يُشْرِكُونَ ﴿٣١﴾ ﴾

《They [Jews and Christians] took their rabbis and their monks to be their lords besides Allah [by obeying them in things which they made lawful or unlawful according to their own desires without being ordered by Allah], and [they also took as their Lord] Messiaḥ, son of Maryam [Mary], while they [Jews and Christians] were commanded [in the *Tawraat* (Torah) and the *Injeel* (Gospel)] to worship none but One *Ilah* [God — Allah] *Laa ilaaha illa Huwa* [none has the right to be worshipped but He]. Praise and glory be to Him [far above is He] from having the partners they associate [with Him].》 *(Qur'an 9: 31)*

Its Connection to *Tawḥeed ar-Ruboobiyah*

Allah (ﷻ) says:

﴿ إِنَّ رَبَّكُمُ ٱللَّهُ ٱلَّذِى خَلَقَ ٱلسَّمَٰوَٰتِ وَٱلْأَرْضَ فِى سِتَّةِ أَيَّامٍ ثُمَّ ٱسْتَوَىٰ عَلَى ٱلْعَرْشِ يُغْشِى ٱلَّيْلَ ٱلنَّهَارَ يَطْلُبُهُۥ حَثِيثًا وَٱلشَّمْسَ وَٱلْقَمَرَ وَٱلنُّجُومَ مُسَخَّرَٰتٍۭ بِأَمْرِهِۦٓ ۗ أَلَا لَهُ ٱلْخَلْقُ وَٱلْأَمْرُ ۗ تَبَارَكَ ٱللَّهُ رَبُّ ٱلْعَٰلَمِينَ ﴿٥٤﴾ ﴾

《Indeed, your Lord is Allah, Who created the heavens and the earth in Six Days, and then He rose over

[*Istawaa*] the Throne [really in a manner that suits His Majesty]. He brings the night as a cover over the day, seeking it rapidly, and [He created] the sun, the moon, the stars subjected to His Command. Surely, His is the creation and commandment. Blessed is Allah, the Lord of the *'Aalameen* [mankind, jinn and all that exists]!》 *(Qur'an 7: 54)*

And Allah (ﷻ) says:

﴿ وَرَبُّكَ يَخْلُقُ مَا يَشَآءُ وَيَخْتَارُ مَا كَانَ لَهُمُ ٱلْخِيَرَةُ سُبْحَـٰنَ ٱللَّهِ وَتَعَـٰلَىٰ عَمَّا يُشْرِكُونَ ﴿٦٨﴾ ﴾

《And your Lord creates whatsoever He wills and chooses, no choice have they [in any matter]. Glorified is Allah, and exalted above all that they associate [as partners with Him].》 *(Qur'an 28: 68)*

— and the like in other places.

Its Connection to *Tawḥeed al-Asmaa' waṣ-Ṣifaat*

The most significant of His Names in this regard are *Al-Ḥakam, Al-Ḥaakim* and *Al-Ḥakeem*.

Allah (ﷻ) says:

﴿ أَفَغَيْرَ ٱللَّهِ أَبْتَغِى حَكَمًا وَهُوَ ٱلَّذِىٓ أَنزَلَ إِلَيْكُمُ ٱلْكِتَـٰبَ مُفَصَّلًا ۚ وَٱلَّذِينَ ءَاتَيْنَـٰهُمُ ٱلْكِتَـٰبَ يَعْلَمُونَ أَنَّهُۥ مُنَزَّلٌ مِّن رَّبِّكَ بِٱلْحَقِّ ۖ فَلَا تَكُونَنَّ مِنَ ٱلْمُمْتَرِينَ ﴿١١٤﴾ ﴾

《'Shall I seek a judge other than Allah while it is He Who has sent down unto you the Book [the Qur'an], explained in detail.' Those unto whom We gave the Scripture [the *Tawraat* (Torah) and the *Injeel* (Gospel)] know that it is revealed from your Lord in truth. So be not you of those who doubt.》 *(Qur'an 6: 114)*

And Allah (ﷻ) says:

﴿ ... ذَٰلِكُمْ حُكْمُ ٱللَّهِ يَحْكُمُ بَيْنَكُمْ وَٱللَّهُ عَلِيمٌ حَكِيمٌ ﴿١٠﴾ ﴾

﴾...That is the Judgement of Allah, He judges between you. And Allah is All-Knowing, All-Wise.﴿ *(Qur'an 60: 10)*

Allah (ﷻ) is also described as:

﴿ ...خَيْرُ ٱلْحَٰكِمِينَ ﴿٨٧﴾ ﴾

﴾..."*Khayr al-Ḥaakimeen* [the Best of judges]".﴿ *(Qur'an 7: 87 — 10: 9 — 12: 80)*

﴿ ... أَحْكَمُ ٱلْحَٰكِمِينَ ﴿٤٥﴾ ﴾

﴾..."*Aḥkam al-Ḥaakimeen* [the Most Just of the Judges]".﴿ *(Qur'an 11: 45 — 95: 8)*

And Allah (ﷻ) says:

﴿ ...وَٱللَّهُ يَحْكُمُ لَا مُعَقِّبَ لِحُكْمِهِۦ وَهُوَ سَرِيعُ ٱلْحِسَابِ ﴿٤١﴾ ﴾

﴾...And Allah judges, there is none to put back His Judgement and He is Swift at reckoning.﴿ *(Qur'an 13: 41)*

And Allah (ﷻ) says:

﴿ ... إِنِ ٱلْحُكْمُ إِلَّا لِلَّهِ يَقُصُّ ٱلْحَقَّ وَهُوَ خَيْرُ ٱلْفَٰصِلِينَ ﴿٥٧﴾ ﴾

﴾...The decision is only for Allah, He declares the truth, and He is the Best of judges.﴿ *(Qur'an 6: 57)*

Its Connection to *Eemaan* (Faith)

Allah (ﷻ) says:

﴿ يَا أَيُّهَا الَّذِينَ آمَنُوا أَطِيعُوا اللَّهَ وَأَطِيعُوا الرَّسُولَ وَأُولِي الْأَمْرِ مِنكُمْ ۖ فَإِن
تَنَازَعْتُمْ فِي شَيْءٍ فَرُدُّوهُ إِلَى اللَّهِ وَالرَّسُولِ إِن كُنتُمْ تُؤْمِنُونَ بِاللَّهِ وَالْيَوْمِ الْآخِرِ ۚ
ذَٰلِكَ خَيْرٌ وَأَحْسَنُ تَأْوِيلًا (٥٩) ﴾

﴾O’ you who believe! Obey Allah and obey the Messenger [Muhammad], and those of you [Muslims] who are in authority. [And] if you differ in anything amongst yourselves, refer it to Allah and His Messenger, if you believe in Allah and in the Last Day. That is better and more suitable for final determination.﴿

(Qur’an 4: 59)

﴿ أَلَمْ تَرَ إِلَى الَّذِينَ يَزْعُمُونَ أَنَّهُمْ آمَنُوا بِمَا أُنزِلَ إِلَيْكَ وَمَا أُنزِلَ
مِن قَبْلِكَ يُرِيدُونَ أَن يَتَحَاكَمُوا إِلَى الطَّاغُوتِ وَقَدْ أُمِرُوا أَن يَكْفُرُوا
بِهِ وَيُرِيدُ الشَّيْطَانُ أَن يُضِلَّهُمْ ضَلَالًا بَعِيدًا (٦٠) وَإِذَا قِيلَ لَهُمْ
تَعَالَوْا إِلَىٰ مَا أَنزَلَ اللَّهُ وَإِلَى الرَّسُولِ رَأَيْتَ الْمُنَافِقِينَ يَصُدُّونَ
عَنكَ صُدُودًا (٦١) فَكَيْفَ إِذَا أَصَابَتْهُم مُّصِيبَةٌ بِمَا قَدَّمَتْ
أَيْدِيهِمْ ثُمَّ جَاءُوكَ يَحْلِفُونَ بِاللَّهِ إِنْ أَرَدْنَا إِلَّا إِحْسَانًا وَتَوْفِيقًا (٦٢)
أُولَٰئِكَ الَّذِينَ يَعْلَمُ اللَّهُ مَا فِي قُلُوبِهِمْ فَأَعْرِضْ عَنْهُمْ وَعِظْهُمْ
وَقُل لَّهُمْ فِي أَنفُسِهِمْ قَوْلًا بَلِيغًا (٦٣) وَمَا أَرْسَلْنَا مِن رَّسُولٍ إِلَّا
لِيُطَاعَ بِإِذْنِ اللَّهِ ۚ وَلَوْ أَنَّهُمْ إِذ ظَّلَمُوا أَنفُسَهُمْ جَاءُوكَ
فَاسْتَغْفَرُوا اللَّهَ وَاسْتَغْفَرَ لَهُمُ الرَّسُولُ لَوَجَدُوا اللَّهَ تَوَّابًا رَّحِيمًا (٦٤)
فَلَا وَرَبِّكَ لَا يُؤْمِنُونَ حَتَّىٰ يُحَكِّمُوكَ فِيمَا شَجَرَ بَيْنَهُمْ ثُمَّ لَا
يَجِدُوا فِي أَنفُسِهِمْ حَرَجًا مِّمَّا قَضَيْتَ وَيُسَلِّمُوا تَسْلِيمًا (٦٥) ﴾

﴾Have you not seen those [hypocrites] who claim that they believe in that which has been sent down to you, and that which was sent down before you, and they wish to go for judgement [in their disputes] to the *ṭaaghoot* [false judges] while they have been ordered to reject them. But *Shayṭaan* [Satan] wishes to lead them far astray. And when it is said to them: 'Come to what Allah has sent down and to the Messenger [Muhammad],' you [Muhammad] see the hypocrites turn away from you [Muhammad] with aversion. How then, when a catastrophe befalls them because of what their hands have sent forth, they come to you swearing by Allah, 'We meant no more than goodwill and conciliation!' They [hypocrites] are those of whom Allah knows what is in their hearts; so turn aside from them [do not punish them] but admonish them, and speak to them an effective word [i.e. to believe in Allah, worship Him, obey Him, and be afraid of Him] to reach their innerselves. We sent no Messenger, but to be obeyed by Allah's Leave. If they [hypocrites], when they had been unjust to themselves, had come to you [Muhammad] and begged Allah's forgiveness, and the Messenger had begged forgiveness for them, indeed, they would have found Allah All-Forgiving [One Who forgives and accepts repentance], Most Merciful. But no, by your Lord, they can have no Faith, until they make you [O' Muhammad] judge in all disputes between them, and find in themselves no resistance against your decisions, and accept [them] with full submission.﴾

(Qur'an 4: 60-65)

And Allah (سبحانه وتعالى) says:

﴿ إِنَّمَا كَانَ قَوْلَ ٱلْمُؤْمِنِينَ إِذَا دُعُوٓاْ إِلَى ٱللَّهِ وَرَسُولِهِۦ لِيَحْكُمَ بَيْنَهُمْ أَن يَقُولُواْ سَمِعْنَا وَأَطَعْنَا ۚ وَأُوْلَٰٓئِكَ هُمُ ٱلْمُفْلِحُونَ ﴿٥١﴾ ﴾

﴿The only saying of the faithful believers, when they are called to Allah [His Words, the Qur'an] and His Messenger, to judge between them, is that they say: 'We hear and we obey.' And such are the successful [who will live forever in Paradise].﴾ *(Qur'an 24: 51)*

Its Connection to Islam

The basis of Islam is submission (*istislaam*) to Allah by obeying Him and by being free of *shirk*.

Allah (ﷻ) says:

﴿ وَمَنْ أَحْسَنُ دِينًا مِّمَّنْ أَسْلَمَ وَجْهَهُۥ لِلَّهِ وَهُوَ مُحْسِنٌ ... ﴿١٢٥﴾ ﴾

﴾And who can be better in religion than one who submits his face [himself] to Allah [i.e. follows Allah's religion of Islamic Monotheism]; and he is a *muḥsin* [a good-doer]...﴿ *(Qur'an 4: 125)*

And Allah (ﷻ) says:

﴿ إِنَّ ٱلدِّينَ عِندَ ٱللَّهِ ٱلْإِسْلَٰمُ ۗ وَمَا ٱخْتَلَفَ ٱلَّذِينَ أُوتُوا۟ ٱلْكِتَٰبَ إِلَّا مِنۢ بَعْدِ مَا جَآءَهُمُ ٱلْعِلْمُ بَغْيًۢا بَيْنَهُمْ ۗ وَمَن يَكْفُرْ بِـَٔايَٰتِ ٱللَّهِ فَإِنَّ ٱللَّهَ سَرِيعُ ٱلْحِسَابِ ﴿١٩﴾ فَإِنْ حَآجُّوكَ فَقُلْ أَسْلَمْتُ وَجْهِىَ لِلَّهِ وَمَنِ ٱتَّبَعَنِ ۗ وَقُل لِّلَّذِينَ أُوتُوا۟ ٱلْكِتَٰبَ وَٱلْأُمِّيِّـۧنَ ءَأَسْلَمْتُمْ ۚ فَإِنْ أَسْلَمُوا۟ فَقَدِ ٱهْتَدَوا۟ ۖ وَّإِن تَوَلَّوْا۟ فَإِنَّمَا عَلَيْكَ ٱلْبَلَٰغُ ۗ وَٱللَّهُ بَصِيرٌۢ بِٱلْعِبَادِ ﴿٢٠﴾ ﴾

﴾Truly, the religion with Allah is Islam. Those who were given the Scripture [Jews and Christians] did not differ except, out of mutual jealousy, after knowledge had come to them. And whoever disbelieves in the *aayaat* [proofs, evidences, verses, signs, revelations, etc.] of Allah, then surely, Allah is Swift in calling to account. So if they dispute with you [Muhammad] say: 'I have submitted myself to Allah [in Islam], and [so have] those who follow me.' And say to those who were given the Scripture [Jews and Christians] and to those who are illiterates [Arab pagans]: 'Do you [also] submit yourselves [to Allah in Islam]?' If they do, they are rightly guided; but if they turn away, your duty is only to convey the Message; and Allah is All-Seer of [His] slaves.﴾ *(Qur'an 3: 19-20)*

And Allah (سبحانه وتعالى) says:

﴿ وَمَن يُسْلِمْ وَجْهَهُۥٓ إِلَى ٱللَّهِ وَهُوَ مُحْسِنٌ فَقَدِ ٱسْتَمْسَكَ بِٱلْعُرْوَةِ ٱلْوُثْقَىٰ ... ﴿٢٢﴾ ﴾

﴿And whosoever submits his face [himself] to Allah, while he is a *muḥsin* [good-doer, i.e. performs good deeds totally for Allah's sake without any show-off or to gain praise or fame and does them in accordance with the Sunnah of Allah's Messenger Muhammad], then he has grasped the most trustworthy handhold [*Laa ilaaha illa-Allah* (none has the right to be worshipped but Allah)]...﴾ *(Qur'an 31: 22)*

And Allah (سبحانه وتعالى) says:

﴿ وَمَن يَبْتَغِ غَيْرَ ٱلْإِسْلَٰمِ دِينًا فَلَن يُقْبَلَ مِنْهُ وَهُوَ فِى ٱلْءَاخِرَةِ مِنَ ٱلْخَٰسِرِينَ ﴿٨٥﴾ ﴾

﴿And whoever seeks a religion other than Islam, it will never be accepted of him, and in the Hereafter he will be one of the losers.﴾ *(Qur'an 3: 85)*

And Allah (سبحانه وتعالى) says:

﴿ ... وَنَزَّلْنَا عَلَيْكَ ٱلْكِتَٰبَ تِبْيَٰنًا لِّكُلِّ شَىْءٍ وَهُدًى وَرَحْمَةً وَبُشْرَىٰ لِلْمُسْلِمِينَ ﴿٨٩﴾ ﴾

﴿...And We have sent down to you the Book [the Qur'an] as an exposition of everything, a guidance, a mercy, and glad tidings for those who have submitted themselves [to Allah as Muslims].﴾ *(Qur'an 16: 89)*

Its Connection to the *Shahaadatayn*

With regard to the testimony that there is no god but Allah, the evidence under the heading of *Tawḥeed al-'Ibaadah* explained that. With regard to the testimony that Muhammad (ﷺ) is the Messenger of Allah:

Allah (ﷻ) says:

﴿ فَلَا وَرَبِّكَ لَا يُؤْمِنُونَ حَتَّىٰ يُحَكِّمُوكَ فِيمَا شَجَرَ بَيْنَهُمْ... ﴿٦٥﴾ ﴾

﴿But no, by your Lord, they can have no Faith, until they make you [O' Muhammad] judge in all disputes between them...﴾ *(Qur'an 4: 65)*

And Allah (ﷻ) says:

﴿ ... وَمَا آتَاكُمُ الرَّسُولُ فَخُذُوهُ وَمَا نَهَاكُمْ عَنْهُ فَانتَهُوا ... ﴿٧﴾ ﴾

﴿...And whatsoever the Messenger [Muhammad] gives you, take it; and whatsoever he forbids you, abstain [from it]...﴾ *(Qur'an 59: 7)*

And Allah (ﷻ) says:

﴿ قُلْ إِن كُنتُمْ تُحِبُّونَ اللَّهَ فَاتَّبِعُونِي يُحْبِبْكُمُ اللَّهُ وَيَغْفِرْ لَكُمْ ذُنُوبَكُمْ ۗ وَاللَّهُ غَفُورٌ رَّحِيمٌ ﴿٣١﴾ قُلْ أَطِيعُوا اللَّهَ وَالرَّسُولَ ۖ فَإِن تَوَلَّوْا فَإِنَّ اللَّهَ لَا يُحِبُّ الْكَافِرِينَ ﴿٣٢﴾ ﴾

﴿Say [O' Muhammad to mankind]: 'If you [really] love Allah, then follow me [i.e. accept Islamic Monotheism, follow the Qur'an and the Sunnah], Allah will love you and forgive you your sins. And Allah is Oft-Forgiving, Most Merciful.' Say [O' Muhammad]: 'Obey Allah and the Messenger [Muhammad].' But if they turn away,

then Allah does not like the disbelievers.﴾
(Qur'an 3: 31-32)

There is Evidence to Indicate that Obedience to Anyone other than Allah and Turning away from His Rulings is *Kufr* and *Shirk*

Allah (ﷻ) says:

﴿ ... وَلَا يُشْرِكُ فِي حُكْمِهِۦٓ أَحَدًا ﴿٢٦﴾ ﴾

﴾...And He makes none to share in His Decision and His Rule.﴾ *(Qur'an 18: 26)*

And Allah (ﷻ) says:

﴿ ... وَإِنْ أَطَعْتُمُوهُمْ إِنَّكُمْ لَمُشْرِكُونَ ﴿١٢١﴾ ﴾

﴾...And if you obey them [the *Shayaaṭeen* (Devils)], then you would indeed be *mushrikoon* [polytheists].﴾
(Qur'an 6: 121)

And Allah (ﷻ) says:

﴿ أَفَحُكْمَ ٱلْجَٰهِلِيَّةِ يَبْغُونَ ۚ وَمَنْ أَحْسَنُ مِنَ ٱللَّهِ حُكْمًا لِّقَوْمٍ يُوقِنُونَ ﴿٥٠﴾ ﴾

﴾Do they then seek the judgement of [the days of] Ignorance? And who is better in judgement than Allah for a people who have firm Faith.﴾ *(Qur'an 5: 50)*

And there are many similar *aayaat* (verses).

This evidence, which is quoted here by way of example — for there is a great deal more than this — explains the extent to which this important matter is connected to *'aqeedah* in all its various issues and principles.

Now we will turn our attention to the words of some of the scholars who connected the issue of ruling by other than that which Allah revealed to *'aqeedah*:

1 - Imam Muhammad ibn Naṣr al-Marwazi said, commenting on the reports of the famous hadith of Jibreel:

"The phrase '*Eemaan* (faith) means to believe in Allah' means to affirm His Unity (*Tawḥeed*) and to believe in Him in one's heart and verbally, and to submit to Him and His commands, by having the resolve to do what He commands and to avoid negligence, arrogance and stubbornness. If you do that, you will be adhering to that which He loves and you will avoid that which angers Him."[5]

Then he said, "With regard to the phrase '...and in His Messengers,' this means believing in those whom Allah has named... and believing in Muhammad (ﷺ). The way in which you should believe in him is different from the way in which you should believe in the other Messengers. Your belief in the other Messengers means affirmation, but your belief in Muhammad (ﷺ) means both affirmation and believing in him, and following that which he brought. If you follow that which he brought, you fulfil the obligatory duties, accept as permissible that which is *ḥalaal* and accept as forbidden that which is *ḥaraam*, you refrain in cases where something is unclear, and you hasten to do good things."[6]

It may be noted that to belief in Allah and *Tawḥeed*, belief in the heart and verbal affirmation, he added the idea of submission to the commands of Allah, then he explained that. In the case of belief in His Messengers, he made a distinction between the other Messengers — who are to be affirmed — and His Messenger Muhammad (ﷺ), in whose case affirmation is not sufficient without following that which he brought.

---

[5] *Ta'ẓeem Qadr aṣ-Ṣalaah*, 1/392-393.

[6] Ibid, 1/393.

2 - Al-'Izz ibn 'Abdus-Salaam (may Allah have mercy on him) said, in his discussion of the principle "Whom it is obligatory to obey, whom it is permissible to obey and whom it is not permissible to obey":

"Only Allah is to be obeyed exclusively, because He is the only One Who bestows the blessings of creation, sustaining and nourishing His creation, and guiding His created beings to the correct path in their religious and worldly affairs. There is nothing good but He brings it, and there is nothing bad but He wards it off. No person deserves to be obeyed more than another, because none of them can bestow any of the blessings mentioned in the case of Allah. By the same token, no one has the right to rule or judge except Him, for His rulings are derived from the Qur'an and Sunnah, and from *ijmaa'* (scholarly consensus) and correct analogy (*qiyaas*), and other means of derivation. So no one has the right to use the method of *istiḥsaan* (discretion) or *al-maṣaaliḥ al-mursalah* (matters which serve the common interests of the Muslims and which do not go against the basic principles of Islam)..."[7] Ibn 'Abdus-Salaam based this matter on *Tawḥeed ar-Ruboobiyah* (Oneness of Divine Lordship): just as the power of creation belongs exclusively to Allah, so too the power of command belongs exclusively to Him.

﴿ ... أَلَا لَهُ ٱلْخَلْقُ وَٱلْأَمْرُ ... ﴿٥٤﴾ ﴾

﴾...Surely, His is the creation and commandment...﴿
(Qur'an 7: 54)

3 - Aṭ-Ṭabari (may Allah have mercy on him) said in his commentary on the *aayah* —

[7] *Qawaa'id al-Aḥkaam*, 2/158. It should be noted that Al-'Izz ibn 'Abdus-Salaam was not rejecting *Al-Maṣaaliḥ al-Mursalah* altogether, especially when they meet their specific conditions, as he explains in the book referred to here and in his other books.

﴿ بَلَىٰ مَنْ أَسْلَمَ وَجْهَهُۥ لِلَّهِ وَهُوَ مُحْسِنٌ ... ﴿١١٢﴾ ﴾

﴾Yes, but whoever submits his face [himself] to Allah [i.e. follows Allah's religion of Islamic Monotheism] and he is a *muḥsin....*﴿ *(Qur'an 2: 112)* —

With regard to the phrase ﴾whoever submits his face﴿, what is meant by submitting the face is humbling oneself and obeying Him, and subjugating oneself to His command. The root meaning of Islam is submission (*istislaam*), because He is the One to Whom you have submitted yourself, which means humbling oneself. The Muslim is so called because he submits all of his faculties in obedience to his Lord."[8] Elsewhere, in his commentary on the *aayah* —

﴿ رَبَّنَا وَٱجْعَلْنَا مُسْلِمَيْنِ لَكَ ... ﴿١٢٨﴾ ﴾

﴾Our Lord! And make us submissive unto You...﴿ *(Qur'an 2: 128)* —

At-Ṭabari says: "Here too, Allah is telling us about the Prophets Ibraaheem and Ismaa'eel, when they were raising the foundations of the House and saying, ﴾Our Lord! And make us submissive unto You﴿, meaning, cause us to submit to Your commands and to humble ourselves in obedience to You; let us not associate anyone other than You in our obedience or our worship. We have referred to above, the meaning of Islam, which is humility in obedience to Allah."[9]

Aṭ-Ṭabari clearly explains the meaning of Islam and the fact that Islam cannot be achieved except through humble submission to Allah Alone in worship and in obedience. This is what *Shaykh al-Islam* (Ibn Taymiyah) mentions frequently, such as when he says in *At-Tadmuriyah* - after he mentions the Qur'anic texts which indicate that

---

[8] *Tafseer aṭ-Ṭabari*, 2/510, edited by Shaakir.

[9] Ibid, 3/73-74, edited by Shaakir.

the religion of all the Messengers was Islam, other than which Allah will not accept any religion from the earlier or later generations — "Islam implies submission (*istislaam*) to Allah Alone. Whoever submits himself to Him and to anyone else is a *mushrik* and whoever does not submit himself to Him is too arrogant to worship Him. Both the *mushrik* and the one who is too arrogant to worship Him are *kaafir*. Submission to Him Alone implies worshipping Him alone and obeying Him alone. This is the religion of Islam, other than which Allah will not accept any religion. Submission is achieved by worshipping Allah at all times by doing that which He has commanded to be done at that particular time..."[10] So Islam implies worship and obedience.

Aṭ-Ṭabari interprets religion (*deen*) as meaning obedience and humility. He states this in his commentary on the *aayah* —

﴿ إِنَّ ٱلدِّينَ عِندَ ٱللَّهِ ٱلْإِسْلَٰمُ ... ﴿١٩﴾ ﴾

﴾Truly, the religion [*deen*] with Allah is Islam...﴿
(Qur'an 3: 19) —

Then he says: "Such is Islam; it means submission and humility. The verb derived from this word is *aslama*, in the sense of entering into Islam. Similarly it is said (in Arabic), *aqḥaṭa al-qawm* when the people (*al-qawm*) enter a period of famine (*qaḥṭ*); or *arba'u* when they enter the season of spring (*ar-rabee'*). So it is said *aslamu* when they enter into Islam, which means submitting and humbling themselves, and giving up resistance. If this is the case, then the interpretation of the *aayah* — ﴾Truly, the religion [*deen*] with Allah is Islam...﴿ is that obedience means obedience to Him, and affirmation on the lips and in the heart of total enslavement (*'uboodiyah*), subjugation and submission to Him by means of obedience to all His

[10] *At-Tadmuriyah*, Pp. 169, edited by Sa'wi.

commands and prohibitions, submission without any arrogance or deviation, without associating any of His creatures in that submission or worship."

Because Aṭ-Ṭabari is the *shaykh* of the *mufassireen*, and the most prominent scholar in knowledge of the Arabic language and the variant readings of the Qur'an, we will quote what he says about this matter. In his commentary on the *aayah* -

﴿ يَٰٓأَيُّهَا ٱلَّذِينَ ءَامَنُوا۟ ٱدْخُلُوا۟ فِى ٱلسِّلْمِ كَآفَّةً ... ﴿٢٠٨﴾ ﴾

> ﴿O' you who believe! Enter into Islam whole heartedly...﴾ *(Qur'an 2: 208* - Yusuf 'Ali's translation)

— after mentioning the scholarly differences in interpreting it and the variant readings of the *aayah*, he says:

"If it is asked, what does it mean when Allah urges the believers to follow Muhammad (ﷺ) and the Islam that he brought? The answer is that it means to follow all His laws and apply all His rulings, without neglecting some whilst doing others. If this is the meaning, then the word ﴿*kaaffatan*﴾ translated here as "perfectly" is an adjective describing *as-silm* (Islam), and the meaning is, enter into action wholeheartedly, and do not omit any part of it, O' you who believe in Muhammad and that which he brought."[11]

Then he mentioned a report from 'Ikrimah concerning the revelation of this *aayah*. Aṭ-Ṭabari said: "Ikrimah stated something similar to that which we have stated above, that the meaning of that call to the believers is to reject all issues that are not part of the rulings of Islam, to follow all its rulings and not to neglect any of them."[12]

---

[11] *Tafseer aṭ-Ṭabari*, 4/255, Edited by Shaakir.
[12] Ibid, 4/356.

He then mentioned the second opinion concerning the *aayah*, that it means that the People of the Book are commanded to enter Islam. He stated that it is more likely that the *aayah* means entering into following all the laws of Islam, and that this is general and applies to both groups.[13]

4 - As this is the case, then it is obligatory to refer all matters to Allah. The connection between this and the attributes of Allah is very clear. Hence Al-Khaṭṭaabi (may Allah have mercy on him) said, commenting on the meanings of the Names of Allah:

"***Al-Ḥakam***: *Al-Ḥakam* (the Judge) means *Al-Ḥaakim*. The true meaning is the One to Whom rulings are submitted and to Whom all matters are referred, as in the *aayaat* (verses):

﴿... لَهُ ٱلْحُكْمُ وَإِلَيْهِ تُرْجَعُونَ ﴿٨٨﴾﴾

﴿...His is the Decision [*al-ḥukm*], and to Him you [all] shall be returned.﴾ *(Qur'an 28: 88)*

﴿... أَنتَ تَحْكُمُ بَيْنَ عِبَادِكَ فِى مَا كَانُوا۟ فِيهِ يَخْتَلِفُونَ ﴿٤٦﴾﴾

﴿...You will judge [*taḥkumu*] between your slaves about that wherein they used to differ.﴾ *(Qur'an 39: 46)*

The word *ḥakam* is mentioned in the *aayah*:

﴿أَفَغَيْرَ ٱللَّهِ أَبْتَغِى حَكَمًا وَهُوَ ٱلَّذِىٓ أَنزَلَ إِلَيْكُمُ ٱلْكِتَٰبَ مُفَصَّلًا ... ﴿١١٤﴾﴾

﴿Shall I seek a judge [*ḥakaman*] other than Allah while it is He Who has sent down unto you the Book [the Qur'an], explained in detail...﴾ *(Qur'an 6: 114)*

---

[13] Ibid, 4/258. See also his commentary on the *aayah*, ﴿...And follow not the footsteps of *Shayṭaan* [Satan]...﴾ *(Qur'an 2: 208)*.

And the word ***Al-Ḥaakim*** is mentioned in several places, but it is mentioned in the plural form where the superlative is used, for example: ﴾...And He is the Best of judges [*Khayr al-Ḥaakimeen*]﴿ *(Qur'an 7: 87; 10: 9; 12: 80),* ﴾...And You are the Most Just of the judges [*Aḥkam al-Ḥaakimeen*].﴿ *(Qur'an 11: 45),* ﴾Is not Allah the Best of judges [*Aḥkam al-Ḥaakimeen*]?﴿ *(Qur'an 95: 8).*

And the word ***Al-Ḥakeem*** is mentioned in very many places, and the words derived from this name, such as *ḥakama, yuḥkumu, taḥkumu, ḥukmuhu, ḥukman* are very many."[14]

Shaykh al-Islam Ibn Taymiyah said, making the connection between this matter and the attributes of Allah:

"Allah is the Judge (*Al-Ḥakam*) Who judges between His slaves; the Decision (*Al-Ḥukm*) belongs to Him Alone. Allah revealed the Books and sent the Messengers to judge between them. Whoever obeys the

[14] Brother Muhammad al-Ḥamad al-Ḥamood has compiled the names of Allah with an explanation of their meanings. He spoke at length about the names of Allah, *Al-Ḥakam* and *Al-Ḥaakim* and *Al-Ḥakeem*. Among the effects of believing in these three names, he mentioned the following:

a) That the Decision belongs to Allah alone with no partner or associate in that decision, just as He has no partner in worship. Allah says: ﴾...And He makes none to share in His Decision and His Rule﴿ *(Qur'an 18: 26).*

b) Allah (سبحانه وتعالى) rules and judges as He wills, because He is One, with no partner or associate.

c) The words of Allah are wise and precise; how could they be otherwise, when He is the Most Just of the judges?

d) Belief in the above dictates referring to the Book of Allah for judgement amongst us, because there is no other book like the Qur'aan that is wise in all aspects.

e) Allah commanded His Messenger (ﷺ) to judge between people according to that which had been revealed to him of the Divine rulings, and to ignore anything else such as opinions and whims and desires...

See *An-Nahj al-Asmaa' fi Sharḥ Asmaa' Allah al-Ḥusnaa* by Muhammad ibn Ḥamad al-Ḥamood, 1/302-308.

Messenger is one of His pious close friends (*awliya'*) and will find happiness in this world and in the Hereafter. Whoever disobeys the Messenger will be one of those who are doomed to torment. Allah (ﷻ) says:

﴿ كَانَ ٱلنَّاسُ أُمَّةً وَٰحِدَةً فَبَعَثَ ٱللَّهُ ٱلنَّبِيِّـۧنَ مُبَشِّرِينَ وَمُنذِرِينَ وَأَنزَلَ مَعَهُمُ ٱلْكِتَـٰبَ بِٱلْحَقِّ لِيَحْكُمَ بَيْنَ ٱلنَّاسِ فِيمَا ٱخْتَلَفُوا۟ فِيهِ ۚ وَمَا ٱخْتَلَفَ فِيهِ إِلَّا ٱلَّذِينَ أُوتُوهُ مِنۢ بَعْدِ مَا جَآءَتْهُمُ ٱلْبَيِّنَـٰتُ بَغْيًۢا بَيْنَهُمْ ۖ فَهَدَى ٱللَّهُ ٱلَّذِينَ ءَامَنُوا۟ لِمَا ٱخْتَلَفُوا۟ فِيهِ... ﴿٢١٣﴾ ﴾

﴾Mankind were one community and Allah sent Prophets with glad tidings and warnings, and with them He sent down the Scripture in truth to judge between people in matters wherein they differed. And only those to whom [the Scripture] was given differed concerning it after clear proofs had come unto them through hatred, one to another. Then Allah by His Leave guided those who believed to the truth of that wherein they differed...﴿ *(Qur'an 2: 213)*

Allah (ﷻ) explains that He sent the Messengers and revealed the Books to them so that they might judge between the people concerning that wherein they differed. Allah (ﷻ) says:

﴿ وَمَا ٱخْتَلَفْتُمْ فِيهِ مِن شَىْءٍ فَحُكْمُهُۥٓ إِلَى ٱللَّهِ ۚ ذَٰلِكُمُ ٱللَّهُ رَبِّى عَلَيْهِ تَوَكَّلْتُ وَإِلَيْهِ أُنِيبُ ﴿١٠﴾ ﴾

﴾And in whatsoever you differ, the decision thereof is with Allah [He is the ruling Judge]. [And say O' Muhammad to these polytheists:] Such is Allah, my Lord in Whom I put my trust, and to Him I turn [in all of my affairs and] in repentance.﴿ *(Qur'an 42: 10)*

And Prophet Yoosuf (عليه السلام) (may Allah's peace be upon him) said:

﴿ يَٰصَٰحِبَيِ ٱلسِّجۡنِ ءَأَرۡبَابٞ مُّتَفَرِّقُونَ خَيۡرٌ أَمِ ٱللَّهُ ٱلۡوَٰحِدُ ٱلۡقَهَّارُ
٣٩ مَا تَعۡبُدُونَ مِن دُونِهِۦٓ إِلَّآ أَسۡمَآءٗ سَمَّيۡتُمُوهَآ أَنتُمۡ وَءَابَآؤُكُم مَّآ
أَنزَلَ ٱللَّهُ بِهَا مِن سُلۡطَٰنٍۚ إِنِ ٱلۡحُكۡمُ إِلَّا لِلَّهِۚ أَمَرَ أَلَّا تَعۡبُدُوٓاْ إِلَّآ إِيَّاهُۚ
ذَٰلِكَ ٱلدِّينُ ٱلۡقَيِّمُ وَلَٰكِنَّ أَكۡثَرَ ٱلنَّاسِ لَا يَعۡلَمُونَ ٤٠ ﴾

﴾O' two companions of the prison! Are many different lords [gods] better or Allah, the One, the Irresistible? You do not worship besides Him but only names which you have named [forged] — you and your fathers — for which Allah has sent down no authority. The command [or the judgement] is for none but Allah. He has commanded that you worship none but Him [i.e. His Monotheism]; that is the [true] straight religion, but most men know not.﴿ *(Qur'an 12: 39-40)*

The Decision belongs to Allah Alone, and His Messengers conveyed that from Him. Their ruling is His ruling, and their command is His command; obeying them means obeying Him. Whatever the Messenger rules or commands them to do or prescribes in the religion, it is obligatory upon all people to follow that and to obey him, for that is the ruling of Allah upon His creation."[15]

Elsewhere, *Shaykh al-Islam* (Ibn Taymiyah) elaborated upon the context of the wording used in the Qur'an, and he defined a principle concerning that, in which he explained that it is obligatory to believe in everything brought by the Messenger (ﷺ). (He stated that) just as disbelief in some of the Messengers is disbelief in the rest of them, so belief in some parts of the Message and not others is also *kufr*. After quoting the evidence (*daleel*) for that, he said: "So He condemned those who had been given a portion of the Scripture (the People of the Book) when they believed in that which went against the Message

---

[15] *Majmoo' al-Fataawa*, 35/361-363; see also Pp. 372, 383.

and preferred those who deviated from the Message to those who believed in it, like those who preferred the Sabian philosophers and the *jaahili* states - the *jaahiliyah* of the Turks, Daylam, Arabs, Persians and others - to those who believed in Allah and His Book and His Messenger. Similarly, He condemned those who claimed to believe in all the Books, but they failed to refer to the Qur'an and Sunnah for judgement, and they referred, instead, to some of the false lawgivers and are venerated instead of Allah, as often happens in the case of those who claim to be Muslims but they refer for judgement to the opinions of the Sabians, philosophers and others, or to the regulations of some of the kings who have gone beyond the pale of Islam, such as the kings of the Tartars and others. When it is said to them, 'Come to the Book of Allah and the Sunnah of His Messenger,' they turn away from that completely."[16]

Because the Decision (*ḥukm*) belongs to Allah Alone, it is obligatory to follow everything that the Messenger (ﷺ) brought, without differentiating. Referring for judgement to the opinions of the Sabians and philosophers, or to anything other than the shari'ah of Allah is referring to false laws (*ṭaaghoot*) for judgement, and it is essential to believe in Allah and to reject the false laws.

5 - This matter is also connected to the testimony that Muhammad is the Messenger of Allah. *Shaykh al-Islam* Ibn Taymiyah said: "The testimony that Muhammad (ﷺ) is the Messenger of Allah implies believing in all that he said and obeying all that he commanded. What he approved of should be approved, and what he denounced should be denounced, just as people should affirm all the names and attributes of Allah that He has affirmed for Himself, and they should reject all the notions of resemblance to His creatures that He has denied, and protect themselves from both *ta'ṭeel* (denying Allah's

[16] *Majmoo' al-Fataawa*, 12/339-340.

attributes) and *tamtheel* (anthropomorphism). When affirming His attributes they must avoid likening Him to any of His creation, and when denying that He resembles any of His creation they must avoid denying any of His attributes. They should do that which He commands and avoid that which He forbids. They must accept as *ḥalaal* that which He has permitted and accept as *ḥaraam* that which He has forbidden. Nothing is *ḥaraam* except that which Allah and His Messenger have forbidden, and there is no religion except that which Allah and His Messenger have prescribed. Hence Allah condemns the *mushrikoon* in *Soorah al-An'aam*, *Soorah al-A'raaf* — the sixth and the seventh chapter of the Qur'an - and elsewhere for forbidding things which Allah has not forbidden and for inventing a religion for which Allah had not sent down any authority, as Allah (ﷻ) says:

﴿ وَجَعَلُوا۟ لِلَّهِ مِمَّا ذَرَأَ مِنَ ٱلْحَرْثِ وَٱلْأَنْعَٰمِ نَصِيبًا... ﴿١٣٦﴾ ﴾

﴿And they assign to Allah a share of the tilth and cattle which He has created...﴾

(Qur'an 6:136 — to the end of the *soorah*)

This is also mentioned at the beginning of *Soorah al-A'raaf*, and Allah (ﷻ) says:

﴿ أَمْ لَهُمْ شُرَكَٰٓؤُا۟ شَرَعُوا۟ لَهُم مِّنَ ٱلدِّينِ مَا لَمْ يَأْذَنۢ بِهِ ٱللَّهُ ... ﴿٢١﴾ ﴾

﴿Or have they partners with Allah [false gods] who have instituted for them a religion which Allah has not ordained?...﴾ *(Qur'an 42: 21)*

And Allah said to His Prophet (ﷺ):

﴿ ... إِنَّآ أَرْسَلْنَٰكَ شَٰهِدًا وَمُبَشِّرًا وَنَذِيرًا ﴿٤٥﴾ وَدَاعِيًا إِلَى ٱللَّهِ بِإِذْنِهِۦ وَسِرَاجًا مُّنِيرًا ﴿٤٦﴾ ﴾

﴿...Verily, We have sent you as witness, and a bearer of glad tidings, and a warner, And as one who invites to Allah [Islamic Monotheism, i.e. to worship none but Allah (Alone)] by His Leave, and as a lamp spreading light [through your instructions from the Qur'an and the Sunnah the legal ways of the Prophet].﴾

(Qur'an 33: 45-46)

So Allah told him that He had sent him to call people to Him by His Leave. So whoever calls people to anyone other than Allah is guilty of *shirk* and whoever calls people to something without His leave or permission is guilty of *bid'ah*. *Shirk* is *bid'ah*, and *bid'ah* ends up in *shirk*. There is no innovator who is not guilty of some kind of *shirk*, as Allah (سبحانه وتعالى) says:

﴿ٱتَّخَذُوٓا۟ أَحْبَارَهُمْ وَرُهْبَـٰنَهُمْ أَرْبَابًا مِّن دُونِ ٱللَّهِ وَٱلْمَسِيحَ ٱبْنَ مَرْيَمَ وَمَآ أُمِرُوٓا۟ إِلَّا لِيَعْبُدُوٓا۟ إِلَـٰهًا وَٰحِدًا ۖ لَّآ إِلَـٰهَ إِلَّا هُوَ ۚ سُبْحَـٰنَهُۥ عَمَّا يُشْرِكُونَ ﴿٣١﴾﴾

﴿They [Jews and Christians] took their rabbis and their monks to be their lords besides Allah [by obeying them in things which they made lawful or unlawful according to their own desires without being ordered by Allah], and [they also took as their Lord] Messiaḥ, son of Maryam [Mary], while they [Jews and Christians] were commanded [in the *Tawraat* (Torah) and the *Injeel* (Gospel)] to worship none but One *Ilaah* [God — Allah] *Laa ilaaha illa Huwa* [none has the right to be worshipped but He]. Praise and glory be to Him [far above is He] from having the partners they associate [with Him].﴾ *(Qur'an 9: 31)*

One of the ways in which they committed *shirk* was that they (the rabbis and the monks) permitted them things which were forbidden, and they obeyed them, and they forbade them things which were permitted, and they obeyed them."[17]

This long comment from *Shaykh al-Islam* (Ibn Taymiyah) clearly explains how the matters of *'aqeedah* are connected to one another. This is because both parts of the *Shahaadatayn*, the testimony that there is no god except Allah and the testimony that Muhammad is the Messenger of Allah, are strongly interconnected. They are like *eemaan* and Islam: if they are mentioned together in the same context, they have different meanings, but if they are mentioned separately, each of them carries the meaning of the other. If the testimony that there is no god but Allah is mentioned on its own, it implies the testimony that Muhammad is the Messenger of Allah, and it cannot be accepted from the person who says it without this belief. Similarly, if the testimony that Muhammad is the Messenger of Allah is mentioned, it implies the testimony that there is no god except Allah, and it cannot be accepted otherwise. If they are mentioned together, then each of them carries its own meaning.

Hence we find that a few lines after saying the words quoted above, *Shaykh al-Islam* (Ibn Taymiyah) made the connection between this matter and Islam. He made a comment similar to the words quoted above from *At-Tadmuriyah*, and said: "The word Islam implies submission and obedience, and it implies sincerity, as Allah (ﷻ) says:

﴿ ضَرَبَ ٱللَّهُ مَثَلًا رَّجُلًا فِيهِ شُرَكَآءُ مُتَشَٰكِسُونَ وَرَجُلًا سَلَمًا ... ﴿٢٩﴾ ﴾

﴿Allah puts forth a similitude: a [slave] man belonging to many partners [like those who worship others along with Allah] disputing with one another, and a [slave] man belonging entirely to one master [like those who worship Allah Alone]...﴾ *(Qur'an 39: 29)*

---

[17] *Iqtiḍaa' aṣ-Ṣiraaṭ al-Mustaqeem*, 2/834-835.

Islam necessarily means submission to Allah Alone, and not submitting to anything or anyone other than Him. This is the true meaning of what we say, Laa ilaaha illa-Allah (There is no god except Allah). Whoever submits to Allah and to someone else is a *mushrik*, and Allah does not forgive the sin of associating anything with Him. Whoever does not submit to Him at all is one who is too arrogant to worship Him. Allah (ﷻ) says:

﴿ وَقَالَ رَبُّكُمُ ادْعُونِي أَسْتَجِبْ لَكُمْ إِنَّ الَّذِينَ يَسْتَكْبِرُونَ عَنْ عِبَادَتِي سَيَدْخُلُونَ جَهَنَّمَ دَاخِرِينَ ﴿٦٠﴾ ﴾

﴿And your Lord said: 'Invoke Me [i.e. believe in My Oneness (Islamic Monotheism) and ask Me for anything] I will respond to your [invocation]. Verily, those who scorn My worship [i.e. do not invoke Me, and do not believe in My Oneness, (Islamic Monotheism)] they will surely enter Hell in humiliation!'﴾[18]

(Qur'an 40: 60)

Undoubtedly the testimony that Muhammad is the Messenger of Allah implies a number of things without which belief in the Messenger cannot be achieved. Among these things is referring to the Messenger (ﷺ) and accepting his ruling. *Shaykh al-Islam* (Ibn Taymiyah) often asserts this, for example, when he says:

"Allah says:

﴿ فَلَا وَرَبِّكَ لَا يُؤْمِنُونَ حَتَّىٰ يُحَكِّمُوكَ فِيمَا شَجَرَ بَيْنَهُمْ ثُمَّ لَا يَجِدُوا فِي أَنفُسِهِمْ حَرَجًا مِّمَّا قَضَيْتَ وَيُسَلِّمُوا تَسْلِيمًا ﴿٦٥﴾ ﴾

﴿But no, by your Lord, they can have no Faith, until they make you [O' Muhammad] judge in all disputes between them, and find in themselves no resistance against your

---

[18] *Iqtiḍaa' aṣ-Ṣiraaṭ al-Mustaqeem*, 2/836.

decisions, and accept [them] with full submission.﴿
(Qur'an 4: 65)

When Allah (ﷻ) denies that anyone has faith until they fulfil this condition, this indicates that this condition is obligatory upon people. Whoever does not meet this condition becomes one of those who are subject to the warning, and has not attained the obligatory level of faith for which those who attain it are promised admission to Paradise with no punishment. Allah has promised that to whoever acts according to what He commands. In the case of those who do some of the obligatory duties and neglect others, they are subject to the warning. It is known from the consensus of the Muslims that it is obligatory to refer to the Messenger for judgement in all disputes that arise among the people in both religious and worldly matters, with regard to both the fundamental issues of their religion and the minor issues. They are all obliged, once he has ruled concerning a matter, to find in themselves no resistance against his decisions, and accept (them) with full submission."[19]

We will discuss the *tafseer* of this *aayah* in more detail below, *In sha Allah*. Our purpose here is to explain the connection between the testimony that Muhammad is the Messenger of Allah and the testimony that there is no god but Allah, and the connection between the obligation to refer for judgement to the Qur'an and Sunnah, and the *Shahaadatayn*.

6 - Ibn al-Qayyim (may Allah have mercy on him) discussed this matter at length. We will limit our discussion here to one topic, where he commented on the *aḥaadeeth*,

> "He has tasted the savour of faith who is content with Allah as his Lord, Islam as his religion and Muhammad

---

[19] *Majmoo' al-Fataawa Shaykh al-Islam*, (vol. *Eemaan*) v/37-38.

> as his Messenger,"[20] and, "Whoever says, when he hears the call (to prayer), 'I bear witness that there is no god but Allah... and I am content with Allah...'"[21]

Ibn al-Qayyim (may Allah have mercy on him) said: "These two hadiths are the focal point around which all the issues of religion revolve, and they form the ultimate goal. They include being content with the Lordship and Divinity of Allah, and being content with His Messenger and following him, and being content with his religion and submitting to it. Whoever combines these four features is truly a *ṣiddeeq* (true believer). It is easy to claim this verbally, but it is one of the most difficult things when it comes to the real test..."[22] Then he commented on both hadiths, then he said: "With regard to being content with His Prophet as a Messenger, implies following him in a complete sense and submitting to him absolutely, so that one gives him preference over one's own self, taking guidance only from what he says, referring for judgement to no one but him, not accepting the judgement of anyone but him, not accepting the judgement of anyone else at all..."[23]

Then he said, commenting on the fourth matter, "With regard to being content with his religion, when he speaks, passes judgement, commands or prohibits, he is completely content with that, and there is no element of resistance in his heart towards that ruling, and he accepts (it) with full submission, even if it goes against his own wishes or desires, or what his leader, *shaykh* or sect say."[24]

---

[20] Muslim: *Kitaab al-Eemaan, Baab ad-Daleel 'ala man raḍaa Billaahi rabban*, hadith no. 34.

[21] Muslim: *Kitaab aṣ-Ṣalaah, Baab istiḥbaab al-Qawl mithl qawl al-mu'adh-dhin*, hadith no. 386.

[22] *Madaarij as-Saalikeen*, 2/172.

[23] Ibid, 2/172-173.

[24] Ibid, 2/173.

This statement made by Ibn al-Qayyim, concerning this matter, is reiterated and commented on further elsewhere in his books,[25] as we shall see below, *In sha Allah*.

7 - Because this matter — the connection between the obligation of referring for judgement to the Qur'an and Sunnah, and *'aqeedah* — is one of the obvious issues, *Shaykh al-Islam* Muhammad ibn 'Abdul-Wahhaab (may Allah have mercy on him) mentioned it in *Kitaab at-Tawḥeed* under the chapter "The interpretation of *Tawḥeed* and the testimony that there is no god except Allah," where he quotes the *aayah*,

﴿ ٱتَّخَذُوٓا۟ أَحْبَارَهُمْ وَرُهْبَـٰنَهُمْ أَرْبَابًا مِّن دُونِ ٱللَّهِ ... ﴿٣١﴾ ﴾

﴿They [Jews and Christians] took their rabbis and their monks to be their lords besides Allah...﴾ *(Qur'an 9: 31)*

He did not stop there, but he also devoted a separate chapter to this topic, entitled "Those who obey the scholars and rulers in regarding *ḥaraam* that which Allah (ﷻ) has permitted and regarding as *ḥalaal* that which Allah (ﷻ) has forbidden, have taken them (those scholars and rulers) as lords besides Allah." In this chapter he mentioned some of the reports (about the Companions) and the hadith of 'Adiy ibn Ḥaaṭim, then he followed that with a chapter entitled, "The *aayah*,

﴿ أَلَمْ تَرَ إِلَى ٱلَّذِينَ يَزْعُمُونَ أَنَّهُمْ ءَامَنُوا۟ بِمَآ أُنزِلَ إِلَيْكَ وَمَآ أُنزِلَ مِن قَبْلِكَ يُرِيدُونَ أَن يَتَحَاكَمُوٓا۟ إِلَى ٱلطَّـٰغُوتِ ... ﴿٦٠﴾ ﴾

﴿Have you not seen those [hypocrites] who claim that they believe in that which has been sent down to you, and that which was sent down before you, and they wish to go for judgement [in their disputes] to the *ṭaaghoot*

---

[25] *Mukhtasar aṣ-Ṣawaa'iq*, 2/351 ff.

[false judges]...﴿ *(Qur'an 4: 60)*",

— in which he mentioned many other *aayaat* and hadiths.

All of those who commented on *Kitaab at-Tawḥeed* made the connection between these two chapters and the matter of *Tawḥeed* and the affirmation of the *Shahaadatayn*. Here we will quote in brief from what *Shaykh* Sulaymaan ibn 'Abdullah ibn Muhammad ibn 'Abdul-Wahhaab said in the first chapter:[26] "Because obedience is a kind of worship, rather worship it is, by doing what Allah commands through the lips of His Messengers (peace be upon them), the author (may Allah have mercy on him) drew attention to the obligation of devoting obedience only to the Creator. No created being should be obeyed except where obeying him comes under the heading of obeying Allah. Otherwise, no created being should be obeyed independently. What is meant here is obedience that has to do specifically with forbidding what is permitted or permitting what is forbidden. Whoever obeys a created being with regard to that, apart from the Messenger (ﷺ) — who does not speak of his own desire — is a *mushrik*, as Allah explains in the *aayah*: ﴾They [Jews and Christians] took their rabbis and their monks i.e., their scholars — to be their lords besides Allah [by obeying them in things which they made lawful or unlawful according to their own desires without being ordered by Allah], and [they also took as their Lord] Messiaḥ, son of Maryam [Mary], while they [Jews and Christians] were commanded [in the *Tawraat* (Torah) and the *Injeel* (Gospel)] to worship none but One *Ilaah* [God — Allah] *Laa ilaaha illa Huwa* [none has the right to be worshipped but He]. Praise and glory be to Him [far above is He] from having the partners they associate [with Him].﴿ *(Qur'an 9: 31)*

The Prophet (Blessings and Peace be upon him) explained this as referring to their obeying them with regard to forbidding what is

---

[26] i.e., the chapter on "Those who obey the scholars and rulers..."

permitted or permitting what is forbidden."[27]

Commenting on the second chapter, *Shaykh* Sulaymaan said: "Because *Tawḥeed*, which is the meaning of the testimony that there is no god except Allah, also includes and is inseparable from belief in the Messenger (ﷺ), and this forms the *Shahaadatayn* or twin testimony of faith, the Prophet (ﷺ) made them a single pillar when he said, "Islam is built on five (pillars)..." In this chapter, (the author) draws attention to the implications and obligations of *Tawḥeed*, which include referring to the Messenger (ﷺ) for judgement in disputed issues. This is the meaning of the testimony that there is no god except Allah, and the inevitable implication which every believer must believe in. Whoever acknowledges that there is no god except Allah is duty-bound to obey the decree of Allah and to submit to His commands which were brought from Him by His Messenger Muhammad (ﷺ). Whoever bears witness that there is no god except Allah then turns for judgement to someone other than the Messenger (ﷺ) concerning disputed issues has nullified the testimony he gave when he bore witness..."[28]

This is clear and does not need further comment.

8 - The contemporary scholars have also spoken a great deal on this issue. It is sufficient here to quote from *Shaykh* Muhammad ibn Ibraaheem Aal ash-Shaykh (may Allah have mercy on him) and *Shaykh* 'Abdul-'Azeez ibn Baaz, and to refer readers to other scholars in the footnotes at the end of this section. *Shaykh* Muhammad ibn Ibraaheem said in a paper entitled *Taḥkeem al-Qawaaneen* (Referring to man-made laws for judgement):

"Allah states that those who do not make the Messenger (ﷺ) judge in all disputes between them do not have faith. This statement is

[27] *Tayseer al-'Azeez al-Ḥameed*, Pp. 543.

[28] Ibid, Pp. 554-555. See the rest of his comments, for they are important.

confirmed by the repeated use of the negative ('no... they can have no faith...') and by the use of an oath ('by your Lord'). Allah (ﷻ) says:

﴿ فَلَا وَرَبِّكَ لَا يُؤْمِنُونَ حَتَّىٰ يُحَكِّمُوكَ فِيمَا شَجَرَ بَيْنَهُمْ ثُمَّ لَا يَجِدُوا۟ فِىٓ أَنفُسِهِمْ حَرَجًا مِّمَّا قَضَيْتَ وَيُسَلِّمُوا۟ تَسْلِيمًا ﴿٦٥﴾ ﴾

﴿But no, by your Lord, they can have no Faith, until they make you [O' Muhammad] judge in all disputes between them, and find in themselves no resistance against your decisions, and accept [them] with full submission.﴾

(Qur'an 4: 65)

But it is not sufficient for them merely to have no resistance in themselves, as Allah (ﷻ) says, ﴿...And find in themselves no resistance against your decisions...﴾. They must also be content and happy with that, and be free of any reservations or objections.

These two factors are also not enough, until submission (*tasleem*) is added to them which means total acceptance of and submission to the Prophet's rulings that is free from any attachment of the soul to the disputed matter, and they submit to this true ruling in the most complete manner. Hence this is emphasized by the use of the verbal noun ﴿*tasleem*﴾ translated here as "with full submission", to show that acceptance is not enough in this case, it must be absolute submission..."[29]

Shaykh 'Abdul-'Azeez ibn Baaz said: "What is meant is that it is essential to devote worship to Allah Alone (*Tawḥeed*), and to disassociate oneself from the worship of anyone else and from the worshippers of anyone else. It is essential to believe that *shirk* is false, and it is essential upon all His slaves, jinn and men alike, to devote their worship to Allah Alone and to fulfil the duty of this *Tawḥeed* by referring for judgement to the shari'ah of Allah. Allah is

[29] *Taḥkeem al-Qawaaneen*, 5-6.

the Judge (*Al-Ḥaakim*), and part of *Tawḥeed* is to believe in that. He is the Judge in this world through His shari'ah and in the Hereafter He Himself will pass judgement, as He (ﷻ) says:

﴿ ... إِنِ ٱلْحُكْمُ إِلَّا لِلَّهِ ... ﴿٥٧﴾ ﴾

﴿...The decision [*al-ḥukm*] is only for Allah...﴾
(Qur'an 6: 57)

﴿ ... فَٱلْحُكْمُ لِلَّهِ ٱلْعَلِيِّ ٱلْكَبِيرِ ﴿١٢﴾ ﴾

﴿...So the judgement [*al-ḥukm*] is only with Allah, the Most High, the Most Great.﴾ *(Qur'an 40: 12)*

﴿ وَمَا ٱخْتَلَفْتُمْ فِيهِ مِن شَىْءٍ فَحُكْمُهُۥٓ إِلَى ٱللَّهِ ... ﴿١٠﴾ ﴾

﴿And in whatsoever you differ, the decision [*al-ḥukm*] thereof is with Allah [He is the ruling Judge]...﴾
(Qur'an 42: 10)."[30]

Elsewhere *Shaykh* Ibn Baaz says: "With regard to the testimony that Muhammad is the Messenger of Allah, many people do not understand it properly, and they refer for judgement to man-made laws and turn away from the shari'ah of Allah. They do not care about that, either because of ignorance or because of negligence. The testimony that Muhammad is the Messenger of Allah implies believing in the Messenger of Allah (ﷺ), obeying his commands, avoiding that which he has forbidden, and believing in what he has told us. Allah cannot be worshipped except in accordance with the shari'ah which he (ﷺ) brought, as Allah (ﷻ) says:

﴿ قُلْ إِن كُنتُمْ تُحِبُّونَ ٱللَّهَ فَٱتَّبِعُونِى يُحْبِبْكُمُ ٱللَّهُ وَيَغْفِرْ لَكُمْ ذُنُوبَكُمْ ... ﴿٣١﴾ ﴾

30 *Majmoo' al-Fataawa Ibn Baaz*, 2/20.

﴾Say [O' Muhammad to mankind]: 'If you [really] love Allah, then follow me [i.e. accept Islamic Monotheism, follow the Qur'an and the Sunnah], Allah will love you and forgive you your sins...'﴿ *(Qur'an 3: 31)*

﴿ وَمَا نَهَىٰكُمْ عَنْهُ فَٱنتَهُوا۟ ... ﴿٧﴾ ﴾

﴾...And whatsoever he forbids you, abstain [from it]...﴿ *(Qur'an 59: 7)*

What is obligatory upon all the Muslims and upon the two races (i.e., mankind and the jinn) is to worship Allah Alone and to refer for judgement to His Prophet Muhammad (ﷺ), as Allah (ﷻ) says: ﴾But no, by your Lord, they can have no Faith, until they make you [O' Muhammad] judge in all disputes between them...﴿ *(Qur'an 4: 65)*."[31]

Shaykh Ibn Baaz clearly states: "Total enslavement (*'uboodiyah*) to Allah Alone, disavowal of the worship of false gods (*ṭaaghoot*) and referring to Him for judgement are among the implications of the testimony that there is no god except Allah Alone, with no partner or associate, and that Muhammad is His slave and Messenger. Allah, glorified be He, is the Lord and God of mankind. He is the One Who created them, and He is the One Who commands them and forbids them, Who gives them life and death, Who brings them to account and rewards or punishes them. He is the One Who deserves to be worshipped, to the exclusion of all others. Allah (ﷻ) says, ﴾...Surely, His is the Creation and Commandment...﴿ *(Qur'an 7: 54)*. Just as Allah is the only Creator, so too He is the Only One to issue commands, and His command must be obeyed. Allah tells us that the Jews took their rabbis as lords instead of Allah..."[32] The issue of referring for judgement to the shari'ah of Allah is connected to

---

[31] *Majmoo' al-Fataawa Ibn Baaz*, 2/337.

[32] *Wujoob Taḥkeem Shar' Allah*, Pp. 7, 4th edition, *Daar al-Iftaa'* 1401 AH.

Tawheed, and it is implied by the *Shahaadatayn* as explained by the *Shaykh* (may Allah bestow abundant mercy upon him).

This is a summary of what some of the scholars have said concerning this matter.[33] From this it is clear that the connection between this matter and *'aqeedah* is something that is agreed upon, and that it is one of the obvious issues. With regard to the details of what is implied by this, this is what we will discuss in the following chapters, *in sha Allah*.

What is important here is to realize that discussing this issue is not the matter of blowing a minor issue out of proportion, as may be claimed by some of those who think that talking a great deal about referring for judgement to the shari'ah of Allah is something which has arisen from political circumstances and the situation of the Islamic movements, and that these movements have taken this issue as a slogan to oppose the rulers and take a stand against deviation and westernization. On the contrary, it is a fundamental issue which is based on evidence (*daleel*).

There is no stronger indication that this issue is obvious to the scholars whose words we have quoted above and others. And Allah is the Guide to the straight path.[34]

---

[33] See also the comments of some contemporary scholars, such as *Shaykh* Aḥmad Shaakir in *Ḥaashiyat 'Umdat at-Tafseer*, 4/147, where he states that this is part of the essence of *'aqeedah*. See also: *Ḥawla Taṭbeeq ash-Sharee'ah* by Prof. Muhammad Quṭb, Pp. 9-23; *Sharee'ah al-Kamaal tashkoo min al-Ihmaal* by 'Abdul-Wahhaab Rasheed Ṣaaliḥ, Pp. 25, 26; *Taḥkeem ash-Sharee'ah wa Da'aawa al-'Ilmaaniyah* by Dr, Ṣalaaḥ aṣ-Ṣaawi, Pp. 35-37, 42, 43; *Al-Ḥadd al-Faaṣil* by 'Abdur-Raḥmaan 'Abdul-Khaaliq, Pp. 42-43; *Ash-Sharee'ah al-Islaamiyah laa al-Qawaaneen al-Waḍa'iyah* by 'Umar al-Ashqar, Pp. 165 ff. And there are many, many others.

[34] The books and papers which explain the importance of applying Islamic shari'ah and warn against ruling by any laws etc. other than that which Allah has revealed are very many. Here I will mention those that I have before me: =

= 1) *Taḥdheer Ahl al-Eemaan 'an al-Ḥukm bi ghayri ma anzala ar-Raḥmaan* by Al-As'ardi, ed. by Saleem al-Hilaali.

2) *Al-Fawaakih al-'Idhaab fi'r-Radd 'ala man lam yuḥakum as-Sunnah wa'l-Kitaab*, by *Shaykh* Ḥamad ibn Naaṣir ibn Mu'ammar, ed. by 'Abdus-Salaam al-Barjas.

3) *Al-Burhaan wa'd-Daleel 'ala Kufr man ḥakama bi ghayr it-Tanzeel*, by *Shaykh* Aḥmad ibn Naaṣir ibn Ghunaym, 1st edition, 1393 AH.

4) *Ash-Sharee'ah laa al-Qaanoon*, by Aḥmad 'Abdul-Ghafoor 'Aṭṭaar, 1st edition, 1384 AH.

5) *Inḥisaar Taṭbeeq ash-Sharee'ah fi Aqṭaar al-'Uroobah wal-Islam*, by Aḥmad 'Abdul-Ghafoor 'Attaar, 1st edition, 1400 AH, *Daar al-Andalus*.

6) *Wujoob Taḥkeem ash-Sharee'ah al-Islamiyah* by Mannaa' al-Qaṭṭaan, 1405 AH edition, Imam University.

7) *Asbaab al-Ḥukm bi ghayri ma anzala Allah wa Nataa'ijuhu*, Dr. Ṣaaliḥ al-Sadlaan, 1st edition, 1413 AH, *Daar al-Muslim*.

8) *Al-Ḥukm bi ghayri ma anzala Allah wa Ahl al-Ghlue*, Muhammad Sarwar Zaynul-'Aabideen, 2vols., *Daar al-Arqam* edition.

9) *Wujoob Taṭbeeq ash-Sharee'ah* by Dr. Muhammad al-Ameen Musṭafa al-Shanqeeṭi, 1412 AH edition, *Maktabat al-'Uloom wa'l-Ḥukm*.

10) *Inna Allah Huwa al-Ḥakam*, by Muhammad Shaakir ash-Shareef, *Daar al-Waṭan* edition.

11) *Al-Ḥukm bi'l-Qur'an wa Qaḍiyat Taṭbeeq ash-Sharee'ah*, by Jamaal al-Banna, *Daar al-Fikr al-Islaami*.

12) *Wujoob Taṭbeeq al-Ḥudood ash-Shar'iyah*, by 'Abdur-Raḥmaan 'Abdul-Khaaliq, *Maktabat Ibn Taymiyah*, Kuwait.

13) *At-Talaazum bayna al-'Aqeedah wa'sh-Sharee'ah*, by Naaṣir al-'Aql, *Daar al-Waṭan*.

14) *Juhood ash-Shaykh Muhammad ibn Ibraaheem fi Mas'alat al-Ḥaakimiyah*, by 'Abdul-'Azeez Aal 'Abdul-Laṭeef, 1st edition, 1412 AH.

15) *Fi Wahj al-Mu'aamarah 'ala Taṭbeeq ash-Sharee'ah al-Islamiyah*, by Muṣṭafa Farghali ash-Shuqayri, *Daar al-Wafaa'*, 1407 AH.

16) *Ash-Shara' wal-Lughah* by Aḥmad Shaakir, 3rd edition, 1987 CE, *'Aalam al-Kutub*.

17) *Al-Qur'an fawqa ad-Dastoor*, by 'Ali Jurayshah, 1406 AH, *Maktabah Wahbah*.

18) *Al-Ḥaakimiyah fi Tafseer Aḍwaa' al-Bayaan*, by 'Abdur-Raḥmaan as-Sudays, *Daar Ṭeebah*.

19) *Abḥaath wa Aḥkaam*, by Aḥmad Shaakir, 2nd edition, 1407 AH, *Maktabah Ibn Taymiyah*, Cairo.

20) *Siyaadah ash-Sharee'at al-Islamiyah fi Miṣr*, by Dr. Tawfeeq ash-Shaawi, *Az-Zahraa' li'l-I'laam al-'Arabi*. =

= 21) *Ḥatta laa taẓill ash-Sharee'ah naṣṣan shakliyyan*, by Dr. 'Ali Ḥasanayn az-Zahraa'.

22) *Al-Ḥukm wat-Taḥaakum fi Khiṭaab al-Waḥy*, by 'Abdul-'Azeez Muṣṭafa, *Daar Ṭeebah*.

23) *Naẓariyah as-Siyaadah wa atharuhaa 'ala Shar'iyat al-Anẓimah al-Waḍ'iyah*, by Dr. Ṣalaaḥ aṣ-Ṣaawi, *Daar Ṭeebah*.

There are many other books which deal with this topic. The point here is to demonstrate the importance of this topic, not to comment on each book.

CHAPTER TWO

THE TEXTS WHICH PROVE THAT IT IS OBLIGATORY TO REFER FOR JUDGEMENT TO THE LAWS OF ALLAH

Most of these texts are in the Qur'an, and those which are narrated in the Sunnah mostly explain the reason for the revelation of the texts (*sabab an-nuzool*) or the meaning of the texts (*tafseer*).

This chapter will be divided into two parts:

1) The general texts which prove that it is obligatory to refer for judgement to the laws of Allah, or which forbid following the laws of anyone other than Him. It will be sufficient to quote some of them, and to quote the comments of some of the *mufassireen* on some of them.

2) The *aayaat* which make it obligatory to refer for judgement to the shari'ah of Allah, or which forbid referring for judgement to any other (laws), but which came with the ruling that the one who goes against this is not a believer, or has taken lords instead of Allah, or is guilty of *shirk*, etc. This will be explained in some detail.

With regard to the *aayah*,

﴿ ... وَمَن لَّمْ يَحْكُم بِمَآ أَنزَلَ ٱللَّهُ فَأُو۟لَـٰٓئِكَ هُمُ ٱلْكَـٰفِرُونَ ﴿٤٤﴾ ﴾

﴾...And whosoever does not judge by what Allah has revealed, such are the *kaafiroon* [i.e. disbelievers].﴿

(Qur'an 5: 44)

— this will be discussed in a separate chapter. And Allah is the Source of strength and the One Whose help we seek.

The General *Aayaat* Which Prove that it is Obligatory to Refer for Judgement to the Laws of Allah

1 - Allah (ﷻ) says:

﴿ وَمِنَ ٱلنَّاسِ مَن يَتَّخِذُ مِن دُونِ ٱللَّهِ أَندَادًا يُحِبُّونَهُمْ كَحُبِّ ٱللَّهِ ... ﴿١٦٥﴾ ﴾

﴿And of mankind are some who take [for worship] others besides Allah as rivals [to Allah]. They love them as they love Allah...﴾ *(Qur'an 2: 165)*

Aṭ-Ṭabari mentioned that the word "*nadd*" (pl. *andaad*, translated here as "rivals") means a peer or one of equal rank. Then he mentioned two views concerning the rivals who used to be worshipped instead of Allah. One view is that they are the gods which are worshipped instead of Allah. Then he said: "Others said that the 'rivals' referred to here are their leaders whom they used to obey in matters that involved disobedience to Allah... (Then he narrated from As-Suddi): ﴿And of mankind are some who take [for worship] others besides Allah as rivals [to Allah]. They love them as they love Allah...﴾. He said, these are rivals among men whom they obey as they should obey Allah; when they issue commands, they obey them and disobey Allah."[1]

The *tafseer* of As-Suddi explains the connection between love and obedience:

﴿ قُلْ إِن كُنتُمْ تُحِبُّونَ ٱللَّهَ فَٱتَّبِعُونِى يُحْبِبْكُمُ ٱللَّهُ ... ﴿٣١﴾ ﴾

﴿Say [O' Muhammad to mankind]: 'If you [really] love Allah, then follow me [i.e. accept Islamic Monotheism, follow the Qur'an and the Sunnah], Allah will love you...'﴾ *(Qur'an 3: 31)*

[1] *Tafseer aṭ-Ṭabari*, 3/280, Ed. by Shaakir.

Hence when Ibn Jareer spoke about the *aayah* of *Soorah al-Baqarah*, the second chapter of the Qur'an (2: 165) quoted above, and the following *aayah*, and about how those who are followed will disown those who follow them, he said, "With regard to the *aayah*:

﴿ إِذْ تَبَرَّأَ ٱلَّذِينَ ٱتُّبِعُوا۟ مِنَ ٱلَّذِينَ ٱتَّبَعُوا۟ ... ﴿١٦٦﴾ ﴾

﴿When those who were followed disown [declare themselves innocent of] those who followed [them]...﴾ *(Qur'an 2: 166)*

— it only refers to the rivals who are taken instead of Allah by those people whom Allah described in the verse, ﴿And of mankind are some who take [for worship] others besides Allah as rivals [to Allah]...﴾ *(Qur'an 2: 165)*. These rivals are the ones who will disown their followers. If the *aayah* indicates this, then the way in which As-Suddi interpreted, it is correct, when he said that in the *aayah*, ﴿And of mankind are some who take [for worship] others besides Allah as rivals [to Allah]...﴾, the word 'rivals' (*andaad*) in this case referred to human rivals whom they obey when they issue commands, and they disobey Allah by obeying them. The believers, in contrast, obey Allah and disobey others besides Him. And the view that the *aayah*, ﴿When those who were followed disown [declare themselves innocent of] those who followed [them]...﴾ *(Qur'an 2: 166)* refers to the *Shayaaṭeen* (devils) who will disown their human followers, is incorrect, because the context of this *aayah* is speaking of those who take rivals."[2]

Ibn al-Qayyim (may Allah have mercy on him) spoke at length about this *aayah* when he discussed the status of love in *Madaarij as-Saalikeen*. Among the things he said was: "Creation and commanding, reward and punishment, all stem from love and are for

---

[2] *Tafseer aṭ-Ṭabari*, 3/288, Ed. by Shaakir.

its sake. This is the truth for which the heavens and the earth were created. This is the truth which includes commands and prohibitions, and this is the secret of being devoted to One God and of loving Him Alone. (This truth) is the testimony that there is no god except Allah."[3] Then he said: "Allah (ﷻ) says: ﴿And of mankind are some who take [for worship] others besides Allah as rivals [to Allah]...﴾.

Here Allah tells us that whoever loves anything else as he loves Allah is one of those who have taken (for worship) rivals besides Allah. This is a rival in love, not in creation or Lordship. For no one among the people of this earth claims that this is a rival in Lordship, unlike the case of a rival in love, for most of the people of this earth have taken rivals in love and veneration to Allah."[4]

After mentioning the two scholarly views concerning the *aayah*, ﴿They love them as they love Allah...﴾ he said: "When Allah describes this making equal, He is telling us about them - and they will be in the Fire, saying to their gods and rivals, who will be sharing the torment with them,

﴿ تَٱللَّهِ إِن كُنَّا لَفِى ضَلَـٰلٍ مُّبِينٍ ﴿٩٧﴾ إِذْ نُسَوِّيكُم بِرَبِّ ٱلْعَـٰلَمِينَ ﴿٩٨﴾ ﴾

> ﴿By Allah, we were truly, in a manifest error, When we held you [false gods] as equals [in worship] with the Lord of the *'Aalameen* [mankind, jinn and all that exists].﴾ *(Qur'an 26: 97-98)*

It is well known that they did not regard them as equal to the Lord of the Worlds with regard to creation and Lordship,[5] rather they made

---

[3] *Madaarij as-Saalikeen*, 3/19.

[4] Ibid, 3/20.

[5] *Shaykh* Al-Fiqqi (may Allah have mercy on him), commented here, "But they regarded them as equal with Him in the characteristics of Lordship, which means issuing laws and legislation... etc."

68451004 PEACOT NAVY

8 81894 18730 1

2 PIECE SET

SIZE 6

C

them equal with Him in love and veneration. This is also holding equal as mentioned in the *aayah*,

﴿... ثُمَّ ٱلَّذِينَ كَفَرُوا۟ بِرَبِّهِمْ يَعْدِلُونَ ١﴾

﴿...Yet those who disbelieve hold others as equal with their Lord.﴾ *(Qur'an 6:1)*,

— i.e., they hold others as equal with Him in worship, which is love and veneration."[6]

Undoubtedly the two views concerning the meaning of *andaad* (rivals) are both correct. The relevant point here is the fact that this word was interpreted as referring to the leaders who are obeyed besides Allah.

2 - Allah (سبحانه وتعالى) says:

﴿كَانَ ٱلنَّاسُ أُمَّةً وَٰحِدَةً فَبَعَثَ ٱللَّهُ ٱلنَّبِيِّـۧنَ مُبَشِّرِينَ وَمُنذِرِينَ وَأَنزَلَ مَعَهُمُ ٱلْكِتَـٰبَ بِٱلْحَقِّ لِيَحْكُمَ بَيْنَ ٱلنَّاسِ فِيمَا ٱخْتَلَفُوا۟ فِيهِ ... ٢١٣﴾

﴿Mankind were one community and Allah sent Prophets with glad tidings and warnings, and with them He sent down the Scripture in truth to judge between people in matters wherein they differed...﴾ *(Qur'an 2: 213)*

Al-Qaasimi said in *Mahaasin at-Ta'weel*: ﴿...And with them He sent down the Scripture...﴾ means, His word which encompassed all that they needed with regard to religion, righteousness and complete guidance, so that they would be characterized with truth in all aspects.' ﴿...To judge between people in matters wherein they differed'...﴾ means, with regard to beliefs and actions, when before that they had been one community..."[7]

---

[6] *Madaarij as-Saalikeen*, 3/21.

[7] *Mahaasin at-Ta'weel* by Al-Qaasimi, 3/528.

Every Prophet was sent to his people and there was sent down with Him a Book so that he might judge between his people in all the matters wherein they differed.

3 - Allah (ﷻ) says:

﴿ ... فَمَن يَكْفُرْ بِٱلطَّٰغُوتِ وَيُؤْمِنۢ بِٱللَّهِ فَقَدِ ٱسْتَمْسَكَ بِٱلْعُرْوَةِ ٱلْوُثْقَىٰ ... ﴿٢٥٦﴾ ﴾

﴿...Whoever disbelieves in *ṭaaghoot* and believes in Allah, then he has grasped the most trustworthy handhold...﴾ *(Qur'an 2: 256)*

There are a number of opinions concerning the word *ṭaaghoot*. It is said that it means the *Shayṭaan*, or that it means the magician or soothsayer; these were suggested by Ibn Jareer,[8] and he quoted reports to support each of them.

When he mentioned the view that it means the soothsayer, he reported that Ibn Jurayj said that ﴿...Whoever disbelieves in *ṭaaghoot...*﴾ means, soothsayers to whom *shayaaṭeen* (devils) come down and cast (words) onto their tongues and into their hearts.

Then he said: "Abuz-Zubayr told me that he heard Jaabir ibn 'Abdullah say, when he was asked about the *ṭaaghoot* to which they used to refer for judgement, 'there was one in Juhaynah, one in Aslam, in every quarter there was one. They were the soothsayers to whom the *Shayṭaan* comes.'"[9]

Then At-Ṭabari stated which he believed to be more correct: "The correct view concerning *ṭaaghoot* in my opinion is that it means everything which is put in the place of Allah and is worshipped instead of Him, whether by force on the part of the one who is

---

[8] *Tafseer aṭ-Ṭabari*, 5/416-418, Ed. by Shaakir.

[9] Ibid, 5/418.

worshipped or by the free will of the worshipper, and whether the one who is so worshipped is a human or a *shayṭaan*, a statue or an idol, or whatever it is."[10]

This is a comprehensive definition of the word *ṭaghoot*. The word *ṭaghoot* is also mentioned in another *aayah*, where Allah (ﷻ) says:

﴿ أَلَمْ تَرَ إِلَى ٱلَّذِينَ أُوتُوا۟ نَصِيبًا مِّنَ ٱلْكِتَٰبِ يُؤْمِنُونَ بِٱلْجِبْتِ وَٱلطَّٰغُوتِ... ﴿٥١﴾ ﴾

﴿Have you not seen those who were given a portion of the Scripture? They believe in *jibt* and *ṭaaghoot...*﴾ [11]

(Qur'an 4: 51)

4 - Allah (ﷻ) says:

﴿ قُلْ إِن كُنتُمْ تُحِبُّونَ ٱللَّهَ فَٱتَّبِعُونِى يُحْبِبْكُمُ ٱللَّهُ وَيَغْفِرْ لَكُمْ ذُنُوبَكُمْ ۗ وَٱللَّهُ غَفُورٌ رَّحِيمٌ ﴿٣١﴾ قُلْ أَطِيعُوا۟ ٱللَّهَ وَٱلرَّسُولَ ۖ فَإِن تَوَلَّوْا۟ فَإِنَّ ٱللَّهَ لَا يُحِبُّ ٱلْكَٰفِرِينَ ﴿٣٢﴾ ﴾

﴿Say [O' Muhammad to mankind]: 'If you [really] love Allah, then follow me [i.e. accept Islamic Monotheism, follow the Qur'an and the Sunnah], Allah will love you and forgive you your sins. And Allah is Oft-Forgiving, Most Merciful.' Say [O' Muhammad]: 'Obey Allah and the Messenger [Muhammad].' But if they turn away, then Allah does not like the disbelievers.﴾

(Qur'an 3: 31-32)

---

[10] *Tafseer aṭ-Ṭabari*, 5/419; 8/465.

[11] The words "*Jibt* and *Ṭaaghoot*" cover wide meanings: They mean anything worshipped other than the Real God (Allah), i.e. all the false deities, it may be an idol, the *Shayṭaan*, graves, stone, the sun, a star, an angel, a saint or any human being. (Footnote from Interpretation of the Meanings of the Noble Qur'an by Dr. Muhammad Muḥsin Khan and Dr. Muhammad Taqi-ud-Din al-Hilali) - Translator.

At-Ṭabari thought it most likely that those who were being addressed here were the Christians of Najraan.[12] But Ibn Katheer thought that it was general in meaning, and said, commenting on it, "This *aayah* states that everyone who claims to love Allah, but does not follow the way of Muhammad, is lying and making a false claim, until he does follow the way of Muhammad and the religion of the Prophet, in all his words, deeds and circumstances. It is reported in *Aṣ-Ṣaḥeeḥ* that the Messenger of Allah (ﷺ) said:

> 'Whoever does any action that is not in accordance with this matter of ours (Islam) will have it rejected.'[13]..."[14]

Then Ibn Katheer said, commenting on the second *aayah* — ﴾Say [O' Muhammad]: 'Obey Allah and the Messenger [Muhammad].' But if they turn away...﴿ i.e., if they go against his command — ﴾...Then Allah does not like the disbelievers﴿ —

"This indicates that going against his way is *kufr*, and Allah does not like anyone who is described as such, even if he claims to love Allah and thinks that he is drawing closer to Him, unless he follows the Messenger, the Unlettered Prophet, the Seal of the Messengers, the Messenger of Allah to the two races of jinn and mankind, who, if the Prophets — and even the Messengers, including the Messengers of strong will[15] — had been alive during his time, they would have had no choice but to follow him and obey him and his laws..."[16]

---

[12] *Tafseer aṭ-Ṭabari*, 6/324, ed. by Shaakir.

[13] Muslim: *Kitaab al-Aqḍiyah, Baab Naqḍ al-Aḥkaam al-Baaṭilah wa Radd Muḥdathaat al-Umoor*, hadith no. 1718. Before it there appears the hadith, "Whoever innovates anything in this matter of ours (Islam) that is not a part of it, will have it rejected."

[14] *Tafseer Ibn Katheer*, 3/25, Ash-Sha'b edition.

[15] i.e., Muhammad, Nooḥ (Noah), Ibraaheem (Abraham), Moosa (Moses) and 'Eesa (Jesus) (peace be upon them all). - Translator

[16] *Tafseer Ibn Katheer*, 3/25.

It is as if Ibn Katheer was referring to some of his contemporaries, as if this is the reaction of one who is dealing with the reality of his own time. Hence he said, "even if he claims to love Allah and thinks that he is drawing closer to Him."

5 - Allah (ﷻ) says, following the *aayaat* about inheritance:

﴿ وَمَن يَعْصِ ٱللَّهَ وَرَسُولَهُۥ وَيَتَعَدَّ حُدُودَهُۥ يُدْخِلْهُ نَارًا خَٰلِدًا فِيهَا وَلَهُۥ عَذَابٌ مُّهِينٌ ﴿١٤﴾ ﴾

﴿And whosoever disobeys Allah and His Messenger [Muhammad], and transgresses His limits, He will cast him into the Fire, to abide therein; and he shall have a disgraceful torment.﴾ *(Qur'an 4: 14)*

After commenting on this *aayah*, and stating that it is most likely that the "abiding" (*khulood*) referred to is eternal, Aṭ-Ṭabari said: "If someone were to ask, will the one who disobeys Allah and His Messenger with regard to inheritance abide forever in Hell? The answer is, yes, if there is, with his disobedience of Allah and His Messenger, any doubt concerning the obligation which Allah enjoins upon His slaves in these two *aayaat*, or who knows that but he opposes them in their command. This is according to what Ibn 'Abbaas (رضي الله عنه)[17] narrated about what was said to the Messenger of Allah (ﷺ) when the following *aayaat* were revealed:

﴿ يُوصِيكُمُ ٱللَّهُ فِىٓ أَوْلَٰدِكُمْ ۖ لِلذَّكَرِ مِثْلُ حَظِّ ٱلْأُنثَيَيْنِ ۚ ... ﴿١١﴾ ﴾

﴿Allah commands you as regards your children's [inheritance]: to the male, a portion equal to that of two females...﴾ *(Qur'an 4: 11-12,* the verses on inheritance)

[17] This is a reference to something he said earlier. See *Tafseer aṭ-Ṭabari*, 8/32, ed. by Shaakir.

Someone said, 'Should the one who does not ride a horse, or fight the enemy, or acquire booty, acquire half or all of the wealth?' This was an objection to the share that Allah allocated to the young children of the deceased and to his womenfolk and daughters, from one who objected to the manner in which Allah dictated that the wealth of the deceased should be divided among the heirs as stated in His Book, and he went against the ruling of Allah and His Messenger. He denounced their ruling as it was denounced by those whom Ibn 'Abbaas mentioned, the hypocrites who were among the Companions of the Messenger of Allah (ﷺ), concerning whom and their like this *aayah* was revealed. So (such a person) is one of those who will abide forever in Hell, because by objecting to the ruling of Allah on this matter he becomes a *kaafir* who disbelieves in Allah, and goes beyond the pale of Islam."[18]

This is how Ibn Katheer understood it, when he said in his *tafseer* of the *aayah*, ﴾And whosoever disobeys Allah and His Messenger [Muhammad], and transgresses His limits, He will cast him into the Fire, to abide therein; and he shall have a disgraceful torment.﴿ *(Qur'an 4: 14)* — "i.e., because he changed the ruling which Allah had given and he opposed Allah with regard to His ruling. This could only stem from a lack of acceptance of the division (of inheritance) which Allah had decreed. Hence He will punish him with humiliation in the eternal, painful torment."[19]

6 - Allah (سبحانه وتعالى) says:

﴿ إِنَّآ أَنزَلْنَآ إِلَيْكَ ٱلْكِتَٰبَ بِٱلْحَقِّ لِتَحْكُمَ بَيْنَ ٱلنَّاسِ بِمَآ أَرَىٰكَ ٱللَّهُ
... ﴿١٠٥﴾ ﴾

﴾Surely, We have sent down to you [O' Muhammad] the

---

[18] *Tafseer aṭ-Ṭabari*, 8/72-73, ed. by Shaakir.

[19] *Tafseer Ibn Katheer*, 2/203, Ash-Sha'b edition.

> Book [this Qur'an] in truth that you might judge between men by that which Allah has shown you...﴾
> *(Qur'an 4: 105)*

At-Ṭabari said: "﴿Surely, We have sent down to you...﴾ — O' Muhammad — ﴿the Book﴾ — meaning the Qur'an — ﴿...That you might judge between men by that which Allah has shown you...﴾ — meaning, by that which Allah has revealed to you of His Book."[20]

Ibn 'Aṭiyah said: ﴿...By that which Allah has shown you...﴾ means, according to the laws of shari'ah, whether based on the *waḥy* and the texts, or in the light of the principles of the *waḥy*, and Allah guaranteed infallibility to His Prophets."[21]

If Allah commanded His Messenger to judge by that which Allah had shown him (i.e., the laws of shari'ah), then this injunction is even more binding on others. Hence Allah (ﷻ) says in another *aayah*:

﴿ لَيْسَ لَكَ مِنَ ٱلْأَمْرِ شَىْءٌ... ﴿١٢٨﴾ ﴾

> ﴿Not for you [O' Muhammad, but for Allah] is the decision...﴾ *(Qur'an 3: 128)*

At-Ṭabari said: ﴿Not for you [O' Muhammad, but for Allah] is the decision...﴾ means, it is not for you, O' Muhammad, to decide concerning My creation; rather it is for you to implement My command concerning them, and to guide them to obey Me. But the decision concerning them is Mine, and the judgement concerning them is in My hand and no one else's. I will decide and rule concerning them as I will..."[22] Although the *aayah* was revealed concerning the battle of Uḥud or the *du'aa'* in which the Messenger (ﷺ) prayed against the *kuffaar* or Quraysh, the wording is general as

[20] *Tafseer aṭ-Ṭabari*, 9/175, ed. by Shaakir.

[21] *Al-Muḥarrar al-Wajeez*, 4/245.

[22] *Tafseer aṭ-Ṭabari*, 7/194, ed. by Shaakir.

reflected at the beginning of the quotation from Aṭ-Ṭabari. This is similar to the *aayah,*

﴿... قُلْ إِنَّ ٱلْأَمْرَ كُلَّهُۥ لِلَّهِ ... ﴿١٥٤﴾﴾

﴾...Say [O' Muhammad]: 'Indeed the affair belongs wholly to Allah'...﴿ *(Qur'an 3: 154)*

— i.e., He directs it as He wills and controls it as He likes, as Aṭ-Ṭabari said.[23]

7 - Allah (ﷻ) says:

﴿أَفَغَيْرَ ٱللَّهِ أَبْتَغِى حَكَمًا ... ﴿١١٤﴾﴾

﴾Shall I seek a judge [*ḥakam*] other than Allah...﴿ *(Qur'an 6: 114)*

Qurṭubi said: "The meaning is: shall I seek someone other than Allah as a judge for you, when He is the One Who has taken care of the issue in the verses that have been revealed from the clear Book? Then it is said, *al-ḥakam* is more emphatic than *al-ḥaakim*, so no one deserves to be called *ḥakam* except one who judges according to the truth, because it is an attribute of veneration and praise, whereas *al-ḥaakim* simply refers to an action, so one who judges according to something other than the truth may also be described as such."[24] The indication and meaning of the *aayah* are clear.

8 - Allah (ﷻ) says:

﴿... أَلَا لَهُ ٱلْخَلْقُ وَٱلْأَمْرُ ... ﴿٥٤﴾﴾

﴾...Surely, His is the creation and commandment...﴿ *(Qur'an 7: 54)*

---

[23] *Tafseer aṭ-Ṭabari*, 7/322.

[24] *Tafseer al-Qurṭubi*, 7/70. See also *Rooḥ al-Ma'aani* by Al-Aloosi, 8/8, 2nd edition.

Undoubtedly the One to Whom alone belongs the creation, to Him alone also will the commandment belong. At-Ṭabari says: "To Allah belongs all of creation, and the command which none may go against or put back. (This belongs exclusively to Him) and to none besides Him at all, and not to the gods and idols whom the *mushrikoon* worship, which can neither harm nor benefit, nor create nor command."[25] Al-Baghawi said: "His is the creation because He created them, and His is the commandment, to command His creation as He wills."[26]

9 - There are very many similar *aayaat*; if we were to contemplate each of them, the discussion would be very long indeed. Perhaps what we have mentioned above is sufficient to provide examples of what the *mufassireen* have said concerning some of these *aayaat*. Below, it will be sufficient simply to refer to some of the *aayaat* and mention the *soorahs* (chapters) in which they are found, then any reader who wishes to learn more about their meanings and what they indicate may consult the books of *tafseer*. But it should be noted that rulings, commandments, permission, etc., as referred to in the Qur'an, are divided into two categories:

a) *Kawni* (universal) or *qadari* (decrees), having to do with His creation.
b) *Deeni* (religious) or *shar'i* (legislative), having to do with His command.

So the *kawni ḥukm* (universal ruling) is reflected in *aayaat* such as:

﴿قَٰلَ رَبِّ ٱحْكُم بِٱلْحَقِّ... ﴿١١٢﴾﴾

﴿He [Muhammad] said: 'My Lord! Judge You in truth!...'﴾ *(Qur'an 21: 112)* —

[25] *Tafseer aṭ-Ṭabari*, 12/483-484, ed. by Shaakir.

[26] *Tafseer al-Baghawi*, 3/286.

meaning, do that which will bring victory to Your slaves and humiliate Your enemies.

The *shar'i hukm* (legislative ruling) is reflected in *aayaat* such as:

﴿...ذَٰلِكُمْ حُكْمُ ٱللَّهِ يَحْكُمُ بَيْنَكُمْ ... ﴿١٠﴾﴾

﴿...That is the Judgement of Allah, He judges between you...﴾ *(Qur'an 60: 10)*

Here we may note three points:

i) That this division serves to explain that there is no conflict between *shar'* (Divine law) and *qadr* (Divine decree). The Divine decree must inevitably come to pass, in which there will be things that go against the laws of Allah, such as the *kufr* of the *kuffaar* and the sin of the sinners. *Shar'* refers to that which Allah commands and is pleased with, but some of it happens and some does not.

ii) Some *aayaat* may combine the two, such as:

﴿... وَلَا يُشْرِكُ فِى حُكْمِهِۦٓ أَحَدًا ﴿٢٦﴾﴾

﴿...And He makes none to share in His Decision and His Rule.﴾ *(Qur'an 18: 26)*

Although some of the *mufassireen*, such as An-Nasafi and Al-Baydaawi, interpret *hukmihi* (translated here as "His Decision and His Rule") as meaning "His Judgement", most of them, including At-Tabari and Ibn Katheer, interpret it as meaning both things (*shar'* and *qadr*). Some of them stated that it includes both things.[27] Al-Shanqeeti said, "It includes all that Allah decrees, which includes *tashree'* (legislation) first and foremost."[28] Then he mentioned many *aayaat* which convey the same meaning — some of which we will

---

[27] They include, Ibn al-Qayyim in *Shifaa' al-'Aleel*, Pp. 280; Ibn Sa'di, 5/27.

[28] *Adwaa' al-Bayaan*, 4/90.

quote below — and some of which may be interpreted as referring to *Al-Ḥukm al-Qadri* (the Divine decree), but they include the idea that Allah Alone has the power of *ḥukm* (ruling) and *tashree'* (legislation), as noted in the next point.

iii) The fact that Allah Alone has the power of universal ruling and decree implies that He alone has the power of legislative ruling, as explained above in the *aayah*: ﴿...Surely, His is the creation and commandment...﴾ *(Qur'an 7: 54)*.

These points are made so that no one will have the right to object by saying that the context of some of these *aayaat* applies only to the Divine decree, even though most of these *aayaat* state that Allah Alone has the power of legislative ruling.

Among the *aayaat* (verses) that have been revealed concerning this are the following:

﴿ ... أَلَا لَهُ ٱلْحُكْمُ وَهُوَ أَسْرَعُ ٱلْحَٰسِبِينَ ﴿٦٢﴾ ﴾

﴿...Surely, for Him is the judgement and He is the Swiftest in taking account.﴾ *(Qur'an 6: 62)*

﴿ ... إِنِ ٱلْحُكْمُ إِلَّا لِلَّهِ يَقُصُّ ٱلْحَقَّ وَهُوَ خَيْرُ ٱلْفَٰصِلِينَ ﴿٥٧﴾ ﴾

﴿...The decision is only for Allah, He declares the truth, and He is the Best of judges.﴾ *(Qur'an 6: 57)*

﴿ ... بَل لِّلَّهِ ٱلْأَمْرُ جَمِيعًا ... ﴿٣١﴾ ﴾

﴿...But the decision of all things is certainly with Allah...﴾ *(Qur'an 13: 31)*

﴿ وَكَذَٰلِكَ أَنزَلْنَٰهُ حُكْمًا عَرَبِيًّا ... ﴿٣٧﴾ ﴾

﴿And thus have We sent it [the Qur'an] down to be a judgement of authority in Arabic...﴾ *(Qur'an 13: 37)*

﴿... وَٱللَّهُ يَحۡكُمُ لَا مُعَقِّبَ لِحُكۡمِهِۦۚ ... ﴿٤١﴾﴾

﴿...And Allah judges, there is none to put back His Judgement...﴾ *(Qur'an 13: 41)*

﴿... إِنِ ٱلۡحُكۡمُ إِلَّا لِلَّهِۚ أَمَرَ أَلَّا تَعۡبُدُوٓاْ إِلَّآ إِيَّاهُۚ ... ﴿٤٠﴾﴾

﴿...The command [or the judgement] is for none but Allah. He has commanded that you worship none but Him...﴾ *(Qur'an 12: 40)*

﴿... إِنِ ٱلۡحُكۡمُ إِلَّا لِلَّهِۖ عَلَيۡهِ تَوَكَّلۡتُۖ ... ﴿٦٧﴾﴾

﴿...Verily, the decision rests only with Allah. In Him, I put my trust...﴾ *(Qur'an 12: 67)*

﴿... وَلَا يُشۡرِكُ فِي حُكۡمِهِۦٓ أَحَدٗا ﴿٢٦﴾﴾

﴿...And He makes none to share in His Decision and His Rule.﴾ *(Qur'an 18: 26)*

﴿لَّقَدۡ أَنزَلۡنَآ ءَايَٰتٖ مُّبَيِّنَٰتٖۚ وَٱللَّهُ يَهۡدِي مَن يَشَآءُ إِلَىٰ صِرَٰطٖ مُّسۡتَقِيمٖ
﴿٤٦﴾ وَيَقُولُونَ ءَامَنَّا بِٱللَّهِ وَبِٱلرَّسُولِ وَأَطَعۡنَا ثُمَّ يَتَوَلَّىٰ فَرِيقٞ مِّنۡهُم مِّنۢ بَعۡدِ
ذَٰلِكَۚ وَمَآ أُوْلَٰٓئِكَ بِٱلۡمُؤۡمِنِينَ ﴿٤٧﴾ وَإِذَا دُعُوٓاْ إِلَى ٱللَّهِ وَرَسُولِهِۦ لِيَحۡكُمَ بَيۡنَهُمۡ
إِذَا فَرِيقٞ مِّنۡهُم مُّعۡرِضُونَ ﴿٤٨﴾ وَإِن يَكُن لَّهُمُ ٱلۡحَقُّ يَأۡتُوٓاْ إِلَيۡهِ مُذۡعِنِينَ ﴿٤٩﴾ أَفِي
قُلُوبِهِم مَّرَضٌ أَمِ ٱرۡتَابُوٓاْ أَمۡ يَخَافُونَ أَن يَحِيفَ ٱللَّهُ عَلَيۡهِمۡ وَرَسُولُهُۥۚ بَلۡ أُوْلَٰٓئِكَ
هُمُ ٱلظَّٰلِمُونَ ﴿٥٠﴾ إِنَّمَا كَانَ قَوۡلَ ٱلۡمُؤۡمِنِينَ إِذَا دُعُوٓاْ إِلَى ٱللَّهِ وَرَسُولِهِۦ
لِيَحۡكُمَ بَيۡنَهُمۡ أَن يَقُولُواْ سَمِعۡنَا وَأَطَعۡنَاۚ وَأُوْلَٰٓئِكَ هُمُ ٱلۡمُفۡلِحُونَ ﴿٥١﴾ وَمَن
يُطِعِ ٱللَّهَ وَرَسُولَهُۥ وَيَخۡشَ ٱللَّهَ وَيَتَّقۡهِ فَأُوْلَٰٓئِكَ هُمُ ٱلۡفَآئِزُونَ ﴿٥٢﴾﴾

﴿We have indeed sent down [in this Qur'an] manifest *aayaat* [proofs, evidences, verses, lessons, signs, revelations, lawful and unlawful things, and the set boundaries of Islamic religion, that make things clear showing the Right Path of Allah]. And Allah guides whom He wills to the Straight Path [i.e. to Allah's religion of Islamic Monotheism]. They [hypocrites] say: 'We have believed in Allah and in the Messenger [Muhammad], and we obey,' then a party of them turn away thereafter, such are not believers. And when they are called to Allah [i.e. His Words, the Qur'an] and His Messenger, to judge between them, lo! a party of them refuses [to come] and turns away. But if the truth is on their side, they come to him willingly with submission. Is there a disease in their hearts? Or do they doubt or fear lest Allah and His Messenger should wrong them in judgement. Nay, it is they themselves who are the *zaalimoon* [polytheists, hypocrites and wrongdoers]. The only saying of the faithful believers, when they are called to Allah [His Words, the Qur'an] and His Messenger, to judge between them, is that they say: 'We hear and we obey.' And such are the successful [who will live forever in Paradise]. And whosoever obeys Allah and His Messenger, fears Allah, and keeps his duty [to Him], such are the successful.﴾

(Qur'an 24: 46-52)

﴿لَا تَجْعَلُوا دُعَاءَ الرَّسُولِ بَيْنَكُمْ كَدُعَاءِ بَعْضِكُم بَعْضًا ۚ قَدْ يَعْلَمُ
اللَّهُ الَّذِينَ يَتَسَلَّلُونَ مِنكُمْ لِوَاذًا ۚ فَلْيَحْذَرِ الَّذِينَ يُخَالِفُونَ عَنْ أَمْرِهِ أَن
تُصِيبَهُمْ فِتْنَةٌ أَوْ يُصِيبَهُمْ عَذَابٌ أَلِيمٌ ﴿٦٣﴾﴾

﴿Make not the calling of the Messenger [Muhammad] among you as your calling one of another. Allah knows those of you who slip away under shelter [of some excuse without taking the permission to leave, from the Messenger]. And let those who oppose the Messenger's [Muhammad's] commandment [i.e. his Sunnah — legal ways, orders, acts of worship, statements] [among the sects] beware, lest some *fitnah* [disbelief, trials, afflictions, earthquakes, killing, overpowered by a tyrant] should befall them or a painful torment be inflicted on them.﴿ *(Qur'an 24: 63)*

﴿ وَرَبُّكَ يَخْلُقُ مَا يَشَآءُ وَيَخْتَارُ مَا كَانَ لَهُمُ ٱلْخِيَرَةُ سُبْحَٰنَ ٱللَّهِ
وَتَعَٰلَىٰ عَمَّا يُشْرِكُونَ ﴿٦٨﴾ وَرَبُّكَ يَعْلَمُ مَا تُكِنُّ صُدُورُهُمْ وَمَا
يُعْلِنُونَ ﴿٦٩﴾ وَهُوَ ٱللَّهُ لَآ إِلَٰهَ إِلَّا هُوَ لَهُ ٱلْحَمْدُ فِى ٱلْأُولَىٰ وَٱلْءَاخِرَةِ
وَلَهُ ٱلْحُكْمُ وَإِلَيْهِ تُرْجَعُونَ ﴿٧٠﴾ ﴾

﴾And your Lord creates whatsoever He wills and chooses, no choice have they [in any matter]. Glorified is Allah, and exalted above all that they associate [as partners with Him]. And your Lord knows what their breasts conceal, and what they reveal. And He is Allah; *Laa ilaaha illa Huwa* [none has the right to be worshipped but He], all praises and thanks be to Him [both] in the first [i.e. in this world] and in the last [i.e. in the Hereafter]. And for Him is the Decision, and to Him shall you [all] be returned.﴿ *(Qur'an 28: 68-70)*

﴿ وَلَا يَصُدُّنَّكَ عَنْ ءَايَٰتِ ٱللَّهِ بَعْدَ إِذْ أُنزِلَتْ إِلَيْكَ وَٱدْعُ إِلَىٰ رَبِّكَ وَلَا
تَكُونَنَّ مِنَ ٱلْمُشْرِكِينَ ﴿٨٧﴾ وَلَا تَدْعُ مَعَ ٱللَّهِ إِلَٰهًا ءَاخَرَ لَآ إِلَٰهَ إِلَّا هُوَ
كُلُّ شَىْءٍ هَالِكٌ إِلَّا وَجْهَهُۥ لَهُ ٱلْحُكْمُ وَإِلَيْهِ تُرْجَعُونَ ﴿٨٨﴾ ﴾

﴾And let them not turn you [O' Muhammad] away from [preaching] the *aayaat* [revelations and verses] of Allah after they have been sent down to you: and invite [men] to [believe in] your Lord and be not of *al-mushrikoon* [those who associate partners with Allah, e.g. polytheists, pagans, idolaters, and those who disbelieve in the Oneness of Allah and deny the Prophethood of Messenger Muhammad]. And invoke not any other *ilaah* [god] along with Allah, *Laa ilaaha illa Huwa* [none has the right to be worshipped but He]. Everything will perish save His Face. His is the Decision, and to Him you [all] shall be returned.﴿ *(Qur'an 28: 87-88)*

﴿ قُلْ أَرَءَيْتُم مَّآ أَنزَلَ ٱللَّهُ لَكُم مِّن رِّزْقٍ فَجَعَلْتُم مِّنْهُ حَرَامًا وَحَلَٰلًا قُلْ ءَآللَّهُ أَذِنَ لَكُمْ أَمْ عَلَى ٱللَّهِ تَفْتَرُونَ ﴿٥٩﴾ وَمَا ظَنُّ ٱلَّذِينَ يَفْتَرُونَ عَلَى ٱللَّهِ ٱلْكَذِبَ يَوْمَ ٱلْقِيَٰمَةِ إِنَّ ٱللَّهَ لَذُو فَضْلٍ عَلَى ٱلنَّاسِ وَلَٰكِنَّ أَكْثَرَهُمْ لَا يَشْكُرُونَ ﴿٦٠﴾ ﴾

﴾Say [O' Muhammad to these polytheists]: 'Tell me, what provision Allah has sent down to you! And you have made of it lawful and unlawful.' Say [O' Muhammad]: 'Has Allah permitted you [to do so], or do you invent a lie against Allah?' And what think those who invent a lie against Allah, on the Day of Resurrection? [i.e. Do they think that they will be forgiven and excused! Nay, they will have an eternal punishment in the fire of Hell]. Truly, Allah is full of bounty to mankind, but most of them are ungrateful.﴿
(Qur'an 10: 59-60)

﴿ وَمَا كَانَ لِمُؤْمِنٍ وَلَا مُؤْمِنَةٍ إِذَا قَضَى ٱللَّهُ وَرَسُولُهُۥٓ أَمْرًا أَن يَكُونَ لَهُمُ ٱلْخِيَرَةُ مِنْ أَمْرِهِمْ وَمَن يَعْصِ ٱللَّهَ وَرَسُولَهُۥ فَقَدْ ضَلَّ ضَلَٰلًا مُّبِينًا ﴿٣٦﴾ ﴾

﴾It is not for a believer, man or woman, when Allah and His Messenger have decreed a matter that they should have any option in their decision. And whoever disobeys Allah and His Messenger, he has indeed strayed into a plain error.﴿ *(Qur'an 33: 36)*

﴿ وَمَا ٱخْتَلَفْتُمْ فِيهِ مِن شَىْءٍ فَحُكْمُهُۥٓ إِلَى ٱللَّهِ ذَٰلِكُمُ ٱللَّهُ رَبِّى عَلَيْهِ تَوَكَّلْتُ وَإِلَيْهِ أُنِيبُ ﴿١٠﴾ ﴾

﴾And in whatsoever you differ, the decision thereof is with Allah [He is the ruling Judge]. [And say O' Muhammad to these polytheists]: Such is Allah, my Lord in Whom I put my trust, and to Him I turn [in all of my affairs and] in repentance.﴿ *(Qur'an 42: 10)*

﴿ ٱللَّهُ ٱلَّذِىٓ أَنزَلَ ٱلْكِتَٰبَ بِٱلْحَقِّ وَٱلْمِيزَانَ ۗ وَمَا يُدْرِيكَ لَعَلَّ ٱلسَّاعَةَ قَرِيبٌ ﴿١٧﴾ ﴾

﴾It is Allah Who has sent down the Book [the Qur'an] in truth, and the Balance [i.e. to act justly]. And what can make you know that perhaps the Hour is close at hand?﴿ *(Qur'an 42: 17)*

﴿ ثُمَّ جَعَلْنَٰكَ عَلَىٰ شَرِيعَةٍ مِّنَ ٱلْأَمْرِ فَٱتَّبِعْهَا وَلَا تَتَّبِعْ أَهْوَآءَ ٱلَّذِينَ لَا
يَعْلَمُونَ ﴿١٨﴾ إِنَّهُمْ لَن يُغْنُوا۟ عَنكَ مِنَ ٱللَّهِ شَيْـًٔا ۚ وَإِنَّ ٱلظَّٰلِمِينَ بَعْضُهُمْ
أَوْلِيَآءُ بَعْضٍ ۖ وَٱللَّهُ وَلِىُّ ٱلْمُتَّقِينَ ﴿١٩﴾ ﴾

﴾Then We have put you [O' Muhammad] on a [plain] way of [Our] commandment [like the one which We commanded Our Messengers before you (i.e. legal ways and laws of the Islamic Monotheism)]. So follow you that [Islamic Monotheism and its laws], and follow not the desires of those who know not. Verily, they can avail you nothing against Allah [if He wants to punish you]. Verily, the *zaalimoon* [polytheists, wrongdoers] are *awliyaa'* [protectors, helpers] of one another, but Allah is the *wali* [Helper, Protector] of the *muttaqoon* [the pious].﴿ *(Qur'an 45: 18-19)*

﴿ يَٰٓأَيُّهَا ٱلَّذِينَ ءَامَنُوا۟ لَا تُقَدِّمُوا۟ بَيْنَ يَدَىِ ٱللَّهِ وَرَسُولِهِۦ ۖ وَٱتَّقُوا۟ ٱللَّهَ ۚ إِنَّ ٱللَّهَ سَمِيعٌ
عَلِيمٌ ﴿١﴾ ﴾

﴾O' you who believe! Make not [a decision] in advance before Allah and His Messenger, and fear Allah. Verily,

Allah is All-Hearing, All-Knowing.﴿ *(Qur'an 49: 1)*

﴿ ... ذَٰلِكُمْ حُكْمُ ٱللَّهِ يَحْكُمُ بَيْنَكُمْ وَٱللَّهُ عَلِيمٌ حَكِيمٌ ۝١٠ ﴾

﴾...That is the Judgement of Allah, He judges between you. And Allah is All-Knowing, All-Wise.﴿

(Qur'an 60: 10)

And there are other *aayaat*, but it is not the point here to list them all. Further *aayaat* will be quoted below, *in sha Allah*.

Contemplating the Meanings of Some of the *Aayaat*

1 - Allah (سُبْحَانَهُ وَتَعَالَىٰ) says:

﴿ أَلَمْ تَرَ إِلَى ٱلَّذِينَ أُوتُوا۟ نَصِيبًا مِّنَ ٱلْكِتَٰبِ يُدْعَوْنَ إِلَىٰ كِتَٰبِ ٱللَّهِ لِيَحْكُمَ بَيْنَهُمْ ثُمَّ يَتَوَلَّىٰ فَرِيقٌ مِّنْهُمْ وَهُم مُّعْرِضُونَ ۝٢٣ ﴾

﴾Have you not seen those who have been given a portion of the Scripture? They are being invited to the Book of Allah to settle their dispute, then a party of them turn away, and they are averse.﴿ *(Qur'an 3: 23)*

There were some scholarly differences of opinion as to what is meant by "the Scripture", and whether it means the Qur'an or the *Tawraat* (Torah). Ibn Jareer thought the latter to be more correct.[29] There was also some scholarly dispute as to the reason for revelation (*sabab an-nuzool*). Aṭ-Ṭabari narrated that Ibn 'Abbaas said: "The Messenger of Allah (ﷺ) passed through a group of Jews in the house of *Al-Madaaris*, and called them to Allah. Na'eem ibn 'Amr and Al-Ḥaarith ibn Zayd said to him, 'What religion do you follow, O' Muhammad?' He said, 'I am of the community of Ibraaheem (Abraham) and I follow his religion.' They said, 'Ibraaheem was a

---

[29] *Tafseer aṭ-Ṭabari*, 6/292,ed. Shaakir. Ibn Katheer mentioned only this view, 2/22, Ash-Sha'b edition.

Jew.' The Messenger of Allah (ﷺ) said to them, 'Come, let us look at the *Tawraat*, (and it will decide) between us and you.' They refused to do that, then Allah revealed the words:

﴿ أَلَمۡ تَرَ إِلَى ٱلَّذِينَ أُوتُواْ نَصِيبٗا مِّنَ ٱلۡكِتَٰبِ يُدۡعَوۡنَ إِلَىٰ كِتَٰبِ ٱللَّهِ
لِيَحۡكُمَ بَيۡنَهُمۡ ثُمَّ يَتَوَلَّىٰ فَرِيقٞ مِّنۡهُمۡ وَهُم مُّعۡرِضُونَ ٢٣ ذَٰلِكَ بِأَنَّهُمۡ قَالُواْ لَن
تَمَسَّنَا ٱلنَّارُ إِلَّآ أَيَّامٗا مَّعۡدُودَٰتٖۖ وَغَرَّهُم فِي دِينِهِم مَّا كَانُواْ يَفۡتَرُونَ
٢٤ ﴾

﴿Have you not seen those who have been given a portion of the Scripture? They are being invited to the Book of Allah to settle their dispute, then a party of them turn away, and they are averse. This is because they say: 'The Fire shall not touch us but for a number of days.' And that which they used to invent regarding their religion has deceived them.﴾ *(Qur'an 3: 23-24)*."[30]

— This indicates that the book to which they were being called was the *Tawraat.*

Aṭ-Ṭabari narrated that Qataadah said concerning this *aayah*: "These are the enemies of Allah, the Jews, who were called to the Book of Allah to settle their dispute, and to His Prophet to judge amongst them, mention of whom they found written in the *Tawraat* and *Injeel*, but they turned away from him and were averse."[31]

---

[30] This is narrated by Aṭ-Ṭabari with two isnads from Ibn 'Abbaas (*Tafseer aṭ-Ṭabari*, 6/289). It is also narrated in a *mursal* report by Ibn Abi Ḥaatim from 'Ikrimah (but Aṭ-Ṭabari made it *mawṣool*). See *Tafseer Ibn Abi Ḥaatim* (published portion), *tafseer* of *Soorah Aal 'Imraan*, Pp. 165, hadith no. 286. This is also mentioned by As-Suyooṭi in *Ad-Durr al-Manthoor*, by Al-Baghawi in *Sharḥ as-Sunnah*, and Al-Waaḥidi in *Asbaab an-Nuzool*, Pp. 99, edited by Al-Ḥumaydi, It is classed as *ḥasan* by the editor of *Tafseer Ibn Abi Ḥaatim*, and also by the editor of *Asbaab an-Nuzool.*

[31] *Tafseer aṭ-Ṭabari*, 6/290, ed. Shaakir, see also *Tafseer al-Qaasimi*, 4/818.

It is narrated that Ibn Jurayj said concerning this *aayah*: "The people of the Book were being called to the Book of Allah to judge amongst them in accordance with the truth and to settle disputes concerning punishments. The Prophet (ﷺ) called them to Islam, but they turned away from that."[32]

This indicates that the Book in question is the Qur'an. The phrase "disputes concerning punishments" is an indication of that which was mentioned by some scholars, that this *aayah* was revealed concerning two Jews who had committed *zina* (adultery); their story will be told when we discuss the verses of *Soorah al-Maa'idah* (the fifth chapter of the Qur'an), and it is to be found in *Aṣ-Ṣaḥeeḥayn* (Bukhari and Muslim) and elsewhere.

Aṭ-Ṭabari said, after mentioning the opinions and reports mentioned above, "In my opinion, the interpretation which is most likely to be correct is the view which says that Allah was speaking of a group of Jews who lived in Madeenah at the time of the Messenger of Allah (ﷺ). They had been given knowledge of the *Tawraat* (Torah), and they were being called to the book of Allah which they believed was from Allah — i.e., the *Tawraat* — in order to settle some of the matters of dispute between them and the Messenger of Allah (ﷺ). It may be that the issue concerning which they were disputing, they were called to refer to the *Tawraat* for judgement and they refused, was the matter of Muhammad (ﷺ) and his Prophethood. It may be that the disputed issue was the matter of Ibraaheem (Abraham), the Close Friend of Allah, and his religion. It may be that the disputed issue was Islam, which they were being called to believe in. Or it may be that the disputed issue was a punishment. All of these are issues concerning which they disputed with the Messenger of Allah (ﷺ), so he called them to the judgement of the *Tawraat*, but they refused to

---

[32] *Tafseer aṭ-Ṭabari*, 6/290, ed. Shaakir, see also *Tafseer al-Qaasimi*, 4/818.

respond and some of them concealed it. There is no indication in the *aayah* to show which was meant (specifically), so that it could be said that it was this and not the other. We do not need to know that, because that to which they were being called to settle the dispute was something to which it was obligatory for them to respond according to their own religion, and they refused to do so. So Allah tells us that they were apostates who had rejected what was in their own Book, and they denied the covenant that they had made. Their rejection of Muhammad and his message of truth is as bad as their rejection of Moosa (Moses) and his message, whom they rejected even though they liked him and approved of him.

The phrase ﴿...Then a party of them turn away, and they are averse﴾ *(cf. Qur'an 3: 23)* means, they turn their backs on the Book of Allah to which they are called in order to settle their dispute, and they turn away from it although they know the truth of the matter and how clear the evidence is."[33]

From what Aṭ-Ṭabari said, we may note a number of points, the most important of which are:

a) That regardless of whether the Book to which they were called to settle the dispute between them was the Qur'an or the *Tawraat* (Torah), the ruling would be one and the same, because they were being called to the Book which they were obliged to follow. If they truly and sincerely believed what was in the *Tawraat*, they would have followed Muhammad (ﷺ).

b) That even though the *aayah* speaks of the People of the Book, it does not apply exclusively to them as far as the ruling is concerned, as we shall see below when we discuss the view of those who said that the *aayah*-

[33] *Tafseer aṭ-Ṭabari*, 6/290-291, ed. Shaakir.

﴿... وَمَن لَّمْ يَحْكُم بِمَآ أَنزَلَ ٱللَّهُ فَأُو۟لَـٰٓئِكَ هُمُ ٱلْكَـٰفِرُونَ ﴿٤٤﴾﴾

﴾...And whosoever does not judge by what Allah has revealed, such are the *kaafiroon* [i.e. disbelievers].﴿ *(Qur'an 5: 44)*

— was speaking of the People of the Book.

c) That the *aayah* is general in terms of the reason for its revelation and the ruling which it points to. What this means — as Aṭ-Ṭabari mentioned — is that whether it is about the Prophethood of Muhammad (ﷺ), or about Islam, or about one of the *ḥadd* punishments, these people were still turning away from the Book of Allah, thus deserved the warning which Allah mentions subsequently.

d) The ruling concerning these people — as Aṭ-Ṭabari mentioned — is that they are apostates who reject what is stated in their own Book and who deny the covenant that they had made, in which they had promised to follow what was in their Book.

e) Finally, we should look again at what Ibn Jareer said: "Their rejection of Muhammad and his message of truth, is as bad as their rejection of Moosa (Moses) and his message, whom they rejected even though they liked him and approved of him." That means that by turning away from what was in the *Tawraat*, they rejected Moosa and the message he brought. Their turning away from the ruling of Allah which Moosa brought in the *Tawraat* was an action of rejection and a negation of their claim to love Moosa and believe in his prophethood. What Aṭ-Ṭabari said is important, as it explains that the *aayah* does not speak only about the People of the Book.

2 - Allah (سبحانه وتعالى) says:

﴿ أَلَمْ تَرَ إِلَى ٱلَّذِينَ أُوتُوا۟ نَصِيبًا مِّنَ ٱلْكِتَـٰبِ يُؤْمِنُونَ بِٱلْجِبْتِ وَٱلطَّـٰغُوتِ وَيَقُولُونَ لِلَّذِينَ كَفَرُوا۟ هَـٰٓؤُلَآءِ أَهْدَىٰ مِنَ ٱلَّذِينَ ءَامَنُوا۟ سَبِيلًا ﴿٥١﴾ ﴾

﴿Have you not seen those who were given a portion of the Scripture? They believe in *jibt* and *ṭaaghoot* and say to the disbelievers that they are better guided as regards the way than the believers [Muslims].﴾ *(Qur'an 4: 51)*

We have already discussed the meaning of *ṭaghoot* above. There are many views concerning the meaning of this word and the word *jibt*.[34] What matters here — after explaining that the *aayah* includes the Muslims too, as we noted in the case of the previous *aayah* — is to quote two of the comments of the *salaf* concerning this verse:

a) The report narrated by Mujaahid in his *Tafseer*, which says: "*Al-Jibt* means *siḥr* (magic or witchcraft) and *aṭ-ṭaaghoot* means the *Shayṭaan* in human form, to whom they refer for judgement. He controls their affairs."[35]

b) What Aṭ-Ṭabari said in his *tafseer* of this *aayah* — after quoting other opinions on it: "The correct view regarding the interpretation of the phrase, ﴿...They believe in *jibt* and *ṭaaghoot*...﴾ *(cf. Qur'an 4: 51)* is that they believe in two gods other than Allah, which they worship instead of Allah, and take them as gods. That is because '*al-jibt*' and '*aṭ-ṭaaghoot*' are

---

[34] It is said that they were two idols; or that *al-jibt* meant the idols and *aṭ-ṭaaghoot* meant the spokesmen of the idols (i.e., the soothsayers who spoke on behalf of the idols); or that *al-jibt* meant magic and witchcraft and *aṭ-ṭaaghoot* meant the *Shayṭaan*; or that *al-jibt* meant the sorcerer and *aṭ-ṭaaghoot* meant the soothsayer; or that *al-jibt* meant the soothsayer and *aṭ-ṭaaghoot* meant the sorcerer; or that *al-jibt* meant Ḥuyay ibn Akhṭab and *aṭ-ṭaaghoot* meant Ka'b ibn al-Ashraf, etc. From *Tafseer aṭ-Ṭabari*, 461-465.

[35] *Tafseer Mujaahid*, 1/161; Ibn Katheer, 1/512 at *Istiqaamah* edition.

> two names for everything that is venerated and worshipped, or obeyed, or submitted to, instead of Allah, regardless of what that venerated thing is, whether it is a stone, a person or a devil. As this is the case, and as the idols which were worshipped during the *jaahiliyah* were venerated with worship instead of Allah, they were '*jibt*' and '*ṭaaghoot*'. The same may be said of the *Shayaaṭeen* (devils) whom the *kuffaar* obey by disobeying Allah, and the sorcerers and soothsayers whose words are accepted by those who associate others with Allah (*shirk*). And it may also be said of Ḥuyay ibn Akhṭab and Ka'b ibn Ashraf because they were obeyed by their fellow-Jews in disobeying Allah and disbelieving in Him and His Messenger, so they were *jibt* and *ṭaaghoot*."[36]

We have already quoted similar words from Aṭ-Ṭabari, but what he says here is clearer and more comprehensive, and more clearly refers to the issue of referring for judgement. This is what was explained by Ibn Sa'di when he said of *al-jibt* and *aṭ-ṭaaghoot*: "This is belief in all worship of anything other than Allah, or ruling by anything other than the laws of Allah; this includes magic or witchcraft, soothsaying or fortune-telling, worshipping anything other than Allah, and obeying the *Shayaaṭeen*."[37]

3 - Allah (سبحانه وتعالى) says:

﴿ يَٰٓأَيُّهَا ٱلَّذِينَ ءَامَنُوٓاْ أَطِيعُواْ ٱللَّهَ وَأَطِيعُواْ ٱلرَّسُولَ وَأُوْلِي ٱلۡأَمۡرِ مِنكُمۡۖ فَإِن
تَنَٰزَعۡتُمۡ فِي شَيۡءٖ فَرُدُّوهُ إِلَى ٱللَّهِ وَٱلرَّسُولِ إِن كُنتُمۡ تُؤۡمِنُونَ بِٱللَّهِ وَٱلۡيَوۡمِ ٱلۡأٓخِرِۚ
ذَٰلِكَ خَيۡرٞ وَأَحۡسَنُ تَأۡوِيلًا ٥٩ أَلَمۡ تَرَ إِلَى ٱلَّذِينَ يَزۡعُمُونَ أَنَّهُمۡ ءَامَنُواْ
بِمَآ أُنزِلَ إِلَيۡكَ وَمَآ أُنزِلَ مِن قَبۡلِكَ يُرِيدُونَ أَن يَتَحَاكَمُوٓاْ إِلَى ٱلطَّٰغُوتِ
وَقَدۡ أُمِرُوٓاْ أَن يَكۡفُرُواْ بِهِۦۖ وَيُرِيدُ ٱلشَّيۡطَٰنُ أَن يُضِلَّهُمۡ ضَلَٰلَۢا بَعِيدٗا

---

[36] *Tafseer aṭ-Ṭabari*, 8/465.

[37] *Tafseer Ibn Sa'di*, 1/358.

﴿٦٠﴾ وَإِذَا قِيلَ لَهُمْ تَعَالَوْا۟ إِلَىٰ مَآ أَنزَلَ ٱللَّهُ وَإِلَى ٱلرَّسُولِ رَأَيْتَ
ٱلْمُنَـٰفِقِينَ يَصُدُّونَ عَنكَ صُدُودًا ﴿٦١﴾ فَكَيْفَ إِذَآ أَصَـٰبَتْهُم
مُّصِيبَةٌۢ بِمَا قَدَّمَتْ أَيْدِيهِمْ ثُمَّ جَآءُوكَ يَحْلِفُونَ بِٱللَّهِ إِنْ أَرَدْنَآ إِلَّآ
إِحْسَـٰنًا وَتَوْفِيقًا ﴿٦٢﴾ أُو۟لَـٰٓئِكَ ٱلَّذِينَ يَعْلَمُ ٱللَّهُ مَا فِى قُلُوبِهِمْ
فَأَعْرِضْ عَنْهُمْ وَعِظْهُمْ وَقُل لَّهُمْ فِىٓ أَنفُسِهِمْ قَوْلًۢا بَلِيغًا ﴿٦٣﴾
وَمَآ أَرْسَلْنَا مِن رَّسُولٍ إِلَّا لِيُطَاعَ بِإِذْنِ ٱللَّهِ ۚ وَلَوْ أَنَّهُمْ إِذ
ظَّلَمُوٓا۟ أَنفُسَهُمْ جَآءُوكَ فَٱسْتَغْفَرُوا۟ ٱللَّهَ وَٱسْتَغْفَرَ لَهُمُ ٱلرَّسُولُ
لَوَجَدُوا۟ ٱللَّهَ تَوَّابًا رَّحِيمًا ﴿٦٤﴾ فَلَا وَرَبِّكَ لَا يُؤْمِنُونَ حَتَّىٰ يُحَكِّمُوكَ
فِيمَا شَجَرَ بَيْنَهُمْ ثُمَّ لَا يَجِدُوا۟ فِىٓ أَنفُسِهِمْ حَرَجًا مِّمَّا قَضَيْتَ
وَيُسَلِّمُوا۟ تَسْلِيمًا ﴿٦٥﴾ ﴾

﴿O' you who believe! Obey Allah and obey the Messenger [Muhammad], and those of you [Muslims] who are in authority. [And] if you differ in anything amongst yourselves, refer it to Allah and His Messenger, if you believe in Allah and in the Last Day. That is better and more suitable for final determination. Have you not seen those [hypocrites] who claim that they believe in that which has been sent down to you, and that which was sent down before you, and they wish to go for judgement [in their disputes] to the *ṭaaghoot* [false judges] while they have been ordered to reject them. But *Shayṭaan* [Satan] wishes to lead them far astray. And when it is said to them: 'Come to what Allah has sent down and to the Messenger [Muhammad],' you [Muhammad] see the hypocrites turn away from you [Muhammad] with aversion. How then, when a catastrophe befalls them because of what their hands have sent forth, they come to you swearing by Allah, 'We meant no more than goodwill and conciliation!' They [hypocrites] are those of whom Allah knows what is in their hearts; so turn aside from them [do not punish them] but admonish them, and speak to them an effective word [i.e. to believe in Allah, worship Him, obey Him, and be afraid of Him] to reach their innerselves. We sent no Messenger, but to be obeyed by Allah's Leave. If they [hypocrites], when they had been unjust to themselves, had come to you [Muhammad] and begged Allah's forgiveness, and the Messenger had begged forgiveness for them, indeed, they would have found Allah All-Forgiving [One Who forgives and accepts repentance], Most Merciful. But no, by your Lord, they can have no Faith, until they make you [O' Muhammad] judge in all disputes between them, and find in themselves no resistance against your decisions, and accept [them] with full submission.﴿

(Qur'an 4: 59-65)

These *aayaat* come in the context of speaking about the *munaafiqeen* (hypocrites) who claimed that they were believers, yet they referred for judgement to the *ṭaaghoot*. Our aim here is not to look in detail at what the *mufassireen* said concerning these verses. But we will pause to look at three verses from this passage:

(i) ﴾[And] if you differ in anything amongst yourselves, refer it to Allah and His Messenger﴿

(ii) ﴾Have you not seen those [hypocrites] who claim that they believe﴿

(iii) ﴾But no, by your Lord, they can have no Faith, until they make you [O' Muhammad] judge in all disputes between them﴿

1) With regard to the first *aayah* (i), Aṭ-Ṭabari said, "What Allah means here is: if you have a difference, O' believers, concerning any matter of your religion, amongst yourselves or between you and

those who are in authority over you, and you are disputing concerning it, ﴾refer it to Allah﴿, i.e., try to find out the ruling on the matter concerning which you are disputing, whether amongst yourselves or between you and those who are in authority over you. Try to find out the ruling from Allah, i.e., from the Book of Allah, and follow what you find. The phrase ﴾and His Messenger﴿ means, if you cannot find that out from the Book of Allah, then try to find out from the Messenger, if he is alive, or if he is dead, from his Sunnah, if you believe in Allah and the Last Day, i.e., if you truly believe in Allah and the Last Day."[38]

We may note from the words of Aṭ-Ṭabari that he connects his comments to the beginning of the *aayah*, which speaks of obedience to those who are in authority, because disputes may arise between the people and their leaders. So all of them are commanded to refer the disputed matter to Allah and the Messenger. This is a confirmation of what the scholars said about the reason why the command ﴾Obey﴿ is not repeated in reference to those who are in authority. It is because obedience to them is conditional upon obedience to Allah and His Messenger.

Ibn Katheer said in his *Tafseer*: "﴾...[And] if you differ in anything amongst yourselves, refer it to Allah and His Messenger...﴿. Mujaahid and more than one of the *salaf* said: this means, refer to the Book of Allah and the Sunnah of His Messenger. This is a command from Allah with regard to any dispute that arises — and may arise — among the people, concerning basic principles or minor issues of religion, the matter should be referred to the Qur'an and Sunnah, as Allah (ﷻ) says:

﴿ وَمَا ٱخْتَلَفْتُمْ فِيهِ مِن شَىْءٍ فَحُكْمُهُۥٓ... ﴿١٠﴾ ﴾

[38] *Tafseer aṭ-Ṭabari*, 8/504, ed. Shaakir.

﴿And in whatsoever you differ, the decision thereof is with Allah [He is the ruling Judge]...﴾*(Qur'an 42: 10)*

Whatever the Qur'an and Sunnah decide and attest to be correct is the truth, and what can there be beyond the truth other than falsehood? Hence Allah (ﷻ) says: ﴿...If you believe in Allah and in the Last Day...﴾, i.e., refer all disputed or unknown matters to the Book of Allah and the Sunnah of His Messenger, and seek judgement from them with regard to matters in which you dispute, ﴿...If you believe in Allah and in the Last Day...﴾ (cf. Qur'an 4: 59). This indicates that whoever does not refer for judgement concerning disputed matters to the Qur'an and Sunnah is not a believer in Allah and the Last Day."[39]

What Ibn Katheer said at the end is what is indicated in the text of the *aayah*, because it states the condition, ﴿...If you believe in Allah and in the Last Day...﴾. So whoever does not refer for judgement to the Qur'an and Sunnah is not a believer. Hence *Shaykh* Ibn Sa'di said: "The religion is based on the Book of Allah and the Sunnah of His Messenger, and belief cannot be sound without them. Referring to them both is a condition of faith. Hence Allah (ﷻ) says: ﴿...If you believe in Allah and in the Last Day...﴾. This indicates that whoever does not refer to them both in disputed matters is not really a believer, rather he is a believer in *ṭaaghoot* as is mentioned in the following *aayah*."[40]

Ibn al-Qayyim mentioned, when discussing this *aayah*, that a number of things may be deduced from it, including:

a) That the believers may dispute concerning some rulings, but that does not mean that they are not believers if they refer the matters concerning which they dispute to Allah and His Messenger, as Allah has enjoined upon them.

---

[39] *Tafseer Ibn Katheer*, 1/518, *Al-Istiqaamah* edition.

[40] *Tafseer Ibn Sa'di*, 1/362.

b) In the *aayah*, ﴿...[And] if you differ in anything...﴾, the use of the indefinite (*shay'in*, translated here as "anything") in a conditional clause indicates that this includes any matters of religion, major or minor, clear or ambiguous, concerning which the believers may dispute.

c) That the people agreed unanimously that referring to Allah and to His Messenger means referring to His Book, and to the Messenger himself during his lifetime, and to his Sunnah after his death.

d) That referring to Allah and His Messenger is a requirement and obligation of faith. If this referring is not done, cancels out faith, because the condition of faith is not fulfilled, therefore faith is cancelled out. The interconnection is especially strong in this case, for each is essential to the other, and if one of them is absent, the other is cancelled out.[41]

This *aayah* indicates that it is not permissible to refer for judgement to anything other than the Qur'an and Sunnah.[42]

2) With regard to the second *aayah* that says:

﴿ أَلَمْ تَرَ إِلَى ٱلَّذِينَ يَزْعُمُونَ أَنَّهُمْ ءَامَنُوا۟ بِمَآ أُنزِلَ إِلَيْكَ وَمَآ أُنزِلَ مِن قَبْلِكَ يُرِيدُونَ أَن يَتَحَاكَمُوٓا۟ إِلَى ٱلطَّٰغُوتِ ... ﴿٦٠﴾ ﴾

﴿Have you not seen those [hypocrites] who claim that they believe in that which has been sent down to you, and that which was sent down before you, and they wish to go for judgement [in their disputes] to the *ṭaaghoot*...﴾
(Qur'an 4: 60)

— we have discussed the meaning of *ṭaaghoot* above, and what the *aayah* indicates concerning the ruling on those who refer for

---

41 *I'laam al-Mawaqqi'een*, 1/51-53, edited by Al-Wakeel.

42 *Aḍwaa' al-Bayaan*, 1/292.

judgement to the *ṭaaghoot*, and we have quoted the words of Aṭ-Ṭabari in more than one place.

Because this *aayah* was revealed concerning some of the hypocrites who claimed to be Muslims, it will suffice us to mention a few reports on the reasons for its revelation.

Aṭ-Ṭabaraani narrated that Ibn 'Abbaas (رضي الله عنه) said: Abu Barzah al-Aslami was a soothsayer who used to judge between the Jews concerning matters that they referred to him. Some of the Muslims also referred to him, so Allah (تعالى) revealed the words: ﴿Have you not seen those [hypocrites] who claim that they believe in that which has been sent down to you, and that which was sent down before you, and they wish to go for judgement [in their disputes] to the *ṭaaghoot* [false judges] while they have been ordered to reject them. But *Shayṭaan* [Satan] wishes to lead them far astray. And when it is said to them: 'Come to what Allah has sent down and to the Messenger [Muhammad],' you [Muhammad] see the hypocrites turn away from you [Muhammad] with aversion. How then, when a catastrophe befalls them because of what their hands have sent forth, they come to you swearing by Allah, 'We meant no more than goodwill and conciliation!'﴾ *(Qur'an 4: 60-62)*[43]

Aṭ-Ṭabari narrated that Qataadah said, concerning this *aayah*, that it was revealed concerning two men, a man from among the Anṣaar called Bishr and a man from among the Jews, with regard to a dispute between them concerning some debt or property. They disputed, then they referred to a soothsayer in Madeenah to judge between them,

---

[43] Aṭ-Ṭabaraani: *Al-Mu'jam al-Kabeer*, 11/373, hadith no. 12045. *Majma' az-Zawaa'id*, 7/6; he said, this is narrated by Aṭ-Ṭabaraani and its men are the men of *Aṣ-Ṣaḥeeḥ*; Al-Waaḥidi in *Asbaab an-Nuzool*, Pp. 160 (and Abu Barzah was a famous *Ṣaḥaabi* - that happened before he became Muslim). *Fatḥ al-Baari*, 5/37, 1st *Salafiyah* edition.

and they did not go to the Prophet (ﷺ), so Allah criticized that. It is reported that the Jew called on him to go to the Prophet (ﷺ), to judge between them, because he knew that the Prophet (ﷺ) would not be unfair, but the Anṣaari refused, even though he claimed to be a Muslim, and he called on him to go to the soothsayer. So Allah revealed these words, and criticized the action of the one who claimed to be a Muslim, and the Jew who was one of the People of the Book, and He (Allah) (ﷻ), the Exalted, All-Glorious, All-Powerful, said: ﴾Have you not seen those [hypocrites] who claim that they believe in that which has been sent down to you... you [Muhammad] see the hypocrites turn away from you [Muhammad] with aversion﴿.[44]

According to a report narrated from Ibn 'Abbaas (رضي الله عنه) (may Allah be pleased with him): "*Aṭ-Ṭaaghoot* was a man among the Jews who was called Ka'b ibn al-Ashraf. When they were called to that which Allah had revealed and to the Messenger to judge between them, they said: 'No, we will ask Ka'b to judge between us.' This is what Allah said, ﴾And they wish to go for judgement [in their disputes] to the *ṭaaghoot* [false judges]﴿.'"[45]

According to a report narrated by Mujaahid in his *Tafseer*, "A man from among the *munaafiqeen* (hypocrites) disputed with a man from among the Jews. The Jew said, 'Let us go to Muhammad.' The hypocrite said, 'Let us go to Ka'b ibn Ashraf.' Then Allah revealed the words, ﴾And they wish to go for judgement [in their disputes] to the *ṭaaghoot*...﴿, which refers to Ka'b ibn Ashraf."[46]

---

[44] *Tafseer aṭ-Ṭabari*, 8/509; *Asbaab an-Nuzool*, Pp. 161, ed. Al-Ḥumaydaan. Here it says that the name of the Anṣaari was Qays, and this is classed as *ṣaḥeeḥ* by Ibn Ḥajar in *Fatḥ al-Baari*, 5/38.

[45] *Tafseer aṭ-Ṭabari*, 8/511; *Fatḥ al-Baari*, 5/37-38, 1st *Salafiyah* edition.

[46] *Tafseer Mujaahid*, 1/163-164; *Tafseer aṭ-Ṭabari*, 8/511.

These examples give us a picture of the kind of referral for judgement which is condemned by Allah, although the *aayah* is general in meaning, as is stated by Ibn Katheer after he quoted — in brief — some of the reports concerning the reason for its revelation. He said: "The *aayah* is more general than all of that, because it condemns anyone who turns away from the Qur'an and Sunnah and refers for judgement to anything else which is false. This is what is meant by *ṭaaghoot* here."[47]

It may be noted that Allah (ﷻ) says, ﴾Those who claim﴿, because if they had been true believers, they would not have wanted to refer for judgement to anyone other than Allah and His Messenger. This indicates that they were claiming to be believers but they were liars.[48]

Allah (ﷻ) says, in the next *aayah*: ﴾And when it is said to them: 'Come to what Allah has sent down and to the Messenger [Muhammad],' you [Muhammad] see the hypocrites turn away from you [Muhammad] with aversion﴿ *(Qur'an 4: 61)*.

Ibn al-Qayyim said: "Here Allah describes turning away from that which the Messenger brought and turning towards something else as being the essence of hypocrisy."[49] And it says in *Tayseer al-'Azeez al-Ḥameed*: "Ibn al-Qayyim said: this indicates that whoever is called to refer for judgement to the Qur'an and Sunnah, and does not accept that and refuses to do so, is one of the hypocrites. The verb *yaṣuddoon* (translated here as 'turn away') is intransitive, i.e., it does not take an object; it means that they turn away, not that they prevent others. If Allah has ruled that the one who turns away from that is a hypocrite, then how about the one who goes further than that and

---

47 *Tafseer Ibn Katheer*, 1/519, *Al-Istiqaamah* edition. *I'laam al-Muwaqqi'een*, 1/53, edited by Al-Wakeel.

48 *Tayseer al-'Azeez al-Ḥameed*, Pp. 556.

49 *Mukhtaṣar aṣ-Ṣawaa'iq*, 2/353.

turns other people away from referring for judgement to the Qur'an and Sunnah through his words, teaching and books, still claims that he means no more than good will and reconciliation, goodwill through his actions and reconciliation between the *ṭaaghoot* to which he refers for judgement and the Qur'an and Sunnah?"[50]

What is indicated by this *aayah* and the *aayaat* that follow may be summed up as under:

a) That *ṭaaghoot* is general in meaning; it may be one man to whom referral for judgement is made, or it may be more than one.

b) That referring to *ṭaaghoot* for judgement is one of the attributes of the hypocrites.

c) That the one who turns away from referring for judgement to the Qur'an and Sunnah has been ruled by Allah to be a hypocrite. So the one who goes further than that by preventing the people from referring for judgement to the Qur'an and Sunnah in any way is even more of a *kaafir* and hypocrite.

3) With regard to the third *aayah*:

﴿ فَلَا وَرَبِّكَ لَا يُؤْمِنُونَ حَتَّىٰ يُحَكِّمُوكَ فِيمَا شَجَرَ بَيْنَهُمْ ثُمَّ لَا يَجِدُوا فِي أَنفُسِهِمْ حَرَجًا مِّمَّا قَضَيْتَ وَيُسَلِّمُوا تَسْلِيمًا ﴿٦٥﴾ ﴾

﴾But no, by your Lord, they can have no Faith, until they make you [O' Muhammad] judge in all disputes between them, and find in themselves no resistance against your decisions, and accept [them] with full submission.﴿

(Qur'an 4: 65)

— the scholars spoke a great deal about this *aayah*. We will limit ourselves to discussion of two topics concerning this verse:

---

[50] *Tayseer al-'Azeez al-Ḥameed*, Pp. 557.

a) The reason for its revelation.

b) Some of the comments of the scholars concerning its meaning.

With regard to the reason for its revelation, Bukhari and others narrated the story of Az-Zubayr and the man from among the Anṣaar. It is narrated from 'Urwah ibn az-Zubayr that a man from among the Anṣaar argued with Az-Zubayr about the channel from Al-Ḥarrah which was used to irrigate the date-palms. The Messenger of Allah (ﷺ) said, "Let the water flow, O' Zubayr" — and he commanded him to be reasonable — "then let it go to your neighbour." The Anṣaari said, "That is because he is your cousin (the son of your paternal aunt)." The face of the Messenger of Allah (ﷺ) changed colour (because of anger) and he said, "O' Zubayr, irrigate (your land) and then stop the water until it reaches the walls between the pits around the trees." Thus he gave Az-Zubayr his full rights (as opposed to telling him to compromise with his neighbour as he did at first). Az-Zubayr said, "By Allah, this *aayah* was revealed concerning that: ﴿But no, by your Lord, they can have no Faith, until they make you [O' Muhammad] judge in all disputes between them...﴾. According to some of the reports, Az-Zubayr said, "I think that this *aayah* was revealed concerning that."[51]

There is another view, that is, the *aayah* was revealed concerning the hypocrite and the Jew concerning whom the *aayah*: ﴿Have you not seen those [hypocrites] who claim that they believe in that which has been sent down to you, and that which was sent down before you,

[51] Bukhari in a number of places. This version is hadith no. 2362 in *Kitaab al-Musaaqaah, Baab Sakr al-Anhaar* and *Baab Sharb al-A'laa qabl al-Asfal*, and *Baab Sharb al-A'laa ilal-Ka'bayn*, hadith nos. 2359-2362 (*Fatḥ al-Baari*), 5/34-39]; also in *Kitaab aṣ-Ṣulḥ, Baab Idha Ashaara al-Imam biṣ-Ṣulḥ*, hadith no. 2708 (*Fatḥ al-Baari* 5/309); and in *Tafseer Soorah an-Nisaa', Baab Falaa wa Rabbika laa yu'minoona...*, hadith no. 4585 (*Fatḥ al-Baari*, 8/254). Muslim, hadith no. 2357.

and they wish to go for judgement [in their disputes] to the *ṭaaghoot*﴿ — was revealed.[52] This is narrated from Mujaahid.[53]

Isḥaaq ibn Raahawayh narrated in his *Tafseer* — with a *ṣaḥeeḥ* isnad, as Ibn Ḥajar said in *Fatḥ al-Baari* — that Ash-Sha'bi said: there was a dispute between a man from among the Jews and a man from among the hypocrites. The Jew called on the hypocrite to go to the Prophet (ﷺ) because he knew that he would not accept a bribe, and the hypocrite called on the Jew to go to a Jewish judge because he knew that he would accept a bribe. So Allah revealed these *aayaat*, to where He says, ﴾But no, by your Lord, they can have no Faith, until they make you [O' Muhammad] judge in all disputes between them, and find in themselves no resistance against your decisions, and accept [them] with full submission﴿ *(Qur'an 4: 65).*

Which of these was the reason for the revelation of the *aayah*?

Aṭ-Ṭabari (may Allah have mercy on him), after quoting the reports, stated that the second view was more likely to be correct, when he said: "The view — I mean the view of those who said that it meant the two who referred for judgement to *ṭaaghoot* whom Allah described in the *aayah*, ﴾Have you not seen those [hypocrites] who claim that they believe in that which has been sent down to you, and that which was sent down before you﴿ — is more likely to be correct, because the *aayah*, ﴾But no, by your Lord, they can have no Faith, until they make you [O' Muhammad] judge in all disputes between them﴿ appears in the context of the story of those whose story Allah started to tell in the *aayah*, ﴾Have you not seen those [hypocrites] who claim that they believe in that which has been sent down to you﴿. There is no evidence of discontinuity as these *aayaat* (verses) follow on from one another. So long as there is no indication of

---

[52] Aṭ-Ṭabaraani from Mujaahid, 8/523, edited by Shaakir.

[53] *Tafseer Mujaahid*, 1/164.

discontinuity, it is more sound to suggest that they are indeed speaking of the same thing."[54]

Then Aṭ-Ṭabari said: "If anyone thinks that there is any indication of discontinuity in the report narrated from Az-Zubayr and Ibn az-Zubayr about the dispute with the Anṣaari concerning the channels from Al-Ḥarrah, or any suggestion that this *aayah* — ﴿But no, by your Lord, they can have no Faith, until they make you [O' Muhammad] judge in all disputes between them﴾ — is unconnected to the story and the rulings mentioned in the preceding *aayaat*, it is not impossible that this *aayah* may have been revealed concerning the story of the two people who referred to *ṭaaghoot* for judgement, but it also explains the issue concerning which Az-Zubayr and his opponent among the Anṣaar referred for judgement, because the *aayah* indicates that, and because that is not impossible. It is more appropriate for them to be connected to one another, so long as the meaning flows in a coherent manner, unless there is evidence to show that there is no continuity between one and the other, in which case it should be understood in a different way."[55]

What Aṭ-Ṭabari mentioned is also pointed out by Ibn Ḥajar when he commented on the report: "Az-Zubayr said: by Allah, this *aayah* was revealed concerning that, and concerning another incident, the *aayah* ﴿But no, by your Lord...﴾ was revealed. Ibn Ḥajar said: "The more correct view is that which is reported by the majority, and that Az-Zubayr was not certain about that."[56] What he meant is: I think that this (the latter) *aayah* was revealed concerning that. Then Ibn Ḥajar said: "But in the report of Umm Salamah narrated by Aṭ-Ṭabari and Aṭ-Ṭabaraani, it shows that he was certain about that and that this is

---

[54] *Tafseer aṭ-Ṭabari*, 8/524.

[55] Ibid, 8/524-525.

[56] *Fatḥ al-Baari*, 5/37, 1st *Salafiyah* edition.

revealed concerning the story of Az-Zubayr and his opponent. This is also shown in the *mursal* report of Sa'eed ibn al-Musayyib... Mujaahid and Ash-Sha'bi were certain that this *aayah* was revealed concerning those concerning whom the previous *aayah* — ﴿Have you not seen those [hypocrites] who claim that they believe in that which has been sent down to you, and that which was sent down before you, and they wish to go for judgement [in their disputes] to the *ṭaaghoot...*﴾ — was revealed."[57]

Then Ibn Ḥajar mentioned that which Aṭ-Tabari thought more likely to be correct, that the reason for revelation of these *aayaat* was all the same, and that they all refer to one thing. There is no reason why the story of Az-Zubayr and his opponent should not have taken place at the same time and not be covered by the general meaning of the *aayah*. And Allah knows best.[58]

Whatever the case — even though what Aṭ-Ṭabari said is correct, especially since it fits the context of the *aayah*, because Allah clearly mentions the hypocrites in it: ﴿...You [Muhammad] see the hypocrites turn away from you [Muhammad] with aversion﴾ *(Qur'an 4: 61)*, whilst the other report states that Az-Zubayr's opponent was a man from among the Anṣaar — what these *aayaat* indicate is very clear, for Allah states that the person who does any such thing is not a believer. So it is general in meaning and applies to everyone who refuses to refer for judgement to the Qur'an and Sunnah, for faith cannot be complete without referring to the Messenger (ﷺ) for judgement and submitting to him.

What Az-Zubayr's opponent said is a serious matter which involves slandering the Messenger (ﷺ) and doubting his justice. Hence An-Nawawi said concerning that: "The scholars said: if such words as

[57] Ibid.

[58] *Fatḥ al-Baari*, 5/38. See also *Sharḥ an-Nawawi 'ala Muslim*, 15/109.

were spoken by this Anṣaari were to be uttered today by any person, suggesting that the Prophet (ﷺ) was following his own desires, that would be *kufr*, and the one who says them would be subject to the rulings on apostates, and he would have to be killed, subject to the relevant conditions. They said that the Prophet (ﷺ) only left this man alone because at the beginning of Islam he used to seek to put the people at ease and respond with that which is better. He put up with the insults of the hypocrites and those in whose hearts was a disease, and he (ﷺ) said,

> 'Be easy-going, not harsh; give glad tidings, do not put people off,' and, 'I do not want the people to say that Muhammad kills his companions.'

And Allah (ﷻ) said:

> ﴿ ... وَلَا تَزَالُ تَطَّلِعُ عَلَىٰ خَآئِنَةٍ مِّنْهُمْ إِلَّا قَلِيلًا مِّنْهُمْ ۖ فَٱعْفُ عَنْهُمْ وَٱصْفَحْ ۚ إِنَّ ٱللَّهَ يُحِبُّ ٱلْمُحْسِنِينَ ﴿١٣﴾ ﴾
>
> ﴾...And you will not cease to discover deceit in them, except a few of them. But forgive them and overlook [their misdeeds]. Verily, Allah loves *al-muḥsinoon* [good-doers].﴿ *(Qur'an 5: 13).*"[59]

Then he mentioned what some of the scholars said, that this man was a *munaafiq* (hypocrite); this issue was discussed by Ibn Hajar in *Fatḥ al-Baari.*[60]

Having discussed what was said concerning the reasons for revelation, we will now move on to the second issue, that is, what the scholars said concerning this *aayah (Qur'an 4: 65)*, and making the connection between that and the issue of referring for judgement.

---

59. *Sharḥ an-Nawawi*, 15/108; see also *Fatḥ al-Baari*, 5/40.

60 *Fatḥ al-Baari*, 5/35-36.

At-Ṭabari (may Allah have mercy on him) said: "What Allah meant when He said, ﴾But no﴿ is, the matter is not as they claim, when they say that they believe in that which has been revealed to you, but they refer for judgement to the *ṭaaghoot*, and they turn away from you when they are called to come to you, O' Muhammad. ﴾They can have no Faith﴿ means, they do not truly believe in Me, in you and in that which was revealed to you, ﴾Until they make you [O' Muhammad] judge in all disputes between them﴿ means, until they make you the judge between them concerning matters of which they are not certain and so they are confused about the rulings..."[61]

Al-Jassaas mentioned a number of texts and the obligation of referring to the Messenger (ﷺ), at the end of which he quoted this *aayah* — ﴾But no, by your Lord, they can have no Faith...﴿. Then he said: "In these *aayaat*, Allah confirmed the obligation of obeying the Messenger (ﷺ) and explained that obedience to him is obedience to Allah, and that disobedience of him is disobedience of Allah. Allah (سبحانه وتعالى) says:

﴿ ... فَلْيَحْذَرِ ٱلَّذِينَ يُخَالِفُونَ عَنْ أَمْرِهِۦٓ أَن تُصِيبَهُمْ فِتْنَةٌ أَوْ يُصِيبَهُمْ عَذَابٌ أَلِيمٌ ﴿٦٣﴾ ﴾

﴾...And let those who oppose the Messenger's [Muhammad's] commandment [i.e. his Sunnah — legal ways, orders, acts of worship, statements] [among the sects] beware, lest some *fitnah* [disbelief, trials, afflictions, earthquakes, killing, overpowered by a tyrant] should befall them or a painful torment be inflicted on them.﴿ *(Qur'an 24: 63)*

So He has warned against going against the commands of the Messenger, and He has stated that going against the commands of the

---

[61] *Tafseer aṭ-Ṭabari*, 8/518, edited by Shaakir.

Messenger, refusing to submit to that which he has brought and doubting it are things that put a person beyond the pale of faith.

Allah (ﷻ) says: ﴾But no, by your Lord, they can have no Faith, until they make you [O' Muhammad] judge in all disputes between them, and find in themselves no resistance against your decisions, and accept [them] with full submission﴿.

It is said that *ḥaraj* (translated here as "resistance") means doubt. This is narrated from Mujaahid. The root meaning of *ḥaraj* is unease. It could be that what is meant is submission without any doubt that submission is obligatory, and no unease in the heart concerning that; rather it should be with an open heart and with insight and certainty. This *aayah* indicates that whoever rejects any of the commands of Allah or of His Messenger (ﷺ) is beyond the pale of Islam, whether he rejects it because of doubt concerning it, or because he does not accept it and refuses to submit. This proves that the *Ṣaḥaabah* were correct when they ruled that those who refused to pay the zakah were apostates, and they killed them and took their women and children into slavery, because Allah ruled that whoever does not submit to the judgement and ruling of the Prophet (ﷺ) is not among the people of faith (the believers)."[62]

Ibn al-Qayyim (may Allah have mercy on him) said: "The obligation of referring to him for judgement did not come to an end when he died; it applies after his death just as it applied during his lifetime. Referring to him for judgement is not something that applies only to practical matters and not to theoretical matters, as the heretics say. Allah begins this *aayah* with an oath which confirms the negation which precedes it, and He swears that they do not have faith until they refer for judgement to the Messenger of Allah (ﷺ) in all matters

---

[62] *Aḥkaam al-Qur'an* by Al-Jaṣṣaaṣ, 1/213-214, *Daar al-Fikr* edition.

concerning which they dispute, whether they are major or minor issues of religion, basic principles or otherwise. This is not sufficient, however, until there is no *ḥaraj* (resistance), i.e., unease concerning the ruling, and until their hearts are open to accepting the ruling in such a manner that there is no longer any unease, and they submit to him completely, i.e., follow his ruling..."[63]

Ibn Katheer said: "Allah (ﷻ) swears by His holy and divine Self that no one believes until he makes the Messenger (ﷺ) judge of all his affairs. So whatever he rules is the truth which must be followed both outwardly and inwardly. Hence Allah says: ﴾And find in themselves no resistance against your decisions, and accept [them] with full submission﴿, i.e., when they make you judge, they should obey you inwardly and find no resistance in themselves to that which you decide. So they should follow you both outwardly and inwardly, and they should submit completely, with no objection or resistance, as is narrated in the hadith,

> 'By the One in Whose hand is my soul, no one of you truly believes until his desire is in accordance with that which I have brought.'"[64]

Shaykh Aḥmad Shaakir (may Allah have mercy on him) commented at length on what Ibn Katheer said concerning these *aayaat*. After a lengthy discussion in which he explained that these *aayaat* are quite clear in their meaning and unambiguous in their wording, that they do not need any lengthy explanation, that there is no room for tampering with their meaning or misinterpreting them, that obedience

---

[63] *Mukhtaṣar aṣ-Ṣawaa'iq*, 2/352; see also *I'laam al-Muwaqqi'een*, 1/54; *Tayseer al-'Azeez al-Ḥameed*, Pp. 562-563, where he quotes some very important comments from Ibn al-Qayyim concerning this topic.

[64] *Tafseer Ibn Katheer*, 1/520. The isnad of this hadith is *ḍa'eef* (weak); it is classed as such by Ibn Rajab in *Jaami' al-'Uloom wal-Ḥikam*.

to Allah and His Messenger is a condition of faith and that whoever turns away from obeying them both and refers for judgement to anything else is a hypocrite, and hypocrisy is the worst kind of *kufr*, then he said:

"Then our Lord swore by His divine and holy Self that the people cannot be believers until they refer for judgement in all their affairs to His Messenger Muhammad (ﷺ), and until they accept his judgement with obedience and submission, and do not find any resistance in themselves, and until they submit in the depths of their hearts to the ruling of Allah and His Messenger with full and complete submission, not acting hypocritically in order to please the believers or submitting because of the power of the ruler or anyone else. Rather they should accept it no matter what difficulty or hardship they face as a result. If they do not do that, then they are not believers at all, rather they are counted among the *kuffaar* and hypocrites..."[65]

Then he spoke of the (man-made) laws in many Muslim countries, and how they are sanctified and called *fiqh* and *tashree'*, and other words that the scholars give to shari'ah. Then, after stating that they have made their laws a new religion instead of Islam, he said: "This new religion has become the basic principle to which the Muslims in most of the Muslim countries refer for judgement and by which they rule. Whether some of its rulings are in accordance with any of the rulings of shari'ah or they go against it, it is all false and goes beyond the pale of Islam, because whatever is in accordance with shari'ah is merely a coincidence; it is not an action of following shari'ah and it is not intended to be an act of obedience to the command of Allah and the command of His Messenger. That which is in accordance with shari'ah and that which goes against it are both sinking in the mire of misguidance which leads a person to Hell. It is not permissible for the

[65] *'Umdat at-Tafseer*, 3/214.

Muslim to submit to this type of law or to accept it."[66]

Shaykh Muhammad ibn Ibraaheem (may Allah have mercy on him) said: "Allah has stated that those who do not refer to the Prophet (ﷺ) for judgement in all disputes between them do not have faith. This statement is confirmed by the repetition of the negative and by the oath (swearing by Allah). Allah (ﷻ) says: ﴾But no, by your Lord, they can have no Faith, until they make you [O' Muhammad] judge in all disputes between them, and find in themselves no resistance against your decisions, and accept [them] with full submission﴿.

Merely referring to the Messenger (ﷺ) for judgement is not sufficient until there is added to that an absence of any element of resistance in their hearts, because Allah (ﷻ) says: ﴾And find in themselves no resistance against your decisions﴿. *Ḥaraj* (translated here as 'resistance') means unease; so their hearts must be open to that and free of any kind of unease or reservation.

And these two things are not sufficient until, as Allah (ﷻ) says, they are accompanied by submission, i.e., complete surrender to his (the Prophet's) rulings, so that there is no longer any attachment of the heart to this matter, and they submit to this true ruling with complete submission. Hence this is emphasized by use of the verbal noun *tasleeman* (translated here as "with full submission"). This shows that mere submission is not enough; it must be absolute submission." Then he said: "Ponder also the general meaning of the second *aayah*, where Allah, the Exated, says, ﴾In all disputes between them﴿, which conveys a general and comprehensive meaning, according to the scholars. This general meaning refers to all types and kinds of issues, whether major or minor, so there is no difference between one kind and another, or between major and minor."[67]

---

[66] Ibid, 3/215.

[67] *Taḥkeem al-Qawaaneen*, Pp. 1-2; see also *Aḍwaa' al-Bayaan*, 1/294.

Whoever ponders this *aayah* and the reports concerning the reasons for its revelation, and what the scholars said concerning its meanings, will understand that this is not only the matter of belief, and that the warning does not apply only to those in whose heart is any element of doubt or dislike of what the Messenger brought. Indeed, if he rejects the ruling of the Messenger (ﷺ) and does not submit to him, then he is subject to the stern warning indicated by the *aayah*, which is that he is not a believer.

4 - Allah (ﷻ) says:

﴿ ٱتَّخَذُوٓا۟ أَحْبَارَهُمْ وَرُهْبَـٰنَهُمْ أَرْبَابًا مِّن دُونِ ٱللَّهِ وَٱلْمَسِيحَ ٱبْنَ مَرْيَمَ وَمَآ أُمِرُوٓا۟ إِلَّا لِيَعْبُدُوٓا۟ إِلَـٰهًا وَٰحِدًا ۖ لَّآ إِلَـٰهَ إِلَّا هُوَ ۚ سُبْحَـٰنَهُۥ عَمَّا يُشْرِكُونَ ﴿٣١﴾ ﴾

﴿They [Jews and Christians] took their rabbis and their monks to be their lords besides Allah [by obeying them in things which they made lawful or unlawful according to their own desires without being ordered by Allah], and [they also took as their Lord] Messiaḥ, son of Maryam [Mary], while they [Jews and Christians] were commanded [in the *Tawraat* (Torah) and the *Injeel* (Gospel)] to worship none but One *Ilaah* [God — Allah] *Laa ilaaha illa Huwa* [none has the right to be worshipped but He]. Praise and glory be to Him [far above is He] from having the partners they associate [with Him].﴾ *(Qur'an 9: 31)*

All of the *mufassireen* interpreted this *aayah* in accordance with what is narrated from the Prophet (ﷺ) and from a group of the *salaf* (the pious predecessors), may Allah have mercy on them. Aṭ-Ṭabari said: ﴿...lords besides Allah...﴾ means, as masters instead of Allah, whom they obey by disobeying Allah, so they accept as permissible that which they permit to them of the things that Allah has forbidden for them, and they regard as forbidden that which they forbid to them of things that Allah has permitted for them."[68]

The hadith narrated concerning that is the hadith of 'Adiy ibn Ḥaatim, who said: I came to the Messenger of Allah (ﷺ) wearing a cross of gold around my neck. He said,

> "O' 'Adiy, throw this idol away from your neck.' So I threw it away, and I came to him whilst he was reciting from *Soorah Baraa'ah* (*Soorah at-Tawbah* — the ninth chapter of the Qur'an) and he recited this *aayah* - ﴿They [Jews and Christians] took their rabbis and their monks to be their lords besides Allah﴾. I said, 'O' Messenger of Allah, we do not worship them.' He said, 'Do they not forbid that which Allah has permitted, so you regard it as forbidden, and they permit that which Allah has forbidden, so you regard it as permissible?' He said, 'Yes.' He said, 'This is worship of them.'"

According to another report, "I said, 'O' Messenger of Allah, they do not pray to them.' He said,

> 'You are right, but they used to permit that which Allah had forbidden, so they regarded it as permissible, and they used to forbid that which Allah has permitted, so they regarded it as forbidden.'"[69]

---

[68] *Tafseer aṭ-Ṭabari*, 14/209, edited by Shaakir.

[69] Tirmidhi, *Kitaab at-Tafseer, Baab Soorah at-Tawbah*, hadith no. 3095. He said, this is a *ghareeb* hadith, which we only know from the hadith of 'Abdus-Salaam ibn Ḥarb, and Ghuṭayf ibn A'yan is not known in this hadith. This is what it says in the edition of 'Aṭwah and Ad-Da'aas. In the Indian edition (published with *Tuḥfat al-Aḥwadhi*), 4/117, it says, this is a *ḥasan ghareeb* hadith.

This hadith is classed as *ḥasan* by *Shaykh al-Islam* Ibn Taymiyah in *Al-Eemaan* (*Majmoo' al-Fataawa*, 7/67. In *Minhaaj as-Sunnah*, 1/48, he said: it was reported in Tirmidhi and elsewhere from the hadith of 'Adiy).

Similar reports were narrated from more than one of the *salaf*. The reports from them were narrated by Aṭ-Ṭabari, Al-Khaṭeeb al-Baghdaadi, As-Suyooṭi and others. These reports include:

— The report from Ḥudhayfah that he was asked about the *aayah*, ﴾They [Jews and Christians] took their rabbis and their monks to be their lords besides Allah﴿ — did they worship them? He (ﷺ) said,

> "No, but if they permitted them something they would take it as permitted, and if they forbade them something, they would take it as forbidden."

According to another report, he said:

> "They did not fast for them or pray to them, but if they permitted them something they would take it as permitted, and if they forbade them something that Allah had permitted to them, they would take it as forbidden, and this is how they took them as lords."[70]

— It is narrated from Ar-Rabee' ibn Anas: "﴾They [Jews and Christians] took their rabbis and their monks to be their lords besides

---

It is also classed as *ḥasan* by Al-Albaani in *Ghaayat al-Maraam*, hadith no. 6. It is also in *Ṣaḥeeḥ at-Tirmidhi, Maktab at-Tarbiyat al-'Arabi* edition, hadith no. 471. The hadith of 'Adiy is also narrated by Al-Bayhaqi in *As-Sunan al-Kubra*, 10/116; by Al-Khaṭeeb in *Al-Faqeeh wa'l-Mutafaqqih*, 1/66-67; by Aṭ-Ṭabari with different isnads, 14/209-211, edited by Shaakir. It is also narrated by As-Suyooṭi in *Ad-Durr al-Manthoor*, 4/174, *Daar al-Fikr* edition; he said: "It is reported by Ibn Sa'd, 'Abd ibn Ḥumayd, Tirmidhi (who classed it as *ḥasan*), Ibn al-Mundhir, Ibn Abi Ḥaatim, Aṭ-Ṭabaraani, Abush-Shaykh, Ibn Mardawayh and Al-Bayhaqi in his *Sunan* from 'Adiy ibn Ḥaatim..." This hadith was classed as *ḥasan* by those who classed it as such because what is narrated from Ḥudhayfah and others are corroborating reports which strengthen it. And this is a matter in which there is no room for opinion.

[70] Aṭ-Ṭabari in his *Tafseer*, 14/211-213; by 'Abdur-Razzaaq in his *Tafseer*, 2/272; by Al-Bayhaqi in his *Sunan*, 10/116; in *Shu'ab al-Eemaan*, 7/45, *Daar al-Kutub al-'Ilmiyah* edition; and by Al-Khateeb in *Al-Faqeeh wal-Mutafaqqih*, 2/67.

Allah﴿ — I said to Abul-'Aaliyah, 'How did the Children of Israel take them as lords?' He said, 'The way in which they took them as lords was that they found commands and prohibitions in the Book of Allah, but they said, we will decide about any matter unless our rabbis tell us first. What they command us to do, we will follow, and what they forbid us to do, we will pay heed to what they say. So they followed what men said and threw away the Book of Allah behind their backs.'''[71]

These reports do not express the personal opinions of the *ṣaḥaabah*; they are *tafseer* which is in accordance with that which is reported from the Prophet (ﷺ) in the hadith of 'Adiy.

For more explanation of the *aayah* in question, let us look at the tafseer of the *aayah*:

﴿ قُلْ يَٰٓأَهْلَ ٱلْكِتَٰبِ تَعَالَوْا۟ إِلَىٰ كَلِمَةٍ سَوَآءٍۭ بَيْنَنَا وَبَيْنَكُمْ أَلَّا نَعْبُدَ إِلَّا ٱللَّهَ وَلَا نُشْرِكَ بِهِۦ شَيْـًٔا وَلَا يَتَّخِذَ بَعْضُنَا بَعْضًا أَرْبَابًا مِّن دُونِ ٱللَّهِ ۚ فَإِن تَوَلَّوْا۟ فَقُولُوا۟ ٱشْهَدُوا۟ بِأَنَّا مُسْلِمُونَ ﴿٦٤﴾ ﴾

﴾Say [O' Muhammad]: 'O' people of the Scripture [Jews and Christians]: Come to a word that is just between us and you, that we worship none but Allah [Alone], and that we associate no partners with Him, and that none of us shall take others as lords besides Allah.' Then, if they turn away, say: 'Bear witness that we are Muslims.'﴿ *(Qur'an 3: 64)*

What is relevant here is the phrase ﴾...And that none of us shall take others as lords besides Allah...﴿, which is interpreted in the same way as the *aayah* from *Soorah at-Tawbah*.

---

[71] *Al-Eemaan* by Ibn Taymiyah, Pp. 64; Aṭ-Ṭabari, 14/212.

At-Ṭabari said: "With regard to the phrase, ﴾...And that none of us shall take others as lords besides Allah...﴿, this taking of others as lords was in the sense of the followers' obedience to their leaders when they commanded them to disobey Allah, and their abstaining from what they forbade them to do of obedience towards Allah, as Allah says: ﴾...They [Jews and Christians] took their rabbis and their monks to be their lords besides Allah...﴿."[72] Then he narrated that Ibn Jurayj said: "﴾...And that none of us shall take others as lords besides Allah...﴿ means, we will not obey one another in disobeying Allah. And it is said that that taking of others as lords meant when the people obeyed their masters and leaders in matters other than worship, even though they did not pray to them."[73]

Qurṭubi said: "﴾...And that none of us shall take others as lords besides Allah...﴿ means, we will not follow them in permitting or forbidding anything except that which Allah has permitted. This is like the *aayah*, ﴾...They [Jews and Christians] took their rabbis and their monks to be their lords besides Allah...﴿, which means that they gave them the status of their Lord by accepting what they forbade and permitted, which Allah had not forbidden or permitted."[74]

Al-Qasṭallaani said in his commentary on Bukhari, when commenting on the letter of the Prophet (ﷺ) to Heraclius, in which this *aayah* — ﴾Say [O' Muhammad]: 'O' people of the Scripture [Jews and Christians]: Come to a word...'﴿ — is mentioned: ﴾And that none of us shall take others as lords besides Allah﴿ means, we should not say that 'Uzayr is the son of Allah, or that the Messiaḥ is the son of Allah; let us not obey the rabbis in their innovations as

---

[72] *Tafseer aṭ-Ṭabari*, 6/488, edited by Shaakir.

[73] Ibid. It is also narrated - in brief - by Ibn Abi Ḥaatim, *Juz' Aal 'Imraan*, Pp. 318, report no. 698.

[74] *Tafseer al-Qurṭubi*, 4/106.

regards what is prohibited and what is permitted, because they are all just like us, they are human like us."[75] Then he quoted the hadith of 'Adiy ibn Ḥaatim as evidence.

Al-Aloosi said concerning this *aayah*: "This means, do not obey one another by disobeying Allah."[76] Then he narrated the report of Tirmidhi and how he classed the hadith of 'Adiy as *ḥasan*.

So what is indicated by these two *aayaat* (the *aayah* from *Aal 'Imraan* and the *aayah* from *At-Tawbah*) is one and the same, which is that taking others as lords means following the rabbis and monks in their innovations concerning what is permitted and what is forbidden, instead of following Allah's rulings. As the *salaf* pointed out, worship of the rabbis and monks does not mean prostrating to them or praying to them; rather it means obeying them instead of Allah. The Jews and Christians — as 'Adiy said to the Messenger (ﷺ) — do not worship their rabbis and monks by prostrating and praying to them.

Hence Ibn Ḥazm narrated this objection and responded to it. He said, "If someone were to say, how can the Jews and Christians take other lords instead of Allah when they deny that? We say, and Allah is the Source of strength, that the way in which things are named is a matter which rests with Allah. When the Jews and Christians accepted as forbidden that which their rabbis and monks forbade them. and accepted as permitted that which they permitted, this was taking them as lords in a real sense and worshipping them in a real sense, which they believed in. So Allah called this action taking of lords besides Allah and worship, and this is indisputably *shirk*."[77]

---

[75] *Irshaad as-Saari*, 1/80.

[76] *Rooḥ al-Ma'aani*, 3/193, 2nd edition.

[77] *Al-Faṣl* by Ibn Ḥazm, 3/266, edited version.

What Ibn Hazm stated is also mentioned by Ibn Katheer in his *Tafseer* of the *aayah*,

﴿ وَلَا تَأْكُلُوا مِمَّا لَمْ يُذْكَرِ اسْمُ اللَّهِ عَلَيْهِ وَإِنَّهُ لَفِسْقٌ وَإِنَّ الشَّيَاطِينَ لَيُوحُونَ إِلَىٰ أَوْلِيَائِهِمْ لِيُجَادِلُوكُمْ وَإِنْ أَطَعْتُمُوهُمْ إِنَّكُمْ لَمُشْرِكُونَ ﴿١٢١﴾ ﴾

﴿Eat not [O' believers] of that [meat] on which Allah's Name has not been pronounced [at the time of the slaughtering of the animal], for sure it is *fisq* [a sin and disobedience of Allah]. And certainly, the *Shayaṭeen* [devils] do inspire their friends [from mankind] to dispute with you, and if you obey them [by making *al-maitah* (a dead animal) legal by eating it], then you would indeed be *mushrikoon* [polytheists]; [because they (devils and their friends) made lawful to you to eat that which Allah has made unlawful to eat and you obeyed them by considering it lawful to eat, and by doing so you worshipped them; and to worship others besides Allah is polytheism].﴾ *(Qur'an 6: 121)*

After a lengthy discussion of its *tafseer* and the reasons for its revelation — narrated in the *Sunans* of Tirmidhi, Abu Dawood, Ibn Maajah and others from Ibn 'Abbaas with *ṣaḥeeḥ* isnads, that the *mushrikeen* objected to the prohibition of eating dead meat, and they said to the Prophet (ﷺ), 'We eat what we kill and we cannot eat what Allah kills?' and according to another report they said, 'You eat what you slaughter by your own hand but you do not eat what Allah slaughters?...'[78] — Ibn Katheer said: "﴿...And if you obey them, then you would indeed be *mushrikoon* [polytheists]...﴾ means, if you turn away from the command of Allah to you and His laws, and turn towards what anyone else says, and you give others preference over

[78] For more details see *Tafseer aṭ-Ṭabari*, 12/76-88, edited by Shaakir; *Tafseer Ibn Katheer*, 3/316-322, Ash-Sha'b edition.

Him, then this is *shirk*, as Allah (ﷻ) says, ﴿...They [Jews and Christians] took their rabbis and their monks to be their lords besides Allah...﴾."[79] Then he mentioned the hadith of 'Adiy ibn Ḥaatim.

These three *aayaat* (verses) (from *Aal 'Imraan, Al-An'aam* and *At-Tawbah*), along with others mentioned in the Qur'an, interpret one another. So it should come as no surprise that the scholars spoke in strong words on this topic, because it is a serious matter which may lead to *shirk* (polytheism i.e., associating deities besides Allah). And Allah is the One Whose help we seek.

We will quote some of what the scholars said on this topic, which will explain the rulings which result from what is indicated by these *aayaat*:

Ash-Shanqeeṭi said — in a clear and unambiguous statement: "According to the guidance of the Qur'an, which guides to that which is most just and right, everyone who follows any laws other than those which were brought by the master of the sons of Adam, Muhammad ibn 'Abdullah (ﷺ), follows a deviant and contradicting laws. This is blatant *kufr* (disbelief) which puts him beyond the pale of Islam. When the *kuffaar* (disbelievers) said to the Prophet (ﷺ), 'When you find a sheep dead in the morning, who killed it?' He said to them. 'Allah killed it.' They said to him, 'What you slaughter by your own hands is *ḥalaal* (permitted), and what Allah kills, you say it is *ḥaraam* (prohibited). Are you then better than Allah?' Allah revealed this *aayah* concerning them: ﴿Eat not [O' believers] of that [meat] on which Allah's Name has not been pronounced [at the time of the slaughtering of the animal], for sure it is *Fisq* [a sin and disobedience of Allah]. And certainly, the *Shayaṭeen* [devils] do inspire their friends [from mankind] to dispute with you, and if you obey them [by making *al-maitah* (a dead animal) legal by eating it],

[79] *Tafseer Ibn Katheer*, 3/322, Ash-Sha'b edition.

then you would indeed be *mushrikoon* [polytheists]﴾.[80]

The fact that there is no *fa'* in the phrase translated as, ﴾then you would indeed be *mushrikoon*﴿ implies an oath. The fulfilment of the conditional clause ﴾if you obey them﴿ would be expected to begin with *fa'*. The fact that there is no *fa'* means that this is not the fulfilment of the conditional clause and is therefore a new sentence.

Allah swears by this oath that whoever follows the *Shayaṭeen* in permitting dead meat is a *mushrik*, and this *shirk* puts a person beyond the pale of Islam, according to scholarly consensus..."[81] So he made the connection between the *aayaat* which spoke of this matter.

Shaykh al-Islam Ibn Taymiyah said concerning this matter: "When a knowledgeable person neglects what he knows of the Book of Allah and the Sunnah of His Messenger, and follows the ruling of a ruler who goes against the rulings of Allah and His Messenger, he is an apostate and a *kaafir* who deserves to be punished in this world and in the Hereafter."[82]

Elsewhere, Ibn Taymiyah explained the ruling concerning those who followed the rabbis and monks. He said: "What He said in the context of the *aayah*,

﴿ إِنَّهُمْ كَانُوٓا۟ إِذَا قِيلَ لَهُمْ لَآ إِلَٰهَ إِلَّا ٱللَّهُ يَسْتَكْبِرُونَ ﴿٣٥﴾ ﴾

> ﴾Truly, when it was said to them: *Laa ilaaha illa-Allah* [none has the right to be worshipped but Allah], they puffed themselves up with pride [i.e. denied it].﴿
> *(Qur'an 37: 35),*

---

[80] See the *Tafseers* of Aṭ-Ṭabari and Ibn Katheer on this *aayah*. See *Ṣaḥeeḥ at-Tirmidhi, Maktab at-Tarbiyah* edition, hadith no. 2454; *Ṣaḥeeḥ Abi Dawood*, hadith nos. 2444, 2445.

[81] *Aḍwaa' al-Bayaan*, 3/439-440.

[82] *Majmoo' al-Fataawa*, 35/372-372.

— undoubtedly refers to both kinds of *shirk*, minor and major, and it also refers to those who reject the commands of Allah and turn away from obeying Him. This is part of the true meaning of *Laa ilaaha illa-Allah*. For the *Ilaah* (God) is the One Who deserves to be worshipped, and every way in which Allah is worshipped is a means of drawing close to Him as the *Ilaah*, so whoever refuses to worship Him in some way, thereby hearing and obeying someone other than Him, has not fully understood and acted upon the phrase *Laa ilaaha illa-Allah* in this case.

Those who took their rabbis and monks as lords when they obeyed them in permitting that which Allah had forbidden and in forbidding that which Allah had permitted, are of two types:

i) Those who knew that they altered the religion of Allah, so they followed them in that alteration, and they believed in their permitting of that which Allah had forbidden and in their forbidding of that which Allah had permitted, following their leaders even though they knew that they had gone against the religion of the Messengers. This is *kufr*, and Allah and His Messenger described it as *shirk*, even though they did not pray to them or prostrate to them. Whoever follows anyone else in going against the religion knowing that he is going against the religion, and believes in what they say instead of in what Allah and His Messenger say, is a *mushrik* (polytheist) like these people.

ii) They clearly understood that their rabbis and monks were prohibiting what was permitted by Allah and permitting what was forbidden by Allah,[83] but they obeyed them by disobeying

---

[83] This is how it appears in the editions of *Kitaab al-Eemaan* and also in *Tayseer al-'Azeez al-Ḥakeem*, where this is quoted from *Shaykh al-Islam* (Ibn Taymiyah). The meaning is: that the belief of those followers in what the rabbis and monks did by forbidding that which was permitted by Allah and permitted that which =

> Allah. This is like the Muslim who commits sins knowing that they are sins, so they come under the category of sinners, as it was reported in *Aṣ-Ṣaḥeeḥ* (Bukhari) that the Prophet (ﷺ) said:
>
> 'Obedience is only with regard to that which is proper and correct...'"[84]

There are other important comments made by Ibn Taymiyah, which we will refer to below. But we will pause here to highlight two points:

The first point is that *Shaykh al-Islam* was not referring — when he mentioned the two cases — to the monks and rabbis themselves who permit and forbid things by themselves. Rather he was speaking only about their followers.

There is no doubt that the rabbis and monks and their like, who change (the religion) and permit that which Allah has forbidden and forbid that which Allah has permitted, are *kuffaar*, indeed they are worse in *kufr* than their followers. But it should be noted that this does not include the *mujtahid* who strives by means of his *ijtihaad* to follow the Messenger and reach the truth that he brought, but reaches a conclusion concerning *ḥalaal* and *ḥaraam* which goes against the view of the majority — or some — of the scholars, because he failed to reach the right conclusion in this case.

Hence Ibn Taymiyah pointed out that: "The one who forbids something which is *ḥalaal* or permits something which is *ḥaraam*, if he is a *mujtahid* whose intention was to follow the Messenger, but he failed to reach the right conclusion in this matter, but he feared Allah as much as he could, then Allah will not punish him for his mistake,

---

= was prohibited by Him is clear to them in the sense that they know what Allah forbids and what He permits, as it came from Him.

In *Fatḥ al-Majeed*, 1/213 (edited by Al-Waleed al-Firyaan) it says: "That their belief in what is *ḥaraam* and what is *ḥalaal* is clear to them."

[84] *Al-Eemaan*, Pp. 67, *Al-Maktab al-Islaami* edition; *Majmoo' al-Fataawa*, 7/70.

rather He will reward him for his *ijtihaad* in which he obeyed his Lord."[85]

Then he went on to explain the ruling concerning those who follow him (the *mujtahid*) in his mistake. He said: "But those who know that it is a mistake and goes against what the Messenger said, still follow him in his mistakes and turn away from what the Messenger said, have a share in that *shirk* which Allah condemns, especially if they are following their whims and desires and they support it by their actions, even though they know that this goes against what the Messenger said. This is *shirk* and the one who does this deserves to be punished for it. Hence the scholars are agreed that if a person knows the truth (the correct view on a matter), it is not permissible for him to follow anyone in going against it..."[86]

The scholars mentioned this issue in the context of following one who goes against the evidence even though the follower knows that he is going against it, as was said by Ibn al-Qayyim in *I'laam al-Muwaqqi'een*, Al-Khaṭeeb in *Al-Faqeeh wal-Mutafaqqih*, and others, who quoted the *aayah* from *Soorah at-Tawbah* — ﴾They [Jews and Christians] took their rabbis and their monks to be their lords﴿ — and the hadith of 'Adiy ibn Ḥaatim. Ibn Taymiyah also referred to this here, when he said. "They have a share in that *shirk*..."

In conclusion, the rabbis and monks who go against the Book of Allah, forbidding what Allah permitted and permitting what Allah forbade, turning away from the truth even though they know what it is, are not the ones whom *Shaykh al-Islam* was discussing here, because there is no doubt concerning their *kufr*.

---

85 *Al-Eemaan*, Pp. 67; *Majmoo' al-Fataawa*, 7/71.

86 Ibid.

The second point is that when Ibn Taymiyah mentioned the second type of people who follow the rabbis and monks, he said, "They clearly understood that their rabbis and monks were prohibiting what was permitted by Allah and permitting what was forbidden by Allah" meaning, they understood what was *ḥalaal* and what was *ḥaraam* according to the way in which it had been revealed by Allah. What this means is that they do not follow the rabbis and monks when they forbid that which is permitted or permit that which is forbidden, rather they accept as permitted that which Allah has permitted and regard as forbidden that which Allah has forbidden. These followers — who believe in that correct belief — may go against what they believe in their actions only, so they obey the rabbis and monks in disobeying Allah, but they are not regarded as *kaafir* because they are like those who commit sins such as adultery or drinking wine or consuming *riba* even though they believe that these are sins and are forbidden. So this is a person who has committed a major sin, and the ruling concerning such a person is well known to *Ahl as-Sunnah wal-Jamaa'ah*.

Ibn Taymiyah's comment, "so they obey them in disobeying Allah" is explained as meaning that this is like what the Muslim does who sins and knows that it is a sin.

So it is obeying them in sin only; it is not obeying and following one who forbids that which is permitted and permits that which is forbidden. There is a great difference between the two things.

The first type follows the rabbis and monks in their alteration of the religion of Allah, and they accept what they say, so they come under the same ruling as them.

The second type does not follow them in that, and they do not accept the changes and alterations that they have introduced, but they follow them by committing sins, so they are like those who commit sins which are less than *shirk*.

The second point is that when Ibn Taymiyah mentioned the second type of people who follow the rabbis and monks, he said, "They clearly understand that their rabbis and monks were prohibiting what was permitted by Allah and permitting what was forbidden by Allah" meaning, they understood what was halal and what was haram according to the way in which it had been revealed by Allah. What this means is that they do not follow the rabbis and monks when they forbid that which is permitted or permit that which is forbidden, rather they accept as permitted that which Allah has permitted and regard as forbidden that which Allah has forbidden. These followers – who believe in that correct belief – may go against what they believe in their actions only, so they obey the rabbis and monks in disobeying Allah, but they are not regarded as *kaafirs* because they are like those who commit sins such as adultery or drinking wine or consuming *riba* even though they believe that these are sinful and forbidden. So this is a person who has committed a major sin, and the ruling concerning such a person is well known to *Ahl as-Sunnah wal-Jamaa'ah*.

Ibn Taymiyah commented, "so they obey them in disobeying Allah," and then he says: "that this is like when the Muslim does this and knows that it is a sin."

So it is obeying them in sin only, it is not obeying and following one who forbids that which is permitted and permits that which is forbidden. There is a great difference between the two things.

The first type follows the rabbis and monks in their alteration of the religion of Allah, and they accept what they say, so they come under the same ruling as them.

The second type does not follow them in that and they do not accept the changes and alterations that they have introduced, but they follow them by committing sins, so they are like those who commit sins which are less than *shirk*.

CHAPTER THREE

THE VERSES FROM *SOORAH AL-MAA'IDAH* CONCERNING RULING BY ANYTHING OTHER THAN THAT WHICH ALLAH HAS REVEALED

The Verses from *Soorah al-Maa'idah*

These verses — concerning ruling by anything other than that which Allah has revealed, and warning against that and against following the misguided People of the Book who have deviated and have distorted the Book of Allah, and who refused to rule according to it, and which enjoin ruling according to the Book of Allah and warn against the *fitnah* of these people and others — these verses all appear in one context, from verse 41 to verse 50. This is the text:

﴿ ۞ يَـٰٓأَيُّهَا ٱلرَّسُولُ لَا يَحْزُنكَ ٱلَّذِينَ يُسَـٰرِعُونَ فِى ٱلْكُفْرِ مِنَ
ٱلَّذِينَ قَالُوٓا۟ ءَامَنَّا بِأَفْوَٰهِهِمْ وَلَمْ تُؤْمِن قُلُوبُهُمْ ۛ وَمِنَ ٱلَّذِينَ هَادُوا۟ ۛ
سَمَّـٰعُونَ لِلْكَذِبِ سَمَّـٰعُونَ لِقَوْمٍ ءَاخَرِينَ لَمْ يَأْتُوكَ ۖ يُحَرِّفُونَ ٱلْكَلِمَ مِنۢ
بَعْدِ مَوَاضِعِهِۦ ۖ يَقُولُونَ إِنْ أُوتِيتُمْ هَـٰذَا فَخُذُوهُ وَإِن لَّمْ تُؤْتَوْهُ
فَٱحْذَرُوا۟ ۚ وَمَن يُرِدِ ٱللَّهُ فِتْنَتَهُۥ فَلَن تَمْلِكَ لَهُۥ مِنَ ٱللَّهِ شَيْـًٔا ۚ
أُو۟لَـٰٓئِكَ ٱلَّذِينَ لَمْ يُرِدِ ٱللَّهُ أَن يُطَهِّرَ قُلُوبَهُمْ ۚ لَهُمْ فِى ٱلدُّنْيَا خِزْىٌ ۖ
وَلَهُمْ فِى ٱلْـَٔاخِرَةِ عَذَابٌ عَظِيمٌ ﴿٤١﴾ سَمَّـٰعُونَ لِلْكَذِبِ أَكَّـٰلُونَ
لِلسُّحْتِ ۚ فَإِن جَآءُوكَ فَٱحْكُم بَيْنَهُمْ أَوْ أَعْرِضْ عَنْهُمْ ۖ وَإِن تُعْرِضْ عَنْهُمْ
فَلَن يَضُرُّوكَ شَيْـًٔا ۖ وَإِنْ حَكَمْتَ فَٱحْكُم بَيْنَهُم بِٱلْقِسْطِ ۚ إِنَّ ٱللَّهَ
يُحِبُّ ٱلْمُقْسِطِينَ ﴿٤٢﴾ وَكَيْفَ يُحَكِّمُونَكَ وَعِندَهُمُ ٱلتَّوْرَىٰةُ فِيهَا حُكْمُ ٱللَّهِ
ثُمَّ يَتَوَلَّوْنَ مِنۢ بَعْدِ ذَٰلِكَ ۚ وَمَآ أُو۟لَـٰٓئِكَ بِٱلْمُؤْمِنِينَ ﴿٤٣﴾ إِنَّآ أَنزَلْنَا

ٱلتَّوۡرَىٰةَ فِيهَا هُدٗى وَنُورٞۚ يَحۡكُمُ بِهَا ٱلنَّبِيُّونَ ٱلَّذِينَ أَسۡلَمُواْ لِلَّذِينَ
هَادُواْ وَٱلرَّبَّٰنِيُّونَ وَٱلۡأَحۡبَارُ بِمَا ٱسۡتُحۡفِظُواْ مِن كِتَٰبِ ٱللَّهِ وَكَانُواْ
عَلَيۡهِ شُهَدَآءَۚ فَلَا تَخۡشَوُاْ ٱلنَّاسَ وَٱخۡشَوۡنِۚ وَلَا تَشۡتَرُواْ بِـَٔايَٰتِي ثَمَنٗا
قَلِيلٗاۚ وَمَن لَّمۡ يَحۡكُم بِمَآ أَنزَلَ ٱللَّهُ فَأُوْلَٰٓئِكَ هُمُ ٱلۡكَٰفِرُونَ ﴿٤٤﴾ وَكَتَبۡنَا
عَلَيۡهِمۡ فِيهَآ أَنَّ ٱلنَّفۡسَ بِٱلنَّفۡسِ وَٱلۡعَيۡنَ بِٱلۡعَيۡنِ وَٱلۡأَنفَ بِٱلۡأَنفِ
وَٱلۡأُذُنَ بِٱلۡأُذُنِ وَٱلسِّنَّ بِٱلسِّنِّ وَٱلۡجُرُوحَ قِصَاصٞۚ فَمَن تَصَدَّقَ
بِهِۦ فَهُوَ كَفَّارَةٞ لَّهُۥۚ وَمَن لَّمۡ يَحۡكُم بِمَآ أَنزَلَ ٱللَّهُ فَأُوْلَٰٓئِكَ هُمُ
ٱلظَّٰلِمُونَ ﴿٤٥﴾ وَقَفَّيۡنَا عَلَىٰٓ ءَاثَٰرِهِم بِعِيسَى ٱبۡنِ مَرۡيَمَ مُصَدِّقٗا لِّمَا بَيۡنَ يَدَيۡهِ مِنَ
ٱلتَّوۡرَىٰةِۖ وَءَاتَيۡنَٰهُ ٱلۡإِنجِيلَ فِيهِ هُدٗى وَنُورٞ وَمُصَدِّقٗا لِّمَا بَيۡنَ يَدَيۡهِ مِنَ ٱلتَّوۡرَىٰةِ
وَهُدٗى وَمَوۡعِظَةٗ لِّلۡمُتَّقِينَ ﴿٤٦﴾ وَلۡيَحۡكُمۡ أَهۡلُ ٱلۡإِنجِيلِ بِمَآ أَنزَلَ ٱللَّهُ فِيهِۚ
وَمَن لَّمۡ يَحۡكُم بِمَآ أَنزَلَ ٱللَّهُ فَأُوْلَٰٓئِكَ هُمُ ٱلۡفَٰسِقُونَ ﴿٤٧﴾ وَأَنزَلۡنَآ إِلَيۡكَ
ٱلۡكِتَٰبَ بِٱلۡحَقِّ مُصَدِّقٗا لِّمَا بَيۡنَ يَدَيۡهِ مِنَ ٱلۡكِتَٰبِ وَمُهَيۡمِنًا عَلَيۡهِۖ
فَٱحۡكُم بَيۡنَهُم بِمَآ أَنزَلَ ٱللَّهُۖ وَلَا تَتَّبِعۡ أَهۡوَآءَهُمۡ عَمَّا جَآءَكَ مِنَ ٱلۡحَقِّۚ
لِكُلّٖ جَعَلۡنَا مِنكُمۡ شِرۡعَةٗ وَمِنۡهَاجٗاۚ وَلَوۡ شَآءَ ٱللَّهُ لَجَعَلَكُمۡ أُمَّةٗ وَٰحِدَةٗ
وَلَٰكِن لِّيَبۡلُوَكُمۡ فِي مَآ ءَاتَىٰكُمۡۖ فَٱسۡتَبِقُواْ ٱلۡخَيۡرَٰتِۚ إِلَى ٱللَّهِ مَرۡجِعُكُمۡ
جَمِيعٗا فَيُنَبِّئُكُم بِمَا كُنتُمۡ فِيهِ تَخۡتَلِفُونَ ﴿٤٨﴾ وَأَنِ ٱحۡكُم بَيۡنَهُم بِمَآ أَنزَلَ
ٱللَّهُ وَلَا تَتَّبِعۡ أَهۡوَآءَهُمۡ وَٱحۡذَرۡهُمۡ أَن يَفۡتِنُوكَ عَنۢ بَعۡضِ مَآ أَنزَلَ ٱللَّهُ
إِلَيۡكَۖ فَإِن تَوَلَّوۡاْ فَٱعۡلَمۡ أَنَّمَا يُرِيدُ ٱللَّهُ أَن يُصِيبَهُم بِبَعۡضِ ذُنُوبِهِمۡۗ وَإِنَّ كَثِيرٗا مِّنَ
ٱلنَّاسِ لَفَٰسِقُونَ ﴿٤٩﴾ أَفَحُكۡمَ ٱلۡجَٰهِلِيَّةِ يَبۡغُونَۚ وَمَنۡ أَحۡسَنُ مِنَ ٱللَّهِ حُكۡمٗا
لِّقَوۡمٖ يُوقِنُونَ ﴿٥٠﴾ ﴾

﴾O' Messenger [Muhammad]! Let not those who hurry to fall into disbelief grieve you, of such who say: 'We believe' with their mouths but their hearts have no Faith. And of the Jews are men who listen much and eagerly to lies — listen to others who have not come to you. They change the words from their places; they say, 'If you are given this, take it, but if you are not given this, then beware!' And whomsoever Allah wants to put in *al-*

fitnah [error, because of his rejecting of Faith], you can do nothing for him against Allah. Those are the ones whose hearts Allah does not want to purify [from disbelief and hypocrisy]; for them there is a disgrace in this world, and in the Hereafter a great torment. [They like to] listen to falsehood, to devour anything forbidden. So if they come to you [O' Muhammad], either judge between them, or turn away from them. If you turn away from them, they cannot hurt you in the least. And if you judge, judge with justice between them. Verily, Allah loves those who act justly. But how do they come to you for decision while they have the *Tawraat* [Torah], in which is the [plain] Decision of Allah; yet even after that, they turn away. For they are not [really] believers. Verily, We did send down the *Tawraat* [Torah] [to Moosa (Moses)], therein was guidance and light, by which the Prophets, who submitted themselves to Allah's Will, judged for the Jews. And the rabbis and the priests [too judged for the Jews by the *Tawraat* (Torah) after those Prophets], for to them was entrusted the protection of Allah's Book, and they were witnesses thereto. Therefore fear not men but fear Me [O' Jews] and sell not My Verses for a miserable price. And whosoever does not judge by what Allah has revealed, such are the *kaafiroon* [i.e. disbelievers — of a lesser degree as they do not act on Allah's Laws]. And We ordained therein for them: Life for life, eye for eye, nose for nose, ear for ear, tooth for tooth, and wounds equal for equal. But if anyone remits the retaliation by way of charity, it shall be for him an expiation. And whosoever does not judge by that which Allah has revealed, such are the *ẓaalimoon* [polytheists and wrongdoers — of a lesser degree]. And in their footsteps, We sent 'Eesa

[Jesus], son of Maryam [Mary], confirming the *Tawraat* [Torah] that had come before him, and We gave him the *Injeel* [Gospel], in which was guidance and light and confirmation of the *Tawraat* [Torah] that had come before it, a guidance and an admonition for *al-muttaqoon* [the pious]. Let the people of the *Injeel* [Gospel] judge by what Allah has revealed therein. And whosoever does not judge by what Allah has revealed [then] such [people] are the *faasiqoon* [the rebellious i.e. disobedient (of a lesser degree)] to Allah. And We have sent down to you [O' Muhammad] the Book [this Qur'an] in truth, confirming the Scripture that came before it and *Mohaymin* [trustworthy in highness and a witness] over it [old Scriptures]. So judge among them by what Allah has revealed, and follow not their vain desires, diverging away from the truth that has come to you. To each among you, We have prescribed a law and a clear way. If Allah had willed, He would have made you one nation, but that [He] may test you in what He has given you; so compete in good deeds. The return of you [all] is to Allah; then He will inform you about that in which you used to differ. And so judge [you O' Muhammad] among them by what Allah has revealed and follow not their vain desires, but beware of them lest they turn you [O' Muhammad] far away from some of that which Allah has sent down to you. And if they turn away, then know that Allah's Will is to punish them for some sins of theirs. And truly, most of men are *faasiqoon* [rebellious and disobedient to Allah]. Do they then seek the judgement of [the days of] Ignorance? And who is better in judgement than Allah for a people who have firm Faith.﴿ *(Qur'an 5: 41-50)*

In this passage the following phrases are to be noted here:

﴾...And whosoever does not judge by what Allah has revealed, such are the *kaafiroon* [i.e. disbelievers].﴿ *(Qur'an 5: 44)*

﴾And whosoever does not judge by that which Allah has revealed, such are the *ẓaalimoon* [polytheists and wrongdoers].﴿ *(Qur'an 5: 45)*

﴾...And whosoever does not judge by what Allah has revealed [then] such [people] are the *faasiqoon* [the rebellious i.e. disobedient].﴿ *(Qur'an 5: 47)*

We will discuss in brief and in general terms these *aayaat* and quote what the scholars said concerning them. For a detailed *tafseer* of each *aayah* and what was said concerning it, refer to the books of *Tafseer*. Because this is a lengthy topic, it is divided into sections.

The Reasons for Revelation

There are a number of opinions concerning the reason for the revelation of these *aayaat*, the most important of which are the two:

The first view is that it was revealed concerning two Jews who committed *zina* (unlawful sexual relations), as was narrated by 'Abdullah ibn 'Umar (may Allah be pleased with them both). He said: "The Jews came to the Messenger of Allah (ﷺ) and told him that a man and a woman from them had committed *zina*. The Messenger of Allah (ﷺ) said to them:

> 'What do you find in the *Tawraat* concerning stoning?' They said, that they should be humiliated and flogged. 'Abdullah ibn Salaam said, 'You are lying; the punishment prescribed in the *Tawraat* is stoning.' They brought the *Tawraat* and opened it, but one of them put his hand over the verse about stoning, and read the verses before it and after it. 'Abdullah ibn Salaam said, 'Lift up your hand.' So he lifted up his hand, and there was the verse about stoning. They said, 'He is speaking

the truth, O' Muhammad, there is the verse about stoning.' So the Messenger of Allah (ﷺ) commanded that they should be stoned, and I saw the man trying to shield the woman from the stones." — This is narrated by Bukhari, Muslim and others.[1]

According to a report narrated by Muslim from Al-Baraa' ibn 'Aazib (رضي الله عنه), "Two Jews were brought to the Prophet (ﷺ) with blackened faces, having been whipped. He said,

'Is this the punishment for *zina* that you find in your Book?' They said, 'Yes.' So he called one of their scholars and said, 'I ask you by the One Who revealed the *Tawraat* to Moosa, is this the punishment for *zina* that you find in your Book?' He said, 'No, if you had not asked me by Allah I would not have told you. The punishment that we find (in the *Tawraat*) is stoning, but *zina* became widespread among our leaders. So if we found a leader doing this, we would leave him alone, and if we found a weaker (member of our community) doing this, we would carry out the punishment on him. So we said, let us agree on some punishment that we could apply equally to the leaders and the weak alike. So we agreed on blackening the face and flogging in place of stoning.' The Messenger of Allah (ﷺ) said: 'O' Allah, I am the first to revive Your command which they had abandoned.' He commanded that they should be stoned, and Allah revealed the words: ﴾O' Messenger

---

[1] Bukhari, in numerous places, *Al-Janaa'iz*, hadith no 1329; *Al-Manaaqib*, hadith no. 3635; *At-Tafseer - Soorah Aal 'Imraan, Baab Qul Fa'tu bil-Tawraat fatloohaa* - hadith no. 4556; *Al-Ḥudood - Baab al-Rajm fil-Balaaṭ* - hadith no. 6819; *Baab Aḥkaam Ahl adh-Dhimmah*, hadith no. 6840, 7332, 7543. Muslim in *Kitaab al-Ḥudood, Baab Rajm al-Yahood*, hadith no. 1699.

> [Muhammad]! Let not those who hurry to fall into disbelief grieve you... If you are given this, take it.﴾ *(Qur'an 5: 41)*. They said: 'Go to Muhammad and if he tells you to blacken their faces and flog them, then accept it, and if he tells you to stone them, then beware.' Then Allah revealed the words, ﴾And whosoever does not judge by what Allah has revealed, such are the *kaafiroon* [i.e. disbelievers].﴾ *(Qur'an 5: 44)*, ﴾And whosoever does not judge by that which Allah has revealed, such are the *zaalimoon* [polytheists and wrongdoers].﴾ *(Qur'an 5: 45)* and ﴾And whosoever does not judge by what Allah has revealed [then] such [people] are the *faasiqoon* [the rebellious i.e. disobedient].﴾ *(Qur'an 5: 47)* concerning all the *kuffaar*."[2]

There are other reports and versions of this hadith, many of which are mentioned by Aṭ-Ṭabari and Ibn Katheer in their *tafseers*. The reports of Al-Baraa' ibn 'Aazib narrated in Muslim and elsewhere clearly states the reason for revelation.

The second view is that is was revealed concerning two groups of Jews with regard to the issue of *diyah* (blood money) between them. One group had defeated the other, so the *diyah* for one of their number who was killed was twice what it was for anyone from the other group, or that for one group a person would be killed in return whereas for the other group only the *diyah* would be paid.

It is narrated that Ibn 'Abbaas (رضي الله عنه) said: "They were Qurayẓah and An-Naḍeer. An-Naḍeer were considered to be of a higher status than Qurayẓah, so that if a man from Qurayẓah killed a man from An-Naḍeer, he would be killed in return, but if a man from An-Naḍeer

---

[2] Muslim, *Kitaab al-Ḥudood, Bab Rajm al-Yahood*, hadith no. 1700, etc.

killed a man from Qurayẓah, he would be ransomed by the payment of one hundred *wasq* of dates. When the Prophet (ﷺ) migrated to Madeenah, a man from An-Naḍeer killed a man from Qurayẓah, and they said, 'Give him to us and we will kill him.' They (An-Naḍeer) said, 'Between you and us (as judge) is the Prophet (ﷺ).' So they came to him, then these words were revealed: 'And if you judge, judge with justice between them'. Justice means, a soul for a soul. Then the words were revealed: ﴾Do they then seek the judgement of [the days of] Ignorance?﴿"[3]

There is another report from Ibn 'Abbaas which we will quote in full because of the additional details it gives and because it speaks of the differences in *diyah*. It is narrated that Ibn 'Abbaas (رضي الله عنه) said: "Allah revealed the words: ﴾And whosoever does not judge by what Allah has revealed, such are the *kaafiroon* [i.e. disbelievers].﴿ *(Qur'an 5: 44)*, ﴾And whosoever does not judge by that which Allah has revealed, such are the *ẓaalimoon* [polytheists and wrongdoers].﴿ *(Qur'an 5: 45)* and ﴾And whosoever does not judge by what Allah has revealed [then] such [people] are the *faasiqoon* [the rebellious i.e. disobedient].﴿ *(Qur'an 5: 47)*. Allah revealed these words concerning two groups of Jews, one of which had subjugated the other during the *jaahiliyah* until they reached an agreement that for every person among the inferior group killed by the superior group, the blood-money would be fifty *wasq*, and for every person among the superior group killed by the inferior group, the blood-money would be one hundred *wasq*. This remained in force until the Prophet (ﷺ) came to Madeenah, and both groups felt that they lost their status when he (ﷺ) came. Then the inferior group killed a man from the

---

[3] Abu Dawood, *Kitaab ad-Diyaat, Baab an-Nafs bi'n-Nafs*, hadith no. 4494. It is also narrated in *Ṣaḥeeḥ Abi Dawood*, hadith no. 3772; Nasaa'i in *Kitaab al-Qisaamah, Baab Ta'weel Qawlihi ta'aala, "Wa in ḥakamta faḥkam baynahum bil-Qisṭ"*, 8/18; *Ṣaḥeeḥ Sunan an-Nasaa'i*, hadith no. 4410.

superior group, so the superior group sent word to the inferior group, telling them to send one hundred *wasq*. The inferior group said, 'Have there ever been two tribes whose religion, lineage and country are the same, where the blood-money of some of them is half the blood-money of the others? We accepted this deal because of our weakness and our fear of you, but now that Muhammad has come, we will no longer accept this.' There was almost war between them, then they agreed to appoint the Messenger of Allah (ﷺ) as the judge between them. Then the superior group said, 'By Allah, Muhammad is not going to approve of this state of affairs whereby you receive double what they receive, and they are right, they only accepted this arrangement because of their fear and weakness. Send someone in disguise to Muhammad so that he can tell you what his opinion is. If he is going to give you what you want, then appoint him as judge, otherwise be cautious and do not appoint him as judge.' So they sent some people from among the hypocrites in disguise to the Messenger of Allah (ﷺ), to find out for them what the opinion of the Messenger of Allah (ﷺ) was.

When they came to the Messenger of Allah (ﷺ), Allah informed His Messenger about them and what they wanted. And Allah revealed the words: ﴿O' Messenger [Muhammad]! Let not those who hurry to fall into disbelief grieve you, of such who say: "We believe"... And whosoever does not judge by what Allah has revealed [then] such [people] are the *faasiqoon* [the rebellious i.e. disobedient].﴾ Then he said,

> "Concerning them (the two groups), by Allah, it was revealed, and they are the ones whom Allah meant."[4]

[4] Imam Aḥmad, 1/246. It is classed as *ṣaḥeeḥ* by Shaakir, hadith no. 2212. Nasaa'i, 8/19; *Ṣaḥeeḥ an-Nasaa'i*, hadith no. 4411; Ibn Jareer, 10/326, edited by Shaakir, report no. 11984.

So long as these two reasons are both proven to be *ṣaḥeeḥ*, it may be said: these two reasons may have existed at the same time, so that these *aayaat* (verse) were revealed concerning all of that, as Ibn Katheer said.[5] And Allah knows best.

There are also other views concerning the reasons for revelation, but they are either *ḍa'eef* (weak), such as the idea that it was revealed concerning the story of Abu Lubaabah and Banu Qurayẓah, or they come under the same heading as the reports narrated above, such that the views that it was revealed concerning the Jew 'Abdullah ibn Ṣooriya who apostatized after becoming Muslim, or that it was revealed concerning the hypocrites.

From this examination of the reasons for revelation, the following points may be noted:

1 - That there is a strong connection between the reasons for revelation and the *aayaat* quoted, for they mention the Jews who distorted words by altering their sequence, and say that if they come to you then judge between them or turn away from them, and how can they appoint you as judge when they have the *Tawraat*, etc. So any story concerning the reason for revelation which does not mention the Jews is unlikely to be correct.

2 - That these *aayaat* which were revealed, exposing the Jews and their allies among the hypocrites, ruling that those who judged or ruled by anything other than that which Allah has revealed are guilty of *kufr, fisq* (rebellion) and *ẓulm* (wrongdoing), and commanding the Messenger (ﷺ) to judge and rule by that which Allah has revealed, and warning against being tempted to ignore some of that which Allah has revealed, etc. - these *aayaat* were revealed concerning only one ruling that the Jews had agreed amongst themselves to change

[5] *Tafseer Ibn Katheer*, 3/110, Ash-Sha'b edition.

and base it on something other than that which Allah had revealed. This ruling concerned either *zina* (adultery) or *qiṣaaṣ* (blood-money). These *aayaat* may also refer to any situation which resembles that of these Jews, regardless of time or place.

3- That agreement between two parties on a matter which goes against the rulings of Allah does not make it permissible. This is a matter concerning which many people are mistaken.

4- The relationship between the hypocrites and the Jews, and the role that each played in waging war against Islam and trying to circumvent the laws of Islam. Anyone who studies history will see that they have persisted in doing these things at all times and in all places.

5- Al-Baraa' ibn 'Aazib said: "It was concerning all the *kuffaar*." We will discuss this in the following section, *in sha Allah*.

Who is Referred to in These Verses? Are They General or Specific in Meaning?

Here we will focus on the phrases: ﴿And whosoever does not judge by what Allah has revealed, such are the *kaafiroon* [i.e. disbelievers] ... the *ẓaalimoon* [polytheists and wrongdoers] ... the *faasiqoon* [the rebellious i.e. disobedient].﴾ *(Qur'an 5: 44-47)*.

The *salaf* (may Allah have mercy on them) differed concerning these verses and had numerous opinions. We will quote some of their views, then we will examine the differences concerning that. And Allah is the Source of strength and help.

These differences may be summed up as follows:

1- That those who are referred to here are the Jews who distorted the Book of Allah and changed His rulings. This view is narrated from Al-Baraa' ibn 'Aazib when he said - as mentioned above from

Ṣaḥeeḥ Muslim — concerning these three *aayaat*, that they were "concerning all the *kuffaar.*"[6]

It is narrated that Abu Ṣaaliḥ said: "The three *aayaat* from *Soorah al-Maa'idah* — ﴿And whosoever does not judge by what Allah has revealed, such are the *kaafiroon* [i.e. disbelievers].﴾ *(Qur'an 5: 44)*, ﴿... such are the *ẓaalimoon* [polytheists and wrongdoers].﴾ *(Qur'an 5: 45)* and ﴿... such [people] are the *faasiqoon* [the rebellious i.e. disobedient].﴾ *(Qur'an 5: 47)* — do not refer to the Muslims at all; they refer to the *kuffaar.*"[7]

It is narrated that Aḍ-Ḍaḥḥaak also said: "These *aayaat* were revealed concerning the People of the Book."[8]

It is narrated that Abu Majlaz said: "They were revealed concerning the Jews, Christians and people of *shirk.*"[9]

It is narrated that 'Ikrimah said: "These *aayaat* are concerning the People of the Book."[10]

It is narrated that Qataadah said: "It was mentioned to us that these *aayaat* were revealed concerning a murdered Jew."[11]

It is narrated that 'Ubaydullah ibn 'Abdullah ibn 'Utbah ibn Mas'ood mentioned the story of the dispute between the two Jewish tribes of Qurayẓah and An-Naḍeer concerning a murder, then he said: "What is meant by that are the Jews, and this was revealed concerning them."[12]

---

6 Quoted above. See also *Tafseer aṭ-Ṭabari*, 1/346, 351, 352, reports nos. 12022, 12034, 12036.

7 *Tafseer aṭ-Ṭabari*, 10/346, report no. 12023.

8 Ibid, 10/347, 350, report nos. 12024, 12028.

9 Ibid, 10/347, report nos. 12025, 12026.

10 Ibid, 10/351, report nos. 12031, 12033.

11 Ibid, 10/351, report no. 12032.

12 Ibid, 10/352, report no. 12037.

This is also narrated from Ibn 'Abbaas,[13] and something similar is narrated from Ḥudhayfah (ﷺ), as it is narrated that he said concerning the *aayah* — ﴾And whosoever does not judge by what Allah has revealed, such are the *kaafiroon* [i.e. disbelievers]﴿ — "What good brothers the Children of Israel are to you. If everything sweet (i.e., words of praise) is for you then everything bitter (i.e., words of condemnation) is for them. And you will certainly follow them, step by step."[14] The phrase "you will certainly follow them" may be understood as meaning that he thought it was revealed concerning the Children of Israel.

Those who state this view quote as evidence the fact that "the Holy Qur'an indicates that it is concerning the Jews, because in the preceding *aayaat*, Allah mentions that they changed some of the words from their places, and that they said, 'If you are given this', meaning the distorted ruling that is not the ruling of Allah, 'take it', 'but if you are not given this', meaning the distorted ruling, but you are given the true ruling of Allah, then beware. So they were enjoining caution in the case of the ruling of Allah which they knew was the truth. Then Allah said, ﴾And We ordained therein for them: Life for life.﴿ This indicates that they are being spoken of here."[15]

This view is also favoured by Az-Zajjaaj, who said in support of it: "Among the best views that were expressed concerning this is the view of Ash-Sha'bi, who said: This is specifically about the Jews.[16] Three things prove what he says: the Jews are mentioned prior to this,

---

[13] *Ad-Durr al-Manthoor*, 3/87-88, where two reports are narrated from him, in one of which he states that it is narrated specifically concerning the Jews.

[14] *Tafseer aṭ-Ṭabari*, 10/349-350, reports nos. 12027, 12029, 12030; *Tafseer 'Abdur-Razzaaq*, 1/191.

[15] *Aḍwaa' al-Bayaan*, 2/90.

[16] This is what Az-Zajjaaj said, quoting from Ash-Sha'bi; there appears below a comment from Ash-Sha'bi which says something different.

in the *aayah*, 'for the Jews', so the pronoun refers back to them; the context of the *aayah* indicates that, because after that it says, ﴿And We ordained therein for them...﴾, and this pronoun refers back to the Jews, according to consensus; and the Jews are the ones who rejected stoning and settling scores (*qiṣaaṣ*)."[17] Then he mentioned some objections and the response to them.

This is what Ibn Jareer thought most likely to be correct, when he thought that it was revealed concerning the *kuffaar* of the People of the Book, then he stated that it was more general in meaning and included everyone who denies (the rulings of Allah).[18]

2 - Some of them said that "the *kaafiroon* (i.e. disbelievers)" meant the Muslims, "the *ẓaalimoon* (polytheists and wrongdoers)" meant the Jews and "the *faasiqoon* (the rebellious i.e. disobedient)" meant the Christians.

Among those who suggested this was Ash-Sha'bi. It is narrated that he said: "One *aayah* referring to us and two *aayaat* referring to the People of the Book. ﴿And whosoever does not judge by what Allah has revealed, such are the *ẓaalimoon* [polytheists and wrongdoers]﴾, and ﴿...the *faasiqoon* [the rebellious i.e. disobedient]﴾ — refers to the People of the Book." According to another comment narrated from him, he said: "The first (*aayah*) refers to the Muslims, the second to the Jews and the third to the Christians."[19] This is the view favoured by Abu Bakr ibn al-'Arabi when he said: "Among them are those who say ﴿the *kaafiroon* [i.e. disbelievers]﴾ refers to the *mushrikeen*,[20] ﴿the

[17] *I'raab al-Qur'an*, 2/21-22, Beirut edition.

[18] *Tafseer aṭ-Ṭabari*, 10/358.

[19] Ibid, 10/353-355, reports 12038-12046.

[20] This is how it appears in *Aḥkaam al-Qur'an* by Ibn al-'Arabi. In *Al-Jaami' li Aḥkaam al-Qur'an* by Qurṭubi, it says, "*Al-Kaafiroon* (the disbelievers) refers to the Muslims..." He was quoting from Ibn al-'Arabi.

zaalimoon [polytheists and wrongdoers]﴿ refers to the Jews and ﴾the *faasiqoon* [the rebellious i.e. disobedient]﴿ refers to the Christians. This is also my opinion, because this is the apparent meaning of the *aayaat*, and it is the view of Ibn 'Abbaas, Jaabir, Ibn Abi Zaa'idah and Ibn Shubrumah."[21]

Ash-Shanqeeti also thought this most likely to be correct, when he said: "The apparent meaning from the context of the *aayaat* is that the phrase ﴾such are the *kaafiroon* [i.e. disbelievers]﴿ refers to the Muslims, because prior to this, Allah said, addressing the Muslims of this ummah: ﴾Therefore fear not men but fear Me and sell not My Verses for a miserable price﴿ *(Qur'an 5: 44)*, then He said: ﴾And whosoever does not judge by what Allah has revealed, such are the *kaafiroon* [i.e. disbelievers]﴿. So those who are being addressed here are the Muslims, as is apparent from the context of the *aayah*, and on this basis the *kufr* mentioned here is either a lesser form of *kufr*, or a major form of *kufr*, when the one who does that does so because he believes it to be permitted, or he aims thereby to deny and reject the rulings of Allah even though he knows them. But in the case of one who rules according to something other than that which Allah revealed, recognizing that he is committing a sin and an evil action, but he is compelled to do that by his whims and desires, he is one of the sinners among the Muslims. The context of the Qur'an also clearly indicates that the *aayah* ﴾such are the *zaalimoon* [polytheists and wrongdoers]﴿ refers to the Jews, because before that Allah (ﷻ) says: ﴾And We ordained therein for them: Life for life, eye for eye, nose for nose, ear for ear, tooth for tooth, and wounds equal for equal. But if anyone remits the retaliation by way of charity, it shall be for him an expiation. And whosoever does not judge by that which Allah has revealed, such are the *zaalimoon* [polytheists and wrongdoers — of a lesser degree]﴿ *(Qur'an 5: 45)*. So this is addressed to them (the

---

[21] *Ahkaam al-Qur'an* by Ibn al-'Arabi, 2/621.

Jews), as is clearly indicated by the context. And the *aayah*, ﴿such [people] are the *faasiqoon* [the rebellious i.e. disobedient]﴾ refers to the Christians, because prior to that Allah says: ﴿Let the people of the *Injeel* [Gospel] judge by what Allah has revealed therein. And whosoever does not judge by what Allah has revealed [then] such [people] are the *faasiqoon* [the rebellious i.e. disobedient (of a lesser degree)] to Allah﴾ *(Qur'an 5: 46)*."[22]

Then he explains that *kufr, ẓulm* (wrongdoing) and *fisq* (rebellion) are all of two types, major and minor. Then he said: "What counts is the general meaning of the words and not the specific reason for revelation. I have stated my opinion above and Allah knows best."[23]

3 - That what is meant by these *aayaat* is a lesser form of *kufr*, a lesser form of *ẓulm* (wrongdoing), a lesser form of *fisq* (rebellion). This is based on the assumption that the *aayaat* are speaking of the Muslims.

This view is narrated from the great scholar of the ummah, Ibn 'Abbaas (رضي الله عنه). It is narrated from him via a number of isnads which strengthen one another, and which, taken all together, are *ṣaḥeeḥ*.[24]

---

[22] *Aḍwaa' al-Bayaan*, 2/92.

[23] Ibid., 2/93.

[24] This is what we think is most likely to be correct, noting that there are those who classify this report from Ibn 'Abbaas as *ḍa'eef* (weak).

The criticisms directed against these reports - and our comments as to what we believe is more likely to be correct - are as follows:

1 - The report of Ibn Abi Ṭalḥah from Ibn 'Abbaas: "Whoever rejects that which Allah has revealed is a *kaafir*, and whoever approves of it but does not judge according to it is a *ẓaalim* and a *faasiq*." It is said that 'Abdullah ibn Ṣaaliḥ, who is in the isnad and was the scribe of Al-Layth was regarded as *thiqah* by some and as *ḍa'eef* by others. Ibn Ḥajar said concerning him: "He is *ṣadooq* but makes many mistakes. He is *thaabit* when he reads from his books but sometimes he is confused."

2 - The report of Sufyaan from a man from Ṭaawoos from Ibn 'Abbaas who said: "*Kufr* which does not put one beyond the pale of Islam." In (this isnad) is an unknown man, so it is *ḍa'eef* (weak). This wording is also narrated from Ṭaawoos.=

= It is narrated from him by Sa'eed al-Makki, which is a sounder isnad.
3 - The report: "It is not the *kufr* which they think it is." According to one version: "It is not the *kufr* which they think it is; it is not the *kufr* which puts one beyond the pale of Islam. ﴾And whosoever does not judge by what Allah has revealed, such are the *kaafiroon* [i.e. disbelievers]﴿ refers to a lesser form of *kufr*." And it is said, these two reports come via Hishaam ibn Ḥujayr from Ibn 'Abbaas. There is some dispute as to whether he is *thiqah* or *ḍa'eef*. Among those who regarded him as *thiqah* were Al-'Ajali, Ibn Ḥibbaan in *Ath-Thiqaat* and Ibn Shaaheen. Among those who regarded him as *ḍa'eef* was Imam Aḥmad who said, "He is not very reliable." I ('Abdullah ibn Aḥmad) said, Is he *ḍa'eef*? He said, he is not very reliable. He said: I asked Yaḥyaa ibn Ma'een about him and he said that he was very *ḍa'eef* (weak). And he is classed as *ḍa'eef* by Yaḥyaa al-Qaṭṭaan. Those who regard him as *ḍa'eef* are more knowledgeable, which means that those who criticize him outweigh those who commend him. Hence Ibn Jareer said concerning him: "He is *ṣadooq* (sincere) but confused." This is narrated in *Al-Hady fiman ṭa'na feehim min Rijaal al-Bukhari*, where he says: "Al-'Ajali and Ibn Sa'd classed him as *thiqah* and Yaḥyaa al-Qaṭṭaan and Yaḥyaa ibn Ma'een classed him as *ḍa'eef*. Aḥmad said: 'He is not very reliable.' Abu Ja'far al-'Aqeeli mentioned him among those who are *ḍa'eef*, and narrated that Sufyaan ibn 'Uyaynah said: 'We do not take anything from him except that which we cannot find with anyone else.' (*Hady as-Saari*, 447-448, 1st *Salafiyah* edition).
Concerning the above, see *Tahdheeb al-Kamaal*, no. 6571 (30/179, edited by Bashshaar 'Awaad)
Even though Hishaam ibn Ḥujayr is one of the men of Bukhari and Muslim, they did not narrate from him except as corroborating reports, as is mentioned by Ibn Ḥajar in his comment on the reports narrated by Bukhari.
4 - The report of Sufyaan ibn Mu'ammar ibn Raashid from Ibn Ṭaawoos from his father, that Ibn 'Abbaas was asked about the *aayah* ﴾And whosoever does not judge by what Allah has revealed﴿, and he said, "It is *kufr* (disbelief)." Ibn Ṭaawoos said: but it is not like disbelief in Allah, His angels, His Books and His Messengers."
Another report is also narrated from Sufyaan from Mu'ammar from Ibn Ṭaawoos from Ibn 'Abbaas: ﴾And whosoever does not judge by what Allah has revealed.﴿ He said: "It is *kufr* (disbelief), but it is not disbelief in Allah, His angels, His Books and His Messengers."
It is said, commenting on these two reports, that the sound report from Ibn 'Abbaas, is the report in which he says "It is *kufr* (disbelief)." The phrase, "but it is not disbelief in Allah, His angels, His Books and His Messengers" may be the words of Ibn Ṭaawoos, as is clearly stated in the first report. =

These include:

— It is narrated that Ibn 'Abbaas said: "﴾And whosoever does not judge by what Allah has revealed, such are the *kaafiroon* [i.e. disbelievers]﴿... this is *kufr* (disbelief), but it is not disbelief in Allah, His angels, His Books and His Messengers."

— That he said: "... *kufr* which does not put a person beyond the pale of Islam."

— (The report) from Ibn Ṭaawoos from his father, who said: "A man said to Ibn 'Abbaas concerning this *aayah* - ﴾And whosoever does not judge by what Allah has revealed, such are the *kaafiroon* [i.e. disbelievers]﴿ — 'Is the one who does that is guilty of *kufr*?' Ibn 'Abbaas said, 'If he does that, it is *kufr*, but he is not like one who disbelieves in Allah and the Last Day, or in such and such.'"

— It is narrated from Ibn Ṭaawoos from his father that he said: "Ibn 'Abbaas was asked about the *aayah*, ﴾And whosoever does not judge by what Allah has revealed, such are the *kaafiroon* [i.e. disbelievers]﴿. He said, 'It is *kufr*.' Ibn Ṭaawoos said, 'But he is not like one who disbelieves in Allah, His angels, His Books and His Messengers.'"

— It is narrated from Ṭaawoos from Ibn 'Abbaas concerning the *aayah* ﴾And whosoever does not judge by what Allah has revealed,

---

= This is a summary of the refutations of these reports, but what we think most likely to be correct is that these reports from Ibn 'Abbaas are sound and trustworthy, for the following three reasons:

1) The report narrated with an isnad from Sufyaan from Mu'ammar from Ibn Ṭaawoos from his father is *ṣaḥeeḥ*. No one casts aspersions on this.

2) These reports are *ṣaḥeeḥ* and are supported by other reports. At the very least, they are *ṣaḥeeḥ* when their isnads are put together.

3) The fact that the scholars have unanimously used the report of Ibn 'Abbaas as evidence and have quoted it when discussing the meaning of the *aayah*.

Our discussion is based on the fact that the report from Ibn 'Abbaas is sound. And Allah knows best.

such are the *kaafiroon* [i.e. disbelievers]﴿, that he said: 'This is not the *kufr* which they think of.'

→ And it is narrated from Ibn 'Abbaas with the wording: "It is not the *kufr* which they think of, it is not the *kufr* which puts a person beyond the pale of Islam.' ﴾And whosoever does not judge by what Allah has revealed, such are the *kaafiroon* [i.e. disbelievers]﴿ is a lesser form of *kufr*." Some of them added: "...and a lesser form of *ẓulm* (wrongdoing) and a lesser form of *fisq* (rebellion)."[25]

This view is also narrated from 'Aṭaa', who said: a lesser form of *kufr*, a lesser form of *fisq* and a lesser form of *ẓulm*.[26] And it was also narrated that Ṭaawoos said: "It is not *kufr* which puts a person beyond the pale of Islam."[27]

4 - That what is meant by the *aayah* ﴾And whosoever does not judge by what Allah has revealed, such are the *kaafiroon* [i.e. disbelievers]﴿ is the one who does not rule by what Allah has revealed because he rejects it. The verses which describe those who do not rule by that which Allah has revealed as *ẓaalimoon* (wrongdoers) and *faasiqoon* (rebels), are referring to those who accept and approve of shari'ah (Islamic law) but do not rule in accordance with it.

This is narrated from Ibn 'Abbaas (رضي الله عنه) (may Allah be pleased with him), who said: "Whoever rejects that which Allah has revealed is guilty of *kufr*, and whoever accepts it and approves of it but does not

---

[25] *Tafseer aṭ-Ṭabari*, 10/355-356; *Ta'zeem Qadr aṣ-Ṣalaah*, 2/521, reports nos. 569-575. See also *Ad-Durr al-Manthoor*, 3/87-88, *Daar al-Fikr*, Beirut, edition. See *Al-Qawl al-Ma'moon fi Takhreej ma warada 'an ibn 'Abbaas fi Tafseer 'Wa man lam yaḥkum bima anzala Allah fa oolaa'ika hum al-kaafiroon*, written by 'Ali Ḥasan 'Abdul-Ḥameed. In this book and in the footnotes of *Ta'zeem Qadr aṣ-Ṣalaah* there is a study of the isnads of these reports.

[26] *Tafseer aṭ-Ṭabari*, 10/355.

[27] Ibid, 10/356; *Tafseer 'Abdur-Razzaaq*, 1/191.

rule by it is a *ẓaalim* (wrongdoer) and a *faasiq* (rebel)."[28]

Many of the *mufassireen* mentioned this view and said that the kind of *kufr* which puts a person beyond the pale of Islam applies only in the case of the one who rejects that which Allah has revealed.

5 - It is said that these *aayaat* were revealed concerning the People of the Book, and that they also refer to all of mankind, Muslims and *kuffaar* alike.

This view is referred to by Ḥudhayfah when he said, concerning the *aayah* from *Soorah al-Maa'idah*, "What good brothers the Children of Israel are to you. If everything sweet is for you then everything bitter is for them. But you will certainly follow them, step by step."[29]

Among those who were also of this view was Ibraaheem an-Nakha'i. He said concerning this *aayah* — ﴿And whosoever does not judge by what Allah has revealed, such are the *kaafiroon* [i.e. disbelievers]﴾ — "These *aayaat* (verses) were revealed concerning the Children of Israel, and Allah included also this ummah in these verses."[30]

It is also narrated that Al-Ḥasan said: "It was revealed concerning the Jews, and it is also applicable to us."[31]

Reports (from the Companions) are narrated from Ibn Mas'ood which indicate that it is general in meaning, and it is narrated from 'Ilqimah and Masrooq that they asked Ibn Mas'ood about bribes, and

---

[28] *Tafseer aṭ-Ṭabari*, 10/357, report no. 12063. It is also narrated from 'Ikrimah; see *Al-Baghawi*, 3/61.

[29] *Tafseer aṭ-Ṭabari*, 10/349-350, reports 12027, 12029, 12030; *Tafseer 'Abdur-Razzaaq*, 1/191. Also narrated by Al-Ḥaakim in *Al-Mustadrak*, 2/312-313. He said, this is a *ṣaḥeeḥ* hadith according to the conditions of the two *shaykhs*, although they did not narrate it, and Adh-Dhahabi agreed with him.

[30] *Tafseer 'Abdur-Razzaaq*, 1/191; Aṭ-Ṭabari, 10/356-357, report no. 12058, 12059; *Ad-Durr al-Manthoor*, 3/87, *Daar al-Fikr* edition.

[31] Aṭ-Ṭabari, 10/357, report no. 12060; *Ad-Durr al-Manthoor*, 3/88.

he said: it is one of the illegal things (cf. Qur'an 5: 62-63). They said, what about when one bribes a judge (to give a wrong ruling)? He said, that is *kufr*, then he recited this *aayah*: ﴿And whosoever does not judge by what Allah has revealed, such are the *kaafiroon* [i.e. disbelievers]﴾.[32]

It is narrated that As-Suddi said: "﴿And whosoever does not judge by what Allah has revealed﴾ — whoever does not judge according to what was revealed and neglects it deliberately, and knowingly passes an unjust ruling, is one of the *kaafireen*."[33]

6 - That this *aayah* is to be interpreted in a manner different to its apparent meaning, as meaning not judging or ruling by all that Allah has revealed, including judging or ruling by *Tawḥeed* and the laws of Islam. This is narrated from 'Abdul-'Azeez al-Kinaani, who said, when he was asked about these *aayaat*: "They apply to all that has been revealed by Allah, not only to part of it. Everyone who does not rule by all that Allah has revealed is a *kaafir*, a *ẓaalim* and a *faasiq*. With regard to one who rules according to what Allah has revealed with regard to *Tawḥeed* and keeping away from *shirk*, but does not rule according to all that Allah has revealed of laws, these *aayaat* are not applicable to him."[34]

7 - There is a view that what is meant are those who deliberately reject a ruling of Allah which is clearly stated in a text, but not those who are confused about a specific ruling or who make a mistake in interpretation.[35]

---

32 *Aṭ-Ṭabari*, 10/321, report no. 11960, 11963; also, 10/357, report no. 12061.

33 *Aṭ-Ṭabari*, 10/357, report no. 12062.

34 *Tafseer al-Baghawi*, 3/61. See also *Tafseer al-Qurṭubi*, 6/190.

35 *Tafseer al-Baghawi*, 3/61.

Az-Zajjaaj said: "﴾And whosoever does not judge by what Allah has revealed, such are the *kaafiroon* [i.e. disbelievers]﴿ means, whoever claims that one of the rulings of Allah which were brought by the Prophets (peace be upon them) is invalid, is a *kaafir*. The *fuqaha'* are agreed that whoever says that married people do not have to be stoned if they commit adultery — and they are free (as opposed to slaves) — is a *kaafir*, and this is the *kufr* of one who rejects one of the rulings of the Prophet because he disbelieves in him, and whoever disbelieves in the Prophet is a *kaafir*."[36]

8 - The *Khawaarij* said that this is *kufr* which puts a person beyond the pale of Islam, and they regarded this as general, applying to every ruling. This is well known from the earliest *Khawaarij*, and from the later *Khawaarij* such as the *Ibaaḍiyah*, who thought that when 'Ali (رضي الله عنه) agreed to accept the two arbitrators, this was ruling by something other than that which Allah had revealed, and was therefore *kufr*.

Now we will examine these viewpoints and indicate which among them is most likely to be correct.

Analysis

The purpose here is not to determine whether ruling by something other than that which Allah has revealed is major *kufr* or minor *kufr*, because this point will be discussed in detail in a following section. Rather the purpose here is to determine whether these *aayaat* speak specifically of the People of the Book, or of the Muslims, or if they apply to all, as suggested in the opinions referred to above.

It is also not the purpose here to determine the reason for the revelation of these *aayaat*, because we have already discussed this

---

[36] *Ma'aani al-Qur'an wa I'raabuhu* by Az-Zajjaaj, 2/178, published by *'Aalam al-Kutub*, Beirut.

matter above and determined — as narrated in the *ṣaḥeeḥ* reports — that they were revealed concerning the People of the Book.

On this basis, we say:

The one who ponders these opinions will notice that they point to only two views:

a) That the ruling of these *aayaat* applies specifically to the People of the Book, and not to the Muslims.
b) That the ruling of these *aayaat* applies to both of them, the People of the Book and, to those Muslims among them who do the deeds of the People of the Book.

With regard to the view that some of these verses apply specifically to the Muslims, some to the Jews and some to the Christians, points to the second view, because our discussion is centred on the first *aayah*, ﴾And whosoever does not judge by what Allah has revealed, such are the *Kaafiroon* [i.e. disbelievers]﴿. The People of the Book are inevitably included in this ruling.

We say that they point to two views because the rest of the views apart from the first one are included in that which we have listed as the second view.

— The view that the first *aayah* — ﴾And whosoever does not judge by what Allah has revealed, such are the *kaafiroon* [i.e. disbelievers]﴿ — is about the Muslims, the second is about the Jews and the third is about the Christians implies that it is general in meaning, because the *ẓulm* (wrongdoing) and *fisq* (rebellion) which the People of the Book committed is of the type which puts one beyond the pale of faith, so the People of the Book are included in the ruling of the first *aayah*, as stated above.

— The third view, that it is a lesser form of *kufr*... is based on the assumption that it is concerning the Muslims, or that they are included along with the People of the Book, so this statement is applicable to the Muslims.

— The same applies to the fourth view, so it may be interpreted as referring to those who reject.

— The fifth view states that it is general in application.

— The sixth view states that it applies to the Muslims.

— The seventh view is like the fourth view.

— The view of the *Khawaarij* is also based on the assumption that it refers only to the Muslims. This is a false view, as we shall see below.

So to sum up, there are two views concerning this matter:

a) That these verses apply only to the People of the Book.
b) That they are general and apply to both of them, the People of the Book and the Muslims - with differences in the way in which they apply to the Muslims.

The view which is more likely to be correct is the second view — that these verses are general in meaning. The evidence for this is as follows:

1 - That the scholars have stated that the reason for revelation and what is indicated by an *aayah* may be interconnected. Undoubtedly the reason for revelation has to do with the Jews who changed the rulings of Allah concerning the married adulterer and concerning *qisaas* (retribution). The context of the *aayah* indicates that, beyond a doubt: ﴾They change the words﴿, ﴾the Jews﴿, ﴾And We ordained therein for them: Life for life﴿, ﴾Let the people of the *Injeel* [Gospel] judge﴿.

All of them indicate that the reason for revelation had to do with the People of the Book, but what is implied by the *aayah* is something different, as stated above. The evidence that these two matters are interconnected is that some of those who were reported to have said that it was about the People of the Book were also reported to have said that these verses were revealed concerning a victim killed by the Jews who was one of them, as is narrated by Qataadah. Some — such as Aḍ-Ḍaḥḥaak — said that these verses were revealed concerning the People of the Book, without being more specific.

We should note that stating that it is more likely to be general in application does not contradict the fact that it was revealed concerning the People of the Book, because the point here is the general applicability of the wording, not the specific reason for revelation. We will discuss this in more detail below.

2 - In the comments of some of those who say that it applies only to the People of the Book, there is the indication that it is general. For example, Ḥudhayfah's comment: "What good brothers the Children of Israel are to you. If everything sweet is for you then everything bitter is for them. But you will certainly follow them, step by step." Similarly, it is narrated that Ibn 'Abbaas said: "What good people you are. If there is something sweet, it is for you, and if it is bitter, it is for the People of the Book." It is as if he thought that these words referred to the Muslims: ﴾And whosoever does not judge by what Allah has revealed, such are the *kaafiroon* [i.e. disbelievers]﴿.[37] Although it is narrated from him that he thought it was specifically concerning the Jews. It is also narrated from him that it was concerning those who reject (the ruling of Allah) or that it referred to a lesser form of *kufr*. This indicates that his statement that it applies specifically to the Jews does not mean that he did not think that it could go beyond them to include the Muslims too. The same may be said concerning the view of Ḥudhayfah.

3 - With regard to the view of Abu Majlaz — "These *aayaat* (verses) were revealed concerning the Jews and Christians" (according to

---

[37] *Ad-Durr al-Manthoor*, 3/88.

another report, "They were revealed concerning the Jews, Christians and people of *shirk*") — it should be borne in mind that Abu Majlaz was discussing the *Ibaaḍiya Khawaarij*. (We will discuss this matter in more detail below *in sha Allah*). At the end of his comment he mentioned the people of *shirk*. Thus he was explaining that whoever acts in a manner similar to the Jews is one of the people of *shirk* and is therefore subject to the ruling of this *aayah*.

4 - With regard to the view of Abu Ṣaaliḥ — "(These *aayaat*) do not refer to the Muslims at all; they refer to the *kuffaar*", and the view of Al-Baraa' ibn 'Aazib (رضي الله عنه) — "They are all about the *kuffaar*" — there is nothing to indicate that they are exclusively about the People of the Book.

Indeed, it might be said:

a) The comments of Abu Majlaz and Abu Ṣaaliḥ indicate that the words in the *aayaat* are addressed to the *kuffaar* of the People of the Book. This does not rule out the idea that they may be general in application, including both the People of the Book and others who do deeds similar to theirs — because the point is the general applicability of the wording.

b) Although it may be understood from the words of Abu Ṣaaliḥ that these words may apply exclusively to the *kuffaar* and that the Muslims are not included in that, it may be the case that he intended to refute those who denounced oppressive rulers as *kaafir*. This is what is implied by the *ṣaḥeeḥ* report from Ibn 'Abbaas (رضي الله عنه). So what is narrated from them both amounts to the same thing.

The conclusion of both is the same, that is, that what is indicated by the *aayaat* is not limited only to the People of the Book. This will be explained in the following points.

5 - The apparent meaning of the wording of the *aayaat* is general, because the word man (whoever) is used, which indicates a general meaning.

Hence when Ibn al-Qayyim mentioned the view that these *aayaat* referred (only) to the People of the Book, he immediately followed that by saying: "This is unlikely, and it goes against the apparent meaning of the words, so it is not valid."[38]

6 - Even if we assume that this was the opinion of some — I mean the view that it applied specifically to the People of the Book — the view of the majority of the *salaf* was that it is general in application. This is also the view of the scholars of Islam who came after them. This is what is indicated by other *aayaat* in the Qur'an, such as the command to judge or rule according to the Book of Allah, and the statement that the one who does not refer for judgement to the Qur'an and Sunnah is not a believer, and the prohibition of referring to *Ṭaaghoot* for judgement, etc.

7 - Whatever may be the case, what counts is the general applicability of the wording, not the specific reason for revelation — as is well known. The point of what those who differ say is that these *aayaat* were revealed concerning the Jews, for a specific reason, so they apply only to them. But in order to refute this, we say that whatever *aayaat* or *aḥaadeeth* came for a specific reason, if the wording

---

[38] *Madaarij as-Saalikeen*, 1/336. Bukhari included a chapter which used this *aayah* as evidence; this chapter is entitled *Baab Ajr man qaḍaa bi'l-Ḥikmah li Qawlihi ta'aala "Wa man lam yaḥkum bimaa anzala Allah fa oolaa'ika hum al-faasiqoon."* Ibn Ḥajar (31/120) said: "From Bukhari's title it appears that he thought it more likely to be general in meaning." Then he narrated that Ismaa'eel al-Qaaḍi said: "The apparent meaning of the *aayaat* indicates that whoever acts in a manner similar to theirs and invents rulings that go against the rulings of Allah, and makes that a way to be followed, is subject to the same warning as them, whether he is a judge or not." (*Fatḥ al-Baari*, 13/120 - 1st *Salafiyah* edition).

indicates whether it is general or specific in meaning, then it should be taken as such. There is no dispute on this point. But if the wording does not indicate one or the other, then the most correct view is that what counts is the general meaning of the words (not the specific reason for revelation). This is the view of the majority of scholars, and their evidence for that is expounded in the books of *Uṣool al-Fiqh*.[39]

This matter may be clarified further by pointing out the following:

a) That the context of the *aayaat* in *Soorah al-Maa'idah* — the fifth chapter of the Qur'an — indicates that the meaning is general and not restricted to the People of the Book. For example:

(i) The phrase begins with the words ﴾And whosoever does not judge by what Allah has revealed﴿ *(Qur'an 5: 44)*. The conditional pronoun man (whosoever) is one of the clearest signs that the meaning is general. Hence some of the *ṣaḥaabah* and a group of the *mufassireen* said that it is general in meaning.

(ii) The words in these *aayaat* are addressed to the Messenger (ﷺ), such as ﴾either judge between them, or turn away from them﴿ *(Qur'an 5: 42)* and ﴾So judge among them by what Allah has revealed, and follow not their vain desires﴿ *(Qur'an 5: 48)*. This wording is addressed to the Messenger and his ummah.

b) It is narrated that the Prophet (ﷺ) and his Companions would refer to verses which had been revealed concerning the People of the Book or the *mushrikeen*, and use them as

---

[39] *Al-Mustaṣfaa* by Al-Ghazaali, 2/20 (*Boolaaq* edition); *Sharḥ al-Kawkab al-Muneer*, 3/177; *Al-Muwaafaqaat*, 3/281 with commentary by Ad-Darraaz., Muṣṭafa Muhammah edition. It is also published by *Daar Ibn 'Affaan*, edited by Ḥasan Salmaan, 4/34.

evidence when debating with Muslims, which indicates that they understood these *aayaat* to be general in application, not specific.

Ash-Shaaṭibi said in *Al-Muwaafaqaat*: "Someone may say that even though the righteous *salaf* knew the aims of shari'ah and were Arabs, they understood the wording as being general in application even though the context may indicate otherwise. This indicates that what counted in their view was the general applicability of the words as they appeared to be, even if the context may indicate otherwise..."[40]

Then Ash-Shaaṭibi mentioned examples, some of which we will quote shortly. Then he said: "This is like the *aayah* — ﴿And whosoever does not judge by what Allah has revealed, such are the *kaafiroon* [i.e. disbelievers]﴾ — even though it was revealed concerning the Jews as is indicated by the context. But the scholars understood it to be general in application, referring not only to the *kuffaar*. They said, this is a lesser form of *kufr*."[41]

In his *tafseer* of the *aayah* —

﴿ ۞ أَجَعَلْتُمْ سِقَايَةَ ٱلْحَآجِّ وَعِمَارَةَ ٱلْمَسْجِدِ ٱلْحَرَامِ كَمَنْ ءَامَنَ بِٱللَّهِ وَٱلْيَوْمِ ٱلْءَاخِرِ وَجَٰهَدَ فِى سَبِيلِ ٱللَّهِ ... ﴿١٩﴾ ﴾

﴿Do you consider the providing of drinking water to the pilgrims and the maintenance of *Al-Masjid al-Haraam* [at Makkah] as equal to the worth of those who believe in Allah and the Last Day, and strive hard and fight in the cause of Allah?...﴾ *(Qur'an 9: 19)* —

Qurṭubi quoted the hadith of An-Nu'maan ibn Basheer (رضي الله عنه) who said: "I was at the *minbar* of the Messenger of Allah (ﷺ) when a man said, 'I wouldn't mind if I don't do anything after becoming Muslim

[40] *Al-Muwaafaqaat*, 4/34 - *Daar Ibn 'Affaan* edition.

[41] Ibid, 4/39.

except providing drinking water to the pilgrims.' Another man said, 'I wouldn't mind if I don't do anything after becoming Muslims except maintaining *Al-Masjid al-Ḥaraam*.' Another man said, 'Jihad for the sake of Allah is better than what you are saying. 'Umar (ﷺ) rebuked him and said, 'Do not raise your voices at the minbar of the Messenger of Allah (ﷺ) on a Friday. But when you pray the *Jumu'ah* prayer, consult him concerning that wherein you differ.' Then Allah revealed the words: ﴿Do you consider the providing of drinking water to the pilgrims and the maintenance of *Al-Masjid al-Ḥaraam* [at Makkah] as equal to the worth of those who believe in Allah and the Last Day...﴾."[42]

Qurṭubi said, after discussing this point:

"If it were said that on this basis it is permissible to use as evidence when debating with Muslims verses which were revealed concerning the *kaafireen* and it is known that the rulings concerning them are different, then it may be said to him that it is not far-fetched to derive rulings concerning the Muslims from that which Allah has revealed concerning the *mushrikeen*. 'Umar said, 'If we wished, we could take fried and grilled food one plate after another, but we have heard the words of Allah,

﴿... أَذْهَبْتُمْ طَيِّبَٰتِكُمْ فِى حَيَاتِكُمُ ٱلدُّنْيَا وَٱسْتَمْتَعْتُم بِهَا ... ۝٢٠﴾

﴿...You received your good things in the life of the world, and you took your pleasure therein...﴾ *(Qur'an 46: 20)*.'

This *aayah* speaks of the *kuffaar*, but 'Umar understood it to be a warning against being like them in some ways, and none of the *ṣaḥaabah* denounced his interpretation. It may be that this *aayah*

---

[42] Muslim in *Kitaaab al-Eemaan, Baab Faḍl ash-Shahaadah fi Sabeel-Allah ta'aala*, hadith no. 1879.

(Qur'an 5: 44) is of this type. This is a valuable point which resolves the problem and dispels confusion. And Allah knows best."[43]

'Umar's comments and reference to the *aayah* ﴿You received your good things...﴾ was also narrated by Ash-Shaaṭibi.[44]

Shaykh al-Islam Ibn Taymiyah said: "The texts of the Qur'an and Sunnah, which comprise the message of Muhammad (ﷺ), convey general meanings which apply to all of mankind through the general applicability of both the wording and the meaning, or of the meaning only. The covenants of Allah in the Book of Allah and the Sunnah of His Prophet apply to the latter generations of this ummah just as they applied to the first generations. Allah has told us the stories of the nations who came before us so that they may be a lesson for us, so that we may liken our situation to theirs and draw analogies between the later generations and the earlier generations of the nations, and so that the believers of the later generations might have an example in the earlier believers, and the *kaafireen* and hypocrites of the later generations might learn from what happened to the *kuffaar* and hypocrites of the earlier generations."[45]

---

[43] *Tafseer al-Qurṭubi*, 8/92, *Daar al-Kutub al-Miṣriyah* edition.

[44] *Al-Muwaafaqaat*, 4/34-35. See the comments on the report in the footnotes, Ḥasan Salmaan edition.

[45] *Majmoo' al-Fataawa*, 28/425. It should be noted that these comments of Ibn Taymiyah appear in an important essay concerning the war with the Tartars and the Muslims' victory over them, and the role which Ibn Taymiyah played in that, and how much the Muslims had suffered prior to that, and how there had been many hypocrites and people who tried to foster discouragement. Ibn Taymiyah drew unique parallels between this situation which arose during his lifetime, and the military campaigns of the Messenger (ﷺ).

Ibn Taymiyah started this essay with the words, "Allah has fulfilled His promise, granted victory to His slave, made His troops victorious and defeated the confederates on His own. ﴿And Allah drove back those who disbelieved in their rage: they gained no advantage [booty]﴾ *(Qur'an 33: 25)* ... This tribulation (*fitnah*) with which the Muslims have been tested with the corrupt enemy who =

Other examples of that include:

i) The report narrated from 'Umar (ﷺ), quoted above.

ii) The way in which the Prophet (ﷺ) quoted the *aayah*,

﴿ ... وَكَانَ ٱلْإِنسَـٰنُ أَكْثَرَ شَىْءٍ جَدَلًا ﴿٥٤﴾ ﴾

﴿...But, man is ever more quarrelsome than anything.﴾
(Qur'an 18: 54)

— in the case of 'Ali (ﷺ) and Faaṭimah, even though this *aayah* was revealed concerning the *kuffaar*. The hadith is narrated in Bukhari.[46]

iii) The way in which Abu Hurayrah (ﷺ) quoted the *aayah*:

﴿ إِنَّ ٱلَّذِينَ يَكْتُمُونَ مَآ أَنزَلْنَا مِنَ ٱلْبَيِّنَـٰتِ وَٱلْهُدَىٰ ... ﴿١٥٩﴾ ﴾

﴿Verily, those who conceal the clear proofs, evidences and the guidance, which We have sent down...﴾
(Qur'an 2: 159)

— when explaining why he narrated the hadith. This is reported in Bukhari.[47]

iv) Abu Bakrah quoted the hadith,

"No people will ever succeed who appoint a woman to rule over them."[48]

= goes against the shari'ah of Islam has its parallel in what happened to the Muslims with their enemies at the time of the Messenger of Allah (ﷺ), in the battles concerning which Allah sent down revelation in His Book..." (*Majmoo' al-Fataawa* 28/424-467). This essay is unique among the essays which Ibn Taymiyah wrote, and it contains a practical example of that which we are discussing here.

[46] Bukhari: *Kitaab at-Tahajjud, Baab Taḥreeḍ an-Nabi* (ﷺ) *'ala Ṣalaat al-Layl*, hadith no. 1127.

[47] Bukhari: *Kitaab al-'Ilm, Baab Ḥifẓ al-'Ilm*, hadith no. 118.

[48] Bukhari: *Kitaab al-Fitan*, chapter no. 18, hadith no. 7099.

— when debating with the Muslims, even though it originally referred to the *kuffaar.*

And there are many other examples.

This indicates what we have said above, that *aayaat* which were revealed for a specific reason may be general in application, and this includes the *aayaat* from *Soorah al-Maa'idah* which speak about judging or ruling by anything other than that which Allah has revealed.

8 - Here there is an inevitable conclusion, that those among the later generations who say that they apply only to the People of the Book, make another mistake in addition to this less valid view, when they claim that the Jews became *kaafir* and were labelled as such — in the *aayaat* of *Soorah al-Maa'idah* which have to do with judging or ruling by anything other than that which Allah has revealed — because they rejected the message of Muhammad (ﷺ) and committed major *shirk.*

This is obviously a mistake, because if it were correct, the Qur'an would have labelled them as *kuffaar* without connecting it to the reason for which these *aayaat* were revealed. Moreover, if that were correct, this *aayah* — ﴾And whosoever does not judge by what Allah has revealed, such are the *kaafiroon* [i.e. disbelievers]﴿, would be meaningless. The ruling in this *aayah* (that they are *kaafir*) is based on the fact that they did not judge or rule according to that which Allah had revealed, and the observation that this view would render meaningless many texts of the Qur'an and Sunnah is sufficient to denounce this view as wrong.

Similar to this is the view of those who claimed that when Ibn Katheer denounced the Tartars as *kaafir* because they ruled according to the *Yaasiq*, he did so because of their *kufr* (disbelief) and *shirk* (polytheism). This is a distortion of and deviation from the words of the scholars. Ibn Katheer connected what he said to the fact that they ruled according to the *Yaasiq*, not to anything else, and his words are not ambiguous.

Based on the above arguments we may state that the correct view is that the Muslims are included in the rulings of these *aayaat*. More details of that will be presented below, *In sha Allah.*

When Does Ruling by Something Other than that Which Allah has Revealed Constitute Major *Kufr* (*Kufr Akbar*)?

Since it is most likely that these *aayaat* (verses) are general in application, does ruling by something other than that which Allah revealed constitute major *shirk* or minor *shirk*? The correct view — that of the majority of scholars — will be described below.

Before we embark upon a more detailed discussion of this matter, I would like to quote two passages, one from Ibn al-Qayyim and one from his *shaykh* Ibn Taymiyah, concerning this topic. The reason why I want to quote them is that they speak of the exact same topic that we are dealing with here, i.e., they discuss the *aayah* — ﴾And whosoever does not judge by what Allah has revealed, such are the *kaafiroon* [i.e. disbelievers]﴿. They explained the root of the dispute concerning this matter and gave examples of situations where it is major *kufr* and where it is minor *kufr*. I have made sure that I have quoted the relevant points.

1- Ibn al-Qayyim (may Allah have mercy on him) said (when he mentioned lesser *kufr*): "This is the interpretation of Ibn 'Abbaas and most of the *ṣaḥaabah* of the *aayah* ﴾And whosoever does not judge by what Allah has revealed, such are the *kaafiroon* [i.e. disbelievers]﴿. Ibn 'Abbaas said: 'This is not the kind of *kufr* which puts one beyond the pale of Islam. It is *kufr* but it is not like disbelieving in Allah and the Last Day.' This was also the view of Ṭaawoos. 'Aṭaa' said: 'It is a lesser form of *kufr*, a lesser form of wrongdoing, a lesser form of rebellion.'"

Some of them interpreted the *aayah* as referring to not ruling by that which Allah has revealed because one rejects it. This is the view of 'Ikrimah. But this view is less likely to be correct, because the very act of rejection is *kufr*, regardless of whether or not he rules by it.

Some of them interpreted the *aayah* as referring to not ruling by anything that Allah revealed at all, which includes not ruling on the basis of *Tawḥeed* and Islam. This is the interpretation of 'Abdul-'Azeez al-Kanaani. This is also unlikely to be correct, because the warning has to do with not ruling according to the revealed ruling, which implies not ruling by shari'ah at all or not ruling by some aspects of shari'ah.

Some of them interpreted it as referring to judging in a manner that goes against the text deliberately, not as a result of ignorance or a mistaken interpretation.. Al-Baghawi narrated this from some of the scholars.

Some of them interpreted it as referring to the People of the Book. This is the view of Qataadah, Aḍ-Ḍaḥḥaak and others. This is unlikely to be correct, and it goes against the apparent meaning of the wording, so it should not be accepted.

Some of them regarded it as meaning the kind of *kufr* which puts a person beyond the pale of Islam.

The correct view is that ruling according to something other than that which Allah has revealed includes both major and minor *kufr*, depending on the position of the judge. If he believes that it is obligatory to rule according to that which Allah has revealed in this case, but he turns away from that out of disobedience, whilst acknowledging that he is deserving of punishment, then this is lesser *kufr*. But if he believes that it is not obligatory and that the choice is his, even though he is certain that this is the ruling of Allah, then this is major *kufr*. If he is unaware of the ruling or makes a mistake, then he is one who is in error and is subject to the rulings of those who err."[49]

From Ibn al-Qayyim's discussion of the matter, the following points may be noted:

— He regards as weak the view of those who limit the meaning of the *aayah* to those who deny (that it is obligatory to rule according to that which Allah has revealed). He says that the very act of rejection is *kufr*, regardless of whether or not he judges or rules by it.

— He regards as weak the view of those who say that what is meant is not ruling by anything that Allah revealed at all.

— He does not comment on what Al-Baghawi narrated, even though it says what it says.

— He regards as weak the view of those who say that it applies only to the People of the Book.

— With regard to lesser *kufr*, he says "in this instance..."

2 - *Shaykh al-Islam* Ibn Taymiyah said, following on from his comments on the texts in which the Messenger (ﷺ) and others are commanded to rule according to that which Allah (سبحانه وتعالى) has revealed:

"(Allah) commanded him to rule by that which Allah has revealed and warned him lest they turn him far away from some of that which Allah had sent down to him. He told him that this was the ruling of Allah, and whoever sought anything other than that was seeking the ruling of *jaahiliyah*. And He said: ﴿And whosoever does not judge by what Allah has revealed, such are the *kaafiroon* [i.e. disbelievers]﴾. Undoubtedly, whoever does not believe that it is obligatory to rule

[49] *Madaarij as-Saalikeen*, 1/336-337.

according to that which Allah has revealed to His Messenger is a *kaafir*, and whoever thinks that it is permissible to rule among people according to his own opinions, turning away and not following that which Allah has revealed is also a *kaafir*. There is no nation which does not enjoin ruling with justice, but justice in their view may be what their leaders think is just. Indeed, many of those who claim to be Muslims rule according to their customs which were not revealed by Allah, such as the customs of the Bedouin or the commands of their leaders. They think that this is what they should rule by, instead of the Qur'an and Sunnah. This is *kufr*. Many people have become Muslim, but they still do not rule by anything except the customs prevalent among them as dictated by their leaders. If they know that it is not permissible to rule by anything except that which Allah has revealed and they do not adhere to that, rather they allow themselves to rule by that which goes against that which Allah has revealed, then they are *kaafir*; otherwise they are ignorant, like those whom we have described above.

Allah has commanded all the Muslims, when they dispute concerning anything, to refer the matter to Allah and His Messenger. Allah (سبحانه وتعالى) says:

﴿ يَا أَيُّهَا الَّذِينَ آمَنُوا أَطِيعُوا اللَّهَ وَأَطِيعُوا الرَّسُولَ وَأُولِي الْأَمْرِ مِنكُمْ ۖ فَإِن تَنَازَعْتُمْ فِي شَيْءٍ فَرُدُّوهُ إِلَى اللَّهِ وَالرَّسُولِ إِن كُنتُمْ تُؤْمِنُونَ بِاللَّهِ وَالْيَوْمِ الْآخِرِ ۚ ذَٰلِكَ خَيْرٌ وَأَحْسَنُ تَأْوِيلًا ﴿٥٩﴾ ﴾

﴿O' you who believe! Obey Allah and obey the Messenger [Muhammad], and those of you [Muslims] who are in authority. [And] if you differ in anything amongst yourselves, refer it to Allah and His Messenger, if you believe in Allah and in the Last Day. That is better and more suitable for final determination.﴾

(Qur'an 4: 59)

﴿ فَلَا وَرَبِّكَ لَا يُؤْمِنُونَ حَتَّىٰ يُحَكِّمُوكَ فِيمَا شَجَرَ بَيْنَهُمْ ثُمَّ لَا يَجِدُوا فِي أَنفُسِهِمْ حَرَجًا مِّمَّا قَضَيْتَ وَيُسَلِّمُوا تَسْلِيمًا ﴿٦٥﴾ ﴾

﴿But no, by your Lord, they can have no Faith, until they make you [O' Muhammad] judge in all disputes between them, and find in themselves no resistance against your decisions, and accept [them] with full submission.﴾

(Qur'an 4: 65)

Whoever does not adhere to referring to Allah and His Messenger for judgement concerning disputes that arise among the people, Allah has sworn by His own self that such a person does not believe. But it he does adhere to the ruling of Allah and His Messenger, both inwardly and outwardly, but he disobeys and follows his own desires, then his status is like that of other sinners.

This *aayah* is one of the things which the *Khawaarij* used as evidence to denounce the authority figures as *kaafir* who did not rule by that which Allah had revealed. Then they (the *Khawaarij*) claimed that their belief was the ruling of Allah. People have expressed many opinions — more than we can list here — but what I have mentioned here is the one that is indicated by the context of the *aayah*.

The point is that ruling justly is absolutely obligatory, at every time and in every place, for every person, in the case of every person. Ruling by that which Allah revealed to Muhammad (ﷺ) is a specific type of justice, it is the best and most perfect form of justice. Ruling according to that is obligatory upon the Prophet (ﷺ) and upon everyone who follows him. Whoever does not adhere to the rulings of Allah and His Messenger is a *kaafir*.

This is obligatory upon the ummah (nation, Muslim community) in all their disputes, whether they be about the matters of belief or practical matters. Allah (ﷻ) says:

﴿ كَانَ ٱلنَّاسُ أُمَّةً وَٰحِدَةً فَبَعَثَ ٱللَّهُ ٱلنَّبِيِّـۧنَ مُبَشِّرِينَ وَمُنذِرِينَ وَأَنزَلَ مَعَهُمُ ٱلْكِتَـٰبَ بِٱلْحَقِّ لِيَحْكُمَ بَيْنَ ٱلنَّاسِ فِيمَا ٱخْتَلَفُوا۟ فِيهِ ... ﴿٢١٣﴾ ﴾

﴾Mankind were one community and Allah sent Prophets with glad tidings and warnings, and with them He sent down the Scripture in truth to judge between people in matters wherein they differed...﴿ *(Qur'an 2: 213)*

So in matters which are common to the ummah as a whole, it is not permissible to rule or judge according to anything except the Qur'an and Sunnah. No one has the right to make the people follow the words of a scholar or *Ameer* or *Shaykh* or king. Whoever believes that he can judge between people according to any such thing, and does not judge between them according to the Qur'an and Sunnah, is a *kaafir*.

The judges of the Muslims judge concerning specific cases, not concerning general matters. If they are judging a specific case, then they must judge according to the book of Allah; if that is not possible, then according to the sunnah of the Messenger of Allah (ﷺ). If they do not find the answer there, then the judge must strive to form his own opinion (ijtihad)."[50]

From what Ibn Taymiyah says, we may note the following:

— He mentions the one who regards it as permissible (to rule by something other than that which Allah has revealed), and states that he is a *kaafir*.

— He mentions those who rule according to their own customs, such as the customs of the bedouin and the commands of their leaders, thinking that this is what they should rule by. This is *kufr*.

---

[50] *Minhaaj as-Sunnah*, 5/130-132.

— Whoever does not adhere to referring for judgement to Allah and His Messenger, Allah has sworn by His own Self that such a person does not believe.

— Whoever does not adhere to the ruling of Allah and His Messenger is a *kaafir.*

— The one who adheres to it both inwardly and outwardly, but disobeys and follows his own desires is in the same position as other sinners. We should note that He (ﷻ) said: "Both inwardly and outwardly".

— We should also note that He refers to matters which are common to the ummah, and that no one has the right to make the people follow the words of a scholar, shaykh or king. Rather judgement should not passed among them by anything other than the Qur'an and Sunnah. Here He is referring to the general law (shari'ah) which applies to everyone.

Following this Introduction, we will now look at this matter in detail, which is examining the cases in which judging by something other than that which Allah has revealed constitutes major *kufr.*

Cases of Major *Kufr*

These cases may be divided into three groups — catagories:

Ideological (denial and regarding forbidden things as permissible)

This is based on a principle which is unanimously agreed upon by the scholars, that whoever denies something which is a well known and well established issue of Islam (which no Muslim has any excuse for not knowing), whether that issue is one of the basic principles of Islam (*uṣool ad-deen*) or one of its minor issues, or who denies even a single letter of the message which the Messenger (ﷺ) brought —

which includes denying the obligations and regarding as permitted that which is forbidden — all of that is major *kufr* which puts one beyond the pale of Islam.

In view of the fact that some people are so confused about the issue of committing *ḥaraam* actions or neglecting obligatory duties without denying that the former are *ḥaraam* or the latter are obligatory, and they think that this comes under the first category (things which put one beyond the pale of Islam), it is essential to clarify this matter. The *Khawaarij* went astray in this matter in the past, and some of those who are too hasty in passing judgement on people may also go astray in a similar manner.

Having quoted these scholarly views, and defining the issue, we will now list the cases in which judging by something other than that which Allah has revealed constitutes major *kufr* in this sense:

1 - It says in *Al-Mughni*: "Whoever believes in the permissibility of a thing on which there is consensus that it is forbidden, and the ruling is well known among the Muslims, and there is no room for confusion because of the clear texts narrated concerning it — such as pork, adultery and other things concerning which there is no dispute — is a *kaafir*, for the same reasons as we have mentioned concerning the one who does not pray..."[51]

2 - Al-Qarraafi said in *Al-Furooq*: "The essence of *kufr* is the specific violation of the sanctity of Lordship, whether by not acknowledging the existence of the Creator, or rejecting something which is a well known and well established issue of Islam (which no Muslim has any excuse for not knowing), such as denying prayer or fasting. This is not limited only to obligatory and other acts of worship; if a person denies something which is permitted and is well known as such, he is a *kaafir*, such as if one were to say that Allah does not allow us to eat

[51] *Al-Mughni*, 12/276 with commentary, published by *Daar Ḥajr*.

figs or grapes. It should not be thought that the one who denies something upon which there is consensus is a *kaafir* in all cases; the thing that is agreed upon should be something that is well established in Islam, to the extent that there is no excuse for not knowing it."[52]

3 - The author of *Nihaayat al-Muḥtaaj* says, discussing that which constitutes apostasy (*riddah*): "... or disbelieving a Messenger... (or permitting something that is forbidden by consensus), when its prohibition is something which is a well known and well established issue of Islam (which no Muslim has any excuse for not knowing), and there is no possible excuse for not knowing it, such as adultery, sodomy, drinking alcohol, etc., — because denying and rejecting something which is well established and proven to be a part of the religion of Muhammad (ﷺ) means that one is disbelieving in him (ﷺ). And the converse also applies, i.e., forbidding something which is permitted according to consensus — even if it is *makrooh* this still applies — such as matters connected to marriage and selling. Or denying an obligation on which there is consensus, such as denying one prostration of the five daily prayers. Or making obligatory something which is known by consensus not to be obligatory, such as adding a sixth prayer; or denying that something is prescribed in shari'ah when it is known by consensus to be so, even if it is *nafl*, such as the regular *nafl* prayers or the 'Eid prayer, as Al-Baghawi clearly stated."[53]

4 - *Shaykh al-Islam* Ibn Taymiyah said: "Whoever does not believe that the five daily prayers, the obligatory zakah, fasting the month of Ramaḍaan and going on pilgrimage to the Ancient House (Ka'bah) are obligatory, and does not regard as forbidden the things that Allah and His Messenger have forbidden of immoral actions, wrongdoing,

---

[52] *Al-Furooq* by *Al-Qarraafi*, 4/115-117, 1st edition, 1346 AH, *Daar Iḥyaa' al-Kutub al-'Arabiyah*, Cairo.

[53] *Nihaayat al-Muḥtaaj Sharḥ al-Minhaaj*, 7/411, *Al-Ḥalabi* edition.

shirk and lying, is a *kaafir* and an apostate. He should be asked to repent; if he repents, all well and good, otherwise he should be killed, according to the consensus of the *aimmah* (Imams, the leading jurists) of the Muslims. The fact that he utters the words of the *Shahaadatayn* does not help him at all."[54]

5 - Because of the seriousness of this issue, I want to quote a lengthy passage from *Shaykh al-Islam* Ibn Taymiyah concerning it, in which he explains the difference between committing sins and thinking of something forbidden as permitted — which makes one a *kaafir*. This is an important comment, especially concerning this topic which we are discussing here. He (may Allah have mercy on him) said:

"It is well-established in the *madhhab* of *Ahl as-Sunnah wal-Jamaa'ah*, based on the evidence of the Qur'an and Sunnah, that they do not regard any of the people of the *Qiblah* (i.e., Muslims) as a *kaafir* because of a sin, and they do not regard him as being out of Islam for doing a forbidden action such as adultery, stealing or drinking wine, unless it also involves his giving up faith. If it involves rejecting some aspect of faith which Allah has enjoined, such as belief in Allah, His angels, His Books, His Messengers and the Resurrection after death, then he becomes a *kaafir* thereby. He also becomes a *kaafir* if he does not believe that the well known and well established duties are obligatory, or if he does not regard as forbidden the things that are well known and well established as being forbidden.

If you say that sins may be divided into not doing that which is commanded and doing that which is forbidden (sins of omission and of commission), I say that if a person fails to do that which is commanded, he either believes that it is obligatory or he does not. If he believes that it is obligatory but he fails to do it, then he is not

---

[54] *Majmoo' al-Fataawa*, 35/105.

neglecting the duty altogether, because he is doing some of it, which is believing in it, and neglecting some of it, which is actually doing it. The same applies to that which is forbidden; if a person does it, either he believes that it is forbidden or he does not. If he believes that it is forbidden but he does it, then he is both fulfilling a duty (i.e., believing it) and doing something forbidden, so he will have both *ḥasanah* (a good deed) and *sayi'ah* (a bad deed). What we are saying here is with regard to issues that are well established and known in Islam, and nobody could be excused for not believing in the obligation or the prohibition. With regard to the one who does not have the correct belief with regard to an action that he is doing or an action from which he is abstaining, because of misinterpretation or ignorance for which he may be excused, the way in which we discuss this lack of proper belief is similar to the way in which we examine whether his action or lack of it is based on misinterpretation or ignorance for which he may be excused.

With regard to the fact that not believing in these laws constitutes *kufr*, but merely doing a *ḥaraam* action does not constitute *kufr* — this is discussed in the appropriate place. This is indicated by the Book of Allah, in the *aayah* (verse):

﴿ فَإِن تَابُوا۟ وَأَقَامُوا۟ ٱلصَّلَوٰةَ وَءَاتَوُا۟ ٱلزَّكَوٰةَ فَإِخْوَٰنُكُمْ فِى ٱلدِّينِ ۗ ... ﴿١١﴾ ﴾

﴾But if they repent [by rejecting *shirk* (polytheism) and accept Islamic Monotheism], perform *Aṣ-Ṣalaah* [*Iqaamat-aṣ-Ṣalaah*] and give Zakah, then they are your brethren in religion...﴿ *(Qur'an 9: 11)*

Accepting and believing (in the laws of Allah) is what is required, according to the consensus; concerning not doing what is commanded there is some dispute. The same applies to the *aayah*:

﴿... وَلِلَّهِ عَلَى ٱلنَّاسِ حِجُّ ٱلْبَيْتِ مَنِ ٱسْتَطَاعَ إِلَيْهِ سَبِيلًا ۚ وَمَن كَفَرَ فَإِنَّ ٱللَّهَ غَنِيٌّ عَنِ ٱلْعَٰلَمِينَ ﴿٩٧﴾﴾

﴾...And Ḥajj [pilgrimage to Makkah] to the House [Ka'bah] is a duty that mankind owes to Allah, those who can afford the expenses [for one's conveyance, provision and residence]; and whoever disbelieves [i.e. denies Ḥajj (pilgrimage to Makkah), then he is a disbeliever of Allah], then Allah stands not in need of any of the *'Aalameen* [mankind, jinn and all that exists].﴿ *(Qur'an 3: 97)*

— not believing that Ḥajj is obligatory and not doing it is *kufr*. Believing that it is obligatory and doing it must be what is meant by this text, as is stated by those among the *salaf* who said: this means the one who does not think that Ḥajj is a good action, or that not doing it is not a sin. But with regard to merely not doing it, there is some scholarly dispute.

There is also the hadith of Abu Bardah ibn Nayyaar, whom the Prophet (ﷺ) sent to the man who had married his father's wife. He ordered him to behead him and to take his wealth and give one-fifth of it to the Muslim state (like war-booty); the fact that his wealth was seized and one-fifth given to the Muslim state indicates that he was a *kaafir* and not merely an evildoer. His *kufr* was because he did not regard as *ḥaraam* that which Allah and His Messenger had forbidden."[55]

Ibn Jareer said, commenting on this incident: "His action was the clearest evidence that he disbelieved in the message that the Messenger of Allah (ﷺ) had brought from Allah, and that he denied the clear, unambiguous *aayah*... Based on his action, he deserved the

[55] *Majmoo' al-Fataawa*, 20/90-92.

ruling of killing and beheading. Hence the Messenger of Allah (ﷺ) commanded that he should be killed and beheaded, because that was his way concerning the apostates who left Islam."[56]

Then *Shaykh al-Islam* said: "The *ṣaḥaabah* - such as 'Umar, 'Ali and others (may Allah be pleased with them all) — did likewise when Qudaamah ibn 'Abdullah drank wine. He was one of those who had fought at Badr, and he thought that this was permitted to the believers who do righteous deeds and that he was one of them, because of his mistaken interpretation of the *aayah*:

﴿ لَيْسَ عَلَى ٱلَّذِينَ ءَامَنُوا۟ وَعَمِلُوا۟ ٱلصَّٰلِحَٰتِ جُنَاحٌ فِيمَا طَعِمُوٓا۟ إِذَا مَا ٱتَّقَوا۟ وَّءَامَنُوا۟ وَعَمِلُوا۟ ٱلصَّٰلِحَٰتِ ... ﴿٩٣﴾ ﴾

﴿Those who believe and do righteous good deeds, there is no sin on them for what they ate [in the past], if they fear Allah [by keeping away from His forbidden things], and believe and do righteous good deeds...﴾

(Qur'an 5: 93)

The *ṣaḥaabah* agreed that if he persisted in that he should be killed, and that if he repented he should be flogged. He repented, so he was flogged.[57]

With regard to sin, the cutting off of the thief's hand and the flogging of the fornicator are mentioned in the Qur'an, but it does not rule that they are *kaafir*. The Qur'an also refers to fighting between two

---

[56] *Tahdheeb al-Athaar*, 2/148, *Ar-Rasheed* edition.

[57] It should be noted that Qudaamah (رضي الله عنه) drank wine thinking that it was permitted, but he was mistaken. The *ṣaḥaabah* agreed that after the ruling had been explained to him and those who were with him, if they persisted, they were to be killed, otherwise they were to be flogged. They repented from thinking that it was permitted, and they were flogged. See *Al-Mughni* by Ibn Qudaamah, 12/276; *Al-I'tiṣaam*, 2/46. The original story is narrated in *Muṣannaf 'Abdur-Razzaaq*, 9/240; *Sunan al-Bayhaqi al-Kubra*, 8/315-316; *Muṣannaf Ibn Abi Shaybah*. 10/39.

groups when one of them is in the wrong, and attests that they are still nonetheless believers and brothers..."[58]

The matter may be clarified further by referring to what Ibn Taymiyah said about differentiating between the believer who goes against shari'ah by committing a sin, and the one who does not believe in something that is well-established and well-known, for which there can be no excuse for not believing in it, whether that belief is accompanied by doing that *ḥaraam* action or neglecting to do that obligatory duty. The former is a believer who is doing wrong, and the latter is a disbeliever and a *kaafir*. Whoever says that *zina* is permitted, when his peers cannot be unaware of the ruling, is rejecting the obligatory belief that Allah has forbidden *zina*, and so on. But whoever believes that *zina* is forbidden, then he commits this sin, is an evildoer who deserves to be punished, but he is not to be denounced as a *kaafir*.

Having introduced the topic of denying well-established obligations and regarding forbidden things as permitted, and the way in which this issue is connected to the issue of faith, we will now turn to the matter of judging by something other than that which Allah has revealed, and how it is connected to this topic.

The scholars (may Allah have mercy on them) included in this matter anything that involves rejecting the laws of Allah, or preferring anything other than the laws of Allah to His laws, or the belief that religion is not relevant to life, because all of that is included in the rejection of the detailed matters of faith and shari'ah which are well established and known from the Book of Allah, the Sunnah of His Messenger and the consensus of the ummah.

Therefore the scholars described as major *kufr* the following:

---

[58] *Majmoo' al-Fataawa*, 20/92.

1 - When the ruler or judge who rules by something other than that which Allah has revealed denies that the ruling of Allah and His Messenger is the one which is to be followed, which is the meaning of that which was narrated from Ibn 'Abbaas (رضي الله عنه).[59] It was also the view of Ibn Jareer that this constitutes rejection of a *shar'i* ruling which was revealed by Allah. This is a matter concerning which there is no dispute among the scholars. The well-established principle upon which they are agreed is that whoever denies and rejects one of the basic principles of the religion, or one of the minor issues on which there is consensus, or denies even a single letter that is definitively narrated from the Messenger (ﷺ), becomes a *kaafir* whose *kufr* puts him beyond the pale of Islam."[60]

The words of Ibn Jareer to which *Shaykh* Muhammad ibn Ibraaheem was referring are: "If someone were to say that the *aayah* refers to all of those who do not rule according to that which Allah has revealed, so how can you now limit it? We would say that Allah stated that in general terms concerning people who, according to the judgement of Allah given in His Book, were denying and rejecting His ruling, so He stated that by turning away from the ruling of Allah in the manner in which they did that, they became *kaafir*. The same might be said of everyone who does not rule according to that which Allah has revealed and rejects it: he is a *kaafir* who disbelieves in Allah, as Ibn 'Abbaas said, because rejecting the ruling of Allah after he has come to know that it has been revealed in His Book is like rejecting His Prophet after coming to know that he is a Prophet."[61]

Think about what Aṭ-Ṭabari said: "... it is like rejecting His Prophet after coming to know that he is a Prophet." Compare that to what is

---

[59] Ibn Jareer, 10/357, report no. 12063.

[60] *Taḥkeem al-Qawaaneen* by *Shaykh* Muhammad ibn Ibraaheem, Pp. 5, 1st edition.

[61] *Tafseer aṭ-Ṭabari*, 10/358.

said above about denial and regarding that which is forbidden (ruling according to something other than that which Allah has revealed) as being permitted.

2 - "When the ruler or judge who rules by something other than that which Allah has revealed does not deny that the ruling of Allah and His Messenger is true, but he believes that the ruling of someone other than the Messenger (ﷺ) is better than his ruling, and more suited to what the people need to judge between them when there is a dispute, whether he believes that in absolute terms or in relation to new developments that have arisen with the passage of time and the change of circumstances. There is no doubt that this too is *kufr*, because it involves giving precedence to the rulings of created beings, which are merely the product of their cheap thought processes, over the ruling of the Most Wise, Most Praiseworthy (Allah)."[62]

3 - When he does not believe that it is better than the ruling of Allah and His Messenger, but he does believe that it is equal to it. This is like the two previous examples, in that it is *kufr* which puts a person beyond the pale of Islam, because that implies that he regards the created being as equal with the Creator, and this goes against the *aayah*,

﴿ ... لَيْسَ كَمِثْلِهِۦ شَىْءٌ ... ﴿١١﴾ ﴾

﴿...There is nothing like Him...﴾ *(Qur'an 42: 11)*

— and other similar *aayaat* which indicate that Allah is unique in His perfection and He is above any resemblance to His creatures in essence, attributes, deeds and judging between people concerning that wherein they dispute.[63]

---

[62] *Taḥkeem al-Qawaaneen*, Pp. 5. See also *Majmoo' al-Fataawa* by Ibn Taymiyah, 27/58.

[63] Ibid, Pp. 5-6.

4 - When he does not believe that the ruling of the ruler or judge who rules according to something other than that which Allah has revealed is equal to the ruling of Allah and His Messenger, let alone believing that it is better, but he believes that it is permissible to rule in a manner that goes against the ruling of Allah. This is like the previous case and the same applies, because he believes that what is well established from the clear and *ṣaḥeeḥ* texts to be forbidden is permitted.[64]

Look at how He connects this matter (the idea that it is permissible to rule in a manner that goes against the ruling of Allah) with the issue of regarding as permitted that which is forbidden, for they are both the which is forbidden, for they are both the same in terms of rejection.

Shaykh 'Abdul-'Azeez ibn Baaz said: "Whoever rules by something other than that which Allah has revealed thinking that that is better than the laws of Allah is a *kaafir* according to all the Muslims. The same applies to one who rules by man-made laws instead of the laws of Allah and thinks that that is permissible — even if he says that referring to the shari'ah for judgement is better — he is a *kaafir* because he regards as permitted something that Allah has forbidden."[65]

Other similar cases also come under the same heading as those mentioned above. They all come under this heading, and they include:

5 - Those who believe that the Islamic system is not fit to be applied in this century.

6 - Or they believe that Islam is the reason for the backwardness of the Muslims.

---

64 *Taḥkeem al-Qawaaneen*, Pp. 6.

65 *Majmoo' al-Fataawa Ibn Baaz*, 4/416.

7 - Or that Islam is limited to the relationship between a person and his Lord, without being involved in other matters of life.

8 - Or they think that applying the ruling of Allah by cutting off the hand of the thief or stoning the married adulterer is not appropriate in the present age.[66]

These cases and examples were mentioned by Ibn Baaz when he was speaking of things which nullify one's Islam. He said: "Included in the fourth category [67] are those who believe that the legal systems which people promulgate are better than the shari'ah of Islam, or that they are equal to it, or that it is permissible to refer to them for judgement — even if he believes that the ruling of shari'ah is superior — or that the Islamic system is not fit to be applied in the twentieth century, or that it was a cause of the backwardness of the Muslims, or that it is limited only to the relationship between a person and his Lord, without being involved in any other affairs of life. Also included in the fourth category are those who think that implementing the ruling of Allah by cutting off the hand of the thief or stoning the married adulterer is not appropriate in the present age. And that also includes everyone who believes that it is permissible to rule by anything other than the shari'ah of Allah in matters of transactions, punishments, etc — even if he does not believe that that is better than the ruling of shari'ah — because by believing this, he has permitted something which Allah has forbidden, according to scholarly consensus, and everyone who regards as permitted something that Allah has forbidden — of things which are well

---

[66] Opt.cit, 1/137.

[67] From *Nawaaqiḍ al-Islam* by *Shaykh* Muhammad ibn 'Abdul-Wahhaab. The wording is: "Whoever believes that the guidance of anyone other than the Prophet (ﷺ) is more perfect than his guidance, or that the ruling of anyone else is better than his rulings, such as those who prefer the ruling of the *ṭawaagheet* (pl. of *ṭaaghoot*, i.e., false judges) to his ruling, is a *kaafir*."

known and well established in Islam as being forbidden, and no one has any excuse for not knowing them, such as adultery, alcohol, riba and ruling by anything other than that which Allah has revealed — is a *kaafir* according to the consensus of the Muslims."[68]

These matters are often referred to by the scholars when they refute the *Baaṭinis* who misinterpret the laws in a esoteric (*baaṭini*) fashion. No one doubts that they are *kaafir*. The scholars also refer to these matters when refuting those among the extreme Sufis and their ilk who claim to have knowledge of the unseen and who claim, based on the story of Moosa and Al-Khiḍr, that it is permissible to go beyond the law of Prophet Muhammad (ﷺ) in the case of those whom they call *awliyaa'* ("saints").

Shaykh al-Islam Ibn Taymiyah said: "If he thinks that something other than the guidance of the Prophet (ﷺ) is more perfect than his guidance, or that among the *awliyaa'* are those who are allowed to go beyond the shari'ah of Muhammad (ﷺ) — as Al-Khiḍr went beyond the law of Moosa (Moses) (عليه السلام) — he is a *kaafir* who must be killed after asking him to repent, because the call of Moosa was not universal and Al-Khiḍr was not obliged to follow Moosa (may peace be upon them both). Indeed, Al-Khiḍr said to Moosa, I know something that Allah has taught me, that you do not know, and you know something that Allah has taught you, that I do not know.

But Muhammad ibn 'Abdullah ibn 'Abdul-Muṭṭalib (ﷺ) is the Messenger of Allah to all of the two races of the jinn and mankind, the Arabs and non-Arabs, near and far, kings and subjects, ascetics and non-ascetics. Allah (سبحانه وتعالى) says:

﴿ وَمَآ أَرْسَلْنَـٰكَ إِلَّا كَآفَّةً لِّلنَّاسِ بَشِيرًا وَنَذِيرًا ... ﴿٢٨﴾ ﴾

﴿And We have not sent you [O' Muhammad] except as a

---

68 *Majmoo' al-Fataawa Ibn Baaz*, 1/137.

giver of glad tidings and a warner to all mankind...﴿

(Qur'an 34: 28)

Whoever believes that anyone among mankind, scholars, slaves or kings, is allowed not to follow him, obey him or take what was given to him of the Book and Wisdom (the Sunnah) is a *kaafir* (disbeliever)."[69]

This matter is clear and there is no dispute concerning it.

Man-made legislation that goes against the laws of Allah

This is one of the examples of ruling by something other than that which Allah has revealed which comes under the heading of major *kufr*. Before going into the details of what the scholars said on this topic, we should first note the following points:

1 - It is clear from what has been said above (in Chapter 2) that ruling and legislation, and the connected matters of commands and prohibitions, deciding what is *ḥalaal* or *ḥaraam* or permitted — whether that is on the individual, familial, communal or state level, in all spheres of life — is the preserved right of Allah alone with no partner or associate.

We have presented above some of the evidences for that, without quoting all of the evidences in detail. What has been stated above is sufficient for those whom Allah has guided to the right path.

2 - When men — instead of Allah — issue laws which apply to everyone and set up systems which go against the laws of Allah, this implies two things:

a) Rejecting the shari'ah of Allah, because if they had not rejected it, why would they replace it with something else?
b) Transgressing upon something which is the exclusive right

---

[69] *Majmoo' al-Fataawa Ibn Taymiyah*, 27/58-59.

of Allah, the right to rule and legislate, which He has reserved for Himself alone.

Hence we find that some of the scholars describe this as making that which is forbidden permissible, because the one who does this thinks that it is permissible to rule by something other than that which Allah has revealed. We will quote some of their comments on the matter below, *In sha Allah.*

3 - Anyone who ponders the story behind the reason for the revelation of the *aayah* ﴿And whosoever does not judge by what Allah has revealed, such are the *kaafiroon* [i.e. disbelievers]﴾ will find that it is not merely the matter of falling into sin;[70] rather it is a major issue, where the Jews agreed to change the ruling of Allah concerning *zina*. It should be noted here that they did not make it permitted in the sense that they thought it was allowed, rather they turned away from the ruling of Allah, that the married adulterer should be stoned, and changed it (the punishment) into flogging and blackening the face. They made this their system which applied to everyone. At the same time, they felt that they were doing something wrong, and they felt guilty too. Hence, when Muhammad ibn 'Abdullah (ﷺ) came to them, and they knew in the depths of their hearts that he was the Messenger of Allah, they wanted, in a devious manner, to attribute their alteration of the ruling of Allah to the Messenger of Allah. That was if he was to rule that (the punishment for adultery) was flogging rather than stoning.

That (the alteration of the ruling on adultery) was one incident but it became part of their system, so Allah described them as hastening to fall into disbelief *(Qur'an 5: 41)*, and judged them to be *kaafir*. Every case which is similar to their case — whether it is on the part of

---

[70] Or injustice, as they used to do before they changed the ruling of Allah concerning the married adulterer, when they used to carry out the punishment on the weak and not on the nobles.

Muslims or others — is subject to the same ruling as that which was applied to the Jews.

It should be noted here that the reason for the ruling was that the Jews had agreed upon that, and it was not an individual matter. Hence in some reports it is said that the Jews said, "We agreed" or "We agreed amongst ourselves to keep it secret"...

4 - The view that it does not make a person *kaafir* unless he regards it as permitted, even if he institutes a legislative system that affects everyone, is a weak view, because the mere act of regarding it as permitted makes him a *kaafir*, regardless of whether he legislates or not. The Jews, by their very actions — as stated in the reason for revelation — became *kaafir*, and their being *kaafir* was not conditional upon whether they actually said that what they were doing was permitted.

5 - The view that it does not make one a *kaafir* unless one believes it to be permitted is the basis of the view of the Murji'ah, who think that faith is in the heart only, and that actions have nothing to do with it. *Shaykh al-Islam* Ibn Taymiyah criticized them for this view and explained in many places (in his writings) what was wrong with it.[71]

6 - It is essential to differentiate between general legislation which affects everyone, such as laws which are applied to all, and individual cases and isolated incidents. This matter will be discussed in more detail below, *in sha Allah.*

Having noted these points, we will move on to a detailed discussion of this topic.

It should be noted that this includes everyone who claims that he has the right to decide what is permitted and forbidden instead of Allah. It also applies to those who institute man-made laws and make them

---

[71] *Al-Eemaan al-Awsaṭ - Majmoo' al-Fataawa*, 7/528, 541, 556, 579, 609 and 616.

into a system for passing judgements, whether that system comes from him, or he imports it in its entirety from the east or the west or elsewhere, from the systems of *jaahiliyah*. All of that comes under the same ruling.

We will quote some of the comments of the scholars on this matter, ending with a general summary.

Ibn Ḥazm

He (may Allah have mercy on him) said: "Allah (ﷻ) says:

﴿ إِنَّمَا ٱلنَّسِىٓءُ زِيَادَةٌ فِى ٱلْكُفْرِ ۖ يُضَلُّ بِهِ ٱلَّذِينَ كَفَرُوا۟ يُحِلُّونَهُۥ عَامًا وَيُحَرِّمُونَهُۥ عَامًا لِّيُوَاطِـُٔوا۟ عِدَّةَ مَا حَرَّمَ ٱللَّهُ ... ﴿٣٧﴾ ﴾

> ﴾The postponing [of a Sacred Month] is indeed an addition to disbelief: thereby the disbelievers are led astray, for they make it lawful one year and forbid it another year in order to adjust the number of months forbidden by Allah...﴿ *(Qur'an 9: 37)*

Abu Muhammad said: According to the rules of the language in which the Qur'an was revealed, the addition of a thing can only be from something of the same nature, not from something else. It is true that the postponing (of a Sacred Month) is *kufr*, and it is a kind of action, which involved making permissible that which Allah had forbidden. Whoever makes permissible that which Allah has forbidden — knowing that Allah has forbidden it — becomes a *kaafir* by virtue of that very action."[72]

This is a clear statement on the part of Ibn Ḥazm that making permissible that which Allah has forbidden and making forbidden that which Allah has permitted is *kufr*, and that it may be *kufr* by virtue of the action only, if it is done by one who knows the *shar'i*

[72] *Al-Faṣl* by Ibn Ḥazm, 3/245, edited version.

ruling then goes against it by making permissible that which Allah has forbidden and making forbidden that which Allah has permitted.

Ash-Shaaṭibi

He speaks a great deal about this topic, such as when he discusses the followers of *bid'ah* (innovation). He quotes the *aayah*,

﴿ يَٰٓأَيُّهَا ٱلَّذِينَ ءَامَنُوا۟ لَا تُحَرِّمُوا۟ طَيِّبَٰتِ مَآ أَحَلَّ ٱللَّهُ لَكُمْ ... ﴿٨٧﴾ ﴾

﴿O' you who believe! Make not unlawful the *Ṭayyibaat* [all that is good as regards foods, things, deeds, beliefs, persons] which Allah has made lawful to you...﴾
(Qur'an 5: 87)

— and mentions the reasons for its revelation, and how some of the *ṣaḥaabah* had resolved not to get married or not to eat meat... He said:

"... there are a number of issues connected to this matter, the first of which is that the prohibition of permitted things and the like may take different forms. The first is when people state that something is believed to be forbidden — which is what the *kuffaar* do — such as the *baḥeerah, saa'ibah, waṣeelah and ḥaami,*[73] and all other cases in

---

[73] These were types of camels concerning which the Arabs of the *Jaahiliyah* had instituted taboos connected to their false religion. The *baḥeerah* was a she-camel whose milk was spared for the sake of idols and nobody was allowed to milk it; the *saa'ibah* was she-camel let loose for free pasture for their false gods, e.g. idols, and nothing was allowed to be carried on it; the *waṣeelah* was a she-camel set free for idols because it had given birth to a she-camel at its first delivery and then again gave birth to a she-camel at its second delivery; and the *ḥaami* was a stallion camel freed from work for the sake of their idols, after it had finished a number of copulations assigned for it.

See *The Translation of the Meanings of the Noble Qur'an* by Dr. Muhammad Muḥsin Khan and Dr. Muhammad Taqi-ud-Din al-Hilali, footnote to *Soorah al-Maa'idah* 5: 103 (Translator).

which Allah has mentioned that the *kuffaar* make something forbidden on the basis of mere opinion. Another example is when Allah (ﷻ) says:

﴿ وَلَا تَقُولُوا۟ لِمَا تَصِفُ أَلْسِنَتُكُمُ ٱلْكَذِبَ هَٰذَا حَلَٰلٌ وَهَٰذَا حَرَامٌ لِّتَفْتَرُوا۟ عَلَى ٱللَّهِ ٱلْكَذِبَ ... ﴿١١٦﴾ ﴾

﴿And say not concerning that which your tongues put forth falsely: 'This is lawful and this is forbidden,' so as to invent lies against Allah...﴾ *(Qur'an 16: 116)*

And there are similar cases where the Muslims forbid things that are permitted on the basis of mere opinion..."[74]

Here Ash-Shaaṭibi is pointing out the difference between a person giving up something because of asceticism, and making things permissible or forbidden in a way that goes against the laws of Allah — which constitutes *kufr*. He compares the actions of the people of the *jaahiliyah*, who forbade the *baḥeerah, saa'ibah*, etc. to what some Muslims do when they make things *ḥalaal* or *ḥaraam* on the basis of mere opinion. This is the essence of what those who institute man-made laws do.

Ash-Shaaṭibi explained this elsewhere, when he said: "If you ponder the basis of *bid'ahs* (innovations), you will find that they vary in degree. Some cases are blatant *kufr*, such as the *bid'ah* of the *jaahiliyah* which the Qur'an refers to in verses such as the following:

﴿ وَجَعَلُوا۟ لِلَّهِ مِمَّا ذَرَأَ مِنَ ٱلْحَرْثِ وَٱلْأَنْعَٰمِ نَصِيبًا فَقَالُوا۟ هَٰذَا لِلَّهِ بِزَعْمِهِمْ وَهَٰذَا لِشُرَكَآئِنَا ... ﴿١٣٦﴾ ﴾

﴿And they assign to Allah a share of the tilth and cattle which He has created, and they say: 'This is for Allah'

[74] *Al-I'tiṣaam*, 1/328.

according to their claim, 'and this is for our [Allah's so-called] partners'...》 *(Qur'an 6: 136)*

﴿ وَقَالُوا۟ مَا فِى بُطُونِ هَٰذِهِ ٱلْأَنْعَٰمِ خَالِصَةٌ لِّذُكُورِنَا وَمُحَرَّمٌ عَلَىٰٓ أَزْوَٰجِنَا ۖ وَإِن يَكُن مَّيْتَةً فَهُمْ فِيهِ شُرَكَآءُ ... ﴿١٣٩﴾ ﴾

《And they say: 'What is in the bellies of such and such cattle [milk or foetus] is for our males alone, and forbidden to our females [girls and women], but if it is born dead, then all have shares therein...》 *(Qur'an 6: 139)*

﴿ مَا جَعَلَ ٱللَّهُ مِنۢ بَحِيرَةٍ وَلَا سَآئِبَةٍ وَلَا وَصِيلَةٍ وَلَا حَامٍ ... ﴿١٠٣﴾ ﴾

《Allah has not instituted things like *baḥeerah* or a *saa'ibah* or a *waṣeelah* or a *ḥaami* [all these animals were liberated in honour of idols as practised by pagan Arabs in the pre-Islamic period]...》 *(Qur'an 5: 103)*

The same is true of the *bid'ah* of the hypocrites when they took Islam as a means of protecting themselves and their wealth, and similar cases where there is no doubt that it is blatant *kufr*."[75]

What is it that is included in his words "and similar cases?" There is no doubt that the man-made laws which go against the laws of Allah should be included in that, first and foremost, and the reason is that these laws, like the laws of the *jaahiliyah*, involve men legislating instead of Allah.

In a third place, Ash-Shaaṭibi said: "It was also reported that the *kuffaar* were guilty of other minor innovations, but these are nonetheless serious matters, such as when they allocated a share of the tilth and cattle to Allah, and a share to their (so-called) partners, then they decided that what was for those (so-called) partners would

---

[75] *Al-I'tiṣaam*, 2/37.

not reach Allah, but what was for Allah would reach the (so-called) partners *(cf. Qur'an 6: 136)*; and their taboos concerning the *baḥeerah, saa'ibah, waṣeelah* and *ḥaami*; and killing their own children from folly, without knowledge *(cf. Qur'an 6: 140)*; and their failing to be just in matters of retaliation (*qaṣaaṣ*) and inheritance; their injustice in matters of marriage and divorce; their consuming orphan's wealth by means of trickery and cheating; and other similar matters which are referred to in shari'ah and mentioned by the scholars — until issuing laws and legislation became a custom for them and it became easy for them to change the religion of Prophet Ibraaheem (Abraham) (ﷺ), which resulted in their adopting and accepting an additional principle which entitled them to issue laws with no restriction, based on their whims and desires..."[76]

Think about what he said: "until issuing laws and legislation became a custom for them..."

Shaykh al-Islam Ibn Taymiyah

We have already quoted a great deal from him on this topic. Here we will quote further from what he said on this matter. As is well known, he is distinguished by the fact that he was contemporary with a real — live example of issuing laws which had entered the Muslim world — which we will look at in a separate section of this book *in sha Allah.*

Ibn Taymiyah described the case of the one who has the audacity to change the shari'ah and make what is true, false and vice versa. He said - and think of the context in which he was speaking: "If the judge is a man of religious commitment, but he passes judgement without knowledge, then he is one of the people of Hell. If he is knowledgeable but he passes a judgement that goes against what he knows to be correct, then he is one of the people of Hell. If he passes

[76] *Al-I'tiṣaam*, 2/210-302.

a judgement with no justice and no knowledge, it is more appropriate that he should be among the people of Hell. This is so if he is ruling in an individual case. But if he is passing a general ruling concerning the religion of the Muslims, making the truth false and falsehood true, making Sunnah *bid'ah* and *bid'ah* Sunnah, making what is good evil and what is evil good, forbidding that which Allah and His Messenger have enjoined and enjoining that which Allah and His Messenger have forbidden, then this is another matter altogether and he will be judged by the Lord of the Worlds, the God of the Messengers, the Only Owner of the Day of Recompense,

﴿ ... لَهُ ٱلْحَمْدُ فِى ٱلْأُولَىٰ وَٱلْءَاخِرَةِ ۖ وَلَهُ ٱلْحُكْمُ وَإِلَيْهِ تُرْجَعُونَ ﴿٧٠﴾ ﴾

﴾...All praises and thanks be to Him [both] in the first [i.e. in this world] and in the last [i.e. in the Hereafter]. And for Him is the Decision, and to Him shall you [all] be returned.﴿ *(Qur'an 28: 70)*

﴿ هُوَ ٱلَّذِىٓ أَرْسَلَ رَسُولَهُۥ بِٱلْهُدَىٰ وَدِينِ ٱلْحَقِّ لِيُظْهِرَهُۥ عَلَى ٱلدِّينِ
كُلِّهِۦ ۚ وَكَفَىٰ بِٱللَّهِ شَهِيدًا ﴿٢٨﴾ ﴾

﴾He it is Who has sent His Messenger [Muhammad] with guidance and the religion of truth [Islam], that He may make it [Islam] superior to all religions. And All-Sufficient is Allah as a Witness.﴿ *(Qur'an 48: 28).*"[77]

Note how he describes a general ruling which goes against shari'ah as being a very serious matter, and how he differentiates between that and a ruling concerning an individual case. We have quoted above what Ibn Taymiyah said in *Minhaaj as-Sunnah* and how it differentiates between matters which are common to the whole ummah, and matters which are specific to the individual.

---

[77] *Majmoo' al-Fataawa*, 35/388, see also 3/267-268.

In many places, Ibn Taymiyah explains that if someone goes beyond any of the well-established laws of Islam, he is to be fought, according to the consensus of the Muslims.[78] We will quote below his comments on this matter.

Ibn al-Qayyim

He said: "The Qur'an and proven consensus state that the religion of Islam abrogated all religions that came before it, and that whoever adheres to that which the *Tawraat* and *Injeel* brought and does not follow the Qur'an is a *kaafir*. Allah has abrogated all the laws in the *Tawraat*, *Injeel* and other nations, and He has made it obligatory upon the two races of the jinn and mankind to adhere to the laws of Islam. So there is nothing forbidden except that which Islam forbids, and there is nothing obligatory except that which Islam enjoins."[79]

Ibn Katheer

He is one of the later scholars who were contemporary with the Tartars. Commenting on the *aayah*:

﴿ أَفَحُكْمَ ٱلْجَٰهِلِيَّةِ يَبْغُونَ ۚ وَمَنْ أَحْسَنُ مِنَ ٱللَّهِ حُكْمًا لِّقَوْمٍ يُوقِنُونَ ﴿٥٠﴾ ﴾

﴾Do they then seek the judgement of [the days of] Ignorance? And who is better in judgement than Allah for a people who have firm Faith?﴿ *(Qur'an 5: 50),*

He said: "Allah denounces those who go beyond the wise and just rulings of Allah which encompass everything that is good and forbid everything that is evil, and turn to other things such as opinions or whims and desires and conventions which people have fabricated with no basis in the laws of Allah, as the people of the *jaahiliyah* used to do when they judged according to the misguided and ignorant

---

[78] Opt.cit, 28/468-471, 35/395.

[79] *Aḥkaam Ahl adh-Dhimmah*, 1/259.

notions which they had fabricated from their own opinions and desires, and as the Tartars do when they rule according to the royal decrees taken from their king Genghis Khan who instituted the *Yaasiq* for them. This *Yaasiq* is a book which is a compilation of laws which he took from the laws of the Jews, Christians and Muslims, and in which there are many rulings which are based solely on his opinion or his whims and desires. So it has become a law to be followed among his children, which they prefer to the rulings of the Book of Allah and the Sunnah of His Messenger (ﷺ). Whoever does that is a *kaafir* and must be fought until he comes back to the ruling of Allah and His Messenger, and does not rule (judge) according to anything else in either minor or major matters."[80]

Simply referring to the *Yaasiq* for judgement is *kufr*; it is not conditional upon uttering words which indicate that one regards it as permissible. Hence Ibn Katheer said in *Al-Bidaayah wan-Nihaayah*: "So whoever neglects the shari'ah which was revealed to Muhammad ibn 'Abdullah (ﷺ), the Seal of the Prophets, and refers for judgement to any other laws which have been abrogated, is a *kaafir*, so how about the one who refers for judgement to the *Yaasiq* and prefers it to (the shari'ah of Islam)? Whoever does that is a *kaafir* according to the consensus of the Muslims..."[81]

See how Ibn Katheer judged the one who refers for judgement to the abrogated laws; with regard to those who refer for judgement to the *Yaasiq* and the contemporary man-made laws, they are even worse.

Whoever thinks that the *fatwa* of Ibn Katheer and his narration of consensus (*ijmaa'*) apply only to the Tartars, or that their *kufr* was due to reasons other than their referring for judgement to the *Yaasiq* is trying too hard to interpret his words in a way other than what was

[80] *Tafseer Ibn Katheer*, 3/122-123, *Ash-Sha'b* edition.
[81] *Al-Bidaayah wan-Nihaayah*, 13/119.

meant. In fact, he meant that it was general when he said: "just like the misguided notions according to which the people of the *jaahiliyah* ruled" and "just like the (royal) decrees to which the Tartars refer for judgement". Then he said: "And whoever does that is a *kaafir.*" So he gave examples, then he indicated that the rulings were general in application. So their view has no basis. O' Allah, we seek refuge in You from being overwhelmed by whims and desires.

Shaykh 'Abdul-Laṭeef ibn 'Abdur-Raḥmaan

He (may Allah have mercy on him) was asked about the customs of fathers and grandfathers by which the traditional people among the Bedouins and others rule: can they be described as *kaafir* because of that, after they have been told (that it is wrong)? He replied: "Whoever refers for judgement to anything other than the Book of Allah and the Sunnah of His Messenger (ﷺ), after being told about that, is a *kaafir.* Allah says: ﴾And whosoever does not judge by what Allah has revealed, such are the *kaafiroon* [i.e. disbelievers]﴿ *(Qur'an 5: 44)*, and He says: ﴾Do they seek other than the religion of Allah...?﴿ *(Qur'an 3: 83)*."[82]

7 - *Shaykh* Ḥamad ibn 'Ateeq

He (may Allah have mercy on him) mentioned the things which make a Muslim an apostate. These include associating anything with Allah (*shirk*); outwardly obeying and agreeing with the *mushrikeen* in their religion; befriending the *mushrikeen*; sitting with the *mushrikeen* in their gatherings of *shirk* without denouncing them; mocking Allah or His Book or His Messenger; expressing dislike or anger when one is called to Allah, or His verses are recited, or when good is enjoined or

[82] *Ad-Durar as-Saniyah*, 8/241. See also 8/271-275, 1st edition, 1356 AH, where he mentions the claim of those who refer for judgement to *ṭaaghoot* (false judges), that if they did not refer to them for judgement the tribes would not accept that and it would lead to fighting amongst them. He refuted this specious argument.

evil is forbidden; disliking what Allah revealed to His Messenger, of the Book and wisdom (the Sunnah); not agreeing with what is indicated in the verses of the Qur'an and the *aḥaadeeth*; disputing concerning that; rejecting anything that is in the Qur'an, even if it is only one *aayah* or part of an *aayah*; turning away from learning the religion of Allah and being negligent concerning it; practising magic or witchcraft (*siḥr*); and denying the resurrection.[83]

Then he said: "The fourteenth issue is: referring for judgement to anything other than the Book of Allah and the Sunnah of His Messenger (ﷺ). Ibn Katheer said: as the people of the *jaahiliyah* used to do when they judged according to the misguided and ignorant notions which they had fabricated from their own opinions and desires, and as the Tartars do when they rule according to the royal decrees taken from their king Genghis Khan who got compiled a book for them comprising laws derived from various sources called *Yaasiq*. It contained laws of the Jews, the Christians and the Muslims, and tribal customs etc.. It has become a law to be followed among his children, which they prefer to the rulings of the Book of Allah and the Sunnah of His Messenger (ﷺ). Whoever does that is a *kaafir* and must be fought until he comes back to the ruling of Allah and His Messenger, and does not rule (judge) according to anything else in either minor or major matters. Allah (ﷻ) says: ﴾Do they then seek the judgement of [the days of] Ignorance? And who is better in judgement than Allah for a people who have firm Faith﴿ *(Qur'an 5: 50)*.

And I say that this is like what the common folk among the Bedouin and their like do, when they refer for judgement to the customs of their forefathers and the accursed rules fabricated by their leaders, which they call *shar' ar-rifaaqah* (the laws of kindness) and give

[83] See the detailed list, with evidence (*daleel*), in *Sabeel an-Najaat wal-Fakaak*, Pp. 74-83, by Al-Waleed ibn 'Abdur-Raḥmaan al-Firyaan.

them precedence over the Book of Allah and the Sunnah of His Messenger (ﷺ). Whoever does that is a *kaafir* who should be fought until he returns to the ruling of Allah and His Messenger. *Shaykh al-Islam* Ibn Taymiyah said: 'Undoubtedly anyone who does not believe that it is obligatory to judge or rule according to that which Allah revealed to His Messenger is a *kaafir*. Whoever believes that it is permissible to judge between people according to what he thinks is just, without following that which Allah revealed, is a *kaafir*. For there is no nation which does not enjoin judging with justice, but according to them, justice may mean that which their leaders think is just. Indeed many of those who claim to be Muslims judge or rule according to their customs which were not revealed by Allah, such as the customs of the Bedouin and the commands of the leaders, and they think that this is what they should judge or rule by, not the Qur'an and Sunnah. This is the essence of *kufr*. Many people became Muslim but they still judge and rule according to their customs as dictated by their leaders. If they knew that it is not permissible for them to judge or rule by anything except that which Allah has revealed, but they do not adhere to that, and they allow themselves to judge or rule by that which goes against what Allah revealed, then they are *kaafir*.' These words are from *Minhaaj as-Sunnah an-Nabawiyah*, and are a commentary on the *aayah*, ﴿And whosoever does not judge by what Allah has revealed, such are the *kaafiroon* [i.e. disbelievers]﴾. May Allah have mercy on him and forgive him."[84]

We have quoted at length from the words of *Shaykh* Ḥamad ibn 'Ateeq, along with his quotations from Ibn Katheer and *Shaykh al-Islam* Ibn Taymiyah — even though we have quoted their words above — in order that the reader may clearly understand what the

---

[84] *Sabeel an-Najaat wal-Fakaak*, Ḥamad ibn 'Ateeq, Pp. 83-84, ed. by Al-Waleed ibn 'Abdur-Raḥmaan al-Firyaan, pub. 1409 AH.

leading scholars said. They were speaking in general terms concerning anyone who does the same as they did; it is not as some people think, that Ibn Katheer was referring to the Tartars and that the matter did not go beyond them to include anyone else. We have pointed that out above.

Shaykh Ash-Shawkaani

Ash-Shawkaani (may Allah have mercy on him) devoted a separate essay to the issue of the alienation of religion in the land of Yemen at his time, whether that was the part which was under Ottoman rule or the other parts. He divided Yemen into three parts, and described the situation of each part and the examples of things that went against Islam and constituted *kufr* which were happening in each part. Among the things that he said about the second part of this country was: "Now that you have a full picture of what is happening in the first of the three parts, let us turn to the second part, concerning the people of the area that is beyond Ottoman control, like the land of the *qiblah* (the north) and the east, etc.

You should know, may Allah bless you, that everything we have mentioned about the first part (of Yemen), where the citizens do not pray or do any of the obligatory duties, apart from a few rare individuals, is also the case in the lands which are beyond Ottoman control; indeed, things are even worse there... but in addition to that there are serious problems and appalling deviations among them, things which are not found in the first part. For example, they refer for judgement to those among them who know the rulings of *ṭaaghoot* (falsehood) concerning all matters that they come across, without anyone denouncing them and without their feeling any shame before Allah or His slaves. They are not afraid of anyone. They may judge in such a manner between any people who come to them. This is well known to all the people, but no one is able to denounce it or ward it off. It is more obvious than a beacon on a hill.

Undoubtedly this is *kufr*, disbelief in Allah and His shari'ah which He enjoined through his Messenger and chose for His slaves in His Book and on the lips of His Messenger. Indeed, they have disbelieved in all the laws from Adam (ﷺ) to the present. It is obligatory to wage jihad against these people and to fight them until they accept the rulings of Islam and submit to them, and judge amongst them according to the pure shari'ah, and give up all the devilish *ṭaaghoot* which they are currently following. In addition to this they are persisting in other matters apart from judging according to the *ṭaaghoot* and referring to it for judgement. Each one of these things on its own is sufficient to condemn them as *kaafir* and put them beyond the pale of Islam. That includes their abolishing women's rights of inheritance, and persisting in that and supporting one another in it. It is stated in the basic principles of Islam that whoever denies something that is definitive and well known in Islam, and rejects it and does that which goes against it, rebelling against it, stubbornly rejecting it, and regarding his action as permissible or taking the matter lightly, is a *kaafir* who disbelieves in Allah and the pure shari'ah which Allah has chosen for His slaves."[85]

What Ash-Shawkaani says indicates a number of things:

a) That referring for judgment to *ṭaaghoot* constitutes major *kufr*.

b) That referring for judgment to *ṭaaghoot* is just one of a number of actions of *kufr*, each of which in its own is sufficient to condemn the one who does it as a *kaafir*.

c) He gives examples of *kufr*, such as their agreeing to deny women their rights of inheritance and their persisting and co-operating in that, and he states that this is major *kufr*.

---

[85] *Risaalah ad-Dawaa' al-'Aajil fi Daf' al-'Adw wa'ṣ-Ṣaa'il*, included in *Ar-Rasaa'il as-Salafiyah* by Ash-Shawkaani, Pp. 33-34.

Shaykh Muhammad ibn Ibraaheem

What he has to say on this topic is clear, that it comes under the heading of major *kufr* which puts a person beyond the pale of Islam, and which is of several types. We have quoted the first four above; he also mentioned two more, which are:

"The fifth is the most serious, and is an obviously stubborn resistance against the shari'ah and its rules, opposing Allah and His Messenger, setting up courts to compete with the shari'ah courts by preparing them, supporting them, establishing principles for them, making them of different types, making their rulings binding, and preparing theoretical bases for them. Just as the shari'ah courts have references which are all based on the Book of Allah and the Sunnah of His Messenger, so too these courts have references which are the laws fabricated from many various laws and legal systems, such as French law, American law, British law and other kinds of laws, and from the *madhhabs* of some of the innovators who claim to belong to Islam, etc.

These courts are now well-established in many Islamic regions. Their doors are open and people are flocking to them so that their judges may judge between them according to these laws that go against the rulings of the Sunnah and the Qur'an. These court rulings are made binding upon them. What *kufr* can be greater than this *kufr*, what contradiction of the testimony that Muhammad is the Messenger of Allah can there be after this contradiction? The evidence for all that we have stated here is available in detail and is well-known, and there is no need to mention it here..."[86]

Then he mentioned the last kind, and said:

---

[86] *Taḥkeem al-Qawaaneen*, Pp. 6-7.

"The sixth kind is that by which many leaders of Bedouin clans and tribes and others rule, based on the stories of their fathers and grandfathers, and their customs, which they call their *salloom* and which they inherited from them. They judge according to this, and they encourage referring to this for judgement when disputes arise, adhering to the rulings of *jaahiliyah* and turning away from and rejecting the rulings of Allah and His Messenger. There is no power and no strength except with Allah."[87]

It is worth pointing out here that the *shaykh* knew the situation of those who advocate (man-made) laws and he referred to the sources of those laws, which are sources that differ from the sources of Islamic shari'ah. This is a basic issue in the case of legislation that goes against the laws of Allah, so there are two important points:

a) The basis from which the law derives its legitimacy.
b) General applicability, which means that the law applies to and is binding upon all the people.

It is clear that man-made laws — and their ilk among the inherited *salloom* of the tribes and Bedouins, which they accept to the exclusion of all other laws and which go against the laws of Allah — stem from complete rejection of the shari'ah of Islam and the One Who revealed it. But this is not the place to discuss this point in further detail.

Shaykh Ash-Shanqeeṭi

He has a great deal to say on this topic, and we have quoted some of his comments above, to which we will add the following. He says, commenting on the *aayah*,

﴿... وَلَا يُشْرِكُ فِي حُكْمِهِۦٓ أَحَدًا ﴿٢٦﴾﴾

[87] *Taḥkeem al-Qawaaneen*, Pp. 6-7.

﴾...And He makes none to share in His Decision and His Rule.﴿ *(Qur'an 18: 26)*:

"It may be understood from this *aayah* that those who follow the rulings of legislators who issue rulings and laws that are not based on the rulings of Allah are *mushrikeen* who associate others with Allah. This concept is stated clearly in other *aayaat* such as the verse concerning the one who follows the law of the *Shayṭaan* (Satan) in allowing the meat of animals which have not been slaughtered correctly on the basis that they were slaughtered by Allah:

﴿ وَلَا تَأْكُلُوا۟ مِمَّا لَمْ يُذْكَرِ ٱسْمُ ٱللَّهِ عَلَيْهِ وَإِنَّهُۥ لَفِسْقٌ ۗ وَإِنَّ ٱلشَّيَـٰطِينَ لَيُوحُونَ إِلَىٰٓ أَوْلِيَآئِهِمْ لِيُجَـٰدِلُوكُمْ ۖ وَإِنْ أَطَعْتُمُوهُمْ إِنَّكُمْ لَمُشْرِكُونَ ﴿١٢١﴾ ﴾

﴾Eat not [O' believers] of that [meat] on which Allah's Name has not been pronounced [at the time of the slaughtering of the animal], for sure it is *fisq* [a sin and disobedience of Allah]. And certainly, the *Shayaaṭeen* [devils] do inspire their friends [from mankind] to dispute with you, and if you obey them [by making *al-maytah* (a dead animal) legal by eating it], then you would indeed be *mushrikoon* [polytheists]; [because they (devils and their friends) made lawful to you to eat that which Allah has made unlawful to eat and you obeyed them by considering it lawful to eat, and by doing so you worshipped them; and to worship others besides Allah is polytheism].﴿ *(Qur'an 6: 121)*

Thus this *aayah* states clearly that they would be *mushrik* if they obeyed the *Shayaaṭeen*, and that this obedience towards others besides Allah and following the laws which go against the laws of Allah is considered the worship of the *Shayṭaan* mentioned in the *aayah* (verse):

﴿ ۞ أَلَمْ أَعْهَدْ إِلَيْكُمْ يَٰبَنِىٓ ءَادَمَ أَن لَّا تَعْبُدُوا۟ ٱلشَّيْطَٰنَ ۖ إِنَّهُۥ لَكُمْ عَدُوٌّ مُّبِينٌ ﴿٦٠﴾ وَأَنِ ٱعْبُدُونِى ۚ هَٰذَا صِرَٰطٌ مُّسْتَقِيمٌ ﴿٦١﴾ ﴾

﴾Did I not command you, O' Children of Adam, that you should not worship *Shayṭaan* [Satan]. Verily, he is a plain enemy to you. And that you should worship Me [Alone Islamic Monotheism, and set up not rivals, associate-gods with Me]. That is the Straight Path.﴿ *(Qur'an 36: 60-61)...*

From these divine texts which we have quoted here, it is abundantly clear that there is no doubt concerning the *kufr* and *shirk* of those who follow the man-made laws which have been instituted by the *Shayṭaan* through his friends and which go against the laws which Allah has instituted through His Messengers (may the blessings and peace of Allah be upon them all). Nobody could doubt that they are *kaafir* and *mushrik* except the one whom Allah has caused to have no understanding and has blinded his eyes, like theirs, to the light of revelation."[88]

The *shaykh* does not state that this is conditional upon their saying that they regard it as permissible or uttering words of denial. We have quoted above that the *shaykh* said: "Everyone who follows laws other than the laws of the leader of the sons of Adam, Muhammad ibn 'Abdullah (ﷺ), his following of those laws, which are opposed to shari'ah, is blatant *kufr...*"[89]

The *shaykh* also comments at length — covering twelve pages — on the *aayah* from *Soorah ash-Shoo'raa*, the 42nd chapter of the Qur'an,

﴿ وَمَا ٱخْتَلَفْتُمْ فِيهِ مِن شَىْءٍ فَحُكْمُهُۥٓ إِلَى ٱللَّهِ ... ﴿١٠﴾ ﴾

[88] *Aḍwaa' al-Bayaan*, 4/91-92.
[89] Ibid, 3/439.

﴿And in whatsoever you differ, the decision thereof is with Allah [He is the ruling Judge]...﴾ *(Qur'an 42: 10)*

He demonstrated the basic principles on which this issue is based, and the connection between it and *Tawḥeed*, and he explained — by examining Qur'anic verses — the attributes of the One who is entitled to have the power of decision, comparing them to the state of the legislators and advocates of man-made laws. This is an important comparison which deserves to be published as a separate book.[90]

One of the comments which he makes — which is worth quoting here — is: "This is a divine decree from the Creator in which He clearly states that the one who follows the law of the *Shayṭaan* which goes against the law of the Most Merciful is a *mushrik* who associates others with Allah."[91]

And he says: "Among the clearest signs of that is that when the *kuffaar* permit something which they know that Allah has forbidden, or forbid something which they know Allah has permitted, they add further *kufr* to their original *kufr*. That is what Allah (سبحانه وتعالى) says: ﴿The postponing [of a Sacred Month] is indeed an addition to disbelief: thereby the disbelievers are led astray, for they make it lawful one year and forbid it another year in order to adjust the number of months forbidden by Allah, and make such forbidden ones lawful. The evil of their deeds is made fair-seeming to them. And Allah guides not the people who disbelieve.﴾ *(Qur'an 9: 37)* Whatever the case, there is no doubt that everyone who obeys someone other than Allah in laws that go against those which Allah has prescribed has associated him with Allah (*shirk*)."[92]

---

[90] *Aḍwaa' al-Bayaan*, 7/162-163.

[91] Ibid, 7/170.

[92] Ibid, 7/173.

If we add this to what the *Shaykh* said in the beginning about those who follow man-made laws and judged them to be *kaafir*, it will be clear that he connected this serious matter to the basics of Islam and *Tawḥeed*, to such an extent that he said that whoever follows any law other than the law of Allah has taken that lawmaker as a lord and associated him with Allah. He said: "The *aayaat* which indicate that are many. We have quoted many of them above and will repeat here only what we need..."[93]

This is only because the *shaykh* felt acute bitterness and deep sorrow concerning the state of the Muslim ummah, and how it had turned its back on the perfect shari'ah of Allah and replaced it with the garbage of lawmakers from the east and the west, and followed the fools and hypocrites.

Shaykh Aḥmad Shaakir and *Shaykh* Maḥmood Shaakir

Shaykh Aḥmad Shaakir (may Allah have mercy on him) wrote a number of footnotes on *'Umdat at-Tafseer*, the abridged version of *Tafseer* Ibn Katheer.[94] Among that is his footnote to Ibn Katheer's commentary on the *aayah*,

﴿ أَفَحُكْمَ ٱلْجَٰهِلِيَّةِ يَبْغُونَ ... ﴿٥٠﴾ ﴾

﴿Do they then seek the judgement of [the days of] Ignorance?...﴾ *(Qur'an 5: 50)*

We have quoted Ibn Katheer's comments above. *Shaykh* Aḥmad Shaakir said, commenting on that (it should be noted that he commented at length and that we are quoting only some of what he said):

---

[93] *Aḍwaa' al-Bayaan*, 7/169.

[94] *Ḥawaashi 'Umdat at-Tafseer*, 3/125, 4/146-147, 155-158 and 165-168.

"I say, how can it be right, according to the laws of Allah, for the Muslims to rule in their land according to the heretic and pagan laws of Europe? Laws which are subject to whims and desires and false opinions, which they change and alter as they wish, and those who institute them do not care whether they are in accordance with Islamic shari'ah or go against it.

The Muslims did not face such a (serious) problem at all — as far as we know from their history — except at that time, the time of the Tartars. Do you not see how *Al-Ḥaafiẓ* Ibn Katheer, in the eighth century (AH) described and condemned in such strong terms the man-made law invented by the enemy of Islam, Genghiz Khan? Do you not think that it also applies to the Muslims of this age, the fourteenth century (AH)? But the Muslims now are in a worse position and are deviating further than they were then, because most of the Muslim nations, now, have virtually fully adopted such laws which go against the shari'ah, which resemble *Yaasiq* made by a *kaafir* whose *kufr* was obvious. These laws are legislated by people who claim to follow Islam. They teach them to the children of the Muslims, and fathers and sons feel proud of that. They entrust their affairs to the followers of this modern *Yaasiq*, and they belittle those who oppose them, describing those who call them to adhere to their religion and their shari'ah as backward and rigid, and use other insulting terms. The matter of these man-made laws is as clear as the light of day: they constitute blatant *kufr......*"[95]

His brother Maḥmood Shaakir (may Allah have mercy on him) commented on Aṭ-Ṭabari's commentary on the *aayah*, ﴿And whosoever does not judge by what Allah has revealed, such are the *kaafiroon* [i.e. disbelievers]﴾ *(Qur'an 5: 44)*, where Aṭ-Ṭabari

[95] *'Umdat at-Tafseer*, 4/173-174. See also his comments on *Sharḥ aṭ-Ṭaḥaawiyah*, Pp. 258, *Daar al-Ma'aarif*, Egypt, edition, 1373 AH, and in the *Al-Maktab al-Islami* edition, Pp. 364, 4th print.

narrated a report of Abu Majlaz with the *Ibaaḍiyah* — which we will refer to below. *Shaykh* Maḥmood added a lengthy footnote, in which he said:

"So their question was not about something that the innovators refer to in our times, of ruling or judging concerning matters of wealth, honour and blood-money according to laws which go against the Islamic shari'ah or of issuing laws obliging the Muslims to refer for judgement to a ruling other than the ruling of Allah in His Book or in the words of His Prophet (ﷺ), because such actions are tantamount to turning away from the ruling of Allah and rejecting His religion, and preferring the rulings of the *kuffaar* (disbelievers) to the rulings of Allah. This is *kufr* and no one among any of the various groups of Muslims doubts that those who say or advocate this are *kaafir*."[96]

These are the words of scholars who lived through the calamities which befell the ummah in Egypt and elsewhere, where the shari'ah of Allah was rejected and man-made laws and *jaahili* systems which go against the laws and rulings of Allah were imposed upon the ummah.

Rasheed Riḍa

A question from India was addressed to him concerning ruling by English law, whether it was permissible for Muslims to rule according to it. He mentioned the differences of opinion concerning the *aayah*: ﴿And whosoever does not judge by what Allah has revealed, such are the *kaafiroon* [i.e. disbelievers]﴾, and the view that it is general in application, he explained that those who expressed this view, interpreted the *aayah* in two ways, one of which was that it was a lesser form of *kufr*. Then he said: "Some of them said that *kufr* is based on one of the general principles, that whoever does not rule according to that which Allah has revealed because he objects to it, or

[96] *Tafseer aṭ-Ṭabari* (footnote), 10/348.

because he is rejecting it and believes it to be unjust, when he knows that it is the ruling of Allah, or the like, which is something that no one could do who has any kind of faith or submission to Allah's religion, is a *kaafir* in the sense of major *kufr*.

No doubt the case of those rulers who promulgate their legislated laws is worse and it is more difficult to justify their actions. This interpretation of *kufr* (as being a lesser form of *kufr*) cannot be applied in their case, and it is difficult to imagine that someone who believes and submits to the religion of Allah and believes that His Book stipulates a certain ruling, would then change it by choice and replace it with another ruling, willingly turning away from it and replacing it with something else, and think that his faith or his Islam still counts for anything. It is clear that the Muslims are obliged, in such a case or with such a ruler, to force him to annul that which he has imposed that goes against the rulings of Allah, and not to be content merely with not helping or supporting him. If they are not able to do that, then the land cannot be considered to be *Daar Islam* (a Muslim land), as it is subject to rulings other than those which apply to *Daar Islam*."[97]

It seems that the *Shaykh* thought that the ruling on the actions of these people was clear. It is very difficult to excuse them by saying that they are not denying or rejecting a ruling of Allah when it is the case that they have willingly changed the ruling of Allah and replaced it with the laws of *jaahiliyah*. With regard to the comments at the end of this quotation that the land cannot be considered to be *Daar Islam*, we have quoted it to demonstrate how far he went by considering that the land ruled by those who impose man-made laws, and refuse to respond to those who advocate annulling those laws and ruling by the shari'ah of Allah, comes to be considered a non-Islamic country.

---

[97] *Fataawa Rasheed Riḍa*, 1/132-133.

However, there is a great deal of debate on this matter, but this is not the place to examine it in detail.[98]

'Abdul-Razzaaq 'Afeefi

In his essay *Al-Ḥukm bi ghayri ma anzala Allah*, he followed his introduction with a list of different types of those who rule by something other than that which Allah has revealed. After mentioning the first and second types, he said: "The third (type) is the one who claims to belong to Islam and knows its rulings, but he legislates — makes laws, for the people and sets up a system to be followed by people and refer to them for judgement, knowing that they go against the rulings of Islam. Such a person is a *kaafir*, is beyond the pale of Islam. The same ruling applies to one who orders the forming of committees or councils for that purpose, and orders the people to refer for judgement to that system and those laws, or forces them to do so, knowing that they go against the shari'ah of Islam. The same applies to the one who passes judgement on that basis and applies it to different cases, and those who obey them in referring to it for judgement by choice, knowing that it goes against Islam. They are all the same in turning away from the ruling of Allah. The same ruling (of *kufr* which puts one beyond the pale of Islam) also applies to those who knowingly make laws to compete with and oppose the laws of Islam, and those who enforce its implementation or force the ummah to follow it, or become judges to judge the people according to those laws or implement rulings according to them. The same ruling applies to those who obey the rulers and accept the laws

---

98 *Shaykh* Muhammad Rasheed Riḍa - may Allah forgive him - made many mistakes in his *fatwa* in which he tried to defend those who do not rule by that which Allah has revealed. What we have quoted here shows that even though he was keen to defend them, the matter is in fact very clear. The points he mentioned has been discussed by *Shaykh* Muhammad Quṭb in his book *Waaqi'unaa al-Mu'aaṣir*, Pp. 231-241.

which they institute for which Allah has not sent down any authority. All of them have followed their own whims and desires, and not the guidance of Allah.

﴿ وَلَقَدْ صَدَّقَ عَلَيْهِمْ إِبْلِيسُ ظَنَّهُۥ فَٱتَّبَعُوهُ إِلَّا فَرِيقًا مِّنَ ٱلْمُؤْمِنِينَ ﴿٢٠﴾ ﴾

﴿And indeed *Iblees* [Devil] did prove true his thought about them, and they followed him...﴾*(Qur'an 34: 20)*.

They are partners in deviation, heresy, *kufr* and transgression; their knowledge of the laws of Allah and their belief in what they contain do not benefit them when they have turned away from them and kept away from their rulings by implementing laws legislated by themselves and referring to them for judgement — just as *Iblees* did not benefit from his knowledge of the truth and his belief in it, when he turned away from it and did not submit to it. In this way they took their own whims and desires as god..."[99]

Then he quoted the *aayaat* (verses) which state that it is obligatory to follow the laws of Allah and judge by that which Allah has revealed, and explained the situation of those who institute man-made laws, and stated that they are opposing the Qur'an and Sunnah and are trying to undermine the shari'ah.

The *Shaykh* clearly states that *kufr* is not limited to believing that ruling by anything other than that which Allah has revealed is permitted, when he says: their knowledge of the laws of Allah and their belief in what they contain did not benefit them when they turned away from them and kept away from their rulings.

---

[99] *Shubahaat ḥawl as-Sunnah* and a dessertation *Al-Ḥukm bi ghayri ma anzala Allah*, Pp. 64-65, *Daar al-Faḍeelah* edition, 1417 AH.

Muḥammad aṣ-Ṣaaliḥ al-'Uthaymeen

In answer to a question about the ruling on one who rules by something other than that which Allah has revealed — after a lengthy and useful introduction — he mentioned the first kind of major *kufr* and said:

"We say: whoever does not rule by that which Allah has revealed because he takes it lightly, or he does not respect it, or he believes that something else is better than it and more beneficial to people, is a *kaafir* whose *kufr* puts him beyond the pale of Islam. Among them are those who impose laws on the people which go against the laws of Islam to be a way for the people to follow. They only impose these laws which go against the Islamic shari'ah because they believe that they are better for the people, because it is simply common sense that a person does not turn from one way to another that goes against it unless he believes that the one to which he is turning is better and the one from which he is turning away is lacking in some respect..."[100]
Then he discussed when ruling by something other than that which Allah has revealed constitutes *ẓulm* (wrongdoing) or *fisq* (rebellion) which does not make a person a *kaafir* — which is the second category.

In a response to yet another question concerning the difference between a specific case and setting out legislation and laws to be applied to all, he said: "Yes, there is a difference. Issues which are considered to be universal legislation cannot be examined in the same way as the above; they belong to the first category only (i.e., major *kufr*), because this legislator who is instituting laws which go against Islam is only doing so because he believes that they are better than Islam and more suited to the people — as we have pointed out above.

---

[100] *Al-Majmoo' ath-Thameen min Fataawa Faḍeelat ash-Shaykh Muhammad ibn Ṣaaliḥ ibn 'Uthaymeen*, 1/36, compiled and edited by Fahd ibn Naaṣir as-Sulaymaan.

Ruling by something other than that which Allah has revealed may take one of the two forms:

1- Replacing a ruling of Allah with a man-made ruling, when the legislator is aware of the ruling of Allah but he thinks that the ruling which goes against it is better and is more beneficial for the people than the ruling of Allah, or that it is equal to the ruling of Allah, or that turning away from the ruling of Allah to the other ruling is permissible, so he promulgates the (man-made) law as that to which referral for judgement is to be made. Such a person is a *kaafir* whose *kufr* puts him beyond the pale of Islam, because the one who does this is not content with Allah as his Lord, Muhammad as his Messenger or Islam as his religion. The following *aayaat* apply to him:

﴿ أَفَحُكْمَ ٱلْجَٰهِلِيَّةِ يَبْغُونَ ۚ وَمَنْ أَحْسَنُ مِنَ ٱللَّهِ حُكْمًا لِّقَوْمٍ يُوقِنُونَ ﴿٥٠﴾ ﴾

﴿Do they then seek the judgement of [the days of] Ignorance? And who is better in judgement than Allah for a people who have firm Faith﴾ *(Qur'an 5: 50)*.

﴿ ...وَمَن لَّمْ يَحْكُم بِمَآ أَنزَلَ ٱللَّهُ فَأُو۟لَٰٓئِكَ هُمُ ٱلْكَٰفِرُونَ ﴿٤٤﴾ ﴾

﴿...And whosoever does not judge by what Allah has revealed, such are the *kaafiroon* [i.e. disbelievers]﴾ *(Qur'an 5: 44)*.

﴿ ذَٰلِكَ بِأَنَّهُمْ قَالُوا۟ لِلَّذِينَ كَرِهُوا۟ مَا نَزَّلَ ٱللَّهُ سَنُطِيعُكُمْ فِى
بَعْضِ ٱلْأَمْرِ ۖ وَٱللَّهُ يَعْلَمُ إِسْرَارَهُمْ ﴿٢٦﴾ فَكَيْفَ إِذَا تَوَفَّتْهُمُ ٱلْمَلَٰٓئِكَةُ
يَضْرِبُونَ وُجُوهَهُمْ وَأَدْبَٰرَهُمْ ﴿٢٧﴾ ذَٰلِكَ بِأَنَّهُمُ ٱتَّبَعُوا۟ مَآ أَسْخَطَ
ٱللَّهَ وَكَرِهُوا۟ رِضْوَٰنَهُۥ فَأَحْبَطَ أَعْمَٰلَهُمْ ﴿٢٨﴾ ﴾

﴿This is because they said to those who hate what Allah has sent down: 'We will obey you in part of the matter.' But Allah knows their secrets. Then how [will it be] when the angels will take their souls at death, smiting their faces and their backs? That is because they followed that which angered Allah and hated that which pleased Him. So He made their deeds fruitless.﴿

(Qur'an 47: 26-28)

So his Prayer, Fasting, Zakah and Ḥajj are of no benefit to him, because the one who rejects part of Islam rejects all of it. Allah (سُبْحَانَهُ وَتَعَالَى) says:

﴿...أَفَتُؤْمِنُونَ بِبَعْضِ ٱلْكِتَٰبِ وَتَكْفُرُونَ بِبَعْضٍ ۚ فَمَا جَزَآءُ مَن يَفْعَلُ ذَٰلِكَ مِنكُمْ إِلَّا خِزْىٌ فِى ٱلْحَيَوٰةِ ٱلدُّنْيَا ۖ وَيَوْمَ ٱلْقِيَٰمَةِ يُرَدُّونَ إِلَىٰٓ أَشَدِّ ٱلْعَذَابِ ۗ وَمَا ٱللَّهُ بِغَٰفِلٍ عَمَّا تَعْمَلُونَ ﴿٨٥﴾﴾

﴿...Then do you believe in a part of the Scripture and reject the rest? Then what is the recompense of those who do so among you, except disgrace in the life of this world, and on the Day of Resurrection they shall be consigned to the most grievous torment. And Allah is not unaware of what you do.﴿ *(Qur'an 2: 85)*

﴿إِنَّ ٱلَّذِينَ يَكْفُرُونَ بِٱللَّهِ وَرُسُلِهِۦ وَيُرِيدُونَ أَن يُفَرِّقُوا۟ بَيْنَ ٱللَّهِ وَرُسُلِهِۦ وَيَقُولُونَ نُؤْمِنُ بِبَعْضٍ وَنَكْفُرُ بِبَعْضٍ وَيُرِيدُونَ أَن يَتَّخِذُوا۟ بَيْنَ ذَٰلِكَ سَبِيلًا ﴿١٥٠﴾ أُو۟لَٰٓئِكَ هُمُ ٱلْكَٰفِرُونَ حَقًّا ۚ وَأَعْتَدْنَا لِلْكَٰفِرِينَ عَذَابًا مُّهِينًا ﴿١٥١﴾﴾

﴿Verily, those who disbelieve in Allah and His Messengers and wish to make distinction between Allah and His Messengers [by believing in Allah and disbelieving in His Messengers] saying, "We believe in some but reject others," and wish to adopt a way in between. They are in truth disbelievers. And We have prepared for the disbelievers a humiliating torment.﴿

(Qur'an 4: 150-151)

2- When the judge passes a judgement which goes against the ruling of Allah in a specific case, without making this ruling universally applicable. This may take three forms:

a) When he does that knowing the ruling of Allah, but he believes that the opposite ruling is better and more beneficial, or that it is equal to it, or that turning away from the ruling of Allah is permissible. This person is a *kaafir* whose *kufr* puts him beyond the pale of Islam, for the same reasons as mentioned in 1-, above.

b) When he does that knowing the ruling of Allah and believing that it is better and more beneficial, but he goes against it with the aim of harming the person against whom judgement is made or benefitting the one in whose favour judgement is passed. Such a person is a *ẓaalim* (wrongdoer, oppressor), not a *kaafir*, and he is the one who is referred to in the *aayah*,

﴿ ... وَمَن لَّمْ يَحْكُم بِمَآ أَنزَلَ ٱللَّهُ فَأُو۟لَـٰٓئِكَ هُمُ ٱلظَّـٰلِمُونَ ﴿٤٥﴾ ﴾

﴿...And whosoever does not judge by what Allah has revealed, such are the *ẓaalimoon* [polytheists and wrongdoers]﴾ *(Qur'an 5: 45).*

c) When he does that, but he goes against (the ruling of Allah) because of his own desires, or for some interest of his that will be served by that. Such a person is a *faasiq* (rebellious, disobedient), not a *kaafir*, and he is the one who is referred to in the *aayah*,

﴿ ... وَمَن لَّمْ يَحْكُم بِمَآ أَنزَلَ ٱللَّهُ فَأُو۟لَـٰٓئِكَ هُمُ ٱلْفَـٰسِقُونَ ﴿٤٧﴾ ﴾

﴿...And whosoever does not judge by what Allah has revealed, such are the *faasiqoon* [the rebellious i.e. disobedient]﴾ *(Qur'an 5: 47).*

This issue — I mean the issue of ruling by something other than that which Allah has revealed — is one of the major issues with which the rulers of this time are being tested. We should not hasten to pass judgement against them undeservedly unless we are sure of the situation, because the matter is serious. We ask Allah to reform the leaders of the Muslims and their advisors. Those to whom Allah has given knowledge must explain it to these rulers so as to establish proof against them and show them the way of Islam, and then those who are to be destroyed (for their rejecting the Faith) might be destroyed after a clear evidence, and those who are to live (i.e. believers) might live after a clear evidence *(cf. Qur'an 8: 42)*. No one should think of himself as insignificant and think that he is unable to speak concerning this issue, and no one should fear anyone else with regard to this matter, for honour, power and glory belong to Allah and His Messenger and the believers. And Allah is the Source of strength."[101]

We have quoted the second *fatwa* in full, so as to give a complete and clear picture of the *fatwa* as issued by the *Shaykh*. But the second category will be discussed in the following section *In sha Allah*.

It is worth pointing out that the *Shaykh* has included in the category of major *kufr* the thinking that judging by something other than that which Allah has revealed is permissible or believing that rulings other than those of Allah are better than or equal to His rulings, or that ruling by them is permissible, whether that involved generally-applicable laws or individual cases.

This is a summary of the views of the scholars concerning this matter, from which it is clear that this category of ruling by anything other than that which Allah has revealed, which constitutes major *kufr*, may include the following cases:

---

[101] *Al-Majmoo' at-Thameen*, 1/37-39.

a) The one who appropriates for himself the right to make laws, and dictate what is permitted and what is prohibited instead of Allah, whether that is an individual, a group, a parliament or something else, so that they promulgate generally-applicable laws which go against the laws of Allah and impose them upon the people, and do not allow them to refer for judgement to the shari'ah of Allah.

b) Those who set up systems or laws which go against the laws of Allah. This is like the man-made laws implemented in many Muslim countries, which impose obligations and dictate what is prohibited and what is permitted, instead of Allah, and go against what is in the Qur'an and Sunnah.

c) Tribal customs, the so-called "*salloom*", which they pass down from one generation to another. If these customs go against the laws of Allah and they know the ruling of Allah, they insist on referring for judgement to their customary laws which go against the ruling of Allah and the ruling of His Messenger (ﷺ).

We should still pay attention to the guidelines and conditions regarding who is to be designated a *kaafir*. This applies both to this type and to others.

Obeying those who change the laws of Allah knowing that they are going against the shari'ah and rulings of Allah

This is a very delicate and subtle issue, hence it should be noted that the title above is somewhat lengthy so as to be specific as to what we intend to discuss in this section, which is one of the categories of ruling by something other than that which Allah has revealed which constitute major *kufr*.

We have described this topic as subtle (lit. slippery) because some of those who speak or issue *fatwa* concerning this matter have, as a result, denounced as *kaafir* entire Muslim societies who are governed by these (man-made) laws, and they have not made any exceptions except for those who oppose them or declare that they are boycotting the entire society. Undoubtedly this is an extreme view which deviates from the proper understanding of the texts and how they are to be applied in the real life.

This issue has been discussed in detail above, when we dealt with the *aayah*,

﴿ ٱتَّخَذُوٓاْ أَحْبَارَهُمْ وَرُهْبَٰنَهُمْ أَرْبَابًا مِّن دُونِ ٱللَّهِ ... ﴿٣١﴾ ﴾

﴾They [Jews and Christians] took their rabbis and their monks to be their lords besides Allah...﴿

(Qur'an 9: 31),[102]

— and similar verses, and the hadith of 'Adiyy ibn Ḥaatim (رضي الله عنه). We have also quoted the comments of Ibn Taymiyah on this *aayah* and this hadith. We will repeat here only the comments of Ibn Taymiyah, because they are so important, so that we may comment on them further:

He said: "Those who took their rabbis and monks as lords when they obeyed them in permitting that which Allah had forbidden and in forbidding that which Allah had permitted, are of two types:

a) Those who knew that they had altered the religion of Allah, so they followed them in that alteration, and they accepted their permitting of that which Allah had forbidden and their forbidding of that which Allah had permitted, following their leaders even though they knew that they had gone against the religion of the Messengers. This is *kufr*, and Allah and His Messenger described it as *shirk*...

[102] See above, Pp. 105-117.

(b) They clearly understood that their rabbis and monks were prohibiting that which was permitted by Allah and permitting that which was forbidden by Allah, but they obeyed them by disobeying Allah. This is like the Muslim who commits sins knowing that they are sins, so they come under the category of sinners..."[103]

On this basis, the followers who are ruled by anything other than that which Allah has revealed cannot be described as *kaafir* unless certain conditions apply, the most important of which are:

(i) They know that the rulers who govern by something other than that which Allah has revealed have altered and changed the laws of Allah, and they follow them in that.

(ii) There is something to indicate that they accept and approve of them, so they have the same belief as those who issue laws instead of Allah concerning what is permitted and what is prohibited, and they follow them.

We cannot say here that the ruling concerning these people is the same as the ruling concerning those who rule by something other than that which Allah has revealed and make it a generally-applicable law, because it may be the case that the one who is so ruled follows them because of some whim or desire of his own, in which case he would come under the same heading as sinners. Or he may be ignorant and thus think that the law promulgated by these leaders is the ruling of Allah; or he may be forced to follow it; or he may have a compelling reason to do so, in order that he may have some right restored to him, etc.

Because all of these cases are possible, we say that there has to be definitive evidence, because the basic principle concerning Muslims

---

[103] Quoted above, Pp. 113-114. From *Al-Eemaan*, Pp. 67, *Al-Maktab al-Islami* edition.

in general is that they are Muslims, and they cannot be regarded as being beyond the pale of Islam unless there is something which obviously nullifies Islam and which fully meets the conditions of nullifying Islam.

The ruling concerning these followers — because they are governed and have no power over the matter — is often similar to the ruling of a judge in a specific case. If he does that believing that what he has done is permissible, then his *kufr* constitutes major *kufr*. Otherwise he is a *faasiq* (rebellious or disobedient) who has committed a major sin. The same applies to these followers. If they follow those who issue laws instead of Allah, knowing what they really are but they obey them because they accept them and approve of what they are doing, then the same ruling (i.e., major *kufr*) applies to them, otherwise they are *faasiq*.

In order to make the matter clearer — lest there be any error or confusion — we will quote the *fatwa* of *Shaykh* Muḥammad ibn Ṣaaliḥ al-'Uthaymeen concerning this topic:

He was asked, what is the ruling on the followers of scholars or governors who permit that which Allah has forbidden or vice versa?

He replied: "The followers of scholars or governors who permit that which Allah has forbidden, or vice versa, may be divided into three categories:

a) Those who follow them in that because they approve of what they say and give it precedence over the ruling of Allah and they dislike the ruling of Allah. Such a person is *kaafir*, because he dislikes that which Allah has revealed, and disliking what Allah has revealed is *kufr*, because Allah (ﷻ) says:

﴿ ذَٰلِكَ بِأَنَّهُمْ كَرِهُوا۟ مَآ أَنزَلَ ٱللَّهُ فَأَحْبَطَ أَعْمَٰلَهُمْ ﴿٩﴾ ﴾

﴾That is because they hate that which Allah has sent down [this Qur'an and Islamic laws]; so He has made their deeds fruitless.﴿ *(Qur'an 47: 9)*

Deeds are only made fruitless by *kufr*, so everyone who hates that which Allah has sent down is a *kaafir*.

b) Those who follow them in that although they approve of the ruling of Allah and know that it is better and more suited for people and for the country, but because of some personal whims and desires they follow them. Such a person is not a *kaafir* but he is a *faasiq* (rebellious, disobedient).

If it were asked, why is he not a *kaafir*? My answer is, because he does not reject the ruling of Allah, but he approves of that which goes against it because of some personal whim or desire, so he is like any other sinner.

c) Those who follow them out of ignorance, thinking that this is the ruling of Allah. These may be further divided into two categories:

i) Those who are able to find out the truth for themselves, but they are negligent and fall short. Such a person is a sinner, because Allah has commanded us to ask the people of knowledge when we do not know something.

ii) Those who are ignorant and are not able to find out the truth for themselves, so they follow them by way of imitation, thinking that this is the truth. Such a person is not to be blamed, because he did that which he was commanded to do, and he is excused for that..."[104]

Based on the above, only the first category comes under the heading of major *kufr*, which is the first category mentioned by Ibn Taymiyah

---

[104] *Al-Majmoo' ath-Thameen*, 2/129-130.

above, subject to the conditions and guidelines which we have referred to. And Allah knows best.

This is a summary of the three categories of major *kufr* which apply to those who rule by something other than that which Allah has revealed:

a) Ideological or connected to belief - i.e., rejecting, believing that ruling by something other than that which Allah has revealed is permissible, and so on. (This includes several categories).

b) Issuing legislation which goes against the laws of Allah (promulgating man-made laws as the law of the country). (This includes several categories).

c) Obeying those who change the laws of Allah, knowing that they are going against the shari'ah of Allah. (This includes one category only).

We have discussed each of them in detail above. Now we will move on to the next topic.

When does it Constitute Minor *Kufr* (A Lesser Form of *Kufr*)?

It is narrated that Ibn 'Abbaas (رضي الله عنه) said concerning the verse from *Soorah al-Maa'idah*, ﴿A lesser form of *kufr*; it is not like one who disbelieves in Allah and the Last Day.﴾ And he said: "It is not the *kufr* which they think it is." We have quoted above the reports concerning this. Here we will discuss the views of those who use this as proof that the comment of Ibn 'Abbaas is general in meaning and applies to all of those who rule by something other than that which Allah (سبحانه وتعالى) (the Exalted) has revealed, so long as he does not regard that as being permissible.

It is clear from the above that the correct view is that the matter requires further discussion.[105] In some cases, ruling by something other than that which Allah has revealed constitutes major *kufr*, and in other cases it constitutes lesser *kufr*. In the previous section, we discussed the cases in which it constitutes major *kufr*. Now we will look at those cases in which the one who judges or rules by something other than that which Allah has revealed is guilty of lesser *kufr*.

From the comments of *Shaykh al-Islam* Ibn Taymiyah, Ash-Shanqeeṭi, Ibn 'Uthaymeen and others that we have quoted above, it will be clear that there are cases in which ruling by something other than that which Allah, the Exalted has revealed may constitute lesser *kufr*. In order to make the matter clearer, in addition to what has been quoted above, it will suffice to quote what one of the scholars has said, then we will follow that with a description of the guidelines and limits governing this issue.

Shaykh Muḥammad ibn Ibraaheem said: "The second type of *kufr* of one who rules by something other than that which Allah has revealed, is that which does not put a person beyond the pale of Islam. We have stated above that the commentary of Ibn 'Abbaas on the *aayah* ﴿And whosoever does not judge by what Allah has revealed, such are the *Kaafiroon* [i.e. disbelievers]﴾ *(Qur'an 5: 44)*, includes this category of *kufr*. That was when he said concerning the *aayah*, ﴿A lesser form of *kufr*﴾, and, ﴿It is not the *kufr* which they think it is﴾. That is because (the judge's) whims and desires may make him judge a case according to something other than that which Allah has revealed, even though he believes that the ruling of Allah and His Messenger is the truth and he acknowledges that he is erring and deviating from true guidance.

---

[105] See Pp. 152 ff.

Even though this *kufr* does not put him beyond the pale of Islam, it is still a grave sin which is more serious than major sins such as adultery, drinking alcohol, stealing, perjury, etc. A sin which Allah describes in His Book as *kufr* is greater than a sin which He does not describe as *kufr*."[106]

We have quoted above the comments of *Shaykh al-Islam* Ibn Taymiyah and Ibn 'Uthaymeen, stating that this comment about lesser *kufr* refers only to specific cases. This is how the words of Ibn 'Abbaas should be interpreted, as we shall see below.

From the words of the scholars and an examination of the texts it is clear that in order for judging or ruling by something other than that which Allah has revealed to constitute lesser *kufr*, the following guidelines must be adhered to:

1- Islamic shari'ah must be prevalent, and the basis of referring for judgement must be based on Qur'an and Sunnah. The ruler or judge should acknowledge and accept that, and should not deny or reject it. He should not believe that judging by something other than that which Allah has revealed is permissible, whether in this particular case where he is passing a judgement which goes against the ruling of Allah, or in any other case, or even if he does not pass a judgement that goes against the shari'ah.

2- It should be with regard to specific cases, not general matters which are imposed on the people so that they become universally-applied laws.[107]

---

106 *Taḥkeem al-Qaanoon*, Pp. 7.

107 The commentator on *Aṭ-Ṭaḥaawiyah*, Ibn Abi'l-'Izz al-Ḥanafi says: "If he [the judge] believes that ruling by something other than that which Allah has revealed is not obligatory or is optional, or he disregards the matter even though he is certain that it is the ruling of Allah, then this is major *kufr*. If he believes that it is obligatory to rule by that which Allah has revealed, and he knows (the ruling)=

3- He should agree that the ruling of Allah is the true ruling, and that it is not permissible to refer for judgement to anything else, and he should agree that if he ignores that ruling in this specific case, he is a sinner who is committing an act of disobedience. But if he believes that his ruling (which goes against shari'ah) is permissible and that he is not sinning by passing this judgement, then his *kufr* is not lesser *kufr*.

Ibn 'Abbaas (ﷺ) and his Comment, *"Kufr doona Kufr* (A Lesser Form of *Kufr*)"

Those who say that the one who rules by something other than that which Allah has revealed does not become a *kaafir* in the absolute sense, unless he believes that it is permissible to do so, quote as evidence for their view the comment narrated from Ibn 'Abbaas concerning the *aayah* in *Soorah al-Maa'idah*: ﴾A lesser form of *kufr*, but it is not like the one who disbelieves in Allah, His angels and the Last Day﴿.

They said, "It indicates that regarding as a *kaafir* in the absolute sense the one who does not believe it is permissible, is the view of the *Khawaarij* as per the report narrated from Abu Majlaz, Laaḥiq ibn Ḥumayd, of the discussion that he had with the *Ibaaḍiyah* concerning the rulers of their time, the application of the *aayah* ﴾And whosoever does not judge by what Allah has revealed, such are the *kaafiroon* [i.e. disbelievers]﴿ *(Qur'an 5: 44)* to them, and how Abu Majlaz did not agree with them and explained that the ones who do this were only sinners, not *kuffaar*."

= in this case, but he turns away from it whilst admitting that he is deserving of punishment, then he is a sinner and is described as a *kaafir* in a metaphorical sense, or a *kaafir* in the sense of lesser *kufr*..." *Sharḥ aṭ-Ṭaḥaawiyah*, Pp. 363-364, 4th edition, *Al-Maktab al-Islami.*

We have referred above to *Shaykh* Mahmood Shaakir's discussion of this argument in his commentary on *Tafseer aṭ-Ṭabari*.[108]

We will quote the reports narrated by Aṭ-Ṭabari concerning the story of Abu Majlaz and the *Ibaaḍiyah*, then we will discuss the matter in some detail.

The story of Abu Majlaz and the *Ibaaḍiyah* and analysis of what happened

Aṭ-Ṭabari narrated that 'Imraan ibn Ḥudayr said: some people from (the tribe of) Bani 'Amr ibn Sadoos came to Abu Majlaz and said: "O' Abu Majlaz, do you think that the *aayah* ﴿And whosoever does not judge by what Allah has revealed, such are the *kaafiroon* [i.e. disbelievers]﴾ *(Qur'an 5: 44)* is true?" He said, "Yes." They said, "And is the *aayah*, ﴿And whosoever does not judge by what Allah has revealed, such are the *ẓaalimoon* [polytheists and wrongdoers]﴾ *(Qur'an 5: 45)* true?" He said, "Yes." They said, "And is the *aayah*, ﴿And whosoever does not judge by what Allah has revealed, ... such [people] are the *faasiqoon* [the rebellious i.e. disobedient]﴾ *(Qur'an 5: 47)* true?" He said, "Yes." They said, "O' Abu Majlaz, are these people (the rulers of that time) ruling by that which Allah has revealed?" He said, "That is their religion which they follow, in which they believe and to which they call others. If they neglect any part of it, they know that they have committed a sin." They said, "No, by Allah, you are scared (of the rulers)." He said, "That is more true in your case than mine. I do not accept this view, but you do and you do not find anything wrong with that. But these *aayaat* were revealed concerning the Jews, Christians and polytheists" — or words to that effect.

---

[108] *Tafseer aṭ-Ṭabari*, 10/348. His brother *Shaykh* Aḥmad Shaakir quoted it in *'Umdat at-Tafseer*, 4/155-158.

According to a report from 'Imraan ibn Ḥudayr, he said: A group of the *Ibaaḍiyah* sat with Abu Majlaz and said to him: "Allah says, ﴿And whosoever does not judge by what Allah has revealed, such are the *kaafiroon* [i.e. disbelievers]﴾ *(Qur'an 5: 44)*, ﴿... such are the *ẓaalimoon* [polytheists and wrongdoers]﴾ *(Qur'an 5: 45)*, ﴿... such [people] are the *faasiqoon* [the rebellious i.e. disobedient]﴾ *(Qur'an 5: 47)*."

Abu Majlaz said: "They do what they do" — referring to the governors — "and they know that it is a sin. These *aayaat* were revealed concerning the Jews and Christians." They said, "By Allah, you know what we know, but you fear them." He said, "You are more deserving than I of this description. I do not accept what you know." They said: "But you do know it, but what is preventing you from following what you know is your fear of them."[109]

Shaykh Maḥmood Shaakir's refutation of those who use these two reports to support their view may be summed up as follows:

1- Laaḥiq ibn Ḥumayd (Abu Majlaz) was a trustworthy *Ṭaabi'i* who loved 'Ali. He was Shaybaani Sadoosi[110] and his people — Bani Shaybaan — were among the supporters of 'Ali at the Battle of the Camel and the Battle of Ṣiffeen. When the *Khawaarij* emerged, there was among them a group from Bani Shaybaan and from Bani Sadoos ibn Shaybaan. Amongst these were some who were followers of 'Abdullah ibn Ibaad, the founder of the *Ibaaḍiyah* sect of the *Khawaarij*. Their view was that 'Ali (رضي الله عنه) became a *kaafir* when he accepted the appointment of the two arbitrators, and they thought that 'Ali had not ruled by that which Allah had revealed when he agreed to refer for judgement to these arbitrators.

---

[109] *Tafseer aṭ-Ṭabari*, 10/347-348, reports nos. 12025 and 12026.

[110] This refers to his tribal affiliation and lineage, as becomes clearer in the remainder of the paragraph (Translator).

These *Ibaaḍiyah* also believed that the lands of their opponents were the lands of *Tawḥeed* (Muslim lands), apart from the seat of the ruler, which was *daar kufr* (abode of disbelief, non-Muslim land), and that whoever committed a major sin was a *kaafir* in the sense of denying the blessing of Allah, but in the Hereafter he would abide in the Fire for eternity.

Summary: the *Ibaaḍiyah* wanted to prove to Abu Majlaz that the governors were *kaafir*, because they were in the camp of the ruler, and because they may have committed sins or some things that Allah had forbidden. Hence, according to the first report (no. 12025) he said to them, "If they neglect any part of it, they know that they have committed a sin" and according to the second report, he said to them, "They do what they do and they know that it is a sin."

So their question did not have anything to do with that which the innovators of our own time use as evidence about passing judgment on matters of wealth, honour and blood according to laws which go against the shari'ah of the Muslims, or promulgating laws which force the Muslims to refer to for judgement to something other than the rulings of Allah revealed in His Book or on the lips of His Prophet (ﷺ). This action is a turning away from the ruling and religion of Allah, preferring the rulings of the *kuffaar* to the rulings of Allah. This is *kufr*, and none of the Muslims, despite their differences, doubts that the one who believes in and advocates this is a *kaafir.*[111]

2 - It never happened in the history of Islam — until recent times — including the time of Abu Majlaz, during the *Umawi* (Umayyad) era, that a ruler promulgated a ruling and made it a law which the people were obliged to refer to for judgement. All that happened were some sins, wrongdoing and oppression on the part of some of the governors. If it so happened that judgement was passed according to

[111] *Tafseer aṭ-Ṭabari*, 10/348, editor's footnote.

something other than that which Allah had revealed, these were incidents that were restricted to specific cases. If this was done on the part of one who was ignorant, then this is the case of one who is ignorant of the shari'ah, and if it was done on the basis of whims and disobedience, then this is a sin which is subject to repentance — that is, if the judge accepts the ruling of Allah and believes that it is the truth. But if his ruling was based on his interpretation which differed from that of the scholars, then this comes under the rulings on one who has a different interpretation. This is what the discussion between Abu Majlaz and the *Ibaaḍiyah* focused on: incidents of wrongdoing and oppression in individual cases. "But to suggest that at the time of Abu Majlaz, or before or after his time, there was a ruler who issued a judgement on the basis of denying one of the rulings of shari'ah, or preferring the rulings of the *kuffaar* over the rulings of Islam — this is something which never happened, and the discussion of Abu Majlaz with the *Ibaaḍiyah* cannot be understood as referring to that."[112]

I would like to add to what *Shaykh* Maḥmood Shaakir said the following points concerning Abu Majlaz and the *Ibaaḍiyah*:

3 - Whoever studies the biography of Abu Majlaz will note the following:[113]

a) He was concerned with the *Khawaarij* and he was one of those who narrated the story of what happened between them

---

[112] *Tafseer aṭ-Ṭabari*, 10/349, editor's footnote.

[113] I studied his biography in order to acquire detailed information about him, but I found that his biography is brief and is centred on what was said about him being *thiqah* (trustworthy) and so on. The most detailed biography that I could find was in the MS of *Taareekh Dimashq* (18/3-10) (MS in *Maktabat ad-Daar*). See his biography in *At-Taareekh al-Kabeer* by Bukhari, 8/58; *Tabaqaat Ibn Sa'd*, 7/216; *At-Thiqaat* by Ibn Ḥibbaan, 5/518; *Al-Jarḥ wat-Ta'deel*, 9/124; *Tahdheeb al-Mazzi* MS; *Tahdheeb at-Tahdheeb* by Ibn Ḥajar, 11/171; *Meezaan al-I'tidaal*, 4/356, etc.

and 'Ali ibn Abi Ṭaalib (ﷺ). He is the one who narrated that he ('Ali) forbade his companions to attack the *Khawaarij* until provocation came from them, that is, when they killed 'Abdullah ibn Khabbaab and his pregnant slave woman, as told in the well-known story.[114]

It is very likely that he played a role with the *Khawaarij* of his time, the *Ibaaḍiyah* and others.

b) He was one of those who were appointed as governors at some time. His biographers mentioned that he came to Khurasaan with Qutaybah ibn Muslim al-Baahili. Indeed Ibn 'Asaakir mentioned that the people of Merv came to Abu Majlaz and appointed him as their governor until Wakee' ibn Abi Aswad came.[115] It is also reported that he used to ride with Qutaybah ibn Muslim in his cavalcade, glorifying Allah twelve times.[116]

Because he was *thiqah* (trustworthy) in narrating hadith, and used to discuss issues of *fiqh* and Sunnah with his companions and was in contact with some of the governors,[117] then it is entirely natural that the *Ibaaḍiyah* would come to him for discussions, especially since they thought that the camp of the ruler — which included the governors — was the camp of *shirk*. He answered them in the manner which he thought was true and in accordance with the *madhhab of Ahl as-Sunnah wal-Jamaa'ah*. This is what he said, according to the reports which Aṭ-Ṭabari narrated from him in his *Tafseer*.

---

[114] *Al-Muṣannaf* by Ibn Abi Shaybah, 15/308, 323, no. 19739 and 19769.

[115] This is what it says in the MS. See *Taareekh Dimashq*, 18/6-7 (MS of *Maktabat ad-Daar* in Madeenah).

[116] Ibid, 18/8.

[117] Ibid. It should be noted that his connection with the governors was based on self-respect. It is narrated that he said: "I never stood at the door of any governor or went to him until he had sent his messenger to me; if he sent for me, I would go in with his messenger." *Taareekh Dimashq*, 18/9.

c) Abu Majlaz was in contact with 'Umar ibn 'Abdul-'Azeez (may Allah have mercy on him). It is narrated that 'Umar said: "I want to know about Khurasaan; find me a truthful man," and he was told to ask Abu Majlaz, so he called for him and asked him.[118]

'Umar ibn 'Abdul-'Azeez also engaged in discussions with the *Khawaarij* of his time. He debated with them and established proof against them, and they were pleased with him in general. Since he regarded Abu Majlaz as trustworthy, it is possible that some of the discussions of the *Khawaarij* were held with him too.

4- With regard to the *Ibaaḍiyah*, we have referred to above to the comments of *Shaykh* Maḥmood Shaakir which describe them. I would like to add the following:

The *Ibaaḍiyah* condemned 'Uthmaan and 'Ali (may Allah be pleased with them both), the two rightly-guided Caliphs, and accused them of ruling by something other than that which Allah revealed, therefore they denounced them as *kaafir*. I will quote some passages from a letter which 'Abdullah ibn Ibaad sent to the Umawi (Umayyad) *khaleefah* 'Abdul-Maalik ibn Marwaan — which is quoted in some of the *Ibaaḍiyah's* books, boasting of it, its style and the courageous attitude of Ibn Ibaaḍ.

Ibn 'Ibaaḍ said, after mentioning the so-called faults of 'Uthmaan (many of which were mentioned by those who held grudges against him and rebelled against him): "One of the things that we hold against him is that he did not let the people of Bahrain and Oman sell any of their food until the food of the state had been sold. This was forbidding something that Allah had permitted, and:

[118] *Taareekh aṭ-Ṭabari*, 6/559-561; *Al-Kaamil* by Ibn al-Atheer, 5/51-52, *Daar Ṣaadir* edition.

﴿... وَأَحَلَّ ٱللَّهُ ٱلْبَيْعَ وَحَرَّمَ ٱلرِّبَوٰا۟ ... ﴿٢٧٥﴾﴾

﴿...Allah has permitted trading and forbidden *ribaa'*...﴾ *(Qur'an 2: 275)*

"Among the things that 'Uthmaan did was to rule according to something other than that which Allah had revealed, and to go against the way of the Messenger of Allah (ﷺ) and his two Companions.

Allah (ﷻ) says:

﴿وَمَن يُشَاقِقِ ٱلرَّسُولَ مِنۢ بَعْدِ مَا تَبَيَّنَ لَهُ ٱلْهُدَىٰ وَيَتَّبِعْ غَيْرَ سَبِيلِ ٱلْمُؤْمِنِينَ نُوَلِّهِۦ مَا تَوَلَّىٰ وَنُصْلِهِۦ جَهَنَّمَ ۖ وَسَآءَتْ مَصِيرًا ﴿١١٥﴾﴾

﴿And whoever contradicts and opposes the Messenger [Muhammad] after the right path has been shown clearly to him, and follows other than the believers' way, We shall keep him in the path he has chosen, and burn him in Hell - what an evil destination!﴾ *(Qur'an 4: 115)*

And: ﴿And whosoever does not judge by what Allah has revealed, such are the *kaafiroon* [i.e. disbelievers]﴾ *(Qur'an 5: 44)*, ﴿... such are the *ẓaalimoon* [polytheists and wrongdoers]﴾ *(Qur'an 5: 45)*, ﴿... such [people] are the *faasiqoon* [the rebellious i.e. disobedient]﴾ *(Qur'an 5: 47)*."[119]

Then he said: "This and similar stories is the reason why the Muslims and the believers denounced 'Uthmaan, and for that reason we also denounce him. They condemned him for that reason and we also condemn him... (Then he criticized 'Ali, then he said:)... Know that the sign that this ummah has returned to *kufr* is when they forsake

---

[119] *Izaalat al-Wa'thaa' 'an Atbaa' Abi'sh-Sha'thaa'* by Saalim ibn Ḥammood as-Samaa'ili, Pp. 92, edited by Sayyid Ismaa'eel Kaashif, Cairo 1979 CE, published by the Sultanate of Oman, Ministry of National Heritage and Culture.

ruling according to that which Allah, the Almighty, All-Powerful, has revealed and rule according to something other than that which He has revealed..."[120]

Then Ibn Ibaaḍ said of his *Khaariji* (Kharijite) predecessors: "They were the opponents of 'Uthmaan who denounced him for the innovations that he introduced and forsook him when he abandoned the ruling of Allah. They were the opponents of Ṭalḥah and Zubayr when they deviated, and the opponents of Mu'aawiyah when he transgressed, and the opponents of 'Ali when he changed the ruling of Allah, and appointed 'Abdullah ibn Qays and 'Amr ibn al-'Aaṣ (as arbitrators). So they forsook all of them. This is the story of the *Khawaarij* (Kharijites), and Allah and His angels bear witness that we are the enemies of those who take them as enemies, and we are the friends of those who take them as friends, (and we will support them) with our words, our actions and in our hearts..."[121]

Then he said: "As for the leaders of misguidance, they are the ones who rule according to something other than that which Allah has revealed, they divide things in a manner other than that which is prescribed by Allah, and they follow their own desires instead of the way of Allah."[122]

This Ibn Ibaaḍ accused the great and prominent *ṣaḥaabah* — above all the rightly-guided *khaleefah* 'Uthmaan ibn 'Affaan and the rightly-guided *khaleefah* 'Ali ibn Abi Ṭaalib — of ruling according to something other than that which Allah had revealed, hence according to him they were *kaafir*, because of the *aayah* revealed concerning that. So what would their attitude be towards those who came after them, such as Mu'aawiyah (رضي الله عنه) and the rest of the Caliphs from Bani

---

[120] Ibid, Pp. 94.

[121] Ibid, Pp. 97.

[122] *Izaalat al-Wa'thaa' 'an Atbaa' Abish-Sha'thaa'*, Pp. 99.

Umayyah? No doubt according to these *Ibaaḍis* their *kufr* would be worse than that (of 'Uthmaan and 'Ali) because they — apart from Mu'aawiyah and 'Umar ibn 'Abdul-'Azeez — committed acts of oppression and injustice, as is well known. The methodology of the *Ibaaḍiyah* is quite obvious. They consider oppression and injustice — even things which according to scholarly consensus are not oppression or injustice, such as the actions of 'Uthmaan and 'Ali's appointing the two arbitrators — to be ruling by something other than that which Allah has revealed, and whoever rules by something other than that which Allah has revealed is a *kaafir.*

The story of Abu Majlaz and his debate with the *Ibaaḍiyah* no doubt involved topics of this nature, and what Abu Majlaz said is true and what the *Ibaaḍi* wanted to prove was false — as stated above. So how can something like this be used as evidence to support what is happening in many Muslim countries, where the ruling of Allah is being rejected and the rule of man-made law is being imposed and the people are being forced to refer to it for judgement?

Ibn 'Abbaas and the *Khawaarij*

From the above it is clear that it is invalid to quote as evidence the story of Ibn Majlaz and the *Ibaaḍiyah* who regarded those who committed injustice as *kaafir* — especially those who were in the ruling camp such as governors and others. It remains for us now to discuss the *ṣaḥeeḥ* reports from Ibn 'Abbaas which state that he commented on the *aayah* and said "A lesser form of *kufr.*" Does this constitute evidence for those who claim that those who replace the shari'ah of Allah with man-made laws and impose them on the people, and give them precedence over the shari'ah of Allah, do not become *kaafir* by doing so?

The truth is that this does not constitute such evidence. This may be explained as follows:

1 - The *Khawaarij* made this *aayah* - ﴾And whosoever does not judge by what Allah has revealed, such are the *kaafiroon* [i.e. disbelievers]﴿ *(Qur'an 5: 44)* — one of their basic grounds for denouncing those who commit major sins as *kaafir* who would abide forever in Hell. Therefore you find that when the scholars discuss this issue, and the views and evidence of the *Khawaarij*, they quote this *aayah* and say that this is the evidence of the *Khawaarij*.

For example, Al-Qaaḍi Abu Ya'laa mentioned the evidence used by the *Khawaarij* and *Mu'tazilah* for their views concerning those who commit major sins. He said: "They quote a number of things as evidence, including the *aayah* (verse), ﴾And whosoever does not judge by what Allah has revealed, such are the *kaafiroon* [i.e. disbelievers]﴿ *(Qur'an 5: 44)*, saying that the apparent meaning of this is that unjust rulers should be denounced as *kaafir*, and this is our view."[123] Then Al-Qaaḍi Abu Ya'laa refuted their view by noting that this *aayah* refers specifically to the Jews. The point here is not to discuss the response of Abu Ya'laa to their views, but to prove that this *aayah* is one of the things that they quote as evidence for denouncing as *kaafir* those who commit major sins, including unjust leaders.

Their arguments were well known to the *khulafa* (Caliphs) and governors of the Umawis (Umayyads) and 'Abbaasis (Abbasids), and there are many stories about that.[124]

2 - The methodology of the *Khawaarij* in quoting these *aayaat* — which is a deviant methodology — was well known to the *ṣaḥaabah*. We will quote some evidence concerning Ibn 'Abbaas below. With regard to other *ṣaḥaabah*, it is narrated by Ibn Wahb from Bukayr

---

[123] *Masaa'il al-Eemaan* by Qaaḍi Abu Ya'laa, Pp. 340, edited by Sa'ood ibn 'Abdul-'Azeez al-Khalaf.

[124] *Taareekh Baghdaad*, 10/186; *Siyar A'laam al-Nubalaa'*, 10/280.

that he asked Naafi', "What was Ibn 'Umar's view of the *Ḥarooriyah* (*Khawaarij*)?" He said, "he believed that they were the worst of Allah's creation, for they referred to *aayaat* that had been revealed concerning the *kuffaar* and applied them to the believers." Sa'eed ibn Jubayr was happy about that, and said: "One of the ambiguous *aayaat* to which the *Ḥarooriyah* refer to is the *aayah*, ﴾And whosoever does not judge by what Allah has revealed, such are the *kaafiroon* [i.e. disbelievers]﴿ *(Qur'an 5: 44)*. They add to it the verse,

﴿ ... ثُمَّ ٱلَّذِينَ كَفَرُواْ بِرَبِّهِمْ يَعْدِلُونَ ۝١ ﴾

> ﴾...Yet those who disbelieve hold others as equal with their Lord.﴿ *(Qur'an 6: 1)*

Then when they see the leader ruling by something other than the truth, they say that he has become a *kaafir*, and the one who becomes a *kaafir* holds others as equal with his Lord, so he is a *mushrik*. So this ummah is *mushrikeen*. They then rebel and kill as you know, because they misinterpret this *aayah*."[125]

The deviant way in which the *Khawaarij* interpreted and used these verses was a major concern of many of the *ṣaḥaabah*, who explained what was wrong with their interpretation, especially when *ṣaḥeeh aḥaadeeth* which condemn them are so many and reach the level of being *mutawaatir.*

3- The *ṣaḥaabah* were well acquainted with the reports of the *Khawaarij*, because they used to mix with them. Many of them did not regard the *Khawaarij* as *kaafir* even though they did what they did. *Shaykh al-Islam* Ibn Taymiyah said: "Among the things which indicate that the *ṣaḥaabah* did not regard the *Khawaarij* as *kaafir* is

---

[125] *Al-I'tiṣaam* by Ash-Shaaṭibi, 2/183-184. What Sa'eed ibn Jubayr said is narrated by Al-Aajurri in *Ash-Sharee'ah*, 1/342, hadith no. 44, edited by Dr. 'Abdullah ad-Dumayji, published by *Daar al-Waṭan.*

that fact that they prayed behind them. 'Abdullah ibn 'Umar (ﷺ) and other *ṣaḥaabah* used to pray behind Najdah al-Ḥaroori. They also used to speak with them, issue *fatwas* to them and address them as one Muslim addresses another. 'Abdullah ibn 'Abbaas used to respond to Najdah al-Ḥaroori when he sent word to him asking about various matters, and his hadith is narrated in Bukhari.[126] Naafi' ibn al-Azraq also answered questions on well-known issues, and Al-Naafi' used to debate with him on matters mentioned in the Qur'an, as he used to debate with other Muslims..."[127] even though the *Khawaarij* denounced the Muslims as *kaafir* and fought them, and the Messenger (ﷺ) had said of them that they were the worst of the slain under the sky, and they regarded people's blood and wealth as permissible, and they even regarded killing women and children as permissible, regarding all of them as *kaafir.*

The point we are trying to make is that when the *ṣaḥaabah* were discussing and interpreting the Qur'an, the issue of the *Khawaarij* and their arguments, was a very real issue with which the *ṣaḥaabah*

---

[126] The question of Najdah to Ibn 'Abbaas is narrated clearly in Muslim (*Al-Jihaad*, hadith no. 1812) with a number of isnads. In Bukhari it is mentioned in *At-Tafseer, Soorah Ḥaa-Meem as-Sajdah*: "Al-Minhaal reported that Sa'eed stated: A man said to Ibn 'Abbaas: 'I find things in the Qur'an about which I am confused...'" In (the *Tafseer* of) *Soorah al-Mursalaat*: "Ibn 'Abbaas was asked..." The commentators on Bukhari think it most likely that this was Naafi' ibn al-Azraq (the subsequent leader of the *Azaariqah*). Ibn Ḥajar narrated in *Fatḥ al-Baari* the report of Aṭ-Ṭabaraani that Naafi' ibn al-Azraq and Najdah ibn 'Uwaymir came to Makkah with a group of *Khaariji* leaders, and they met Ibn 'Abbaas... (*Fatḥ al-Baari*, 8/557). Concerning the above, see *Fatḥ al-Baari*, 8/686, first *Salafi* edition; *'Umdat al-Qaari'*, 19/150, *Muneeriyah* edition; *Irshaad as-Saari*, 7/260, 2nd *Boolaaq* edition; *Tuḥfat al-Baari* by Zakariya al-Anṣaari, 9/107, *Al-Maymaniyah* edition published in one volume with Irshaad as-Saari. The report of Al-Minhaal from Sa'eed and the question of Naafi' and Najdah are both narrated in Aṭ-Ṭabaraani, 10/300, 304, hadith nos. 10594 and 10597.

[127] *Minhaaj as-Sunnah*, 5/247.

were dealing directly. One of their most famous arguments was based on the verse from *Soorah al-Maa'idah* which they used to prove that those who differed with them were *kaafir*. The response of Ibn 'Abbaas and his comments on the interpretation of this *aayah* should not be understood outside of this context.

4 - One fact which will explain the matter further is that Ibn 'Abbaas, according to some of the reports narrated from him, said, "It is not the *kufr* which they think it is." Undoubtedly this is a reference to the *Khawaarij*. The evidence for that is the fact that he engaged in debates with them, as was narrated by the scholars of hadith with *ṣaḥeeḥ* isnads. This is after the two arbitrators were appointed and the *Khawaarij* had split from the army of 'Ali (رضي الله عنه), denouncing him as a *kaafir* because he had appointed men as judges, and judging or ruling by anything other than that which Allah has revealed is *kufr*. It is narrated that 'Ali ibn Abi Ṭaalib mounted the *minbar* (pulpit) on a Friday and praised Allah, then he gave a sermon in which he mentioned the *Khawaarij* and criticized them, and he mentioned the issue of creating division among the people, and the issue concerning which this division had arisen. (Abu Razeen) said: "When he came down from the *minbar*, they called out from all across the mosque, 'The judgement is only for Allah.' 'Ali said, 'I am waiting for the judgement of Allah concerning you.' Then he gestured with his hand that they should be silent, and remained on the *minbar* until a man came forward putting his fingers in his ears, saying,

﴿... لَئِنْ أَشْرَكْتَ لَيَحْبَطَنَّ عَمَلُكَ وَلَتَكُونَنَّ مِنَ ٱلْخَٰسِرِينَ ﴿٦٥﴾﴾

﴿...If you join others in worship with Allah, [then] surely, [all] your deeds will be in vain, and you will certainly be among the losers.﴾ *(Qur'an 39: 65)*."[128]

---

[128] *Muṣannaf Ibn Abi Shaybah*, 15/312-313, no. 19746.

It is narrated that he engaged directly in debates with them. 'Ali sent Ibn 'Abbaas to them to debate with them, then Ibn 'Abbaas came to them and discussed their specious arguments one by one until most of them recanted, then a few of them were left, whom 'Ali (رضي الله عنه) fought against.

We will quote relevant parts of the debates which Ibn 'Abbaas had with them, which was their most famous argument, and the response given by Ibn 'Abbaas to it.

Ibn 'Abbaas said (after he came to them, which is narrated in a lengthy story): "I said, 'Tell me, why are you so upset with the cousin and son-in-law of the Messenger of Allah (ﷺ), and the *muhaajireen* and the Anṣaar?' They said, 'For three reasons.' I said, 'What are they?' They said: 'The first is that he appointed men to judge concerning the command of Allah, and Allah (سبحانه وتعالى) says,

﴿ ... إِنِ ٱلْحُكْمُ إِلَّا لِلَّهِ ... ۝٥٧ ﴾

﴿...The decision is only for Allah...﴾
(Qur'an 6: 57; 12: 40, 67).

What do men have to do with the decision or ruling?' I said, 'That is fine — what else?...' I said to them, 'Do you think that if I recite to you from the Book of Allah and the Sunnah of His Prophet (ﷺ) that which refutes what you say, that you will accept it?' They said, 'Yes.' I said, 'With regard to your view that he appointed men to judge concerning the ruling of Allah, I will recite to you an *aayah* which says that we should refer the judgement to men concerning a rabbit, which is worth no more than a quarter of a dirham, or other game. Allah (سبحانه وتعالى) says:

﴿ يَٰٓأَيُّهَا ٱلَّذِينَ ءَامَنُوا۟ لَا تَقْتُلُوا۟ ٱلصَّيْدَ وَأَنتُمْ حُرُمٌ ۚ وَمَن قَتَلَهُۥ مِنكُم مُّتَعَمِّدًا فَجَزَآءٌ مِّثْلُ مَا قَتَلَ مِنَ ٱلنَّعَمِ يَحْكُمُ بِهِۦ ذَوَا عَدْلٍ مِّنكُمْ ... ۝٩٥ ﴾

﴿O' you who believe! Kill not the game while you are in

a state of *Iḥraam* [for Ḥajj or 'Umrah (pilgrimage)], and whosoever of you kills it intentionally, the penalty is an offering, brought to the Ka'bah, of an eatable animal [i.e. sheep, goat, cow] equivalent to the one he killed, as adjudged by two just men among you...﴿ *(Qur'an 5: 95)*

Tell me for the sake of Allah, is the appointment of two men to judge concerning a rabbit or similar game more important than appointing men to judge concerning the issue of preventing bloodshed and reconciling between people? You know that if Allah had willed, He could have ruled Himself, and He would not have delegated that to men. Concerning a woman and her husband, Allah (ﷻ) says:

﴿ وَإِنْ خِفْتُمْ شِقَاقَ بَيْنِهِمَا فَٱبْعَثُوا۟ حَكَمًا مِّنْ أَهْلِهِۦ وَحَكَمًا مِّنْ أَهْلِهَآ إِن يُرِيدَآ إِصْلَٰحًا يُوَفِّقِ ٱللَّهُ بَيْنَهُمَآ ... ﴿٣٥﴾ ﴾

﴾If you fear a breach between them twain [the man and his wife], appoint [two] arbitrators, one from his family and the other from hers; if they both wish for peace, Allah will cause their reconciliation...﴿ *(Qur'an 4: 35)*

So Allah has made the appointment of men as arbitrators the method to be used all the time. 'Have we finished with this issue?' They said, 'Yes.'..."[129]

---

[129] This is narrated by Al-Ḥaakim in *Al-Mustadrak*, 2/150-152; he said, it is *ṣaḥeeḥ* according to the conditions of Muslim although they (Bukhari and Muslim) did not narrate it, and Adh-Dhahabi agreed with him. It is also narrated by Aḥmad in *Al-Musnad*, 1/342, in brief. Its number according to Aḥmad Shaakir is 3187, and he said, its isnad is *ṣaḥeeḥ*. It is narrated by Al-Bayhaqi in *As-Sunan al-Kubra*, 8/179; Aṭ-Ṭabaraani in *Al-Mu'jam al-Kabeer*, 10/312, no. 10598; 'Abdur-Razzaaq in *Al-Muṣannaf*, 10/157, no. 18678. Also narrated by Al-Fasawi in *Al-Ma'rifah wat-Taareekh*, 1/522, *Maktabat ad-Daar* edition; Ibn 'Abdul-Barr in *Jaami' al-Bayaan al-'Ilm*, Pp. 375-377, edited by 'Abdul-Kareem al-Khaṭeeb, or 2/103 *Al-Muneeriyah* edition. Narrated by Al-Balaadhuri in *Ansaab al-Ashraaf*, part 3, Pp. 43-44, edited by 'Abdul-'Azeez ad-Doori.

This indicates that Ibn 'Abbaas (رضي الله عنه) used to engage in debates with these *Khawaarij* and respond to their specious arguments, including the matter of referring to men for judgement, and their denouncing 'Ali (رضي الله عنه) and those who were with him as *kaafir*. He wanted to protect the Muslims from the danger they represented and from their specious arguments, therefore he explained to them where they had gone wrong in their using the *aayah* ﴿And whosoever does not judge by what Allah has revealed, such are the *kaafiroon* [i.e. disbelievers]﴾ *(Qur'an 5: 44)* to prove that 'Ali and his companions were *kaafir*, and why their argument was false. What Ibn 'Abbaas said, commenting on this *aayah* — ﴿A lesser form of *kufr*﴾; it is not the *kufr* which they think it is — should be understood as meaning that he was referring to these people who accused unjust rulers, and even the noblest of the *ṣaḥaabah* (may Allah be pleased with them), of being *kaafir*.

Although Ibn 'Abbaas had some contact with them, as stated above, in the sense that he responded to their questions and debated with them, he still, like the rest of the *ṣaḥaabah*, understood the danger that they posed to the Muslim ummah. Hence Ibn Abi Shaybah narrated from 'Abdullah ibn Abi Yazeed from Ibn 'Abbaas that when he talked to him about the *Khawaarij* and told him how hard they strove in worship, he (Ibn 'Abbaas) said: "They do not strive harder than the Jews and the Christians in their worship, but still they are misguided."[130] Ṭaawoos narrated from his father that Ibn 'Abbaas mentioned how the *Khawaarij* reacted when they heard the Qur'an (i.e., with humility), then he said: "They are believers when they hear the unambiguous verses but they are doomed when they hear the ambiguous verses."[131] The rest of the *ṣaḥaabah*

---

[130] Ibn Abi Shaybah, 15/313, no. 19737; Al-Laalkaa'i in *Sharḥ as-Sunnah*, 8/1322, hadith no. 2315.

[131] Ibn Abi Shaybah, 15/313, no. 19748.

(Companions of the last Prophet) also spoke a great deal about the *Khawaarij*.

5 - What Ibn 'Abbaas said may also be understood as referring to the *Khawaarij* who denounced people as *kaafir* for every sin. So his comment "a lesser form of *kufr*" could refer to one who judged unjustly, according to something other than that which Allah revealed, in an individual case. This is how it was understood by the scholars, including *Shaykh* Muhammad ibn Ibraaheem and others, as we have quoted from them above.

6 - What has been said concerning the story of Abu Majlaz and the *Ibaaḍiyah*[132] may also be said concerning the words of Ibn 'Abbaas. Indeed, it is more appropriate in this case, because the *Khawaarij* at his time denounced the great and reputed *ṣaḥaabah*, including some of the Rightly-Guided Caliphs (*Al-Khulafa' ar-Raashidoon*), as *kaafir*. Hence *Shaykh* Aḥmad Shaakir co-related the two matters and said, commenting on the report from Ibn 'Abbaas, "These reports — from Ibn 'Abbaas and others — are things with which the misleading elements of our own times are toying, those who claim to have knowledge and those who have the audacity to say things which undermine the principles of Islam. They make these things an excuse to permit the introduction of idolatrous man-made laws which they impose on the Muslim lands.

There is a report from Abu Majlaz concerning the debate which the *Khaariji Ibaaḍiyah* had with him, concerning the unjust actions of some of the governors. In some cases they ruled in a manner that went against the shari'ah, either deliberately because of some whim or desire, or because they were ignorant of the ruling. According to the *madhhab* of the *Khawaarij*, whoever committed a major sin was a *kaafir*, so in their debates with Abu Majlaz, they wanted to make him

[132] See the debate mentioned above, Pp. 210-219.

agree with them in condemning those governors as *kaafir*, because that was their excuse for mounting an armed rebellion against them."[133] Then the *Shaykh* quoted two reports from *Tafseer aṭ-Ṭabari*, and the comments of his brother Maḥmood on them. We have referred to this above.

At the time of Ibn 'Abbaas — whether during the time of 'Ali (رضي الله عنه) or after — there was no one who thought that the Muslims could be ruled by anything other than the shari'ah of Allah, or that anyone could promulgate laws which went against the Qur'an and Sunnah, then force the people to refer to them for judgement. Since this was the case — and the *Khawaarij* were following a wrong method of deriving evidence from the texts, and their understanding was incorrect[134] — Ibn 'Abbaas explained that this *aayah* was not referring to them and that what it referred to was lesser *kufr*.

---

[133] *'Umdat at-Tafseer*, 4/156.

[134] With regard to the mistaken methodology of the *Khawaarij* concerning rulings and that the Decision is only for Allah, *(Qur'an 6: 57)*, etc., see *Al-I'tisaam* by Ash-Shaaṭibi, 1/238, 2/311.

CHAPTER FOUR

EXAMPLES OF THE SCHOLARS' VIEWS ON THOSE WHO ALTER THE LAWS OF ALLAH

In this chapter we will refer to in brief to some of the views of the scholars and how they stood against those who altered and changed the laws of Allah. Even though the Muslim world had not, at that time, gone through the things that it is going through now, where people have turned away from the laws of Allah and are openly replacing them with laws and systems that go against the laws and religion of Allah, the Muslim world has experienced this kind of problem to varying degrees. So what was the ummah's attitude towards these attempts to change the laws of Allah? This is what we shall examine below.

The *Riddah* (Apostasy) Movement

This happened after the death of the Prophet (ﷺ). Bukhari said in his *Ṣaḥeeḥ*: "*Baab Qatl man abaa Qubool al-Faraa'iḍ wa ma nusiboo ila ar-Riddah* (Chapter on Killing those who refuse to accept the obligatory duties and how they were labelled as apostates). Then he narrated, with his isnad, that Abu Hurayrah said: 'When the Prophet (ﷺ) died, and Abu Bakr was appointed as *Khaleefah*, and those Arabs who apostatized did so, 'Umar said: 'O' Abu Bakr, how can you fight the people when the Messenger of Allah (ﷺ) said,

> 'I have been commanded to fight the people until they say, *Laa ilaaha illa-Allah*, and whoever says *Laa ilaaha illa-Allah*, his property and his life are safe from me,

> unless he trespasses the law (he does something for which he receives legal punishment justly), and his account will be with Allah'?'

Abu Bakr said: 'By Allah, I will fight whoever differentiates between Prayer and Zakah, for zakah is the right to be taken from property. By Allah, if they refuse to give me even so much as a kid (young goat) (*i'naaqan*) that they used to give to the Messenger of Allah (ﷺ) (in zakah), I will fight them for withholding it.' 'Umar said: 'By Allah, I could see that Allah had opened Abu Bakr's heart to the idea of fighting, so I realized that he was right.'"[1]

Ibn Ḥajar said: "The fact that he said 'Chapter on Killing those who refuse to accept the obligatory duties' means that it is permissible to kill those who refuse to adhere to the obligatory rulings and follow them. Al-Muhallab said: 'Whoever refuses to accept the obligatory duties, his case should be examined, and if he agrees that zakah is obligatory, for example, it should be taken from him by force, but he should not be killed. But if in addition to refusing to pay he also fights and resists, then he should be fought until he recants. Maalik said in *Al-Muwaṭṭa'*: in our opinion, if people refuse to obey one of the obligatory duties enjoined by Allah, and the Muslims cannot take it from them, then it is their duty to wage jihad against them. Ibn Baṭṭaal said: this applies even if they accept that it is obligatory, and there is no scholarly dispute concerning that."[2]

Al-Baaji said, commenting on the words of Imam Maalik quoted above: "This is as he said: whoever withholds some of the dues of

---

[1] Bukhari: *Kitaab Istitaabah al-Murtaddeen wa'l-Mu'aanideen wa Qitaalihim*, hadith no. 6924, 6925 (*Fatḥ al-Baari*, 12/275, 1st *Salafiyah* edition).

[2] *Fatḥ al-Baari* 12/275-276. What he narrated from Imam Maalik in *Al-Muwaṭṭa'* is in *Kitaab az-Zakaah, Baab maa jaa'a fi Akhdh aṣ-Ṣadaqaat wa't-Tashdeed feehaa*, 1/269, edited by Fu'aad 'Abdul-Baaqi.

Allah concerning which there is no dispute that they are obligatory, the Muslims must wage jihad against him until they take these dues. This is what Abu Bakr did with the apostates (*Ahl ar-Riddah*), especially when they withheld the zakah. It may have meant all the dues concerning which the rulings are the same as the rulings on zakah."[3]

As is well known, the apostates were of various types:

— Those who went back to idol-worship.

— Those who followed the false prophets Al-Aswad, Musaylimah and Sajjaah.

— Those who denied that zakah was obligatory.

— Those who did not deny that it is obligatory but they refused to pay it to Abu Bakr.

The difference of opinion between Abu Bakr and 'Umar — in the beginning — was concerning the fourth category only. With regard to the first three types, there was no dispute concerning that the fact that they were *kuffaar* who must be fought. What these people did was considered by Bukhari to be tampering with the religion and altering its rulings. He said: "The *aimmah* (the most reputed religious scholars, Imams) after the Prophet (ﷺ) used to consult trustworthy scholars concerning permissible matters so that they might adopt the easiest option. But if the Qur'an and Sunnah were clear, they would not look for any other opinion, following the example of the Prophet (ﷺ). Abu Bakr thought that he should fight those who withheld the zakah but 'Umar said, 'How can you fight the people when...' Then 'Umar followed his opinion. Abu Bakr did not resort to consultation, because he had the ruling of the Messenger of Allah (ﷺ) concerning those who differentiated between prayer and zakah, and who wanted to change the religion and its rulings. The Prophet (ﷺ) said:

---

[3] *Al-Muntaqaa* by Abul-Waleed al-Baaji, 2/157.

'Whoever changes his religion, execute him...'"[4]

The point here is not to discuss the issue of *riddah* (apostasy) in detail, but to explain two matters which are relevant to our own discussion:

1- The consensus of the *ṣaḥaabah* that those who withheld the zakah were to be fought. They did not differ concerning this matter, which indicates that the one who refuses to carry out one of the obligatory duties of Islam is to be fought.

Whether these people are judged to be *kaafir* or not, this is an indication of how serious the matter is. This is the case when the people agree to reject one of the rulings of Allah, so how about when they cast aside the entire shari'ah of Allah and replace it with man-made laws?

2- With regard to whether or not one who refuses to pay zakah although he believes that it is obligatory is a *kaafir*, this is a well-known controversy. It is narrated that when the delegation of Buzaakhah came to Abu Bakr seeking peace, after he had fought them, he gave them the choice between all-out war or a humiliating peace. They said, 'We know what all-out war means, but what is this humiliating peace?' He said, 'We will take away from you your weapons and horses, we will keep as booty that which we have taken from you, but you will have to return to us that which you have taken from us, you will have to pay us blood money for our slain, but your slain are in Hell...'[5] Those who thought that they were apostates

---

[4] Bukhari: *Kitaab al-I'tiṣaam bil-Kitaab was-Sunnah, Baab Qawl Allah: "wa amruhum shoora baynahum"* (*Fatḥ al-Baari* 13/339), 1st *Salafiyah* edition.

[5] Al-Burqaani in his *Mustakhraj*, and quoted from him by Al-Ḥumaydi in *Al-Jama' bayna aṣ-Ṣaḥeeḥayn*, 1/96, hadith no. 17, edited by 'Ali Ḥusayn al-Bawwaab, 1st edition, 1419 AH. A shorter version is narrated by Bukhari: *Kitaab al-Aḥkaam, Baab al-Istikhlaaf*, no. 7221 (*Fatḥ al-Baari*, 13/206, 210), 1st *Salafiyah* edition.

quoted this as evidence, but it is said in *Al-Mughni* that this evidence was open to interpretation; it could be understood as meaning that they were apostates (even if they believed that zakah was obligatory), or it could be understood as meaning that they denied that zakah is obligatory, etc..."[6]

There are two views narrated from Imam Aḥmad concerning this matter. Al-Qaaḍi Abu Ya'laa said concerning the two reports and the two views: "There are different reports from Aḥmad (may Allah have mercy on him) concerning those who believe that zakah is obligatory, but refuse to pay and fight for that purpose — are they to be denounced as *kaafir*? Al-Maymooni narrated concerning those who withhold the zakah and fight for that purpose — as they refused to pay it to Abu Bakr and fought him for that purpose — that no one should inherit from them and the funeral prayer should not be offered for them (i.e., they are not Muslim). Whoever withholds it because of stinginess or negligence, but does not fight for not paying it, may be inherited from and the funeral prayer may be offered for him (i.e., he is a Muslim). The apparent meaning of this is that if they fight for the purpose of withholding it, then they become *kaafir* by doing that, because Abu Bakr (عنه) stated definitively that those who withheld the zakah were *kaafir*, and said, 'No, not until they bear witness that their slain are in Hell.'

Al-Athram said, concerning the question whether those who do not fast in Ramaḍaan are like those who do not pray, 'Prayer is more important, it is not like other things.' It was said to him, '(What about) the one who does not pay zakah?' He said, 'It is narrated from 'Abdullah[7] that the one who does not pray is not a Muslim. Abu Bakr

---

[6] *Al-Mughni* by Ibn Qudaamah, 4/9.

[7] This means Ibn Mas'ood. This report is narrated from him by Ibn Abi Shaybah in *Al-Muṣanaaf*, 3/114. See also *Al-Mughni*, 4/9.

fought them for not paying zakah (obligatory charity, one of the pillars of Islam), but the hadith is about prayer.'

From this it seems that he narrated what 'Abdullah said and what Abu Bakr did, but he did not give a definitive verdict on this matter, because he said, "the hadith is about prayer" — the hadith which was narrated concerning their being *kaafir*. The Prophet (ﷺ) said:

> 'Between a person and *kufr* there stands his giving up prayer. Whoever gives up prayer becomes a *kaafir*.'[8]

Zakah is something which is an obligation upon people's wealth; they do not become *kaafir* by withholding it and fighting for that purpose, as is the case with not paying *kafaarah* (expiation) and things owed to other people."[9]

These two reports were referred to by *Shaykh al-Islam* Ibn Taymiyah (may Allah's mercy be upon him) when he discussed this topic; he mentioned that there were also two scholarly views.[10] The two reports were also quoted and discussed in detail by the author of *Al-Mughni*. It appears that he thought it more likely that this does not make one a *kaafir* (disbeliever), as is indicated by the context of his comments, his discussion of the evidence for this view, and his response to the evidence of those who say that it does make one a *kaafir*.[11] What Ibn Taymiyah thought more likely to be correct is that if it is a group who is refusing to pay zakah and is fighting for that purpose, then they are to be regarded as *kaafir*, because of what Abu Bakr did with the apostates (*Ahl ar-Riddah*) when the *ṣaḥaabah* did

---

[8] Muslim: *Al-Eemaan, Baab Iṭlaaq Ism al-Kufr 'ala Taarik aṣ-Ṣalaah*, hadith no. 82.

[9] *Kitaab ar-Riwaayatayn wal-Wajhayn* by Abu Ya'laa, 1/221-222, edited by 'Abdul-Kareem al-Laaḥim.

[10] *Majmoo' al-Fataawa*, 28/518, 35/57.

[11] *Al-Mughni*, 4/8, 9.

not differentiate between those who were withholding their zakah and others.

With regard to the difference of opinion mentioned by the *fuqahaa'* (scholars of Islamic jurisprudence), this has to do with individuals who withhold their zakah but do not fight. There is evidence to support that view, that such a person is not a *kaafir*, for example: "We are going to take it and half of his wealth," and the hadith, "What is wrong with Ibn Jameel...?" etc.

In order to explain the matter further, I will quote what *Shaykh al-Islam* Ibn Taymiyah said, which will explain what is meant. He (may Allah have mercy on him) said: "The *ṣaḥaabah* and the *aimmah* (the reputed jurists) after them were agreed that those who withhold the zakah should be fought, even if they pray the five daily prayers and fast the month of Ramaḍaan, for such people do not have any justifiable reason, and hence they are apostates; they should be fought for withholding their zakah even if they state that it is obligatory as enjoined by Allah. It is narrated that they said: 'Allah commanded His Prophet to take the zakah when He said,

﴿خُذْ مِنْ أَمْوَٰلِهِمْ صَدَقَةً ... ﴿١٠٣﴾﴾

﴾Take *Ṣadaqah* [alms] from their wealth...﴿
(Qur'an 9: 103),

— but now that he has died this no longer applies.'"[12] And he also said: "With regard to fighting the *Khawaarij*, those who withheld their zakah and the people of Aṭ-Ṭaa'if who did not give up dealing in *riba*, such people are to be fought until they implement all the rulings that were proven from the Prophet (ﷺ). If they form a group and refuse to implement (some aspects of shari'ah), there is no doubt that

---

[12] *Majmoo' al-Fataawa*, 28/519.

it is permissible to kill their prisoners, pursue those who flee the battlefield, finish off their wounded, and if they stayed in their own land doing what they were doing, it would be obligatory upon the Muslims to go to where they are and fight them until they submit completely..."[13]

One of the clearest comments that I have seen from Ibn Taymiyah is that which was quoted from him in *Ad-Durar as-Sanniyah*: "The *Ṣaḥaabah* did not ask, 'Do you believe that it is obligatory or do you deny that?' Such a thing was not known among the *ṣaḥaabah* at all. Rather *aṣ-ṣiddeeq* (Abu Bakr) said to 'Umar: 'By Allah, if they refuse to give me even so much as a kid (young goat) that they used to give to the Messenger of Allah (ﷺ), I will fight them for withholding it.'" So his view was that simply refusing to pay — not denying that it is obligatory — was grounds for fighting them. It is narrated that some groups among them used to believe that it was obligatory, but they were too stingy to pay. Nevertheless, the way in which all the *khulafaa'* dealt with them was the same, that is, to kill their fighting men, take their women and children prisoner, seize their wealth as booty and they testify that their slain were in Hell. They called all of them *Ahl ar-Riddah* (apostates). One of the greatest virtues of *aṣ-ṣiddeeq* (Abu Bakr) was that Allah made him steadfast in fighting them and he did not hesitate as others did, debating with them until they agreed with him. With regard to those who affirmed the prophethood of Musaylimah, there was no dispute that it was obligatory to fight them. This is the evidence of those scholars who said that if they (those who withhold the zakah) fight the *khaleefah* they become *kaafir*, otherwise they do not. The labelling of these people as *kaafir* and their inclusion among the apostates was approved by the *ṣaḥaabah* on the basis of the texts of the Qur'an and

---

[13] *Majmoo' al-Fataawa*, 28/551.

Sunnah, unlike those who did not fight the *khaleefah* for this reason. It is narrated in *Aṣ-Ṣaḥeeḥ* (Bukhari) that it was said to the Prophet (ﷺ), "Ibn Jameel is withholding (his zakah)." He said, "All that is wrong with Ibn Jameel is that he was poor and Allah made him rich." He did not issue orders that he be killed, nor did he state that he was a *kaafir*. In *As-Sunan* it is narrated from Bahz ibn Ḥakeem from his father from his grandfather that the Prophet (ﷺ) said:

> "Whoever withholds it (zakah), we will take it and half of his wealth..."[14]

I want to explain something which was referred to by Ibn Taymiyah in one of the above quotations from him, where he mentions the people of Aṭ-Ṭaa'if and how they did not give up dealing in *riba*. He explained this elsewhere, and because it is relevant to our discussion, we will quote it here. He said, in response to (a question) about the Tartars: "Fighting the Tartars who have come to Syria is obligatory according to the Qur'an and Sunnah. Allah (ﷻ) the Exalted, All-Powerful, says in the Qur'an:

﴿ وَقَٰتِلُوهُمْ حَتَّىٰ لَا تَكُونَ فِتْنَةٌ وَيَكُونَ ٱلدِّينُ كُلُّهُۥ لِلَّهِ ... ﴿٣٩﴾ ﴾

> ﴾And fight them until there is no more *fitnah* [disbelief and polytheism, i.e. worshipping others besides Allah], and the religion [worship] will all be for Allah Alone...﴿
>
> *(Qur'an 8: 39)*

Religion here means obedience, so if part of the religion is for Allah and part is for someone other than Allah, then it is obligatory to fight them until the religion is all for Allah. Hence Allah (ﷻ) says:

---

[14] *Ad-Durar as-Sanniyah*, 8/131, from a letter to *Shaykh* 'Abdullah ibn Muhammad ibn 'Abdul-Wahhaab (may Allah have mercy on him).

﴿ يَٰٓأَيُّهَا ٱلَّذِينَ ءَامَنُوا۟ ٱتَّقُوا۟ ٱللَّهَ وَذَرُوا۟ مَا بَقِىَ مِنَ ٱلرِّبَوٰٓا۟ إِن كُنتُم مُّؤْمِنِينَ ﴿٢٧٨﴾ فَإِن لَّمْ تَفْعَلُوا۟ فَأْذَنُوا۟ بِحَرْبٍ مِّنَ ٱللَّهِ وَرَسُولِهِۦ ... ﴿٢٧٩﴾ ﴾

﴿O' you who believe! Be afraid of Allah and give up what remains [due to you] from *riba* [from now onward] if you are [really] believers. And if you do not do it, then take a notice of war from Allah and His Messenger...﴾ *(Qur'an 2: 278-279)*

This *aayah* was revealed concerning the people of Aṭ-Ṭaa'if, when they entered Islam and observed prayer and fasting, but they refused to give up *riba*. Allah explained that they would be at war with Him and His Messenger if they did not give up *riba*. *Riba* is the last of the things that Allah forbade; it means money which is taken with the owner's consent. If these people were in a state of war with Allah and His Messenger and it is obligatory to wage jihad against them, then how about those who ignore many or most of the laws of Islam, such as the Tartars?"[15]

In conclusion, the *ṣaḥaabah* were unanimous that in the case of those who withheld zakah — including those who did not deny that it was obligatory — it was obligatory to fight them and that they were apostates, but this does not apply unless the following two conditions are also met:

a) That they form a group which is refusing to pay zakah.
b) That they are fighting the *khaleefah* (Caliphs) for the purpose of withholding it.

If these two conditions are present, then all the *ṣaḥaabah* ruled that they are apostates.

[15] *Majmoo' al-Fataawa*, 28/544. Concerning the reason for revelation of the *aayah*, see *Tafseer aṭ-Ṭabari*, 6/23, edited by Shaakir; *Tafseer Ibn Katheer*, 1/489-490, published by Ash-Sha'b.

This issue explains what was mentioned above about judging or ruling by something other than that which Allah has revealed, where a distinction is made between individual cases and cases where a general system is imposed upon a society as a whole. The two issues are similar. The ruling of *kufr* and apostasy may be applied to the one who does that, but this is subject to certain conditions.

The scholars often point out the difference between individuals and groups, between individual cases and things that affect the whole ummah. Ibn Taymiyah said concerning the obligation of fighting the extreme Raafidis and those who exaggerate about their *shaykhs* etc., "All of these people are *kaafir* and must be fought according to the consensus of the Muslims; individuals must be killed when it is possible to do so. But with regard to killing individuals from among the *Khawaarij* and *Raafiḍis* when it is possible to do so, it is narrated from them — i.e., 'Umar and 'Ali — that they should also be killed. Although the *fuqaha'* differed concerning killing individuals from among these groups when it is possible to do so, they did not dispute that it is obligatory to fight them if they are rebels. And fighting is broader in meaning than killing..."[16]

This is a very important guideline concerning this matter and others. The *ṣaḥaabah's* ruling that those who withheld their zakah were apostates — without differentiating between those who believed it to be obligatory and those who did not — was based on this principle.

There remains another issue connected to those who withheld their zakah, which was often quoted as proof by those who have a different opinion. They say that during his reign as *khaleefah*, 'Umar ibn al-Khaṭṭaab (رضي الله عنه) went back on his first opinion that those who withheld their zakah were *kaafir* whose children could be taken prisoner and whose wealth could be kept as war-booty, because he returned to

[16] *Majmoo' al-Fataawa*, 28/475-476.

them that which he had taken from them; on this basis it is not correct to say that there was consensus among the *ṣaḥaabah* [Companions of the Prophet (ﷺ)] concerning that.

This issue confused me for a long time, until I came across an answer given by Ibn Taymiyah concerning this matter.

This specious argument was mentioned by the *Raafiḍi* author of *Minhaaj al-Karaamah*, where in a discussion of the differences of opinion that arose among the *ṣaḥaabah*, he said: "The sixth difference of opinion was concerning those who withheld their zakah. Abu Bakr fought them, and 'Umar reviewed their case during the days of his reign as *khaleefah*, then he returned the prisoners and property to them, and released the detainees." Ibn Taymiyah refuted this by saying:

"This is a lie, as is obvious to anyone who knows about the circumstances of the Muslims. Abu Bakr and 'Umar were agreed that those who withheld the zakah were to be fought, after 'Umar had discussed the matter with Abu Bakr, as is narrated in *Aṣ-Ṣaḥeeḥayn* (Bukhari and Muslim). So 'Umar agreed with Abu Bakr that the apostates who withheld the zakah were to be fought, and all the *ṣaḥaabah* agreed with that. Then those people agreed to pay the zakah after having withheld it, and their women and children were not taken prisoner, neither were any of them detained. There was no prison in Madeenah, either during the time of the Messenger (ﷺ) or the time of Abu Bakr, so how could he have died whilst they were being detained by him? The first prison in Islam was in Makkah, where 'Umar bought the house of Safwaan ibn Umayyah and made it into a prison.

But there are some people who say: Abu Bakr took their women and children prisoner, then 'Umar returned them to them. Even if this did happen, it does not show that there was a difference of opinion concerning them. It may be that 'Umar agreed that it was permissible to take their women and children prisoner, but he returned the prisoners to them just as the Prophet (ﷺ) returned the women and children of Hawaazin to them after they had been divided among the Muslims; whoever was willing to return them did so, otherwise the Prophet (ﷺ) commanded that they be returned to them and he offered compensation for that. That was when Hawaazin came to the Prophet (ﷺ) declaring their Islam and demanding that their families be returned to them.

Abu Bakr, 'Umar and all the *ṣaḥaabah* were unanimous that the apostates should not be allowed to ride horses or bear arms, rather they should be left to engage in agricultural pursuits until Allah showed the successor to His Messenger and the believers that they were indeed good Muslims.[17] When it became clear to 'Umar that they were now good Muslims, he returned the prisoners (their women and children) to them because it was permissible to do so."[18]

We have dwelt at length on this point — the attitude of the *ṣaḥaabah* towards fighting the apostates, including those who withheld the zakah — because this is considered to be the first movement to turn away from Islam and tried to change the religion and its rulings, as is stated by Bukhari (may Allah have mercy on him).

The *Yaasiq* of the Tartars and Ibn Taymiyah

This is one of the important issues that characterized the time of *Shaykh al-Islam* Ibn Taymiyah and made it distinct from the preceding eras. From the beginning of Islam, and as the religion spread in the conquered lands, the Muslims had never known any system or rule other than that which was brought by the shari'ah of

---

[17] Bukhari: *Kitaab al-Aḥkaam, Baab al-Istikhlaaf*, hadith no. 7221. See also *Fatḥ al-Baari*, 13/210, 1st *Salafiyah* edition.

[18] *Minhaaj as-Sunnah*, 6/347-349.

Islam. This does not mean that injustice or oppression never happened, or that blood was never shed and property was never seized wrongfully. There was injustice on the part of some rulers — during Umawi and 'Abbaasi times, and others — and there was a great deal of oppression on the part of rulers and others in positions of authority. There were trials and tribulations in various regions of the Muslim world, as is detailed in the books of history written by Muslim historians. But despite all that, these things happened with the knowledge that they were against Islam and were the result of whims and desires, a wish for vengeance, or other reasons, and when a new, just ruler came to power, he would set matters straight and restore people's rights in accordance with Islamic shari'ah. The view of *Ahl as-Sunnah wal-Jamaa'ah* is that it is not permitted to rebel against the rulers even if they are unjust. This acknowledges that oppression and injustice may occur, but if they do occur, it is not permissible to take that as an excuse to rebel against them and to stop obeying them, unless they commit acts of blatant *kufr*.

But to have a system of law which goes against shari'ah, and to have a group or state referring to it for judgement, even though they call themselves Muslims — this is something which never happened except in the period which we are discussing here. If there were some groups who ruled over some parts of the Muslim world and imposed beliefs and promulgated laws which went against Islam, these groups were beyond the pale of Islam, such as the *'Ubaydiyah* (*'Faaṭimiyah'* — the Fatimids) of whom Ibn Taymiyah said:

"For nearly two hundred years, Cairo was ruled by something other than the shari'ah of Islam; its rulers were outwardly *Raafiḍis*, but inwardly they were *baaṭini Ismaa'eelis, Nuṣayris, Qaraamiṭah*. As Al-Ghazaali (may Allah have mercy on him) said in his book which he wrote to refute them: 'Outwardly they follow the way of *Ar-Rafḍ*, but inwardly it is pure *kufr*.'

All the various groups of Muslims, their scholars, kings and common folk, Ḥanafis, Maalikis, Shaaf'is and Ḥanbalis and others are unanimous that they were beyond the pale of Islam and that fighting them was permissible. Indeed they stated that their claims of descent from Faaṭimah were false... The *Ismaa'eelis, Nuṣayris, Druze* etc. who were present in the Muslim lands were the ones who helped the Tartars to fight the Muslims.[19] The adviser of Hulagu, An-Naṣeer aṭ-Ṭoosi, was one of their Imams."[20]

This new development which appeared at this time came with the emergence of the Tartars and their attacks on the Islamic world. These Tartars were governed by a system and law which had been set out for them by their leader Genghis Khan, and was known as *Al-Yaasaa* or *Al-Yaasiq*. They used to apply this law in totality, and it became sacred to them. During their attacks on the Muslims they carried it with them and followed it.

The word *Yaasaa* - which also appears as *Yaasah*, *Yasaaq* or *Yasaq*[21] — is a Mongol (Turkish) word which means the laws of the Tartars set out by their leader.

---

[19] It is amazing - when Ibn Taymiyah was referring to the cooperation of the *Raafiḍis* with the Tartars - that in the texts of the Tartar law, the *Yaasiq*, parts of which were quoted by Al-Maqreezi in his MS, there are clauses which say that preferential treatment is to be given to the children of 'Ali ibn Abi Ṭaalib (رضي الله عنه), and that no hardships or tasks are to be imposed on them. It says: "And the condition is that no hardships or tasks are to be imposed on any of the children of 'Ali ibn Abi Ṭaalib (رضي الله عنه)." MSS 2/220, *Boolaaq* edition.

[20] *Majmoo' al-Fataawa*, 28/635-636.

[21] In *Taaj al-'Aroos* (7/98), it adds in the section on " *yaa*' with *qaaf* ": the word *Yasaaq* may also be pronounced as *yasaq*, without the long *alif*. The word was originally *yasaagh*, with a *ghayn*, which may be changed to a *qaaf*. This is a Turkish word which means setting out laws governing dealings between people. Because most of the punishments dictated in the system of the *Yaasaa* were death, the word came to be known as synonymous with killing or death. See *Al-Mughul fil-Taareekh*, 1/338.

Al-Maqreezi said — in his discussion of the role of the *ḥaajibs* (literally the gatekeepers of the rulers) of his period — that "the task of the person who held such a position was to judge between the commanders and soldiers, sometimes acting on his own initiative and sometimes in consultation with the ruler or his deputy. But the judgement of the *ḥaajib* did not go beyond the soldiers' disputes and differences among them concerning allocation of land and the like. None of the *ḥaajibs* in the past interfered in passing judgement concerning matters of shari'ah such as disputes between spouses or between lenders and debtors. They would refer such matters to the *qaaḍis* (judges) of shari'ah. It was usually the case that one of the scribes or guarantors would try to run from the door of the *ḥaajib*, trying to reach the door of one of the qaadis, seeking their ruling of shari'ah, after which no one would be able to take him from the door of the *qaaḍi*..."[22]

Then Al-Maqreezi mentioned the subsequent developments in the role of the *ḥaajib*. He said: "Then all that changed, so that now[23] the name of *ḥaajib* is applied to many of the commanders who have set themselves up to pass judgement among the people... Nowadays the *ḥaajib* passes judgement on any major or minor issue among the people, whether the ruling is according to shari'ah or according to *'siyaasah'* as they claim. If any of the *qaaḍis* of shari'ah tries to take the plaintiff away from the *ḥaajib*, he will not be able to do that."[24] Then he said: "The rulings of the *ḥaajibs* were the first to be described as the ruling of *siyaasah*.' This is a devilish term, the origins of which most people do not know, and they use it without

---

[22] *Al-Khuṭaṭ*, 2/219, *Boolaaq* edition.

[23] Al-Maqreezi died in 845 AH. His full name was Taqiy ad-Deen Abul-'Abbaas Aḥmad ibn 'Ali; he was born in 766 AH. See *Aḍ-Ḍaw' al-Laami'*, 2/21; *Al-Badr aṭ-Ṭaali'*, 1/79; *Al-A'laam*, 1/177.

[24] *Al-Khuṭaṭ*, 2/219,220.

thinking. They say, 'This matter could not be resolved on the basis of the rulings of shari'ah, so it is one of the rulings of *siyaasah*.' They count it a little thing, while with Allah it is very great (i.e., serious, cf. *Qur'an 24: 15)*."

Then Al-Maqreezi discussed the meaning of *shar'* and of *siyaasah* in the Arabic language. He states that *siyaasah* is of two types: *siyaasah 'aadilah* or just *siyaasah*, which is the *siyaasah* of shari'ah, on which many books have been written, and *siyaasah ẓaalimah* or oppressive *siyaasah*, which is forbidden by shari'ah. Then he discussed the origins of this word and the mistaken belief of those who think that it is originally an Arabic word. He said: "What the people of our own times say concerning that is not true at all. Rather it is a verb which was originally *yaasah*, then the people of Egypt changed it and added the letter seen to the beginning, so they said *siyaasah*. Then they added the definite article *al-* to it, so that those who have no knowledge think that it is an Arabic word, but the matter is no more than what I have mentioned. Look now at how this word has spread until it is well known in Egypt and Syria. That is because when Genghis Khan, the leader of the Tartar state in the east, defeated the king Ong Khan, and he developed an empire, he established principles and punishments which he wrote down in a book called *Yaasah*, which some people call *Yasaq*, although it is originally *Yaasah*. When he had finished writing it, he had it engraved on steel plates, and he made it a law for his people. They adhered to that after he died, until Allah destroyed them. Genghis Khan did not follow any of the religions of the people of earth, as you will know if you have any knowledge of their history. The *Yaasah* continued to govern the subsequent generations and they never deviated from his rulings."[25]

---

[25] *Al-Khuṭaṭ*, 2/220.

Al-Qalqashandi [26] narrated that 'Ala ad-Deen al-Juwayni [27] — who was one of the closest scribes to the Tartar leader Arghoon, during whose time Halagu's attack on Baghdaad took place — said: "Among the customs of the people of Genghis Khan is that everyone among them who follows a particular religion will not be denounced by another for that."[28] Then Al-Qalqashandi mentioned the *Yaasah* and said: "Then the way that was followed by Genghis Khan was followed by the subsequent generations, who adhered to the *Yaasah* that he had written. This is composed of laws which he formed from his own ideas, in which he stipulated rulings and punishments, very few of which are in accordance with the shari'ah of Muhammad, and most of which go against that. He called it *Al-Yaasah al-Kubra* (the greater *Yaasah*), which he wrote down and issued orders that it was to be placed in a chest which would be inherited by subsequent generations and be taught to the children of his household."[29]

Ibn Katheer said: "With regard to his book *Al-Yaasah*, it is written in two volumes in a large hand, and carried on a camel with them."[30]

---

[26] Aḥmad ibn 'Ali ibn Aḥmad al-Fazaari, b. 756 AH, d. 821 AH. *Aḍ-Ḍaw' al-Laami'*, 2/8; *Al-A'laam*, 1/177.

[27] 'Ala' ad-Deen 'Ata' Malik al-Juwayni. He and his father worked for the Mongols. He was born in 623 AH and died in 686 AH. *Ad-Dawlah al-Ismaa'eeliyah fil-Iran*, Pp. 127-138. Al-Juwayni was one of those who wrote the history of the Mongols. Many historians relied on his writings and on the writings of another historian, Rasheed ad-Deen, when writing the history of the Mongols, including Ibn Katheer in his biography of Genghis Khan, in *Al-Bidaayah wan-Nihaayah*, 13/117.

[28] *Subḥ al-A'sha*, 4/310. See a further explanation of this in the history written by 'Ata' Malik al-Juwayni himself, which is entitled *Taareekh Faatiḥ al-'Aalam Jahaankuashay*, 1/62-63, translated and edited by Dr. Muhammad at-Tuwanji, 1st edition, 1405 AH/1985 CE, *Daar al-Malaaḥ* publishers.

[29] Ibid, 4/310-311. For more details on the development of this law, see the book by Al-Juwayni - *Taareekh Faatiḥ al-'Aalam*, 1/61-68.

[30] *Al-Bidaayah wan-Nihaayah*, 13/118.

Among the laws of this *Yaasah* are the following: "Whoever commits adultery is to be killed — and no differentiation is made between a married and an unmarried adulterer. Whoever commits sodomy is to be killed. Whoever deliberately tells a lie, practises magic, spies on anyone, or interferes between two people who are arguing and helps one of them against the other, is to be killed. Whoever urinates into water or onto ashes is to be killed. Whoever is given some trade goods and makes a loss on them is to be killed if this happens the third time. Whoever feeds or clothes the prisoner of some people without their permission is to be killed... Whoever slaughters an animal in the manner of the Muslims is to be slaughtered [31]... He enjoined respect for all religions, without being devoted to any one of them rather than another... He enjoined upon them that no one should put his hand into water, but should drink water by using something to scoop it up. He forbade them to wash their clothes, and said that they should wear them until they wore out.[32] He forbade calling anything impure *najis*, and said: all things are pure. He did not differentiate between pure and impure, and he forced them not to be devoted to any one sect."[33] It is worth noting that among these laws was one which stipulated that the ruler had to establish a mail system so that news of the kingdom might be gathered quickly.[34]

This was the system of the *Yaasah* which was established by the leader of the Tartars. "When he died, those who came after him, his children and followers, adhered to the ruling of the *Yaasah* just as the

---

[31] See some of these strange laws in *Taareekh 'Ataa' Malik al-Juwayni*, 1/191, 248.

[32] Ibid.

[33] *Al-Khuṭaṭ* , 2/220-221.

[34] Ibid. It is also worth noting that at the end of the 'Abbaasi (Abassid) period, the mail system was abolished. This was one of the factors which helped to weaken resistance against the Tartars.

early Muslims adhered to the ruling of the Qur'an. They made that a religion which none of them opposed in any way."[35]

This was the system which the Tartars followed when they attacked the Muslim world, but an important development occurred, many of them entered Islam and their leader, Qaazaan, declared his Islam. But their claim to be Muslim was accompanied by a number of things which were contrary to the behaviour expected of a Muslim, for example:

a) Their attacks against the Muslim lands in Syria and elsewhere, when they fought the Muslims, confiscated their wealth and committed other acts of mischief.

b) Their veneration of their *Yaasiq* system, and their implementation of some of its clauses even though they went against Islamic shari'ah.

c) Their failure to implement some of the laws of Islam, such as establishing regular prayer, paying the zakah, refraining from shedding the blood of the Muslims, imposing the jizyah on the Jews and the Christians, etc.

d) Approving evil things such as taverns and brothels, and allowing the Christians to display their crosses openly, as happened in *Bayt al-Maqdis* (Jerusalem) and *Al-Khaleel* (Hebron) at the time of the Tartars.

Despite this they declared that they were Muslims and affirmed the *Shahaadatayn*. Indeed, Qaazaan claimed in his letters to sultan An-Naaṣir Qalaaqoon that they were all of one religion, Allah had honoured them the religion of Islam, and that he had defended the people of Mardeen when they were attacked by some of the Mamlook troops, and the only reason why he had done so was for the

---

[35] *Al-Khuṭaṭ*, 2/221.

purpose of Islamic solidarity. In another letter which he wrote when he took over Damascus, he accused the rulers of Egypt and Syria of deviating from the religion and not adhering to the rulings of Islam.[36]

Because of these circumstances and claims, and because of the outbreak of war between the people of Syria and the Tartars, people became confused. How could they fight the Tartars when they claimed to be Muslims and proclaimed the *Shahaadatayn*?[37] This confusion was not restricted to the common folk; the scholars and *fuqaha'* were also confused. The matter needed someone to explain the ruling on this real-life issue, and to explain the truth concerning it, so that the people might be guided. Among those who were asked to do so and who came forward to explain this matter was *Shaykh al-Islam* Ibn Taymiyah (may Allah have mercy on him), who dealt with the matter from two angles:

The theoretical angle

He explained the ruling on these Tartars. A number of questions were directed to Ibn Taymiyah concerning these people who proclaimed the *Shahaadatayn* but killed the Muslims and took prisoner some of the women and children of the Muslims, and violated the things that Islam held sacred, by humiliating the Muslims and desecrating the mosques, especially *Bayt al-Maqdis* (Jerusalem)... and at the same time, some Muslims claimed that it was *ḥaraam* to fight the Tartar fighters because they claimed in principle to be Muslim — so was it permissible to fight them?

In another question, in addition to the above (it was asked): what is the ruling on those who are among their soldiers and claim to have

---

[36] See the letters of Qaazaan to An-Naaṣir Qalaawoon and his responses to them in *Wathaa'iq al-Ḥuroob aṣ-Ṣaleebiyah wal-Ghazw al-Mughooli*, Pp. 383-403.

[37] *Shahaadatayn*: Declaration and witnessing the two things that (a) there is no god/deity but Allah alone and (b) Muhammad is Allah's messenger.

knowledge and understanding (of Islam), or claim to be mystics or Sufis, and so on? What may be said concerning those who claim that the Tartars are Muslims, and that the ones who are fighting them are Muslims, and both parties are wrongdoers so we should not fight on either side?... Give us a clear detailed answer that will help us, for this matter is confusing to many of the Muslims, indeed for most of them, either because they do not know how these people really are or because they do not know the ruling of Allah and His Messenger (ﷺ) concerning such people.

In another question, he was asked about the troops who refused to fight the Tartars, saying that among them were those who were forced to march with them, and if anyone deserted the battlefield should he be pursued?

In another question, he was asked about their wealth — was it permitted or forbidden to confiscate it?

Ibn Taymiyah answered these questions with all clarity, based on an important principle which everyone who is in a position to issue *fatwa* (the religious verdict on particular issue/s) — especially concerning new issues — should adhere to.

In one of his answers, he said: "Yes, it is obligatory to fight these people, according to the Book of Allah and the Sunnah of His Messenger, and the consensus of the *aimmah* (the most reputed Muslim jurists) of the Muslims. This is based on two principles:

i) Knowledge of how they are.
ii) Knowledge of the ruling of Allah concerning such people.

With regard to the first (principle): everyone who mixes with these people knows what they are, and those who do not mix with them know what they are through the well-established reports and reports of truthful people that he hears. We will discuss what they are in some detail, after we explain another principle which is only for people who understand the Islamic shari'ah to know. We say: every group which rebels against one of the clear, well-established issues of Islam must be fought, according to the consensus of the *aimmah* (the most reputed Muslim jurists) of the Muslims, even if they have uttered the *Shahaadatayn*. If they affirm the *Shahaadatayn* but refuse to pray the five daily prayers, then they must be fought until they do pray; if they refuse to pay zakah, they must be fought until they do pray zakah. The same applies if they refuse to fast the month of Ramaḍaan or to perform pilgrimage to the Ancient House (Ka'bah), or if they refuse to accept that immoral actions, *zina*, gambling, wine, or other things that are prohibited by shari'ah are *ḥaraam*. The same applies if they refuse to follow the ruling of the Qur'an and Sunnah concerning people's blood, property, honour and wounds, etc. The same applies if they refuse to enjoin what is good and forbid what is evil, or to engage in jihad against the *kuffaar* until they submit and pay the *jizyah* with willing submission, and feel themselves subdued *(cf. Qur'an 9: 29)*. The same applies if they openly practise *bid'ahs* (innovations) which go against the Qur'an and Sunnah and the way of the early generation of this ummah and their leaders, such as openly denying (or uttering impious words against) the names and signs of Allah *(cf. Qur'an 7: 180)*, or disbelieving in the names and attributes of Allah, or disbelieving in His will and decree, or disbelieving in that which was followed by the majority of the Muslims at the time of the Rightly-Guided *Khulafah* (Caliphs), or slandering the first Muslims, the *muhaajireen* and Anṣaar, and those who followed them in truth, or fighting the Muslims until they are forced to obey them, which implies that they must be deviating from the laws of Islam, and other similar matters..."[38]

---

[38] *Majmoo' al-Fataawa*, 28/510-511.

Then he mentioned the evidence from the Qur'an and Sunnah, and the way in which the *ṣaḥaabah* dealt with the apostates, *Khawaarij* and others. Then he said: "The last principle is to know how they (i.e. the Tartars) are. It is known that they attacked Syria for the first time in 699 (AH), and they gave the people assurances of safety which were proclaimed from the minbar in Damascus, despite that they took some of the women and children of the Muslims as prisoners, and it is said that the number reached one hundred thousand or more. What they did in *Bayt al-Maqdis, Jabal aṣ-Ṣaaliḥiyah, Nablus, Ḥomṣ, Daariya* and elsewhere of killing and taking prisoners, only Allah knows. It is said that they took nearly one hundred thousand Muslim prisoners, and they raped the righteous Muslim women in the mosques and elsewhere, such as in *Al-Masjid al-Aqṣa* (in Jerusalem) and *Al-Masjid al-Umawi* (the Umayyad Mosque, in Damascus) and elsewhere, and they reduced to rubble the mosque which used to be in 'Uqaybah.

We have seen the troops of these people, and we saw that most of them do not pray. We have never seen a *muadh-dhin* or an Imam in their camp. What they have taken of the property of the Muslims, and their women and children, and what they have destroyed of their lands, only Allah knows... They are fighting to establish the kingdom of Genghis Khan, and whoever obeys them they take as a friend, even if he is a *kaafir*, and whoever does not obey them, they take him as an enemy, even if he is one of the best of the Muslims. They are not fighting for the sake of Islam and they do not impose *jizyah* or subdue (the People of the Book)."[39]

Then he explained how they venerated Genghis Khan and compared him to the Prophet (ﷺ), and regarded his teachings as sacred, then he said: "It is well known in the religion of Islam, that no Muslim has

---

[39] *Majmoo' al-Fataawa*, 28/519-521.

any excuse for not knowing, that whoever justifies following any religion other than the religion of Islam is a *kaafir*. This is like the *kufr* of one who believes in part of the Book and disbelieves in part of the Book."[40] Then he spoke of their advisors, and how they manifest their *Raafiḍi* beliefs, then he answered the rest of the questions and confusing issues.[41]

This is the first angle. The second angle is the practical angle.

The practical angle

This took the form of urging jihad against these Tartars and declaring war against them. He travelled from Syria to Egypt in order to meet the sultan and his governors and advisors in order to urge them to engage in jihad against them and to gather armies to fight them. Ibn Taymiyah played a leading role in this jihad and in the preparations for it, and he led some of the troops himself, as is well known.

Ibn Katheer (may Allah have mercy on him) also referred to this issue — the issue of the confusion about fighting the Tartars who claimed to be Muslim. He discussed a little about how they were, and he said concerning the battle of Shaqhab: "The people spoke about fighting these Tartars and asked of what type it is, for they make an outward show of Islam and they are not rebelling against the *khaleefah* because they never promised to obey him at one time and then rebelled against him. *Shaykh* Taqiy ad-Deen (Ibn Taymiyah) said: 'They are like the *Khawaarij* who rebelled against 'Ali and Mu'aawiyah, and thought that they were more entitled to be in a position of authority than them. They claim that they are more entitled to be in a position of authority than the Muslims, and they criticize the Muslims for the sins and wrongdoings that they do, but they are doing things that are many times worse.' He drew the

---

[40] *Majmoo' al-Fataawa*, 28/524.

[41] Ibid, 28/501-553, 589.

attention of the scholars and the people to that, and he used to say to the people: 'If you see me on that side with the *Muṣ-ḥaf* on my head, kill me.' So he encouraged the people to fight the Tartars, and he strengthened their hearts and their intention, to Allah be praise."[42]

When the *Yaasah* and some of its rulings were mentioned, Ibn Katheer said: "All of that goes against the laws of Allah which He revealed to His slaves the Prophets, upon whom be blessings and peace. Whoever leaves the perfect laws which were revealed to Muhammad ibn 'Abdullah (ﷺ), the Seal of the Prophets, and refers for judgement to anything else among the abrogated laws, is a *kaafir*, so how about one who refers for judgement to the *Yaasah* and gives it precedence? Whoever does that is a *kaafir* according to the consensus of the Muslims."[43]

In his commentary on the *aayah* — ﴾Do they then seek the judgement of [the days of] Ignorance? And who is better in judgement than Allah for a people who have firm Faith.﴿ *(Qur'an 5: 50)* — he said: "Allah denounces the one who rebels against the perfect ruling of Allah, which encompasses all that is good and forbids all that is evil, and turns to anything else, be it opinions, whims and desires or traditions that people have established without basing them on the shari'ah of Allah, as the people of the *jaahiliyah* used to refer for judgement to misguided and ignorant ideas which they made up from their own opinions and whims and desires, as the Tartars do with the royal decrees which they took from their king Genghis Khan, who wrote the *Yaasiq* for them. This is the name of a book which is a collection of rulings which he gathered from various laws of the Jews, the Christians and the Muslims, and it includes many rulings which are taken from his own opinions and whims and desires. This

---

[42] *Al-Bidaayah wan-Nihaayah*, 14/23-24.

[43] Ibid, 13/119.

became a law to be followed among his people, to which they give precedence over the rulings of the Book of Allah and the Sunnah of His Messenger (ﷺ). Whoever among them does that is a *kaafir* who must be fought until he returns to the ruling of Allah and His Messenger and does not refer to anything else for judgement, whether in a minor or a major issue."[44]

In this manner, Ibn Taymiyah, and his students after him, made clear the ruling on this issue. Their answers decisively explained the ruling, and strongly urged jihad against these Tartars to remove the danger they posed to the Muslims.

Other Examples

There are other examples of attempts to reject the shari'ah of Allah, but they were of a lesser degree than the previous examples, either because of the confusion that characterized them, or because their proponents were not able to implement what they believed in. It will suffice here to give just three examples:

> a) The *baaṭini* (esoteric) movements whose various groups spread throughout different regions of the Muslim world. What distinguished all of them as Al-Ghazaali described in *Faḍaa'iḥ al-Baaṭiniyah*, where he said: "The fifth aspect of their belief concerning the obligations of shari'ah. It is narrated from them that they believe in absolute license, eliminating *ḥijaab*, permitting forbidden things and regarding them as permissible, rejecting the laws of shari'ah..."[45]

Their *baaṭini* (esoteric) misinterpretations of the clear laws of Islam such as Prayer, Fasting, Ḥajj and Jihad are well known.

---

[44] *Tafseer Ibn Katheer*, 3/122-123, Ash-Sha'b edition. See *'Umdat at-Tafseer* by Aḥmad Shaakir, 4/173, and his comment on this topic.

[45] *Faḍaa'iḥ al-Baaṭiniyah*, Pp. 46.

But the fact that their *kufr* is so obvious, and that the people of the Sunnah — Sunnis, took such a strong stand against them, meant that the ruling on their being apostates and *kaafir* was clear to everyone. This led to their being secretive and concealing their beliefs, and taking a gradual approach in spreading their views.

> b) What Al-Juwayni mentioned concerning some of the *zindeeq* (heretics) of his time (who could also be described as secularists). Al-Juwayni said, — addressing *Ghiyaath ad-Dawlah Niẓaam al-Mulk*, the famous 'Abbaasi advisor — "What I want to convey to His Excellency, after mentioning the news from the various regions, is a serious *fitnah* (tribulation) which is affecting the religion. If it is not stopped, it will reach most of the Muslims and the problem will go beyond our control and will be very difficult to deal with later on. This is one of the most serious problems facing the common folk.

It is the duty of the one whom Allah has put in a position to support Islam, to watch and protect the ummah night and day. The best that I can do is to try to extinguish (this *fitnah*) the way it started. The responsibility of the one to whom Allah has given authority is to strive to protect the people from the means of destruction.

There has spread throughout various regions and cities — may Allah protect our leaders — a group of heretics and those who deny the attributes of Allah, who are striving to call people to cast aside true guidance. In making this call, they rely on groups of misguided notables who have become their protectors and supporters. Those deluded persons, who are enjoying the blessings of Allah (سبحانه وتعالى) — the Exalted, All-Merciful — and a life of ease, started to use the jokes made in their gatherings to belittle religion, criticizing the shari'ah of the Muslims by hints and gestures. Their behaviour and attitudes passed to their followers among the ignorant commoners who imitate them, and the specious arguments of the heretics and misguidance of the deniers have spread amongst the common folk of the Muslims. Discussions and debates aimed at undermining and criticizing Islam have become widespread..."[46]

To whom was Al-Juwayni referring when he mentioned these *zindeeq* groups? Were they the *baaṭiniyah* or others? All of that is possible, but what he says elsewhere indicates that he was referring to people other than the *baaṭinis*. He says:

> "In conclusion, whoever thinks that the shari'ah may be derived from what people agree upon, of reason or from the opinions of wise men, has rejected the shari'ah and has taken this principle as a means to reject the shari'ah.
>
> If this is acceptable, then it would be acceptable to stone the unmarried fornicator who commits fornication in our times, based on this argument. And it would be permissible to execute a person on the basis of suspicion. And it would be justifiable to kill a person whom it was feared would betray the ummah, if there were signs and indications to that effect. And it would be permissible to increase the rate of zakah if there appeared to be a need to do so...
>
> These arguments have no strong foundation. If they were to form the foundation of religion, then you would find that everyone who has some rational power would take his own ideas and thoughts as shari'ah, and thus ideas and thoughts would take the place of the Revelation sent to the Messengers. These ideas and thoughts would vary according to time and place, thus the shari'ah would have no stability..."[47]

---

[46] *Al-Ghiyaathi* by Al-Juwayni, Pp. 381-382, edited by Dr. 'Abdul-'Azeem ad-Deeb.

[47] Ibid, Pp. 220-221.

It is clear that the *Shaykh* was referring to some of those who believed that using excessive force and harshness against those who commit major sins and their like was a more effective deterrent, and so wanted to add to the rulings of shari'ah. For example, they wanted to stone the unmarried fornicator, or execute on the basis of mere suspicion, and so on. Look at what he says concerning such people — even though they had good intentions. He said:

> "Anyone who oversteps the limits set by shari'ah should be viewed as definitely deviating from the religion of the Prophet (ﷺ). Whoever transgresses, knowing that he is committing a sin and engaging in a wrongful action, is a sinner but he should not despair of the mercy of Allah.
>
> Woe to those who commit major sins and, based on their own ideas and what they think is correct, decide that it is part of the religion of the Prophet. For the truth is that which has been defined by the prominent scholars, following the Prophet (ﷺ), and anything else is misguidance. And after the truth, what else can there be, save error? *(cf. Qur'an 10: 32)*
>
> This way of thinking is similar to the one who takes the traditions of Chosroes and extinct kings as the basis for religion. Whoever adheres to such a thing has cast aside Islam as easily as one who pulls a hair from the dough."[48]

This is what he (may Allah have mercy on him) said about the people who wanted and tried to change the religion, but did not succeed. Rather the Muslim ummah continued to refer to nothing but the

---

[48] *Al-Ghiyaathi*, Pp. 221-222. What Al-Juwayni describes here is similar to the man-made laws which have become widespread among the Muslims, for they are the ways and laws of the *kaafir* west, the Christians and others. Al-Juwayni stated that the one who takes the laws of Chosroes as a reference point and basis for religion is a *kaafir*, who is beyond the pale of Islam.

shari'ah of Allah for judgement, during Al-Juwayni's time and subsequently; despite the incidents of oppression and injustice that occurred, and despite the spread of evil actions, the ruling and laws of Allah were the prevailing system.

Al-Juwayni then mentioned the reason why he told the story of the scholar who gave a *fatwa* to one of the kings concerning intercourse during the day in Ramaḍaan, and told him to fast (for sixty consecutive days), so that this would be a deterrent. He did not tell him to follow the first option, which is to free a slave — although this is the ruling of shari'ah — because that would be too easy for the ruler. Al-Juwayni commented on this *fatwa* in strong terms.[49]

c) The followers of *bid'ah*. Ash-Shaaṭibi mentions this in his book *Al-I'tiṣaam*, and makes the connection between this issue and the issue of the perfection and soundness of the shari'ah, because the people of *bid'ah* claim, in effect, that the shari'ah is not complete. Because the book of Ash-Shaaṭibi is so well known, we do not need to speak about it at length; it is sufficient merely to refer to it here.

[49] *Al-Ghiyaathi*, 222-226.

CHAPTER FIVE

SPECIOUS ARGUMENTS AND RESPONSES TO THEM

In this chapter we will examine the important specious arguments which have been put forward concerning the topic which we have examined in detail above, especially those which have to do with legislation that goes against the laws of Allah, or with ruling by something other than that which Allah has revealed, in the sense of permanent, binding laws which are referred to for judgement and which, as is clear from the above discussion, constitute major *kufr*. With regard to the one who denies that which Allah has revealed and regards it as permissible to refer for judgement to something other than that which Allah has revealed, hardly anyone whose opinion carries any weight holds a different view.

The important specious arguments that have been put forward by those who hold differing views and which they use as evidence are as follows:

1) The reports from Ibn 'Abbaas (رضي الله عنه) that he said concerning the *aayah (Qur'an 5: 44)*, ﴿A lesser form of *kufr*﴾.

2) That the *aayaat* which speak of ruling by something other than that which Allah has revealed refer exclusively to the People of the Book.

3) That referring for judgement to (man-made) laws is the matter of *kufr* of action (*al-kufr al-'amali)*, and *kufr* of action does not put a person beyond the pale of Islam; that which puts a person beyond the pale of Islam is *kufr* of belief (*al-kufr al-i'tiqaadi*).

4) That only the one who thinks that it is permissible to rule by something other than that which Allah has revealed, or rejects that which Allah has revealed, is a *kaafir*.

5) The attitude of the *salaf* towards the people of *bid'ah* (innovation), whereby they said that some *bid'ah* make one a *kaafir* and some *bid'ah* do not do that, and the one who rules by something other than that which Allah has revealed is like one who innovates.

6) The reports of scholarly consensus that it does not constitute *kufr*.

7) Applying the ruling of *kufr* in all cases so that it even includes minor issues.

These are the very important specious arguments that have been raised concerning this topic. In order to complete the picture and explain the truth concerning this matter, we will examine them further, as follows.

The First Specious Argument

The reports from Ibn 'Abbaas that he said concerning the *aayah* ﴾A lesser form of *kufr*﴿

We have discussed this matter above, in section 5 of Chapter 3, where we discussed it in detail from a number of angles, some of which are sufficient to refute those who use the words of Ibn 'Abbaas (رضي الله عنه) as evidence and make them the basis of their argument, and they do not pay attention to other things he said, or to the words of other *ṣaḥaabah*.[1]

[1] See above, Pp. 209 ff.

The Second Specious Argument

The claim that the *aayaat* refer exclusively to the people of the book, and that the Muslims are not included in the rulings of these *aayaat*

We have discussed this view above, in the second part of Chapter 3, where we discussed the verses of *Soorah al-Maa'idah*, the reasons for their revelation and the comments (of the scholars) on them.

Knowing that the view that they are exclusive was narrated concerning the verses from *Soorah al-Maa'idah*, there is no dispute that other verses which were revealed concerning ruling by that which Allah has revealed and connected matters are general in application. In the Introduction to this book we have quoted many *aayaat* on this topic.

The Third Specious Argument

That ruling by something other than that which Allah has revealed is *kufr* of action, and *kufr* of action does not put one beyond the pale of Islam

This is based on the fact that the one who rules by something other than that which Allah has revealed but does not deny (that ruling by that which Allah has revealed is obligatory) is a *kaafir* in the sense of *kufr* of action, and *kufr* of action differs from *kufr* of belief in that it does not put one beyond the pale of Islam. In response to this it is sufficient to explain the basis of this argument, which is the claim that *kufr* is of two types, *kufr* of belief which puts a person beyond the pale of Islam, and *kufr* of action which does not put a person beyond the pale of Islam — but no guidelines or explanation is offered.

Before we discuss the matter further in order to refute this argument, I would like to explain how this terminology developed — I mean the terminology of *kufr* of belief and *kufr* of action. It is known that the texts of the Qur'an and Sunnah which describe certain things as *kufr* may refer to matters which put a person beyond the pale of Islam, or things which do not do so. In contrast to the *Khawaarij* and the *Wa'eediyah*, whose views were similar, the *salaf* and the *aimmah* (the great Muslim jurists and scholars) spoke of the difference between the two matters and distinguished between the two types of *kufr*, so that the truth became clear and so that the *Khawaarij* were refuted. So they divided *kufr* into two types, one of which puts a person beyond the pale of Islam and one which does not. But the phrases used by the *salaf* and *aimmah* to describe that varied:

— Some of them distinguished between them by calling one of them *kufr akbar* (major or greater *kufr*) and the other *kufr aṣghar* (minor or lesser *kufr*).

— Some of them distinguished between them by calling one of them *kufr* which puts a person beyond the pale of Islam and the other *kufr* which does not put a person beyond the pale of Islam.

— Some of them distinguished between them by calling the second type — that which does not put a person beyond the pale of Islam — ﴾a lesser form of *kufr*﴿.

— Some of them distinguished between them by calling one of them *kufr* of belief (*al-kufr al-i'tiqaadi*, lit. ideological *kufr*) and the other *kufr* of action (*al-kufr al-'amali*, lit. practical *kufr*). By 'practical' they meant that which has to do with actions — doing or not doing them — such as the obligations of zakah, fasting and honouring one's parents, and abstaining from forbidden things such as adultery, theft, drinking alcohol and killing a soul wrongfully. They regarded all of these as coming under the heading of *kufr* of action which does not put a person beyond the pale of Islam, unless he believes these actions to be permitted.

These expressions which have been narrated from the *salaf* concerning the differentiation between major and minor *kufr* are synonymous, and all boil down to the same meaning, that is, what they all understood and what they were all referring to, and none of them disputed these meanings — unlike those who differed from them such as the *Khawaarij* and *Murji'ah*.

But in later times there were those who were influenced to a great extent by some of the views of the *Murji'ah*, either in general terms or in a specific issue, so they would pay attention to the phrases of some of the *aimmah* that they had picked up concerning the differentiation between major and minor *kufr*, namely the words *al-kufr al-i'tiqaadi* (*kufr* of belief) and *al-kufr al-'amali* (*kufr* of action). They made this into a principle which they then applied in general terms, basing on that the specious argument that no one could be classified as a *kaafir* except the one who believed that the forbidden action he was doing was permitted, and they applied this specious argument to all the things that may constitute *kufr*.

It became the habit of these people, when commenting on matters of faith or when refuting the *Khawaarij*, to quote this guideline and say: this is the matter of *kufr* of action, and *kufr* of action does not put a person beyond the pale of Islam. For example, it might be said that ruling by something other than that which Allah has revealed, such as man-made laws — so long as one does not regard that as being permissible — is the matter of *kufr* of action, and *kufr* of action does not put one beyond the pale of Islam. Thus the matter for them would be settled in definitive terms (and would not require any further discussion), because it was based — or so they claimed — on one of the principles set out by the *salaf*.

As I have said, there is no problem with the terminology itself, unless it leads to misunderstanding which in turn could lead to defective understanding of the issues of *'aqeedah*, or of some of them, including the issue under discussion here.

In order to refute this specious argument and explain the truth, we will explain the confusion surrounding the matter in the following two ways:

1- The scholars who used this terminology — *kufr* of belief and *kufr* of action — explained the correct meaning of these words, and they explained the confusion that might arise from them, so they went back and commented further on it, and explained the truth of the matter. I will quote from two of the major scholars of *Ahl as-Sunnah wal-Jamaa'ah*:

Ibn al-Qayyim (may Allah have mercy on him) said in *Kitaab aṣ-Ṣalaah*: "Faith of action (*al-eemaan al-'amali*, lit. practical faith) is diametrically opposed by *kufr* of action, and faith of belief (*al-eemaan al-i'tiqaadi*, lit. ideological faith) is diametrically opposed by *kufr* of belief. The Prophet (ﷺ) stated this when he said in the *ṣaḥeeḥ* hadith,

> 'Trading insults with a Muslim is *fusooq* (evil doing) and fighting him is *kufr*.'

He differentiated between fighting and trading insults, describing one of them as being *fusooq* which does not make one a *kaafir*, and the other as *kufr*. Of course, he meant *kufr* of action, not *kufr* of belief, and this type of *kufr* does not put one completely beyond the pale of Islam, just as the adulterer, thief or wine-drinker does not go beyond the pale of Islam, even though the description of having faith does not apply to them."[2]

What Ibn al-Qayyim says is correct and is in accordance with the view of the *aimmah* of the *salaf*, when he gives examples to explain

---

[2] *Kitaab aṣ-Ṣalaah*, Pp. 407.

the terminology that he uses. But Ibn al-Qayyim understood that this terminology might cause confusion, so he went back and commented on it and explained it further. This explanation came before these comments, where he said: "Just as one may become a *kaafir* by uttering words of *kufr* willingly, which is one of the branches of *kufr*, so too one may become a *kaafir* by doing an action which is one of the branches of *kufr*, such as prostrating to idols or showing disrespect to the *Muṣ-ḥaf*."[3]

These two examples — prostrating to the idols and showing disrespect to the *Muṣ-ḥaf* — undermine the basis used by those who generalize this rule and apply it to all cases by saying that *kufr* of action does not put one beyond the pale of Islam, because these two actions make one a *kaafir*, according to scholarly consensus, and these are actions, according to scholarly consensus.

Ibn al-Qayyim clarified the matter further by saying: "*Kufr* of action may be divided into that which is diametrically opposed to faith and that which is not diametrically opposed to faith. Prostrating to idols, showing disrespect to the *Muṣ-ḥaf* and killing or insulting the Prophet are all diametrically opposed to faith."[4] In other words, even though they are actions.

Stating in absolute terms, without further explanation, that all cases of *kufr* of action come under the category of minor *kufr* is undermined by the examples given by Ibn al-Qayyim, referred to above. Anyone who describes minor *kufr* as "*kufr* of action" must accompany that with examples of things that the *salaf* unanimously agreed to be a kind of lesser *kufr*, such as fighting a believer, casting aspersions upon a person's lineage, wailing over the dead, *zina* (adultery or fornication), theft, etc.

---

[3] *Kitaab aṣ-Ṣalaah*, Pp. 405.

[4] Ibid, Pp. 406.

This is similar to the well-known phrases which were used in general terms to refute the *Khawaarij*: "we do not label anyone as a *kaafir* because of sin" or, "we do not label anyone as a *kaafir* because of major sin," etc. Some people thought that the view of the *salaf* was not to label a person as a *kaafir* for any sin or for any major sin, even though sins and major sins include *shirk* or the association of others with Allah, which no one disputes is major *kufr*. The Prophet (ﷺ) described it as a sin in the hadith where he was asked, "Which sin is the greatest?" and he (ﷺ) said,

> "To set up a rival to Allah."

He also described it as a major sin, as in the hadith,

> "Shall I not tell you of the greatest of major sins?" then he said, "Associating others with Allah, and disobeying one's parents..."

In the case of those who used these phrases in general terms, all that they wanted to do was to refute the *Khawaarij* who denounced people as *kaafirs* for any type of sins or any type of major sins.

The other scholar is *Shaykh* Ḥaafiẓ Ḥakami (may Allah have mercy on him) who mentioned in his famous book, *A'laam as-Sunnah al-Manshoorah*, the various kinds of *kufr*, and said: "*Kufr* is of two types, major *kufr* which puts a person beyond the pale of Islam, the *kufr* of belief that contradicts the beliefs and actions of the heart, or one of them; and minor *kufr* which undermines the perfection of faith but does not cancel out faith altogether — this is the *kufr* of action which does not contradict the beliefs and actions of the heart and does not necessarily imply that."[5] Then he mentioned a question — what is the *kufr* of action which does not put a person beyond the pale

[5] *A'laam as-Sunnah al-Manshoorah*, Pp. 179, edited by Aḥmad 'Aloosh Madkhali, published by *Maktabah ar-Rushd*.

of Islam? — and replied: "It is every sin which the Lawgiver has described as *kufr*, but the one who does it is still regarded as having faith..."[6]

What the *Shaykh* says perfectly explains why the phrase "*kufr* of action" is used to describe minor *kufr*. This is sufficient to explain the matter and to dispel any confusion that may arise. However, he went back and explained it further by quoting a second question: "If it is said to us: 'Prostrating to idols, showing disrespect to the *Muṣ-ḥaf*, insulting the Messenger, mocking the religion, etc., all appear to be *kufr* of action, so they would not put a person beyond the pale of Islam, as you have defined minor *kufr* as *kufr* of action?' —

The answer is that these four things and other similar actions are not *kufr* of action except in the sense that they happen as physical actions that people may see. But they could not take place unless all belief in the heart has been destroyed, such as good intention, sincerity, love and submission, so that nothing of that is left. Although it appears to be *kufr* of action, it inevitably implies *kufr* of belief... We do not define minor *kufr* as being *kufr* of action in all cases; rather we define it as referring to that which is purely physical and does not undermine faith or contradict the belief or actions of the heart."[7]

This further clarification from *Shaykh* Ḥaafiẓ explains that the phrase "*kufr* of action" is not absolute and that it must be further qualified.

As there are phrases used by the *salaf* which do not cause confusion — such as "minor *kufr*", or "a lesser form of *kufr*," or "*kufr* which does not put one beyond the pale of Islam" — it would be a good idea to avoid using the phrase "*kufr* of action" because it is confusing, as we have seen above.

---

[6] *A'laam as-Sunnah al-Manshoorah*, Pp. 179.

[7] Ibid, Pp. 181-182.

2 - Uttering the *Shahaadatayn* — which is a physical action — is a prerequisite of faith. Whoever does not utter them — although he is able to do so — is a *kaafir*. This is in contrast to what the *Murji'ah* say. *Shaykh al-Islam* Ibn Taymiyah (may Allah have mercy on him) said: "With regard to the *Shahaadatayn*, if a person does not utter them although he is able to do so, then he is a *kaafir*, according to the consensus of the Muslims. He is a *kaafir* both outwardly and inwardly according to the *Salaf* of the ummah and the majority of its scholars. A group of the *Murji'ah* — the *Jahamiyah* of the *Murji'ah* such as *Jaham aṣ-Ṣaaliḥi* and his followers — said that if he believes in his heart, then he is outwardly a *kaafir* but not inwardly. We have pointed out above the origin of this belief, that this is an innovated belief that has been introduced into Islam. This was not the belief of any of the *aimmah* — the reputed Muslim jurists and scholars. We have stated above that inward belief must be confirmed by outward words of acknowledgement rather more than that, and that the existence of inward faith, belief and love without any outward confirmation is not possible."[8]

Would anyone say that not uttering the *Shahaadatayn* — which is a physical action — does not put a person beyond the pale of Islam because it is *kufr* of action? This is contrary to scholarly consensus. If we add to this what we have mentioned above, that the one who insults Allah or His Messenger, or shows disrespect towards the *Muṣḥaf*, etc., is a *kaafir*, and that this is *kufr* according to scholarly consensus, although it is a kind of action, then the matter is explained clearly.

What we are going to discuss in the next section and the answer we are going to give, complements the two points discussed above.

---

[8] *Al-Eemaan al-Awsaṭ*, Pp. 151.

The Fourth Specious Argument

A person does not become a *kaafir* unless he regards it to be permissible to rule by something other than that which Allah has revealed and rejects that which Allah has revealed

Some researchers connect this to that which is more general and more comprehensive, namely the claim that no one who commits an act of *kufr* becomes a *kaafir* unless he rejects and denies (the ruling of Allah). They quote as evidence for that things like the words of Aṭ-Ṭaḥaawi, who was quoting from the *a'immah* before him, "We do not regard any of the people of the *Qiblah* (i.e., Muslims) as a *kaafir* for committing a sin so long he does not regard it as being permissible." The one who rules or judges by something other than that which Allah has revealed is included in this general statement so he is not regarded as a *kaafir* unless he regards his action as being permissible.

This issue and the response to it may be discussed from several angles:

1- The *aimmah* — the reputed Muslim jurists and scholars (may Allah have mercy on them), did not speak in general terms in the way that some have understood from the words of Aṭ-Ṭaḥaawi and others.

For example, Imam Bukhari gave one of the chapters in *Kitaab al-Eemaan* in his *Ṣaḥeeḥ* the title *Baab al-Ma'aaṣi min Amr al-Jaahiliyah wa laa yakfur Ṣaaḥibuhaa bi irtikaabihaa illaa bish-Shirk* (Chapter: Sin is the matter of *Jaahiliyah* and the one who commits sin is not a *kaafir* unless he commits *shirk*).[9] Here Imam Bukhari is pointing out that *shirk* on its own is *kufr*, although it is also a type of sin. What may be noted here is that Bukhari did not mention the one who believes sins to be permissible, so does this mean that he did not

---

[9] Bukhari, *Kitab al-Eemaan*, Chapter 22.

regard the one who believed sins to be permissible as a *kaafir*? Bukhari, like other *aimmah*, was speaking in general terms and did not mean that this was the only way of labelling a person *kaafir*; what he intended here was to refute the *Khawaarij* who labelled all sinners as *kaafir*.

Barbahaari said in *Sharḥ as-Sunnah*: "No Muslim goes beyond the pale of Islam unless he rejects one or more verses of the Book of Allah, or rejects any of the hadith of the Messenger of Allah (ﷺ), or prays to anyone other than Allah, or offers a sacrifice to anyone other than Allah. If he does any of these things, then you must regard him as being beyond the pale of Islam, but if he does not do any of these things, then he is a believer and a Muslim in name, if not in reality."[10]

He mentioned praying to anyone other than Allah and offering sacrifices to anyone other than Allah. These are sins and they are also actions, and the one who does them is beyond the pale of Islam. Barbahaari meant to give examples, but he did not intend to list all the examples. By the same token, when the scholars said that the adulterer and the thief are not *kaafirs*, they did not limit that to those people; they were merely giving examples. This is clear.

2 - Similarly, the *aimmah* (may Allah have mercy on them) explained the correct meaning of the phrases used by Aṭ-Ṭaḥaawi and others, and that the intention was to refute the *Khawaarij*; they did not mean that this applies to all sins and that no sins could make one a *kaafir*. It is sufficient to mention a few brief examples of what the scholars said concerning that.

Among them *Shaykh al-Islam* Ibn Taymiyah said: "Hence the *Sunni* scholars said, when describing the belief of *Ahl as-Sunnah wal-Jamaa'ah*, that they did not denounce any Muslim as a *kaafir* for

---

[10] *Sharḥ as-Sunnah*, Pp. 31, edited by Dr. Muhammad Sa'eed al-Qaḥṭaani.

sinning, referring to the *bid'ah* (innovation) of the *Khawaarij* who denounced people as *kaafirs* for any sin."[11] The phrase "denounced people as *kaafir* for any sin" refers to what we mentioned above, which is that the *Khawaarij* denounced people as *kaafir* for any sin; in contrast, the *Ahl al-Sunnah* do not denounce people as *kaafir* for all sins, only for some sins, for which there is clear evidence that the one who does them is a *kaafir*.

Ibn Taymiyah also said: "What is indicated by the Qur'an and Sunnah is an established principle of *Ahl as-Sunnah wal-Jamaa'ah*, that they do not denounce any Muslim as a *kaafir* because of sin, and they do not regard him as being beyond the pale of Islam because of his actions, if he does something that is not allowed, such as committing adultery or stealing or drinking alcohol, so long as it does not imply that he no longer believes"[12] — i.e., by doing something which nullifies faith, such as regarding the forbidden thing he is doing as being permissible, etc.

He also said: "If we say that the *Ahl as-Sunnah* are agreed that a person is not to be denounced as a *kaafir* because of sin, we mean that the sins such as adultery and drinking wine. But with regard to these basic issues, there is a well known dispute as to whether the one who neglects them is to be denounced as a *kaafir*."[13]

What he means by "these basic issues" is the four pillars of Prayer, Zakah, Fasting and Ḥajj.

Shaykh Muhammad ibn 'Abdul-Wahhaab (may Allah have mercy on him) said, refuting those who use the fact that the scholars said that it is not permissible to denounce a Muslim as *kaafir* because of sin (to support their own specious arguments): "This is true, but this is not

---

[11] *Majmoo' al-Fataawa*, 12/474.

[12] Ibid, 20/90.

[13] Ibid, 7/302.

the issue which we are dealing with here. The *Khawaarij* used to denounce as a *kaafir* the one who committed adultery, stole or shed blood, indeed (their view was that) if a Muslim committed any major sin, he became a *kaafir*. But the view of the *Ahl as-Sunnah* was that a Muslim becomes a *kaafir* only if he commits *shirk*. We did not denounce the misguided leaders and their followers as *kaafirs* for anything but their *shirk*. You are one of the most ignorant of men if you think that a person who prays and claims to be a Muslim can never be denounced as a *kaafir...*"[14]

He further said, refuting the same idea: "Do you not see that when the Companions of the Messenger of Allah (ﷺ) fought those who withheld the zakah, when they wanted to repent, Abu Bakr said, 'We will not accept your repentance until you bear witness that our slain are in Paradise and your slain are in Hell.' Do you think that Abu Bakr and his companions did not understand and that you and your father are the ones who understand? Woe to you, O' deeply ignorant one, if you think that!"[15]

He mentioned *shirk* and withholding the zakah, and he explained the meaning of the words of the *salaf*, "we do not denounce anyone as a *kaafir* for sins." This *Shaykh* is the author of a well-known essay entitled Nawaaqiḍ al-Islam (What nullifies Islam), which includes things other than regarding as permissible that which is forbidden, such as practising witchcraft or magic, and ruling by anything other than that which Allah has revealed.

Shaykh 'Abdul-Laṭeef ibn 'Abdur-Raḥmaan ibn Ḥasan (may Allah have mercy on them) said, refuting Dawood ibn Jarjees al-'Iraaqi: "With regard to his saying that *Shaykh* Aḥmad ibn Taymiyah and his student Ibn al-Qayyim did not denounce any of the people of the

---

[14] *Ma'llifaat Muhammad ibn 'Abdul-Wahhaab, Ar-Rasaa'il ash-Shakhṣiyah*, Pp. 233.
[15] Ibid, Pp. 234.

qiblah as *kaafir*, it has to be said: if only he knew who were the people of the *qiblah* mentioned in this context and what is meant by this phrase, he would not have mentioned it here as evidence to support those who call upon anyone other than Allah and to say that they are not to be denounced as *kaafir*.

Whoever turns away from the words of the scholars and thinks that anyone who prays and says *Laa ilaaha illa-Allah* is one of the people of the *qiblah* (i.e., a Muslim) even though he does what he does of things that indicate that he is guilty of *shirk* and has left the religion of Islam, is calling attention to his own ignorance and misguidance, and is exposing his lack of knowledge and religion by saying that. Imam Aḥmad (may Allah have mercy on him) denounced the one who says, we do not label those who sin as *kaafir*,[16] but this person claims to be following the *madhhab* of Imam Aḥmad. This phrase meant a disavowal of the belief of the *Khawaarij* who denounced people as *kaafir* simply for committing sin. This is quoting words out of context and distorting the meaning, because it is mistakenly applied to those who commit *shirk* and pray to righteous people. Thus he became confused and did not understand what the *salaf* meant by these words. This incorrect understanding is refuted by the Book of Allah, the Sunnah of His Messenger and the consensus of the scholars. The leading *fuqahaa'* of the *madhahib* (*madhhabs*) devoted a separate chapter to this issue, where they mentioned the ruling concerning apostates from Islam and listed many actions which make one a *kaafir*, which are less serious than the issue we are dealing with here. They affirmed that the means of protection against *kufr* is adherence to Islam and its pillars and basic principles, not merely

[16] I say: perhaps when Ibn Abil-'Izz mentioned in *Sharḥ aṭ-Ṭaḥaawiyah* that many of the *Sunni* scholars disallowed use of the phrase "we do not denounce those who sin as *kaafir*" (as we will refer to in point 3 below), he was referring to the saying of Imam Aḥmad as quoted from him by *Shaykh* 'Abdul-Laṭeef.

saying words and praying whilst still persisting in things that go against Islam. Students who have only just begun their studies know this, and it is mentioned in the summaries of the books of the Ḥanbalis and others. This person does not know what young boys in school know. This claim is baseless and his lack of intellectual ability is obvious."[17]

What *Shaykh* 'Abdul-Laṭeef says is applicable to the matter we are discussing here, when he refutes those who quote as evidence the comments of Aṭ-Ṭaḥaawi and the conclusion that no one becomes a *kaafir* except the one who regards that which is forbidden as being permissible.

3 - When the *aimmah* (Imams) said, "we do not denounce anyone as a *kaafir* for sins", they intended thereby to refute the *Khawaarij*. The error stems from a misunderstanding of this phrase and using it in general terms to refer to all sins. That is not what the *aimmah* intended when they said this. The confusion surrounding this phrase may be dispelled in two ways:

a) The commentator on *Aṭ-Ṭaḥaawiyah*, Ibn Abil-'Izz, said that many of the scholars of *Ahl as-Sunnah* stopped using this phrase in general terms, and that the correct thing to say in this case is "we do not denounce people as *kaafir* for all sins."[18] This is in order to differentiate between the view of the *Khawaarij*, who denounce people as *kaafir* for all sins, and the view of *Ahl as-Sunnah*, who denounce people as *kaafir* for some sins which imply *kufr*, for which there is clear evidence that the one who does them is a *kaafir*, but they do not denounce people as *kaafir* for all sins.

b) What is meant by sins is acts of disobedience to Allah which

---

[17] *Ad-Durar as-Sanniyah* (*Ar-Rudood*), vol. 9, Pp. 290-291, 1st edition.

[18] *Sharḥ aṭ-Ṭaḥaawiyah*, Pp. 433-434, edited by At-Turki, Al-Arnaa'ooṭ.

do not make the person who does them a *kaafir*, such as adultery, stealing, drinking alcohol, killing unlawfully, disobeying one's parents, casting aspersions upon a person's lineage, wailing for the dead, etc. These do not make the one who does them a *kaafir* unless he believes that they are permissible. The sins which do make one a *kaafir*, such as insulting Allah, worshipping idols, showing disrespect to the *Muṣ-ḥaf*, make the one who does them a *kaafir* regardless of whether he believes them to be permissible or not.

Perhaps the phrase used by Aṭ-Ṭaḥaawi, "from among the people of the *qiblah*" indicates that "the people of the *qiblah*" includes those who commit sins which do not nullify their Islam, such as those who commits sin like adultery, theft, consuming *riba*, etc. These people do not become *kaafir* because of their sins, unless they believe that they are permissible.

By taking these two points into consideration, what Aṭ-Ṭaḥaawi meant becomes clear.

4 - Saying that no one is a *kaafir* except the one who rejects (the ruling) is the view of the *Murji'ah* of all kinds. The reason for that is that when they defined faith as being belief, they limited *kufr* to the opposite of faith, which is disbelief and denial.

The *salaf* were unanimous in condemning all the *Murji'ah*, whether they were the *Jahamiyah* or the 'Islamic philosophers' (*mutakallimoon*) such as the *Ash'ariyah* and *Al-Maaturidiyah*, or the *Murji'ah al-Fuqahaa'*. But unfortunately there are people among those who claim to follow the *salaf* who express the same view as the *Murji'ah* with regard to some issues of faith.

Shaykh al-Islam Ibn Taymiyah said: "Jaham used to say that faith is simply belief in the heart, even if one does not speak the words of faith. This view is unknown from any of the scholars or *aimmah*

(Imams) of this ummah. Indeed, Aḥmad, Wakee' and others regarded *kaafir* those who expressed this view. But this view was supported by *Al-Ash'ari* and most of his followers, despite that they said that everyone who is judged by shari'ah to be a *kaafir*, we also judge him to be a *kaafir*, and we take the fact that the shari'ah judges him to be a *kaafir* as evidence that his heart is devoid of knowledge."[19]

The view that no one becomes a *kaafir* except the one who rejects (the ruling) is the view of the extreme *Murji'ah*, but it should be noted that even when the *Murji'ah al-Fuqahaa'* and the *mutakallimoon* went along with this principle, they did not take it as an absolute rule. Rather, they said: whoever is judged by the Lawgiver to be a *kaafir* (i.e., because of any of the types of *kufr* apart from denial), we also judge him to be a *kaafir*. This, in general, is in accordance with the view of the *salaf*, but they introduced a *bid'ah* (innovation) and said: whoever is judged by the Lawgiver to be a *kaafir*, this is an indication that his heart is devoid of knowledge — which goes against common sense, reason and *shar'*.

We are not discussing the issues that have to do with classifying a person as a *kaafir*, but I shall quote one principle — on which there is consensus — to refute clearly the issue that we are discussing, and to settle the dispute between *Ahl as-Sunnah* and the *Murji'ah* of various kinds.

I have limited this to one issue for the sake of brevity, because in the case of what nullifies faith, quantity is irrelevant, as *Shaykh al-Islam* Ibn Taymiyah says: "In the case of words that nullify faith, it does not matter whether it is one or many, even if the person does not utter words of blatant *kufr*, for example, if he rejects one *aayah*, or denies one obligatory duty, or insults the Messenger once, even if he does not state that he disbelieves in the Messenger. The same applies to

---

[19] *Majmoo' al-Fatawa*, 13/47.

words which nullify faith if they are uttered, such as saying, 'I nullify the covenant' or 'I have nothing to do with you.' The covenant (of Islam) becomes null and void because of this, even if he does not repeat it. Similarly, insulting the religion etc., does not need to be repeated."[20]

These are matters concerning which there is no dispute. If a person disbelieves in Prophet Nooḥ (Noah) (ﷺ), then he is a *kaafir*, even if he believes in the rest of the Prophets, just as *ṭahaarah* (purity) and *ṣalaah* (prayer) may be nullified by one of the things that nullify them. Similarly, a Muslim may be one of those who profess the *Shahaadatayn* and perform all the other pillars of Islam, but if he commits one action that nullifies Islam — such as denying that adultery or drinking alcohol is *ḥaraam* — then he is a *kaafir*, according to scholarly consensus.

Insulting the Messenger (ﷺ)

The one issue which we will examine here is that of insulting the Messenger (ﷺ). The scholars are unanimous that whoever clearly insults the Messenger (ﷺ) is a *kaafir.* Among those who stated that there is a consensus, are:

1 - Isḥaaq ibn Raahawayh, the famous Imam. *Shaykh al-Islam* Ibn Taymiyah said: "Imam Isḥaaq ibn Raahawayh, one of the prominent *aimmah* (Imams), said: the Muslims are agreed that whoever insults Allah or His Messenger, or rejects anything that Allah has revealed, or kills one of the Prophets of Allah, is a *kaafir* by virtue of that, even if he believes in everything that Allah has revealed."[21]

2 - Ibn al-Mundhir and Al-Faarisi. Ibn Ḥijr said in *Fatḥ al-Baari*:

---

[20] *Aṣ-Ṣaarim al-Maslool*, 2/178.

[21] Ibid, 2/15, 3/955. The words of Isḥaaq are mentioned in *At-Tamḥeed* by Ibn 'Abdul-Barr, 4/226.

"Ibn al-Mundhir narrated that there was consensus that whoever insults the Prophet (ﷺ) in clear terms must be killed. Abu Bakr al-Faarisi, one of the Shaafa'i Imams, narrated in *Kitaab al-Ijmaa'* that whoever insults the Prophet (ﷺ) in a manner that is clearly slander, is a *kaafir* according to scholarly consensus."[22]

3- Muhammad ibn Saḥnoon who said: "The scholars are agreed that whoever insults the Prophet (ﷺ) and shows disrespect to him is a *kaafir* and is subject to the warning of Allah's punishment. According to the view of the ummah, he is to be killed, and whoever doubts that he is a *kaafir* and deserves punishment is also a *kaafir.*"[23]

This ruling of *kufr*, which is agreed upon concerning the one who insults the Messenger (ﷺ), is applicable simply for the action of insulting, regardless of whether he believes it to be permissible or thinks that it is forbidden. His *kufr* is both outward and inward, in contrast to the view of the *Murji'ah*. *Shaykh al-Islam* Ibn Taymiyah said: "We say: that insulting Allah or insulting His Messenger is *kufr* both outwardly and inwardly, whether the one who does that believes that it is forbidden or he thinks that it is permissible, or if he does not have any opinion on that. This is the view of the *fuqahaa'* (Muslim jurists) and all of the *Ahl as-Sunnah*, who say that faith is both words and deeds."[24] In this case, there is no difference between one who is joking and the one who is serious.[25]

The mere act of insulting is major *kufr*, whether one believes it to be permissible or not. Whoever says that it is *kufr* only in the case of one who believes it to be permissible has taken that from the *Murji'ah*,

---

[22] *Fatḥ al-Baari*, commentary on hadith no. 6928 of *Ṣaḥeeḥ al-Bukhari*. (*Fatḥ al-Baari*, 12/281, 1st *Salafiyah* edition)

[23] *Aṣ-Ṣaarim al-Maslool*, 2/15-16; 3/956.

[24] Ibid, 3/955.

[25] Ibid, 3/957.

whom Ibn Taymiyah criticized severely when he said: "It must be noted that saying the reason why the one who insults (Allah or His Messenger) is a *kaafir* is his belief that this is permissible, is a serious mistake and a grave error. May Allah have mercy on Al-Qaaḍi Abu Ya'laa who mentioned in more than one place in his books things that contradict what he said here. The reason why they fell into this pit is what they learned from a group of the later *mutakallimoon* (Scholastics), who were influenced by the *Jahamiyah* in saying faith is merely the matter of belief in the heart, even if it is not accompanied by words on the lips and even if it does not lead to any action of the heart or physical action..."[26]

This consensus of the scholars and their comments on this issue indicate a number of things:

a) That *kufr* is not limited only to rejection.
b) That *kufr* may take the form of words or deeds.
c) That *kufr* is not only dependent on a person believing something forbidden to be permitted.
d) That this kind of *kufr* — which is described as such in a text — is both inward and outward *kufr*, and that it is *kufr* in and of itself, not because it indicates that the person believes something forbidden to be permissible.
e) Those who go against this view are kinds of *Murji'ah*, extreme or otherwise.

In order to distinguish the view of *Ahl as-Sunnah wal-Jamaa'ah* — concerning the issue of insulting the Prophet (ﷺ) — from the views of the *Murji'ah*, we will mention various views on the matter, and the views of each group which went against the view of the *salaf*. These views (which are opposed to the view of the *salaf*) are as follows:

---

[26] *Aṣ-Ṣaarim al-Maslool*, 3/960.

The first view: That a person who insults the Prophet (ﷺ) is not considered to be a *kaafir* (disbeliever) in this world unless he clearly states that he rejects (the ruling) or believes that uttering such insults is permissible. This is the view of the extreme *Murji'ah* who say that whoever is described by shari'ah as being a *kaafir* because he does or says something that implies *kufr* should not be judged to be a *kaafir* in this world unless he clearly states that he rejects (the ruling).

This group was accused of *bid'ah* (innovation) by the *salaf* because of their extreme *Murji'i* views which went against the texts which describe the one who commits an action that implies *kufr* (disbelief)as being a *kaafir* without stipulating the condition that it should be accompanied by denial or rejection. Thus they made rejection a condition for classifying a person as a *kaafir*, so that no one could be described as *kaafir* unless he clearly stated that he denied or rejected (the ruling).

The second view: That the one who insults the Prophet (ﷺ) is a *kaafir* outwardly — i.e., as far as the rulings of this world are concerned — but he may be a believer on the inside, if he believes in his heart. These people say that everyone who is described in shari'ah as being a *kaafir* must be judged as such outwardly, and the rulings of *kufr* must be applied to him in this world, but it may be that inwardly he is a believer, if he believes in his heart and does not reject (the ruling). This view is well known among the extreme *Murji'ah* who say that faith is knowledge. Their justification for that is "that he may say with his lips something that is not in his heart. If there is respect and veneration of the Messenger in his heart, what is inward cannot be undermined by his contrary outward speech, just as the hypocrite does not gain anything by making an outward show that goes against what is in his heart."[27]

---

[27] *Aṣ-Ṣaarim al-Masloool*, 3/966.

Shaykh al-Islam Ibn Taymiyah refuted the specious arguments of these people from three angles, of which the first one concerns us here. "The implication of this is that whoever utters words of rejection and denial, or any kind of *kufr*, without being forced to do so, may nevertheless still be a believer. Whoever believes this has cast aside the covenant of Islam (i.e., become a *kaafir*)."[28]

Because of the seriousness of this specious argument — I mean the argument of the *Jahamiyah* — and the extent to which it spread in later periods, I will quote what Ibn Taymiyah said about it, and how groups among the *Ahl al-Kalaam* (Scholastics) other than the *Jahamiyah* were influenced by it. He said: "Hence it is clear that Jaham ibn Ṣafwaan and his followers erred when they thought that faith is simply the matter of belief and knowledge in the heart, and they did not regard actions of the heart as being part of faith. They thought that a person could have perfect faith in his heart, yet at the same time he could insult Allah and His Messenger, or oppose Allah and His Messenger, and oppose the friends (*awliya'*) of Allah and take the enemies of Allah as friends, and kill the Prophets, and destroy mosques, and show disrespect towards the *Muṣ-ḥaf*, and show the utmost respect to the *kuffaar*, and the utmost disrespect towards the believers. They said, all of that is sin which does not nullify faith which is in the heart, indeed a person may do that whilst inwardly and before Allah he is a believer. They said: indeed the rulings on the *kuffaar* may be applied to him in this world because these words[29] are sign of *kufr*, so he should be judged on outward appearance just as judgement may be based on confession and the testimony of witnesses, even though inwardly he may be different from that which he has confessed and that the witnesses have testified. If the Qur'an, Sunnah and scholarly consensus are quoted to

[28] *Aṣ-Ṣaarim al-Maslool*, 3/973.

[29] In *Al-'Abeekaan* edition, Pp. 212, it says "deeds".

them to prove that one of these people is a *kaafir* because of doing these actions and he will be punished in the Hereafter, they say: these actions are an indication of the absence of belief and knowledge in his heart. So in their view *kufr* means only one thing, namely ignorance, and belief means only one thing, namely knowledge, or rejection or belief in the heart. So they dispute as to whether belief in the heart is anything other than knowledge, or is it merely knowledge?

Though this is the most corrupt statement ever uttered concerning faith, it is the view of many of the scholars of *kalaam* who were influenced by the *Murji'ah*. The *salaf*, such as Wakee' ibn al-Jarraaḥ, Aḥmad ibn Ḥanbal, Abu 'Ubayd and others described as *kaafir* those who expressed this view. They said: *Iblees* is a *kaafir* according to the text of the Qur'an, and he became a *kaafir* because of his arrogance and his refusal to prostrate to Adam, not because he disbelieved in any text. The same applies to Pharaoh and his people, concerning whom Allah (سبحانه وتعالى) said:

﴿ وَجَحَدُوا۟ بِهَا وَٱسْتَيْقَنَتْهَآ أَنفُسُهُمْ ظُلْمًا وَعُلُوًّا ... ﴿١٤﴾ ﴾

> ﴿And they belied them [those *aayaat*] wrongfully and arrogantly, though their ownselves were convinced thereof [i.e. those (*aayaat*) are from Allah, and Moosa (Moses) is the Messenger of Allah in truth, but they disliked to obey Moosa (Moses), and hated to believe in his Message of Monotheism...].﴾ *(Qur'an 27:14)*."[30]

The difference between this group of the *Murji'ah* and that which came before — both of whom are among the extreme *Murji'ah* — is that the first group did not regard a person as *kaafir*, either in this world or in the Hereafter, unless he denied and rejected (the ruling),

[30] *Al-Eemaan*, in *Majmoo' al-Fataawa*, 7/188-189.

whereas the second group said: whoever is judged to be a *kaafir* according to shari'ah, we also regard him as a *kaafir* in this world, but inwardly he may be a believer so before Allah he is a believer.

These two groups were regarded by some of the *salaf* as *kaafir*, as stated above, because of their extreme views and because they went against the clear text (of the Qur'an and Sunnah).

The third view: That whoever is judged by the texts to be a *kaafir* — such as one who insults the Prophet (ﷺ) — is a *kaafir* both outwardly and inwardly, both in this world and in the Hereafter, but if his *kufr* is because of an action such as words or deeds, it is not because of the action itself, but because the action is indicative of the absence of belief in his heart, i.e., his action indicates that there is disbelief in his heart. This is the view of the *kalaami Murji'ah* such as the *Ash'aris* and others, who wanted to reconcile between their view that *kufr* is merely rejection or disbelief and their agreement with shari'ah that such people are *kaafir*. So they said: this action is major *kufr*, but *kufr* happens because it is a sign of disbelief in the heart.

This is the view of those who say that the *kufr* of the one who insults the Prophet (ﷺ) is essentially because he believes it to be permissible to utter such insults. This is what Ibn Taymiyah described as a serious mistake and a grave error, and he attributed this view to the later *Jahamiyah* who followed the views of the early *Jahamiyah*. We have quoted above what he said concerning this matter and how he criticized this specious argument.

They agreed with *Ahl as-Sunnah wal-Jamaa'ah* concerning the ruling, that whoever does this is a *kaafir* both outwardly and inwardly, but they differed from them concerning the reason for that. *Ahl as-Sunnah* said that he is a *kaafir* by virtue of the very action or words which imply *kufr*, whereas these people said that he is a *kaafir* because this action or these words are a sign of the absence of belief in his heart, and that is the reason why he became a *kaafir*. This is false, because not every *kaafir* disbelieves in his heart. *Iblees*, Pharaoh, the Jews, Heraclius and others believed and knew in their hearts, but they were *kaafirs* (disbelievers) because of their actions of refusal and turning away.

The *aimmah* (Imams) engaged in debate with them, especially Ibn Taymiyah in his two books *Al-Eemaan* and *Aṣ-Ṣaarim al-Maslool*. Among the things that he said concerning these people was: "The words of Allah contain information and commands. With regard to the information, it is to be believed, and the commands are to be obeyed and submitted to. This is an action in the heart, based on submission to the command even if one does not do what is commanded... (Then he said): if there is any element of belittling or disrespect in the heart then there cannot be submission to the command, and thus there can be no faith in the heart. This is the very nature of the *kufr* of *Iblees*, for he heard the command of Allah and he did not disbelieve in any messenger, but he did not obey the command or submit to it, and he was too arrogant to obey, so he became a *kaafir*. This is an issue concerning which some of the later generations were confused. They imagined that faith is basically nothing more than belief, then they thought like *Iblees* and Pharaoh and others who did not disbelieve as such, either verbally or in their hearts, but their *kufr* was of the most extreme type. So they became confused, but if they had followed the guidance followed by the righteous *salaf*, they would have known that faith is both words and deeds..." After mentioning that both belief and obedience are essential, he said: "He cannot be a believer unless both conditions are met, for if he fails to obey and submit he is being arrogant, so he is one of the *kaafirs* (disbelievers) even if he believes. For *kufr* is more general than rejection. It may mean rejection and ignorance, or arrogance and wrongdoing. Hence *Iblees* was described as a *kaafir* and as being arrogant, but he was not described as rejecting or disbelieving. Hence the *kufr* of those who had knowledge, like the Jews and their ilk, is described as being like the *kufr* of *Iblees*, and the *kufr* of those who were ignorant, like the Christians and their ilk, is described as misguidance, which is ignorance. Do you not see that a group of the Jews came to the Prophet (ﷺ) and asked him about some things, and when he told them, they said, 'We bear witness that you are a Prophet,' but they did not follow him.[31] The same is true of Heraclius and others. This knowledge and belief did not benefit them..."

Then he mentioned the *Shahaadatayn* (the twin testimony of faith): the testimony that there is no god except Allah, and the testimony that Muhammad is the Messenger of Allah, then he said: "Since belief must be based on both parts of the *Shahaadatayn*, — which simply means that one has accepted the Message — there were some who thought that this is the only foundation of faith, and they forgot the other essential principle, which is submission. So he may believe in the Messenger both outwardly and inwardly, but he still refuses to submit to the commands. All he achieves by believing in the Messenger is that he becomes like the one who heard the message directly from Allah, like *Iblees*.[32] This explains to you that mocking Allah and His Messenger essentially contradicts submission and obedience to Him, and it contradicts belief by implication, because it contradicts the consequences and implications of belief and prevents him from reaping its benefits.[33]

These *Murji'ah* and those who agreed with them thought that there could be no *kufr* unless it was accompanied by disbelief or rejection.

---

[31] This story is narrated by Tirmidhi, hadith no. 2877. He said, this is a *ṣaḥeeḥ ḥasan* hadith.

[32] i.e., without any intermediary such as an angel or Prophet. This is the highest level of establishing evidence, since *Iblees* heard the command to prostrate (to Adam) directly from Allah.

[33] *Aṣ-Ṣaarim al-Maslool*, 3/967-969.

When these cases were quoted to them, in which there is definitive proof that the people who commit these sins are *kaafir*, they said: this is *kufr*, but then they introduced a *bid'ah* (innovation) which goes against the view of *Ahl as-Sunnah wal-Jamaa'ah*, when they said: but it is *kufr* because doing that is an indication of the lack of belief in his heart. So they went against the evidence of shari'ah which stated that there is belief in their hearts, and they also went against the evidence of common sense, for a man may believe in his heart but his words and actions may demonstrate something other than what is in his heart.

The fourth view: *Ahl as-Sunnah wal-Jamaa'ah* say: just as faith is the matter of what is in the heart and what one says and does, the same applies to its opposite. *Kufr* is the matter of what is in the heart or what one says and does, or all of them. If a person does something which implies *kufr* — whether it is verbal, such as insulting Allah, or a physical action, such as showing disrespect towards the Qur'an — by virtue of this very action, he becomes a *kaafir*, both inwardly and outwardly, according to the rulings of both this world and the Hereafter. What is in his heart does not matter, because he may have belief or disbelief in his heart. What Allah tells us is true both outwardly and inwardly. So when Allah tells us about the *kufr* of those who say that Allah is one of three, or that Allah is the *Messiaḥ* son of Maryam, or as He told us about those who mocked the religion:

﴿لَا تَعْتَذِرُوا۟ قَدْ كَفَرْتُم بَعْدَ إِيمَـٰنِكُمْ ... ﴿٦٦﴾﴾

﴾Make no excuse; you disbelieved after you had believed...﴿ (*Qur'an 9: 66*)

— these statements are true, and the *kufr* of such a person is real; the fact that the one who does it believes that Allah is One, or that the *Messiaḥ* is not God, etc., will not avail him anything.

These views — which I have discussed in detail, with examples — explain the difference between the view of *Ahl as-Sunnah wal-Jamaa'ah* and the views of the *Murji'i* groups.

Conclusion

— *Ahl as-Sunnah wal-Jamaa'ah* say: this action which constitutes *kufr* is *kufr* in and of itself.

— The *Ahl al-Kalaam* (Scholastics) who were influenced by the *Murji'ah* said that this was major *kufr* — which is in accordance with the view of *Ahl as-Sunnah wal-Jamaa'ah* — but they also said that it was *kufr* because it was indicative of disbelief or rejection in the heart. Thus they went against the view of *Ahl as-Sunnah wal-Jamaa'ah* in this sense, because they restricted the meaning of *kufr* to disbelief and rejection.

— One group went to extremes and said that it was *kufr* in an outward sense, according to the rulings of this world, but inwardly such a person may be a believer. This is a false view, as stated above.

— Another group went to extremes by saying that in principle, no one was a *kaafir* except the one who believed that the action he was doing, which constituted *kufr*, is permissible and who disbelieved in the sense that he clearly rejected (the ruling). This is also a false view.

Let those who speak or write about these topics think long and hard lest they express these false views without realizing, and then attribute what they say to the view of the *salaf*.

5- *Kufr* is not restricted only to disbelief or rejection. It may mean disbelief or it may mean some other action which implies *kufr*, whether that takes the form of words spoken or physical actions. There follow some examples of what the scholars have said on this matter:

a) Whoever mocks Allah or His religion or the Messenger is a *kaafir*. Allah (ﷻ) says:

﴿ وَلَئِن سَأَلْتَهُمْ لَيَقُولُنَّ إِنَّمَا كُنَّا نَخُوضُ وَنَلْعَبُ ۚ قُلْ أَبِاللَّهِ وَآيَاتِهِ وَرَسُولِهِ كُنتُمْ تَسْتَهْزِئُونَ ﴿٦٥﴾ لَا تَعْتَذِرُوا قَدْ كَفَرْتُم بَعْدَ إِيمَانِكُمْ ۚ إِن نَّعْفُ عَن طَائِفَةٍ مِّنكُمْ نُعَذِّبْ طَائِفَةً بِأَنَّهُمْ كَانُوا مُجْرِمِينَ ﴿٦٦﴾ ﴾

﴾If you ask them [about this], they declare: 'We were only talking idly and joking.' Say: 'Was it at Allah, and His *aayaat* [proofs, evidences, verses, lessons, signs, revelations, etc.] and His Messenger that you were mocking?' Make no excuse; you disbelieved after you had believed. If We pardon some of you, We will punish others amongst you because they were *mujrimoon* [disbelievers, polytheists, sinners, criminals].﴿

(Qur'an 9: 65-66)

Shaykh al-Islam Ibn Taymiyah said:

"Allah tells them that they disbelieved (became *kaafir*) after they had believed, even though they said, 'we were speaking of *kufr* but we did not believe in it; we were only talking idly and joking.' He explains that mocking the signs or verses of Allah is *kufr*."[34]

Ibn Taymiyah also said:

"Allah says: ﴾If you ask them [about this], they declare: 'We were only talking idly and joking...'﴿ *(Qur'an 9: 65)* so they admitted it and made excuses, hence Allah says: ﴾Make no excuse; you disbelieved after you had believed. If We pardon some of you, We will punish others amongst you because they were *mujrimoon* [disbelievers, polytheists, sinners, criminals].﴿ *(Qur'an 9: 66)*.

[34] *Al-Eemaan*, Pp. 208, *Al-Maktab al-Islami* edition.

This indicates that in their own view, they were not guilty of *kufr*, rather they thought that this was not *kufr*. So Allah explained that mocking Allah, His signs or verses and His Messengers is *kufr* which makes the one who does it a *kaafir* after he had believed. This indicates that they had weak faith and they committed his forbidden action, which they knew was *ḥaraam*, but they did not think that it would constitute *kufr*. But it did constitute *kufr* and they became *kaafir* because of it, even though they did not believe that it was permissible. This was the view of more than one of the *Salaf* concerning the description of the hypocrites of whom analogies are given in *Soorah al-Baqarah*, where they are described as seeing then being blind, as knowing then denying, as believing then disbelieving..."[35]

They became *kaafir* because of this mocking; no attention was paid to what they believed; in fact, the apparent meaning of the *aayah* is that they did not believe in the words that they were saying.

b) *Iblees* became a *kaafir* because of his refusal to prostrate to Adam, although he acknowledged Allah and had sworn an oath by His Glory, and asked Him to give him respite until the Day when they would be resurrected. So He believed in Allah, had knowledge of Him and believed in the Last Day. Allah (ﷻ) says:

﴿ وَإِذْ قُلْنَا لِلْمَلَٰٓئِكَةِ ٱسْجُدُوا۟ لِءَادَمَ فَسَجَدُوٓا۟ إِلَّآ إِبْلِيسَ أَبَىٰ وَٱسْتَكْبَرَ وَكَانَ مِنَ ٱلْكَٰفِرِينَ ﴿٣٤﴾ ﴾

﴾And [remember] when We said to the angels: 'Prostrate yourselves before Adam.' And they prostrated except *Iblees* [Satan], he refused and was proud and was one of the disbelievers [disobedient to Allah].﴿ *(Qur'an 2: 34)*

---

[35] *Al-Eemaan*, Pp. 260.

His *kufr* was the *kufr* of disdain and arrogance, caused by his refusal to prostrate (to Adam). He is a *kaafir* (disbeliever) simply because of this action, and the fact that he believed and did not deny is of no avail to him.

c) Allah has described some people as *kaafir* because of things that they have said. Allah (ﷻ) says:

﴿ لَّقَدْ كَفَرَ ٱلَّذِينَ قَالُوٓا۟ إِنَّ ٱللَّهَ هُوَ ٱلْمَسِيحُ ٱبْنُ مَرْيَمَ ... ﴿١٧﴾ ﴾

﴾Surely, in disbelief are they who say that Allah is the Messiah, son of Maryam [Mary]...﴿ *(Qur'an 5: 17,72)*

And He (ﷻ) says:

﴿ لَّقَدْ كَفَرَ ٱلَّذِينَ قَالُوٓا۟ إِنَّ ٱللَّهَ ثَالِثُ ثَلَٰثَةٍ ... ﴿٧٣﴾ ﴾

﴾Surely, disbelievers are those who said: 'Allah is the third of the three [in a Trinity]...'﴿ *(Qur'an 5: 73)*

These are words that in and of themselves constitute major *kufr*, and the fact that the one who says them believes in his heart is of no avail, even if he believes that Allah is One with no partner or associate.

d) Those who worship graves, calling upon someone other than Allah, offering sacrifices to them and seeking their help are *kaafir* simply because of these actions, even if they claim to believe in *Tawḥeed* and that they believe in their hearts that benefit and harm are in the hand of Allah Alone, and they say that there is no god but Allah and Muhammad is the Messenger of Allah. All of that is of no benefit to them.

The evidence for this is well known, and the scholars, in the past and more recently, have discussed this matter a great deal. They have refuted the specious arguments of the grave-worshippers who quoted the evidence of the *Murji'ah* as proof that praying to graves, offering sacrifices and making vows to them is not *shirk* or *kufr* if the one who does that believes in his heart and utters the *Shahaadatayn*.

The point here is that the action on its own constitutes major *kufr*, regardless of whether he regards it as being permissible or not.

This nullifies the claim of the one who says that no sin makes the one who does it a *kaafir* unless he regards it as being permitted.

e) Insulting Allah or the Messenger (ﷺ) is major *kufr*, regardless of whether one regards it as permissible or not. More than one scholar has reported consensus on this point, as we have quoted above.[36]

f) The *ṣaḥaabah* unanimously agreed that those who withheld the zakah and fought to do so were *kaafir*. We have discussed this matter in detail in Chapter 4. The point is that those who withheld the zakah became *kaafir* simply by withholding it — whether they denied (the obligation) or not was not relevant.

g) Whoever claims that any created being, whether a *wali* ("saint") or anyone else, is allowed to go against the shari'ah of Muhammad (ﷺ) is a *kaafir* [37] — regardless of whether he believes that in his heart or not.

h) There is consensus that the one who deliberately mishandles the Qur'an or shows disrespect towards it is a *kaafir*,[38] regardless of whether he means that in his heart or not.

i) The one who does not pray — we are referring here to the one who does not deny that it is obligatory, because concerning

---

[36] *Al-Eemaan*, Pp. 295 ff.

[37] *Al-Iqnaa'* by Al-Ḥajaawi, 4/299; *Majmoo' al-Fataawa*, 3/422.

[38] *Ash-Shifaa'* by Al-Qaaḍi 'Iyaaḍ, 2/1101, where he narrated that there is consensus on this point. See also *Rawḍah aṭ-Ṭaalibeen* by An-Nawawi, 10/64; *Al-'Iqnaa'*, 4/297.

> the one who does deny that, there is no dispute (that he is a *kaafir*). The evidence of the Qur'an and Sunnah indicates that the one who does not pray is a *kaafir*. This evidence is listed by Al-Marwazi in *Ta'ẓeem Qadr aṣ-Ṣalaah*,[39] Ibn al-Qayyim in *Kitaab aṣ-Ṣalaah*,[40] and others.

What concerns us here is the fact that some scholars narrated that there was consensus on the *kufr* of the one who does not pray, even if he does not deny (that it is obligatory). This refutes the *Murji'ah* who said that no sin makes a person a *kaafir* unless he believes it to be permissible, without differentiating between major sins of action such as *zina*, stealing, etc., which do not make a person a *kaafir* unless he believes them to be permitted, and major sins which constitute *kufr* and make a person a *kaafir* regardless of whether he regards it as permissible or not — as in the examples given above. In the case of prayer, even though there is a dispute concerning it among the *aimmah* (Imams), especially after the time of the *ṣaḥaabah*, more than one scholar narrated that there was consensus that the one who does not pray is a *kaafir*. It is narrated that Ayyoob said: not praying is *kufr* and there is no dispute on this point.[41] Isḥaaq ibn Raahawayh also narrated that there was consensus on this point,[42] and he refuted the *Murji'ah* who said that denial or rejection of the ruling was a prerequisite for denouncing anyone as a *kaafir*,[43] even though not every scholar who did not denounce the one who does not pray as a *kaafir* was a *Murji'i*.

Ibn Rajab (may Allah have mercy on him) said: "Many of the scholars of *Ahl al-Ḥadeeth* think that the one who does not pray is a

---

[39] 2/873 ff., no. 886 ff.

[40] Pp. 395 ff., in *Majmoo' al-Ḥadeeth an-Najdiyah*, *As-Salafiyah* edition.

[41] *Ta'ẓeem Qadr aṣ-Ṣalaah*, 2/925, hadith no. 978; *Ṣaḥeeḥ at-Targheeb*, 1/230.

[42] Ibid, 2/929, hadith no. 990.

[43] Ibid, 2/930 ff.

kaafir. Isḥaaq ibn Raahawayh narrated that there was consensus among them on this point, and he even described the view of those who say that the one who neglects these pillars but believes in them is not a *kaafir*, as being the view of the *Murji'ah*. Similarly, Sufyaan ibn 'Uyaynah said that the *Murji'ah* called not doing the obligatory duties a sin, equivalent to committing forbidden actions. But they are not the same, because committing *ḥaraam* actions deliberately, without believing that they are permitted, is a sin, but not doing the obligatory duties, without being ignorant of them and with no excuse, is *kufr*. This is clear in the story of Adam and *Iblees*, and the Jewish scholars who verbally affirmed the mission of the Prophet (ﷺ) but did not follow his shari'ah. It is narrated that 'Aṭaa' and Naafi', the freed slave of Ibn 'Umar, were asked about the one who says, prayer is obligatory but I do not pray. They said: he is a *kaafir*. This is the view of Imam Aḥmad..."[44]

Then he mentioned some of the views concerning the *kufr* of the one who does not abide by the four pillars — Prayer, Zakah, Fasting and Ḥajj — then he said: "Most of the scholars of hadith are of the view that not praying is *kufr*, unlike the case with the other pillars. Muḥammad ibn Naṣr al-Marwazi and others also narrated this view from them. Among those who said this was Ibn al-Mubaarak, and Aḥmad — in the well-known view narrated from him — and Isḥaaq. It is narrated that there was consensus among the scholars on this point, as stated above. Ayyoob said: not praying is *kufr*, and there is no dispute on this point. 'Abdullah ibn Shaqeeq said: the Companions of the Messenger of Allah (ﷺ) did not think that neglecting any deed was *kufr*, except in the case of prayer. This is narrated by Tirmidhi, who narrated that 'Ali, Sa'd, Ibn Mas'ood and others said: whoever does not pray is guilty of *kufr*. 'Umar (رضي الله عنه)

[44] *Fatḥ al-Baari* by Ibn Rajab al-Ḥanbali, 1/23, *Maktabat al-Ghuraba'* edition.

said: there is no share of Islam for the one who does not pray..."[45]

We are not discussing the dispute concerning this matter here — although the most correct view, based on the evidence, is that one who does not pray is a *kaafir* even if he does not deny (that it is obligatory) — but we would like to mention here a number of points:

a) The fact that consensus is reported on the point that the one who does not pray is a *kaafir*, even if he does not deny (that it is obligatory), or at the very least this is the view of the majority of the *salaf* of *Ahl al-Ḥadeeth* (i.e., early hadith scholars) destroys the view of the *Murji'ah* completely, because this is a sin of action, and whoever commits it, even if he does not deny (that prayer is obligatory) is a *kaafir* in the sense of major *kufr* according to these *aimmah* (Imams). So what is left of the *Murji'i* claim whose scholars say that no one can be denounced as a *kaafir* except the one who thinks that it is permissible for him to do (that sin), without differentiating between sins which constitute *kufr* and sins which are acts of disobedience but do not constitute *kufr* unless one believes them to be permissible.

b) If (a scholar) denounces the one who does not pray as a *kaafir* even though he does not deny (that it is obligatory), can it be said that he is going against the well-known principle that no one can be denounced as a *kaafir* for committing sin, so long as he does not regard that as permissible? Or can it be said that he is one of the *Khawaarij* who denounce people as *kaafir* for committing sins even though they do not regard them as permissible?

Those who set up these principles and rules say that no one can be denounced as a *kaafir* except the one who denies (obligations, etc.), and they make this a *salafi* principle, such that those who differ from

[45] *Fatḥ al-Baari* by Ibn Rajab al-Ḥanbali, 1/25.

it are viewed as being *Khawaarij*. This is the accusation which they make against those great *aimmah* (Imams) of the past and present. The same is also said with regard to the issue of ruling by something other than that which Allah has revealed without denying (the obligation of ruling by shari'ah).

c) Some of those who liked the views of the *Murji'ah* were keen to support the view that the one who does not pray is not a *kaafir* unless he denies (that prayer is obligatory). This was so as not to undermine the principles of the *Murji'ah*, which state that no-one can be denounced as a *kaafir* unless he denies and rejects (the obligations and prohibitions etc). I do not know what makes him reject the view of those *aimmah* (Imams) — of *Ahl al-Ḥadeeth* — and the *salaf* and *aimmah* (Imams) of this ummah. Theirs are the views which destroy the false and innovated views of the *Murji'ah*.

They did not stop at opposing the *aimmah's* (Imams') views concerning the issue of one who does not pray. They also opposed them with regard to another aspect of the issues of faith, namely the actions which constitute *kufr*, concerning which the *aimmah* (Imams) are unanimous that the one who does them is a *kaafir* — such as insulting Allah and His Messenger, or showing disrespect towards the *Muṣ-ḥaf*. They said that the one who does that is not a *kaafir* unless he believes that it is permissible. This was so as not to undermine their basic principles, even though there is scholarly consensus on this matter, as stated above when we discussed the issue of insulting Allah and His Messenger, etc.

We said "some of them", because not everyone who said that the one who does not pray is not a *kaafir* was following the view of the *Murji'ah*. We have noted this point above.

d) We have quoted from Ibn Rajab, some of which was mentioned by Al-Marwazi in *Ta'ẓeem Qadr aṣ-Ṣalaah* , there is an indication that the *aimmah* (Imams) of the *salaf* were aware of and understood the views of the *Murji'ah* who said that no one was to be denounced as *kaafir* except the one who denied (the obligations or prohibitions). The fact that they mentioned the *Murji'ah* in connection with the issue of prayer is an indication that those who applied the principle that no one was to be denounced as a *kaafir* for sinning except the one who denies (that the sin is forbidden) to all cases of sin, are *Murji'ah* or express the same views as they did.

In conclusion: the view of the majority, if not all, of the *salaf*, that the one who does not pray is a *kaafir* even if he does not deny (that prayer is obligatory), refutes the principle mentioned by those who oppose this view and go along with the *Murji'ah*, knowingly or otherwise.

6 - From discussion of the previous points concerning this specious argument, it is clear that the view that no one can be denounced as a *kaafir* except the one who denies that which Allah has revealed,[46] is a view which is based on false principles which they set out so that they could apply them to the issue of ruling by something other than that which Allah has revealed. Concerning this matter we say the following:

It is clear that this principle, which they set out and applied to all sins, is false, and that this applies only to sins of action, such as adultery, stealing and drinking alcohol, for which a person does not become a *kaafir* unless he regards that action as permissible, unlike the view of the *Khawaarij*. With regard to words and actions which constitute *kufr* and which nullify faith — examples of which we have given

---

[46] *Shaykh* Muhammad ibn Ibraaheem said in his *Fataawa* (6/189): "If the one who judges according to man-made laws says, 'I believe that this is false,' this does not change the ruling, rather he is abolishing the Shari'ah. It is like a person saying, 'I worship idols but I believe that they are false.'"

above - this principle does not apply to them; rather the one who does such things is a *kaafir* regardless of whether or not he regards them as being permissible. If this is clear, then we say: the ruler who rules by something other than that which Allah has revealed, at the national level — without regarding that as being permissible — is, according to the evidence, a *kaafir*. We have discussed this in detail above, in the previous section, and quoted the comments of scholars of the past and present. This shows that they think it more correct to view such a person as a *kaafir* in the sense of major *kufr*. This is the whole point of this book.

Our purpose in mentioning this specious argument and refuting it is to undermine the principle on which those who hold the opposite view base their view and which they use as definitive evidence. This has been explained in the previous section.

Thus the issue of ruling by something other than that which Allah has revealed clearly does not come under the same heading as the principle referred to above, rather it is similar to the issue of the one who does not pray, and it is to be examined and judged in the light of the same evidence, i.e., the relevant evidence and the view of the *aimmah* — the reputed jurists and scholars, then we may see which view is more correct and preferrable.

The preferred view concerning this issue (ruling by something other than that which Allah has revealed) and concerning the ruling on the one who does not pray is that both constitute major *kufr*. Praise be to Allah, in thinking that this is the preferred view, that we have the example of many of the *aimmah* (Imams) who came before us. Indeed, it has been narrated that there is consensus, as stated above concerning the issue of prayer, and as we shall see below concerning the issue of ruling by something other than that which Allah has revealed, when we respond to the sixth specious argument. And Allah knows best.

The Fifth Specious Argument

Comparing ruling by something other than that which Allah has revealed to *bid'ah*

This may be summed up as follows: that the innovator is, in effect, trying to compete with the shari'ah by means of his *bid'ah*, trying to fill gaps in it and claiming that it is imperfect. The innovator is opposing shari'ah and diverting from it, and the one who rules by something other than that which Allah has revealed is also like this: he thinks that the shari'ah is imperfect, and he is trying to match it with his man-made laws, claiming implicitly and explicitly that the shari'ah is incomplete.

If this be the case, the proponents of this specious argument say that the innovator is more opposed to the shari'ah than the one who rules by something other than that which Allah has revealed, and he is more dangerous, because he attributes his innovation to Islam, unlike the one who rules by something other than that which Allah has revealed, because he does not attribute the man-made laws to shari'ah. The danger posed by the innovator to the common folk is greater because he is dividing the ummah and splitting it into various groups and factions.

Then they say that the *aimmah* (Imams) divided *bid'ah* into two categories:

1 - *Bid'ah* which constitutes *kufr* and puts a person beyond the pale of Islam, such as the *bid'ah* of those who deny something which is a well known and well established part of Islam, and which no Muslim has any excuse for not knowing, or believe the opposite of such a thing.

2 - *Bid'ah* which does not constitute *kufr* and does not put a person beyond the pale of Islam; this is apart from that described above.

They then seek to apply this to the issue of ruling by anything other than that which Allah has revealed, which they divide into two categories:

a) That which constitutes major *kufr*, that is, when the ruler regards ruling by anything other than that which Allah has revealed as being permissible, and rejects (the ruling of Islam).
b) That which constitutes lesser *kufr*, which is the case of the ruler who rules by something other than that which Allah has revealed, without regarding that as being permissible, even if he promulgates man-made laws and enforces them.

This is the summary of the specious argument of those who compare ruling by something other than that which Allah revealed to *bid'ah* and the people who do it, and the view of the *salaf* concerning them.

At the end of Chapter 4 we referred to the issue of *bid'ah* and the attitude of the *salaf* towards it and those who followed it. We said that this was an example of the attitude of the scholars towards those who alter the shari'ah; as Ash-Shaaṭibi said, those who follow *bid'ah* are accusing the shari'ah of being imperfect.

Undoubtedly the similarities between *bid'ah* and man-made laws are many.[47] How could it be otherwise, when the man-made laws are innovations that have been introduced into Islam?

This specious argument is based on the previous comparison, but it contains a number of contradictions and errors which we have no choice but to examine. These include the following:

---

[47] See *Al-I'tiṣaam*, 1/46-53, where he describes in detail the perfection of shari'ah and the fact that human minds cannot independently know people's best interests. He describes therein the opposition of the followers of *bid'ah* towards the shari'ah, and how they try to compete with it by means of their innovations and following of their whims and desires.

1) Promulgating man-made laws which go against the Islamic shari'ah is a kind of innovation that has been introduced into Islam, indeed it is a kind of innovation that never happened to the Muslim ummah — in the way it is happening now — except in the most recent times, whereas some of the other kinds of *bid'ah* had emerged during the time of the *ṣaḥaabah* (may Allah be pleased with them).

It may be said: how can one *bid'ah* be compared and contrasted with another, based on the general wording of the scholars concerning innovation? This is imprecise and inaccurate. It is more appropriate to say that these man-made laws are a kind of newly-invented innovation, then we should examine the evidence in the words of the scholars concerning them, to see whether they regarded it as constituting *kufr* or not.

The comparison made by some between man-made laws and *bid'ah* is like one who says that the issue of worshipping graves is something which, like *bid'ah*, may be divided into that which constitutes *kufr* and that which does not constitute *kufr*; or that the issue of celebrating the *Mawlid* (Prophet's birthday) is something which, like *bid'ah*, may be divided into that which constitutes *kufr* and that which does not constitute *kufr*; or that giving the *adhaan* for the 'Eid prayer is something which, like *bid'ah*, may be divided into that which constitutes *kufr* and that which does not constitute *kufr* ... and so on. This involves a significant degree of mixing unrelated issues and making mistakes.

The correct view is to say that this is a kind of newly invented *bid'ah*, we should then examine what kind of *bid'ah* it is, whether it constitutes *kufr* or not, by examining it in the light of the evidence, correct principles and the comments of the scholars.

2) Even though ruling by something other than that which Allah has revealed is a kind of newly invented innovation, it is still incorrect to

compare it to the well-known general kinds of *bid'ah*, because there are differences between the two. These differences include:

> a) That the one who rules by something other than that which Allah has revealed is blatantly opposing the shari'ah because he is basing his judgement on mere opinion, not on any kind of evidence. He does not have any evidence, or anything that even resembles evidence, for his laws which clearly go against Islamic shari'ah.

But the one who follows *bid'ah* — as he claims — is basing his view on shari'ah, or so he says. Hence he presents evidences from the Qur'an or Sunnah or *qiyaas* (scholarly analogy), or the words of a scholar. Indeed, he — as Ash-Shaaṭibi says[48] — "can never think of it as being *bid'ah*; rather in his view it is something which is a part of that which is prescribed by shari'ah, like the view of the one who allocates Mondays for fasting because that is the day on which the Prophet (ﷺ) was born, or who regards the twelfth day of *Rabee' al-Awwal* as an *'Eid* day because the Prophet (ﷺ) was born on that day..."[49] He also says concerning the followers of *bid'ah* — in the context of explaining why the scholars have some considerations in some cases for the views those who follow *bid'ah* —

"If we accept the fact that they sometimes have some consideration for the views of the innovators, this is because they are not following their whims and desires in an absolute sense. But those who do follow their whims and desires in an absolute sense do not believe in shari'ah in the first place. But in the case of the one whose belief is so strong that one may think that he is only following that which the

---

[48] We have quoted what Ash-Shaaṭibi says because he is one of the most well known scholars who explained in detail that those who follow *bid'ah* are opposed to shari'ah and accuse it of being incomplete, as stated above.

[49] *Al-I'tiṣaam*, 2/63.

evidence (*daleel*) leads him to, it cannot be said that he is following his whims and desires in an absolute sense, rather he is following the shari'ah, but in another sense he is following his whims and desires because he is following something that is unclear. So in a way he has something in common with those who follow their whims and desires, and he has something in common with those who follow the truth, in the sense that in general he does not accept anything but that which is based on evidence. It also seems that in general they have the same intention as the followers of truth, which is to follow the shari'ah..."[50]

The one who follows *bid'ah* attributes his innovation to Islam, and looks to shari'ah for evidence,[51] whereas the one who replaces shari'ah with man-made laws is going against shari'ah and he has no evidence for his laws.

Thus the difference between the one who follows *bid'ah* and the one who invents laws which oppose shari'ah becomes clear. Hence Ash-Shaaṭibi called (the latter) the one who follows his whims and desires in an absolute sense, and the one who does not believe in shari'ah in the first place, because he is not following evidence or any interpretation of any text.

b) Innovations (*bid'ah*) may be major or minor; they vary in degree. Some of them may make the one who does them a *kaafir* and some of them may not. But changing the shari'ah is *kufr* in every case, minor or major. Ash-Shaaṭibi said, referring to the fact that *bid'ah* contains some element of introducing new laws — which he mentioned in the context of listing

[50] *Al-Muwaafaqaat*, 5/222. Ed. by Mashhoor Ḥasan Salmaan.

[51] This is one of the very serious aspects of the danger which innovation poses to Islam, because its proponents claim to be Muslims, thus they deceive the common folk and their like. But Islam is free of any innovation, and Allah is the One Whose help we seek. (Author)

questions and answers on the matter of dividing *bid'ah* into major and minor, and the dispute concerning that — "Every *bid'ah* — even if it is minor — involves adding or taking away laws and rituals, or changing their original form. All of that may be with regard to one issue of shari'ah or it may be with regard to something that is connected to shari'ah, thus undermining that which is prescribed. If anyone does this deliberately with regard to shari'ah, then he is a *kaafir*, because adding to it, taking away from it or changing it — whether that is to a greater or lesser extent — is *kufr*. Whether that is done to a greater or lesser extent makes no difference. But if a person does that because of a misinterpretation or a wrong opinion which he formed or ascribed to shari'ah, even though we do not regard him as a *kaafir*, what he does is still wrong regardless of its extent, because all of that is a sin that cannot be tolerated by shari'ah, regardless of its extent."[52]

From pondering the comments of Ash-Shaaṭibi, the following points become clear:

— There is a similarity between the action of introducing *bid'ah* and the action of making laws which go against shari'ah. This is true.

— Whether this is done to a greater or lesser extent, both are a manifest going astray.

— There are two-pronged differences between the innovator and the one who promulgates laws over and above the laws of Allah:

a) The innovator tries to base his opinion on evidence, albeit a misinterpretation or an incorrect opinion, whereas the one who promulgates laws has no evidence, rather he is deliberately going against shari'ah.

---

[52] *Al-I'tiṣaam*, 2/61.

This difference between the innovator and the promulgator of laws is quite obvious.

b) With regard to the ruling on each, the one who invents laws deliberately and adds to or takes away from the shari'ah becomes a *kaafir*, whereas a mere innovator may or may not become a *kaafir*. In either case — whether the innovator becomes or does not become a *kaafir* — there is no difference whether the *bid'ah* is done on a large or small scale.

Thus it becomes clear that there is a difference between the one who rules by something other than that which Allah has revealed, and the one who introduces *bid'ah*. How can we compare the one to the other in absolute terms? Any comparison made when these differences exist is a false comparison, I mean the comparison made by the proponent of this specious argument, which led him to the conclusion that the one who rules by something other than that which Allah has revealed and who changes the laws of Allah — without denying them or believing that to be permissible — comes under the same category as *bid'ah* that does not constitute *kufr*. We will explain this further in the following section.

3) The comparison made by the proponent of this specious argument leads to incorrect conclusions. This is clear from the fact that he divides *bid'ah* into two categories, that which constitutes *kufr*, which includes disbelieving in or denying well known and well established matters of shari'ah which no Muslim has any excuse for not knowing; and that which does not constitute *kufr*, which is any other kind of *bid'ah* — i.e., *bid'ah* in word or deed which does not involve disbelieving in or denying matters which no Muslim has any excuse for not knowing. By the same token, he also divided ruling by something other than that which Allah has revealed into two categories: that which constitutes major *kufr*, which involves regarding that which is forbidden as permissible and denying or

rejecting (the rulings of Allah); and that which constitutes minor *kufr* which means ruling by something other than that which Allah has revealed and changing the laws of Allah without denying or rejecting (the ruling of Allah).

It should be noted that this leads to two incorrect conclusions:

a) That the implication of major *kufr* attached to ruling by something other than that which Allah has revealed is limited to matters of belief, i.e., denial and disbelieving. So he should be consistent in applying this principle to *bid'ah*, so that every *bid'ah* that involves belief would be denounced as major *kufr*. Therefore the label of major *kufr* would be applied to everyone who misinterprets some of the attributes of Allah; or who says that we cannot know what they mean, so we should leave this matter to Allah; or who believes that 'Ali is superior to Abu Bakr and 'Umar (may Allah be pleased with them all), whilst believing that all of them are good; or who denies some aspects of *Al-Qadr* (Divine Decree), like the *Qadari Mu'tazilah* and others. This argument implies that everyone whose *bid'ah* involves some aspect of belief (*'aqeedah*) should be denounced as a *kaafir*, and this is obviously false and incorrect.

b) In addition, this implies that just as he does not regard as a *kaafir* the one who rules by (man-made) laws, so long as he does not believe that it is permissible for him to do so, by the same token he should not denounce anyone as a *kaafir* because of a *bid'ah* that takes the form of action, no matter how serious the *kufr* involved, such as worshipping graves and offering sacrifices to them, or saying that the *'aarif* and *wali* are not subject to the obligations of Islam, or worshipping *Al-Ḥaakim bi Amr-Allah*,[53] like the Druze, or prostrating to idols — especially if, in addition to doing those things,

[53] The sixth *Faaṭimi* (Fatimid) *khaleefah* (and *Isma'ili* Imam) who died in Cairo in 411 AH/1021 CE. (Translator)

they say that they venerate Allah alone and that they do not believe that those whom they worship can bring benefit or ward off harm — or other actions which are *kufr* according to the consensus of the Muslims.

These are the two false implications which result from this specious argument. The reason is — as in the case of the previous specious arguments — that this opinion is based on the division of *kufr* into major *kufr* or *kufr* of belief, and minor *kufr* or *kufr* of action. See how these specious arguments are interconnected:

— The specious argument which says that promulgating man-made laws is *kufr* of action, and *kufr* of action does not put one beyond the pale of Islam.

— The specious argument which says that as a general principle, no one is a *kaafir* except the one who denies and rejects (the ruling of Allah) in the case of ruling by something other than that which Allah has revealed and in other cases, meaning that no one can ever be denounced as a *kaafir* for an action.

— This specious argument which says that just as no one can be denounced as a *kaafir* except the innovator who rejects (the ruling of Allah), so, too, no one can be denounced as a *kaafir* except the one who denies and rejects that which Allah has revealed.

These lead to false conclusions, as stated above.

4) What has been said concerning the definition of *bid'ah* which makes one a *kaafir* and puts one beyond the pale of Islam is that it means one who denies and rejects something which is a well known and well established part of shari'ah, something which no Muslim has any excuse for not knowing, or who believes the opposite of such a thing. It may be said concerning this:

(i) That this definition is based on the principles of the *Murji'ah* , who said that no one should be denounced as a *kaafir* except the one who denies and rejects (the rulings of Allah) — the response to this view appears above, in the discussion of the third and fourth specious arguments.

(ii) That what, as the reputed scholars and *aimmah* said, divides *bid'ah* into that which constitutes *kufr* and that which does not constitute *kufr*. They based their arguments on matters which have to do with the *bid'ah* itself, and they did not connect the reasons for denouncing someone as a *kaafir* or not to the issue of whether it was the matter of belief or action. This is also their approach to whether words, actions or belief constitute *kufr* or not.

The following examples will make the matter more clear:

a) The extreme *Jahamiyah*, denied all the attributes of Allah. The well known view of Imam Aḥmad and the reputed scholars of the *salaf* is that they were *kaafir*, whereas those who misinterpreted some of the attributes of Allah, like the *Ash'aris*, were not regarded as *kaafirs*, according to the well known views of the *aimmah* — the well-reputed theologians and jurists of Islam.

(Both cases are concerned with the misinterpretation of the aspects of belief.)

b) The *bid'ah* of rejecting any of the pillars of Islam, or denying any of the clear prohibitions such as theft, adultery and drinking alcohol, or denying the resurrection after death. All of that is major *kufr*, according to the consensus. Whoever denies the Balance (*al-meezaan*) or some of the kinds of intercession, or some of the matters which have been narrated in the *aaḥaad aḥaadeeth* — there is some dispute as to whether such a one is a *kaafir*, and the majority of scholars say that he is not a *kaafir*.

(Both cases have to do with the matters of belief.)

c) The *baaṭini* (esoteric) misinterpretations of the prayer and fasting constitute major *kufr*, and the views of some of those who misinterpret the divine attributes or divine decree or some aspects of faith are not considered to constitute major *kufr*.

d) The *bid'ah* of the *Ṣufi zindeeqs* (heretics) who say that the obligations of shari'ah do not apply to the *wali* constitutes *kufr* according to consensus, whilst their innovations in rituals and practices and asceticism, etc., that are not prescribed by shari'ah do not constitute major *kufr*.

e) The innovations of offering sacrifices at graves, circumambulating them and praying to their occupants constitute major *kufr*, whilst the innovations of the *Mawlid* (Prophet's birthday), spending the night of the 15th of *Sha'baan* (*laylat an-nisf min Sha'baan*) in prayer, reciting *dhikr* in unison, reciting the *niyah* (intention for prayer) out loud and giving the *adhaan* for the *'Eid* prayer do not constitute major *kufr*.[54] (All of these are innovations of action)

The *aimmah* — the reputed scholars, did not divide *bid'ah* into matters of belief which constitute *kufr* and matters of action which do not constitute *kufr*; rather innovations of both belief and action were divided by the scholars into those which constitute major *kufr* and those which constitute minor *kufr*. The examples preceded above. We have explained where this specious argument goes wrong with regard to the comparison it makes — where it limits major *kufr* to matters of disbelief and denial — it is made clear that whatever is based on it is also false, namely the notion that no one can be regarded as a *kaafir* except the one who denies and rejects that which Allah revealed.

---

[54] For more details on which innovations do and do not imply *kufr*, and the comments of the *aimmah* on that. See in the desertation *Ḥaqeeqat al-Bid'ah wa Aḥkaamuhaa* by *Shaykh* Sa'eed ibn Naaṣir al-Ghaamidi, 2/190-305, published by *Maktabat ar-Rushd*.

5) The correct view on this matter — according to what we have mentioned, that ruling by anything other than that which Allah has revealed is a kind of *bid'ah*, or for the sake of argument, comparing ruling by anything other than that which Allah has revealed to *bid'ah* — is to say that just as *bid'ah* may be divided into two categories —

> i) *Bid'ah* which constitute *kufr* in the sense of major *kufr*, are all those concerning which the evidence indicates that the one who invents them is a *kaafir*, whether they are innovations of belief or of action;
>
> ii) *Bid'ah* which do not constitute *kufr* are lesser forms of innovation of belief or action, which do not reach the level of being major *kufr* —

Similarly the matter of ruling by anything other than that which Allah has revealed may also be divided into two categories:

> i) That which constitutes major *kufr* , such as denying and rejecting that which Allah has revealed, or issuing laws and legislation with no authority from Allah, or ruling by something other than that which Allah has revealed, namely man-made laws, and referring to those laws for judgement and forcing the people to do so.
>
> ii) That which constitutes lesser *kufr*, which has to do with minor matters and individual cases of judging or ruling by something other than that which Allah has revealed, on the condition that this is accompanied by affirmation and belief in the shari'ah of Allah.

Thus we cannot judge as *kaafir* all those who rule by something other than that which Allah has revealed. Rather the matter is subject to examination as we have discussed above, and this is in accordance with the division of *bid'ah* into that which constitutes *kufr* and that which does not constitute *kufr*. And Allah knows best.

The discussion on this specious argument may be summed up as follows:

a) That whoever bases his view and judgement of the people of *bid'ah* on the proper principles — that *bid'ah* may take the form of words, beliefs or actions, and that it may be divided into that which constitutes major *kufr* and that which constitutes minor *kufr*, even in the case of actions — then says that this also applies to the issue of ruling by something other than that which Allah has revealed — which may also take the form of words, beliefs or actions, and may be divided into that which constitutes major *kufr* and that which constitutes minor *kufr* — comes to the conclusion that the one who denies and rejects on his lips or in his heart that which Allah has revealed, and similarly the one who by man-made laws and adheres to them, is a *kaafir* who is guilty of major *kufr*. The one who rules (or judges) according to his own whims and desires in a minor issue — but does not deny or reject (the ruling of Allah) — is guilty of a lesser form of *kufr*.

Whoever says this is saying the right thing, and in accordance with the views of the *aimmah*.

b) But whoever bases his views on the notion that *bid'ah* does not constitute *kufr* unless one also denies and rejects something which is a well established fact of Islam which no Muslim has any excuse for not knowing, then makes an analogy on that basis and says that no one can be described as a *kaafir* except the one who denies and rejects that which Allah has revealed, has gone against the Imams and what he says leads to incorrect implications, as described above.

c) The one who came up with this specious argument based his view on a principle which he adheres to steadfastly and is unable to let go of, otherwise his conclusions would become baseless and he would contradict himself. Do you not see — as in the case of the previous specious arguments — that he does not stop repeating the idea that *kufr* can only apply in the case of rejection and denial — which is one of the basic principles of the *Murji'ah* — but he will never give up this idea. Every time he is cornered by the evidence and words of the scholars, he refers again to this corrupt principle and says that no one may be described as a *kaafir* except the one who denies and rejects (the ruling of Allah), and that no one may be described as a *kaafir* for judging by something other than that which Allah has revealed except the one who denies and rejects (the ruling of Allah), and that the one who follows *bid'ah* cannot be described as a *kaafir* unless he denies and rejects (the ruling of Allah), and so on.

In our discussion of the previous specious argument we have already explained what is wrong with this principle, which goes against the views of the *aimmah* (Imams) of the *salaf*.

The Sixth Specious Argument

The narration of consensus that the one who rules by something other than that which Allah has revealed is not a *kaafir*, except in the case of one who denies and rejects (that which Allah has revealed)

This is explained by saying that ruling by something other than that which Allah (ﷻ) has revealed is of two types:

a) Where the person regards it as permissible to rule by something other than that which Allah has revealed, or denies and rejects (the idea of) ruling by that which Allah has revealed. There is no dispute that the one who does this is a *kaafir* in the sense of major *kufr*, and the consensus of the *salaf* on this point is well known. He is a *kaafir* in all cases, whether he rules by something other than that which Allah has revealed or not, so long as he is denying and rejecting (the ruling of Allah).

b) The one who rules by something other than that which Allah has revealed, but he does not regard that as being permissible. This may be one of two cases:

The first case is where he sets up a general system of binding legislation or man-made laws which go against the shari'ah. Such a person, as we have explained in this book, is guilty of major *kufr.*

The second case is where he rules (judges) in an individual case by something other than that which Allah has revealed, because of some whim or desire, whilst he believes in and adheres to ruling by that which Allah has revealed. Such a person commits a major sin, but his *kufr* is a lesser form of *kufr* which does not put him beyond the pale of Islam.

So there are three cases:

a) Regarding ruling by something other than that which Allah has revealed as being permissible, and denying or rejecting the ruling of Allah.

b) Promulgating general legislation and laws — without regarding that as being permissible.

c) Ruling in an individual case according to one's whims and desires, without regarding that as being permissible.

With regard to the first case: there is no dispute concerning this; there is consensus that the one who is guilty of this is a *kaafir.*

With regard to the third case: there are those who consider him a *kaafir.* In the following section, when discussing the responses to these specious arguments, we will explain why this view is weak, and that the one who does this is not guilty of major *kufr*, rather it is a lesser form of *kufr.*

With regard to the second case: This is the focal point of the discussion and disagreement, especially among the later scholars. We have already mentioned the various kinds of evidence from the Qur'an, the Sunnah and the words of the scholars, both classical and modern, whose words carry weight, to show that in these cases the ruling is that this constitutes major *kufr*.

Those of the later scholars whose view on this matter is that the one who rules by something other than that which Allah has revealed by promulgating man-made laws and making them binding is not a *kaafir* — unless he regards that as being permissible — can do no more than quote some of the words of the scholars and use them as evidence to support their view.

Would that the matter stopped at this point, then it would not be so serious. But to claim that there is consensus on that which they say is incredibly strange!

The reason why this is so strange is that no scholar has been quoted as saying that there is consensus that the one who rules by something other than that which Allah has revealed is not a *kaafir* — except in the case of the one who regards that as being permissible. In fact, more than one scholar has narrated that there is consensus that such a person is a *kaafir* in the sense of major *kufr*, so how could this matter be reversed?

Nevertheless, we will pause to examine the claim of consensus made by those who holds the opposing view. Here we will discuss the second case only, since this is the focal point of the dispute.

Those who hold the opposing view claim that there is consensus among the earlier and later generations of *Ahl as-Sunnah* and others[55] that the one who rules by something other than that which Allah has

[55] This is his wording. I do not know what he would say about the *Khawaarij*, and whether he would include them or not. Whatever be the case, there is some contradiction in what he says.

revealed, but does not reject it or regard what he does as being permissible, is not a *kaafir*. They base this on a number of things, as they claim, which may be summed up as follows:

> (i) The consensus of the *salaf* that no Muslim may be described as a *kaafir* for committing a major sin unless he believes it to be permissible or denies that it is forbidden.
> (ii) There is no dispute among the *mufassireen* of the earlier and later generations concerning the interpretation of the *aayah* from *Soorah al-Maa'idah*, ﴿And whosoever does not judge by what Allah has revealed, such are the *kaafiroon* [i.e. disbelievers]﴾ (*Qur'an 5: 44)*, that a differentiation should be made between the one who denies and the one who does not deny: the former is a *kaafir* in the sense of major *kufr* and the latter is a *kaafir* in the sense of lesser *kufr*.
> (iii) The *Ahl as-Sunnah* are agreed that *bid'ah* is of two types: that which constitutes *kufr* and that which does not constitute *kufr*; the same is true of ruling by anything other than that which Allah has revealed.

It may be noted that there is no report from any scholar that there is consensus on this view; rather this (alleged) consensus is his deduction, and then he forbade anyone to disagree with him.

This is one aspect of the argument against this claim, especially when it comes from a seeker of knowledge (*ṭaalib al-'ilm*) who has not reached the level of the scholars and *mujtahids* who know the views and opinions (of the scholars and schools of thought) and the evidence for them. So what about the fact that there is a variety of evidence and statements of the scholars, both classical and modern, which go against and undermine this claim?

We shall explain the matter further in order to refute this claim:

1- Where are the quotations from the scholars who said that there is consensus? Narrating scholarly consensus is not something to be taken lightly, unless someone believes in an idea and thinks that no one would disagree with him on that, so he claims that there is consensus on that. This happened a great deal to some people, then it became clear that the matter was not as they thought. So what about the cases where it has been narrated that there is consensus on the opposite of what is being claimed?

2- The claim that the *salaf* were unanimously agreed that the one who commits a major sin is not a *kaafir* — unless he regards that as being permissible. We have discussed this matter above when discussing the third and fourth specious arguments. The *salaf* unanimously agreed on this point with regard to major sins that do not constitute *kufr* — such as adultery, theft, drinking wine and disobeying one's parents. These sins do not mean that the one who commits them is a *kaafir*, so long as he does not regard them as being permissible. If he does regard them as being permissible then he becomes a *kaafir*, even if he does not commit them.

But sins which constitute *kufr* — such as associating others with Allah (*shirk*), worshipping idols, offering sacrifices to them, insulting Allah, insulting the Messenger (ﷺ), showing disrespect towards the *Muṣ-ḥaf* , etc. — are major sins which also constitute major *kufr*, regardless of whether the one who does them believes them to be permissible or not. This is according to the consensus of the *salaf*, and no one disputed that except the extreme *Murji'ah*.

Apart from the extreme *mutakallimoon* (scholastics) among the *Murji'ah* and others, there is scholarly agreement with the *salaf* concerning the ruling - even though they differed as to the justification.

Therefore the principle referred to cannot be used as evidence with regard to major sins which constitute major *kufr* — as discussed above.

What would the one who uses this idea as evidence (to support his argument) and the one who derives the idea of consensus from it say if a grave-worshipper were to say to them, "praying to the dead and offering sacrifices to them does not constitute major *kufr*, according to scholarly consensus, unless one believes that to be permissible, and the evidence for consensus is the principle of the *salaf* that no Muslim can be regarded as a *kaafir* for a major sin unless he regards it as being permissible"?

What if he were to say something similar concerning the one who insults Allah or shows disrespect towards the *Muṣ-ḥaf*?

The one who claims such consensus has to choose one of the following:

Either he has to be consistent and say that the one who prays to someone other than Allah, or insults Him, or shows disrespect towards the *Muṣ-ḥaf*, is not a *kaafir* unless he regards that as being permissible, based on the principle mentioned.

If he does that, then he has gone against scholarly consensus and has expressed the view of the extreme *Murji'ah* such as the *Jahamiyah* and others.

Or he has to make an exception in the case of these major sins which constitute *kufr*, and express the view of the *salaf*, that the one who commits that is a *kaafir* in the sense of major *kufr*, regardless of whether he regards that as being permissible or not.

In this case, his use of that principle becomes baseless (his whole argument collapses), let alone his suggestion of consensus on the topic under discussion here.

Thus it becomes obvious that his using this principle is false. And Allah is the Guide to the straight path.

3 - His suggestion of consensus based on the comments of the *mufassireen* on the verse from *Al-Maa'idah* is also shown to be false in two ways.

a) What some of the scholars, such as Ismaa'eel al-Qaaḍi said. He said: 'The apparent meaning of the *aayah* indicates that whoever does what they did and invents a law that goes against the ruling of Allah and makes it a way to be followed, is subject to the same warning as was issued to them, whether he is a ruler or not."[56]

He did not mention the issue of regarding ruling by something other than that which Allah has revealed as being permissible, rather he mentioned the issue of inventing laws and making them a way to be followed. The Jews became *kaafir* by doing the action mentioned in the reason for revelation, but they did not regard it as being permissible, because they felt guilty for their action. They tried to find some approval from the Prophet Muhammad (ﷺ) to support their misguided notion and their ruling by something other than that which Allah had revealed.

Although some of the *mufassireen* mentioned the condition of regarding ruling by something other than that which Allah has revealed as being permissible, there are others who did not mention it, so where does this consensus come from?

If we add to that the comments of Imaams such as Ibn Katheer and others, it will become apparent that the claim that there is consensus among them is a claim that is to be rejected. This is sufficient here — the verse from *Al-Maa'idah* has been discussed in detail above, to which the discussion may refer to.

---

[56] *Fatḥ al-Baari* by Ibn Ḥajar, *Kitaab al-Aḥkaam, Baab Ajr man qaḍaa bil-ḥikmah*, hadith no. 7141.

b) It is narrated from Ash-Shu'bi that by *al-kaafireen* (disbelievers) Allah meant the Muslims; *aẓ-ẓaalimeen* (wrongdoers) meant the Jews and *al-faasiqeen* (rebellious) the Christians. This view was also favoured by Ibn al-'Arabi al-Maaliki and by *Shaykh* Ash-Shanqeeṭi in *Aḍwaa' al-Bayaan*, as quoted from them above.[57]

Ash-Shu'bi thought that the most likely meaning of *al-kaafireen* here is the Muslims, because *kufr* is mentioned here with the definite article *al-*. No distinction is made between the one who regards ruling by something other than that which Allah has revealed as being permissible and the one who does not. Indeed, he thought that what was meant by *aẓ-ẓaalimeen* was the Jews and what was meant by *al-faasiqeen* was the Christians, and *ẓulm* (wrongdoing) and *fisq* (rebellion), in his view, can only mean that which accompanies major *kufr*. But it is known that in the Qur'an, *ẓulm*, *fisq* and *kufr* may all be divided into major and minor.

What would the one who claims consensus say about the view of Ash-Shu'bi and the views of two of the Imams of *tafseer*, both classical and modern? If someone were to say that Ash-Shu'bi meant lesser *kufr* we would say that the context of his words does not indicate that, rather it indicates the other view. If we assume that it is possible, what to say then about the claim of consensus in view of this and other comments?

4- With regard to the claim of consensus based on the view of the *salaf* (pious predecessors) regarding the rulings on those who commit *bid'ah*, we have discussed above in our response to the sixth specious argument.

If the ruling on the people of *bid'ah* were to be used as evidence concerning the issue of ruling by something other than that which

---

[57] See above, p. 132 ff.

Allah has revealed in the manner claimed — falsely — by those who hold the opposing view, as discussed in detail above, then their derivation of consensus becomes more far-fetched and more apparently false to the one who thinks deeply and is objective. if we reverse their claim of consensus and say that the *salaf* were unanimous, that some of those who committed *bid'ah* of action became *kaafir* in the sense of major *kufr* — such as offering sacrifices at graves and showing disrespect towards the *Muṣ-ḥaf*, and also ruling by something other than that which Allah has revealed, even if he did not believe that this is permissible — this would be more acceptable than the claim of the one who holds the opposing view. but we do not say this in the sense that we compare ruling by something other than that which Allah has revealed to grave worship in the sense that both are actions. rather we say that each *bid'ah* should be examined by itself, then judged as appropriate, whilst noting that the *salaf* denounced some actions as *kufr* without stipulating any condition that the action should be regarded as being permissible — as has been discussed above more than once.

5- The scholars are unanimously agreed that the one who rules by something other than that which Allah has revealed is a *kaafir*, even if he does not regard that as being permissible. This consensus is narrated by more than one scholar.

This aspect alone is sufficient to refute the claim of those who hold the opposing view, who say that there is consensus that the one who rules by something other than that which Allah has revealed is not a *kaafir*, unless he regards that as being permissible. Because if we assume that it is narrated from one of the scholars that there was consensus as he claims, we should say to him that there are also reports of consensus on the opposite view, so we cannot say that one carries more weight than the other.

Moreover, the one who holds this opposing view does not narrate consensus from any scholar to support his claim. Rather it is something that he has deduced by himself, and we have explained above the weaknesses and faults in his notion.

Hence we say that more than one of the scholars has narrated that there was consensus to the effect that the one who rules by something other than that which Allah has revealed is a *kaafir*; this applies to all those who promulgate the laws of *jaahiliyah* and other systems, even if they do not regard that as being permissible. These scholars include *Shaykh al-Islam* Ibn Taymiyah, Ibn al-Qayyim and Al-Ḥaafiẓ ibn Katheer (may Allah have mercy on them), as we shall see below.

If someone were to ask, what about the scholars who came before Ibn Taymiyah and Ibn Katheer; what did they say about this matter and are there any reports of consensus from them?

Our response is that the Muslim ummah did not witness any alteration of the shari'ah or referral to any other laws for judgement until the Tartars came with their *Yaasiq* which they made a law to which they referred for judgement. But it should be noted that they did not oblige the rest of the Muslim ummah to refer to it. At there time there were regions of the Islamic world which continued to be ruled only by the pure shari'ah, but when these Tartars adhered to the law of their grandfather, the Imams (reputed scholars and jurists) — including Ibn Taymiyah, as mentioned above — took a stand and explained the ruling of Allah concerning them.

Here we will point out the following:

a) That when Islam came and the Prophet (ﷺ) was sent, there were those who did not obey Allah, such as the *mushrikeen* of Makkah who used to refer for judgement to their *jaahili* customs and false laws (*ṭaaghoot*), and the Jews in Madeenah who had distorted their scriptures and changed their rulings, agreeing amongst themselves to do so. It was concerning them that the verses of *Al-Maa'idah* were revealed.

The Qur'an was sent down to the Muslims, warning against obeying the *mushrikeen* or the People of the Book, or following them in their *kaafir* rulings; it stated that whoever did what they did was like them.

b) Amongst the Muslims, there was no one who referred for judgement to anything other than the Qur'an and Sunnah, apart from a few cases among the hypocrites, whom Allah exposed with regard to this matter — i.e., the matter of referring for judgement — in many *aayaat*, and pointed out the corrupt nature of their attitude. One of the most prominent features of the hypocrites was their refusal to refer for judgement to the Qur'an and Sunnah, and their referral to *ṭaaghoot* (false laws or false judges) instead.

The Muslim ummah continued to refer only to the Qur'an and Sunnah for judgement, except for some individual cases of injustice and oppression on the part of some rulers and judges.

c) With regard to the practical aspect, the matter was clear to the Muslims because of the clarity and unambiguous nature of the evidence concerning this important matter.

The ummah continued to follow this clear way until *bid'ah* began to emerge. The most prominent followers of *bid'ah* with regard to this matter were of two groups:

(i) Those who went to extremes in this matter and regarded injustice on the part of the rulers and judges to be ruling according to something other than that which Allah had revealed, so they regarded the one who did that as a *kaafir*. They even went to the extent to say that one who committed adultery, stole, or drank alcohol — and other major sins — was ruling by something other than that which Allah had revealed, and they judged such people to be guilty of major *kufr*.

The *aimmah* — the reputed jurists and theologians — confronted this misguided group of the *Khawaarij* and refuted their claims that injustice and committing major sins constituted ruling by something other than that which Allah had revealed in the sense of *kufr* (disbelief).

They said that this injustice was a lesser form of *kufr*, or *kufr* which did not put one beyond the pale of Islam. We have discussed this in detail above, when we examined what has been narrated from Ibn 'Abbaas concerning that.

(ii) Those who went to the other extreme and said that all actions — doing obligatory duties and not doing that which is forbidden — had nothing to do with faith. These are the *Murji'ah*. The *aimmah* confronted them and explained where they were going wrong, and they even denounced the extreme *Murji'ah* as *kaafir*.

d) With regard to practical matters and implementation, the Muslim ummah never knew of any referral for judgement to man-made laws and rejection of the Islamic shari'ah until two later times:

The first time was when the Tartars came with their law, the *Yaasiq*, to which they referred for judgement instead of shari'ah, even though they claimed to be Muslims.

This was one of the new phenomena, the like of which had never been known before on such a scale.

The scholars resisted this and issued *fataawa* concerning it, based on what they knew of the *Yaasiq* and its rulings and what they knew of the rulings of Allah concerning that.

Even though the Tartars did not impose the *Yaasiq* on the Muslim ummah,[58] and the pure shari'ah continued to rule all regions of the Islamic world, when they adhered to their *Yaasiq* and referred to it for judgement instead of to the shari'ah, the Imams considered this action of theirs to be changing and altering the shari'ah, so they judged this to be major *kufr*.

This is the point on which it is narrated that there was consensus among these *aimmah*. It was not the issue of injustice or oppression, as had been the case previously, for which the followers of *bid'ah* among the *Khawaarij* condemned people as *kaafir*. The action of the Tartars was a binding law to which they referred for judgement instead of the laws of Allah. So those *aimmah* (Imams) explained that this action of their constituted major *kufr* according to consensus, and that anyone who did the same as they did would be subject to the same ruling as them.

The second time was the modern times, when the Muslim ummah became weak and divided, and its enemies among the Christians and others attacked it. One of the most serious effects and elements of *kufr* which they transferred to the Muslims was these man-made laws - the historical details of which would take too long to explain here. The contemporary *aimmah*, like their brothers in the past, confronted these laws and explained the position of the laws and of those who refer to them for judgement instead of the laws of Allah.

This was another incident, more serious than the first, and the need to explain (the ruling of Islam) was more urgent, especially because it is so widespread in the Muslim lands and there are groups of Muslims

---

[58] It should be noted that this law quickly became extinct, so it cannot be regarded as a ruling which was applied in general terms. Perhaps the reason for that was the strongly worded and decisive *fataawa* issued by the scholars on this matter, and the fact that the Tartars were absorbed and assimilated into the Muslim ummah.

who promote these laws and give them precedence over the shari'ah of Allah. And Allah is the One Whose help we seek.

After noting these brief but important points, we will return to the issue of the narration of consensus from some of the *aimmah*, and quote what they said concerning this matter:

1) *Shaykh al-Islam* Ibn Taymiyah said:

"When a person regards as permissible something which is agreed by consensus to be forbidden, or he regards as forbidden something which is agreed by consensus to be permitted, or he alters a ruling of shari'ah which is agreed upon by consensus, then he is a *kaafir* according to the consensus of the *fuqahaa'*."[59]

2) He also said:

"It is also known that whoever disregards the commands and prohibitions with which Allah sent His Messengers is a *kaafir* according to the consensus of the Muslims, Jews and Christians."[60]

3) Ibn al-Qayyim (may Allah have mercy on him) said:

"It is stated in the Qur'an and in sound reports of scholarly consensus that the religion of Islam abrogates all religions which came before it, and that whoever adheres to that which is in the *Tawraat* (Torah) and *Injeel* (Gospel), and does not follow the Qur'an, is a *kaafir*."[61]

4) Ibn Katheer (may Allah have mercy on him) said:

"Whoever turns away from the laws which were revealed to Muhammad ibn 'Abdullah, the Seal of the Prophets (ﷺ), and refers for judgement to any of the abrogated laws (of earlier Prophets) is a *kaafir*, so how about one who refers for judgement to the *Yaasaa*

---

[59] *Majmoo' al-Fataawa*, 3/267.

[60] Ibid, 8/106.

[61] *Aḥkaam Ahl adh-Dhimmah*, 1/259.

(*Yaasiq*) and gives it precedence over (the shari'ah)? Whoever does that is a *kaafir* according to the consensus of the Muslims."[62]

These are the reports of scholarly consensus that the one who refers to something other than the shari'ah is a *kaafir*. Modern man-made laws are not the abrogated laws of earlier Prophets, rather they are more like the *Yaasiq* of the Tartars which was composed of the laws from the Jews, the Christians and the Muslims etc.

The modern *jaahili* laws are a more extreme form of *kufr* than the *Yaasiq* of the Tartars, so the ruling of *kufr* is more applicable in this case, as is pointed out by Aḥmad Shaakir and *Shaykh* Ash-Shanqeeṭi — as stated above.

Conclusion: The claims of consensus made by the one who holds the opposing view is a claim that is to be rejected. What is narrated from the *aimmah* (Imams) — leading Muslim jurists — concerning consensus is the opposite of this claim and thus refutes it.

The Seventh Specious Argument

Extending the judgement of *kufr* to include minor incidents

This specious argument goes to the opposite extreme compared to the previous specious arguments. This happened in the case of some contemporary writers, who extended the ruling of the *aayah* from *Soorah al-Maa'idah* — the fifth chapter of the Noble Qur'an — to apply to all cases in such a way that major *kufr* included the following:

1) Denying or rejecting that which Allah has revealed or legalising things as per rule other than that which Allah has revealed.

2) Promulgating general legislation or laws which go against shari'ah, even if that is not regarded as being permissible.

---

[62] *Al-Bidaayah wan-Nihaayah*, 13/119.

3) Ruling by something other than that which Allah has revealed, even if that is in only one case, or a person judged on one occasion by something other than that which Allah has revealed because of his own whims and desires, or because of a bribe, or for some other reason, even if he did not regard that as being permissible.

They do not make any exception, apart from the *mujtahid* who commits a mistake in deciding something; he is not to be regarded as a *kaafir*, rather he will be rewarded for his *ijtihaad*.

We disagree with what they say concerning a judgement made in an individual case or concerning a minor issue — as we have explained in detail above, in part four of Chapter Three, where we said: it is lesser *kufr* and a major sin, so long as he does not regard that as being permissible.

The reasons why they reached this incorrect conclusion by believing that the one who judges by something other than that which Allah has revealed in an isolated case were:

1) They regarded the report narrated from Ibn 'Abbaas concerning his comment on the *aayah*, "A lesser form of *kufr*" as being weak, so it could not be used as evidence to say that ruling by something other than that which Allah has revealed is lesser *kufr*.

2) The reason for the revelation of the *aayah* of *Al-Maa'idah* had to do with a single case, which was their altering of the ruling on adultery, which happened in the case of one of the Jews, so Allah described them as *kaafir* because of that, when He said: ﴾And whosoever does not judge by what Allah has revealed, such are the *kaafiroon* [i.e. disbelievers]...﴿ *(Qur'an 5: 44).*

This specious argument may be answered, with evidence, as follows:

1- The preferred view is that what Ibn 'Abbaas said was sound, when he said, "A lesser form of *kufr*", or, "it is not the *kufr* which they think it is." That is when the isnads of the report from Ibn 'Abbaas are taken together.

Moreover, the statement that it is a lesser form of *kufr* is narrated in *ṣaḥeeḥ* reports from Ṭaawoos, who was one of the *taabi'een* (generation after the Companions of the Prophet).

So this is a statement which has been narrated from the *salaf.* It is narrated in order to refute the *Khawaarij* who regarded unjust rulers and judges as being *kaafir*, and it is correct. Whoever adheres to shari'ah, then in an individual case he is guilty of injustice because of some whim or desire or some other reason, this is a major sin and is lesser *kufr*, but it does not put him beyond the pale of Islam.

2- The *kufr* of the Jews — as is stated in the reason for revelation — was not only in one case, as suggested by the one who holds the opposing view; rather they had agreed, in general, to change the ruling of Allah concerning the punishment of the adulterer, whereby they made blackening the face an universally applied ruling which was applied to every adulterer. Thus they changed the law in a way that was applicable to all. They did not — as some people claim — change it in just one case. No one who studies the reasons for revelation would say that the Jews were adhering to the ruling of Allah in a complete and general sense, then when one of them committed adultery they were unjust in their ruling concerning him. Rather what happened in their case was that they agreed to change the shari'ah and replace it with a law to be applied to and enforced upon all.

Whoever passes an unfair judgement in an individual case — concerning the punishment for adultery, for example — and goes against the ruling of Allah, although, generally speaking he adheres to that which Allah has revealed, is not like the one who changes the entire ruling and enforces that which goes against shari'ah in every case that he comes across — of the punishment of adultery — and adheres to that and forces it upon others.

The difference between the two is very clear, praise be to Allah.

3- The claim that what the Jews did was concerning one specific case is mistaken. Whoever examines the reports concerning the reasons for revelation will understand the following:

Concerning the report of Al-Baraa' ibn 'Aazib — the story of the face — blackened and flogged Jew who passed by the Prophet (ﷺ) — one of the Jew scholars said to the Prophet (ﷺ), when he asked him about the punishment for adultery among them, "Adultery became widespread amongst our nobles, so if we caught one of our nobles we would let him get away with it, but if we caught one of the lowly amongst us, we would carry out the punishment on him. Then we said, come, let us get together and agree upon something instead of stoning that may be applied to noble and common people alike. So we instituted blackening of the face and flogging instead of stoning..."[63]

Look at the differences between the two cases of the Jews:

In the first case, they adhered to the ruling of Allah concerning the punishment for adultery, but they were unjust in that they did not apply it to their nobles. This was injustice and a grave major sin on their part, though they did not regard that as being permissible.

In the second case, they changed the ruling of Allah concerning the punishment for adultery, and they thought, that it was better for them than their previous situation. They agreed to institute another ruling instead of stoning, to be a general ruling applied to everyone.

---

[63] *Tafseer aṭ-Ṭabari*, 10/305, hadith no. 11922; also 10/351, hadith no. 12033, edited by Shaakir.

This general law which they agreed upon and made binding upon everyone was a general law which was an alteration of the shari'ah. This constituted major *kufr*, and it was concerning this that the verses of *Al-Maa'idah* were revealed.

The difference between the two cases is very great. Whoever confuses them and applies one ruling to both cases is making a mistake.

4 - This is explained further by another report concerning the reason for revelation narrated from Abu Hurayrah (رضي الله عنه), in which it says: "The Messenger of Allah (ﷺ) said:

> 'What was the first thing in which you made an exception to the ruling of Allah?' He said: 'A nephew of a king committed adultery, and he was not stoned. Then a man from an ordinary family committed adultery, and that king wanted to have him stoned. Some of the people came to him and said, 'By Allah you will not stone him until you stone So-and-so, the king's nephew.' Then they agreed amongst themselves on a punishment other than stoning, and they forsook the punishment of stoning.' The Messenger of Allah (ﷺ) said: 'I pass judgement according to what is in the *Tawraat*.'

Then Allah (سبحانه وتعالى) revealed the words:

﴿ ۞ يَٰٓأَيُّهَا ٱلرَّسُولُ لَا يَحۡزُنكَ ٱلَّذِينَ يُسَٰرِعُونَ فِي ٱلۡكُفۡرِ مِنَ
ٱلَّذِينَ قَالُوٓاْ ءَامَنَّا بِأَفۡوَٰهِهِمۡ وَلَمۡ تُؤۡمِن قُلُوبُهُمۡۛ وَمِنَ ٱلَّذِينَ هَادُواْۛ
سَمَّٰعُونَ لِلۡكَذِبِ سَمَّٰعُونَ لِقَوۡمٍ ءَاخَرِينَ لَمۡ يَأۡتُوكَۖ يُحَرِّفُونَ ٱلۡكَلِمَ مِنۢ
بَعۡدِ مَوَاضِعِهِۦۖ يَقُولُونَ إِنۡ أُوتِيتُمۡ هَٰذَا فَخُذُوهُ وَإِن لَّمۡ تُؤۡتَوۡهُ
فَٱحۡذَرُواْۚ وَمَن يُرِدِ ٱللَّهُ فِتۡنَتَهُۥ فَلَن تَمۡلِكَ لَهُۥ مِنَ ٱللَّهِ شَيۡـًٔاۚ
أُوْلَٰٓئِكَ ٱلَّذِينَ لَمۡ يُرِدِ ٱللَّهُ أَن يُطَهِّرَ قُلُوبَهُمۡۚ لَهُمۡ فِي ٱلدُّنۡيَا خِزۡيٞۖ

وَلَهُمْ فِي ٱلْآخِرَةِ عَذَابٌ عَظِيمٌ ﴿٤١﴾ سَمَّٰعُونَ لِلْكَذِبِ أَكَّٰلُونَ
لِلسُّحْتِ ۚ فَإِن جَآءُوكَ فَٱحْكُم بَيْنَهُمْ أَوْ أَعْرِضْ عَنْهُمْ ۖ وَإِن تُعْرِضْ عَنْهُمْ
فَلَن يَضُرُّوكَ شَيْـًٔا ۖ وَإِنْ حَكَمْتَ فَٱحْكُم بَيْنَهُم بِٱلْقِسْطِ ۚ إِنَّ ٱللَّهَ
يُحِبُّ ٱلْمُقْسِطِينَ ﴿٤٢﴾ وَكَيْفَ يُحَكِّمُونَكَ وَعِندَهُمُ ٱلتَّوْرَىٰةُ فِيهَا حُكْمُ ٱللَّهِ
ثُمَّ يَتَوَلَّوْنَ مِنۢ بَعْدِ ذَٰلِكَ ۚ وَمَآ أُو۟لَٰٓئِكَ بِٱلْمُؤْمِنِينَ ﴿٤٣﴾ إِنَّآ أَنزَلْنَا
ٱلتَّوْرَىٰةَ فِيهَا هُدًى وَنُورٌ ۚ يَحْكُمُ بِهَا ٱلنَّبِيُّونَ ٱلَّذِينَ أَسْلَمُوا۟ لِلَّذِينَ
هَادُوا۟ وَٱلرَّبَّٰنِيُّونَ وَٱلْأَحْبَارُ بِمَا ٱسْتُحْفِظُوا۟ مِن كِتَٰبِ ٱللَّهِ وَكَانُوا۟
عَلَيْهِ شُهَدَآءَ ۚ فَلَا تَخْشَوُا۟ ٱلنَّاسَ وَٱخْشَوْنِ وَلَا تَشْتَرُوا۟ بِـَٔايَٰتِى ثَمَنًا
قَلِيلًا ۚ وَمَن لَّمْ يَحْكُم بِمَآ أَنزَلَ ٱللَّهُ فَأُو۟لَٰٓئِكَ هُمُ ٱلْكَٰفِرُونَ ﴿٤٤﴾ ﴾

﴾O' Messenger [Muhammad]! Let not those who hurry to fall into disbelief grieve you, of such who say: 'We believe' with their mouths but their hearts have no Faith. And of the Jews are men who listen much and eagerly to lies — listen to others who have not come to you. They change the words from their places; they say, 'If you are given this, take it, but if you are not given this, then beware!' And whomsoever Allah wants to put in *al-fitnah* [error, because of his rejecting of Faith], you can do nothing for him against Allah. Those are the ones whose hearts Allah does not want to purify [from disbelief and hypocrisy]; for them there is a disgrace in this world, and in the Hereafter a great torment. [They like to] listen to falsehood, to devour anything forbidden. So if they come to you [O' Muhammad], either judge between them, or turn away from them. If you turn away from them, they cannot hurt you in the least. And if you judge, judge with justice between them. Verily, Allah loves those who act justly. But how do they come to you for decision while they have the *Tawraat* [Torah], in which is the [plain] Decision of Allah; yet even after that, they turn away. For they are not [really] believers. Verily, We did send down the *Tawraat* [Torah] [to Moosa (Moses)], therein was guidance and light, by which the Prophets, who submitted themselves to Allah's Will, judged for the Jews. And the rabbis and the priests [too judged for the Jews by the *Tawraat* (Torah) after those Prophets], for to them was entrusted the protection of Allah's Book, and they were witnesses thereto. Therefore fear not men but fear Me [O' Jews] and sell not My Verses for a miserable price. And whosoever does not judge by what Allah has revealed, such are the *kaafiroon* [i.e. disbelievers — of a lesser degree as they do not act on Allah's Laws].

(Qur'an 5: 41-44)."[64]

This report, like the report quoted previously, indicates that they — at first — were adhering to the ruling of Allah concerning the punishment for adultery, but that they were unjust in that they did not carry out the punishment on some of their nobles, such as the king's nephew. The evidence that they were adhering to the ruling is the fact that the king wanted to stone the adulterer from amongst the ordinary people. So they did not change the ruling or institute something else in its place, rather they were adhering to it in general, but they were unjust in some cases. This is a major sin and is a lesser form of *kufr*.

Then matters changed and they altered the ruling of Allah by agreeing amongst themselves upon a punishment other than stoning. They made this punishment a generally applicable system to be applied to everyone, nobles and others. This action of theirs was changing the shari'ah, and this constituted major *kufr*.

---

[64] *Tafseer aṭ-Ṭabari*, 10/306, hadith no. 11924, edited by Shaakir.

Thus it is clear that the argument of those who oppose this view is weak, and that what we have established, that there is a difference between promulgating laws to be applied in all cases and judgements passed in individual cases, is correct. And Allah knows best.

5 - Injustice in judgements passed in individual cases was well known in the Muslim lands, especially after the time of the Rightly-Guided *khulafa'* (Caliphs), when Islam spread east and west. In every city and town of the Muslim world there were governors and judges, on whose part there may have been cases of injustice — for various reasons — in some individual cases, in which they went against the ruling of Allah because of some whims and desires, or a bribe, or for some other reason.

Because these incidents are something which is well-known, none of the *aimmah* of Islam are known to have classified any of these (rulers or judges) as being *kaafir* in the sense of *kufr* which puts one beyond the pale of Islam. If any such thing had happened, it would have been well-known and widely-reported.

This indicates that injustice in judging by something other than that which Allah has revealed in an individual case, when one adheres to the shari'ah and applies it, comes under the heading of major sins which are forbidden, but that does not mean that the one who does that is beyond the pale of Islam, unless he regards this judging by something other than that which Allah has revealed as being permissible.

Injustice on the part of rulers is something well known. It may occur to a lesser extent at some times and a greater extent at others. The same applies to injustice on the part of judges, it may happen to a greater extent at some times and a lesser extent at others, depending on the circumstances of the Islamic state. But the general principle in all cases was adherence to Islam and its shari'ah, and if there were instances of rulers or judges going beyond the boundaries of Islam, this did not happen in any general and widespread fashion, rather these were isolated incidents.

The leading Muslim jurists and theologians of Islam in every period knew of that and heard of it. Indeed in some cases they themselves were subjected to injustice. But they did not think of this as being anything more than injustice and oppression; they did not regard it as reaching the level of major *kufr*.

6 - It is known that the basis of the *bid'ah* of the *Khawaarij* who rebelled at the time of 'Ali ibn Abi Ṭaalib (رضي الله عنه), and of those who staged successive rebellions during the time of the Umawis (Umaayads) — during which many historical events and great battles happened — and their reason for rebelling, was the injustice and oppression of the rulers. This is what they called ruling by something other than that which Allah had revealed and they applied the ruling of *kufr* to all of them, based on their interpretation of the *aayah*.

Although it is known that some of the Umawis,[65] and their governors in the various regions, committed acts of injustice — as is well known and well-established — the Imams of the *salaf* at that time, most of whom were from among the *taabi'een* and the succeeding generation, did not agree with the *Khawaarij* and their labeling of the rulers as *kaafir* and fighting them. Rather, they opposed the methodology of the *Khawaarij* and this opposition took the following forms:

a) Classifying the *Khawaarij* as innovators whose *bid'ah* took the form of words, such as their denouncing as *kaafir* those who committed major sins, or of actions, such as their rebelling

---

[65] The word "some" is used because of the exceptions of Mu'aawiyah (رضي الله عنه), 'Umar ibn 'Abdul-'Azeez (may Allah have mercy on him) and others who were known for their justice.

against and fighting the leaders who were unjust. The books of Sunnah — most of which were compiled after the time of the *Umawis* — contain warnings against the innovations of the *Khawaarij*.

b) They did not denounce those unjust rulers and judges as *kaafir*, rather they viewed them as Muslims and prayed behind them, and they believed that it was obligatory to obey them with regard to matters that involved obedience towards Allah.

Even though injustice may be prevalent at some times, this does not undermine the basic principle. Although there may be some scholars who denounced one of these rulers as a *kaafir*, such as Al-Ḥajjaaj, that was an exceptional and isolated case in which he learned something about Al-Ḥajjaaj which none of the other scholars knew, even though his view differed from that of the majority.

Thus it becomes clear that those who apply the ruling of *kufr* to everyone who rules by something other than that which Allah has revealed, including those who do so with regard to individual cases, is mistaken. And Allah knows best.

CHAPTER SIX

RELATED TOPICS AND ISSUES

There are some issues which have to do with ruling by something other than that which Allah has revealed, concerning which some people may be mistaken. Therefore we will examine them briefly in this chapter.

The most important of these issues are as follows:

Differentiating between the *Shar'i* System and the Administrative System

Two groups make mistakes concerning this issue.

The first group thinks that every system devised by the ruler is a case of ruling by something other than that which Allah has revealed, even if it is a purely administrative system which does not lead to permitting that which Allah has forbidden or forbidding that which Allah has permitted, or does not go against the laws of Allah.

The other group thinks that so long as the ruler is permitted to issue administrative regulations, then every system that the ruler devises with the intention of serving the society is justifiable, so long as the ruler declares his commitment to Islam, even if these laws and systems involve something that goes against the laws of Allah, because they are matters of necessity, and other such justifications.

Both groups have misunderstood this issue. The correct way is to differentiate between systems which go against the laws of Allah, and administrative systems which do not involve going against the rulings of Allah. The former is not permissible whilst there is nothing wrong with the latter.

One of those who drew attention to this fact is *Shaykh* Ash-Shanqeeṭi (may Allah have mercy on him), who after discussing the issue of promulgating legislation without any authority from Allah and ruling by something other than that which Allah has revealed, said:

"It should be noted that we should differentiate between man-made systems, promulgating which constitutes *kufr* or disbelief in the Creator of the heavens and the earth, and systems which do not constitute *kufr*.

This may be clarified by pointing out that systems are of two types, administrative and legislative. Administrative systems are those intended for the purposes of organization and efficiency, without going against the shari'ah. There is nothing wrong with this, and there was no dispute concerning this among the *ṣaḥaabah* and those who came after them. 'Umar (﷡) did many such things which were not done at the time of the Prophet (ﷺ), such as recording the names of the troops in a book so as to keep track of who was absent and who was present, even though the Prophet (ﷺ) did not do that, and he did not know that Ka'b ibn Maalik had stayed behind from the campaign of Tabook until after he reached Tabook. And 'Umar (﷡) bought the house of Ṣafwaan ibn Umayyah and made it into a prison in Makkah, although neither the Prophet (ﷺ) nor Abu Bakr (﷡) had established a prison.

There is nothing wrong with administrative matters such as these, which are done for the sake of efficiency and do not go against shari'ah, such as organizing the affairs of employees or organizing the administration of work in a manner that does not go against shari'ah. This kind of man-made system is fine, and it does not go against the *shar'i* aims of taking care of the general interests of people.

But promulgating legislative systems that go against the shari'ah of the Creator of the heavens and the earth, and referring to them for judgement, constitutes *kufr* or disbelief in the Creator of the heavens and the earth, such as claiming that giving preference to males over females in matters of inheritance is not fair, and that they should be given equal shares; or claiming that plurality of marriage is oppression, or that divorce is unfair to women, or that stoning and amputation of hands, etc., are bestial acts which cannot be justifiably done to anyone, and so on.

Imposing this kind of system on the members of a society and on their wealth, honour, lineage, minds and ways constitutes *kufr* and disbelief in the Creator of the heavens and the earth. It is a rebellion against the divine system which was designed by the One Who created all of mankind and Who knows best what is in their interests, Glorified and Exalted be He far above having any partner in legislation."[1]

The difference between what is man-made legislation which goes against shari'ah, and what is administrative but does not go against shari'ah, will be made clearer by noting three things:

a) Who has the right, according to the system and constitution of the state, to issue laws and legislation? Is there any authority, be it a council, body or individual, that possesses the right to issue laws and legislation? Is there any council that has the power to issue legislation, without whose approval legislation cannot be passed, but with whose approval laws may be passed even if they go against the ruling of Allah and the ruling of His Messenger (ﷺ)? Or is the foundation of the systems and laws that it promulgates the shari'ah of Allah, so that the shari'ah of Allah is ruling and everyone submits to that, as is the case when Islam rules and it is applied in the correct manner?

---

[1] *Aḍwaa' al-Bayaan*, 4/92-93.

Undoubtedly the purely administrative systems will differ based on the above, depending on examining any given system and the overlapping of rulings.

b) Does this system include anything that goes against shari'ah or not? Going against shari'ah here refers to all matters of life concerning which *shar'i* evidence has been narrated, whether in a text or by derivation and ijtihaad.

c) Matters which are the subject of scholarly dispute are not trivial matters with which those who make laws can play about as they like; rather they must be examined from two aspects:

(i) What we have mentioned first above, which is the source of legislation in the state.
(ii) What the evidence indicates is most likely to be correct, through the ijtihaad of the scholars and *mujtahideen*.

The Method of the *Salaf* in Classifying People as *Kaafir*

The view of the *salaf* with regard to this matter — the issue of classifying people as *kaafir* — is distinguished by a clear method which treads a middle path between the view of the *Murji'ah* and that of the *Khawaarij*. It should be noted that the dispute concerning that is based on the dispute concerning faith and its implications. Our intention here is not to discuss the issues of faith in detail, because that requires a book of its own, but we will refer to the matter in brief so as to demonstrate clearly the moderate nature of the view of the *salaf* (pious predecessors — may Allah have mercy on them).

This mistake which both the *Khawaarij* and the *Murji'ah* made was to think that faith is one indivisible entity, and that if one part of it was lacking, faith would be annulled altogether.

The *Khawaarij* and those who agreed with them said: the texts indicate that deeds are a part of faith, and based on this principle which they had set out, they said that if a deed or part of it is lacking, faith is lacking altogether; therefore they said that the one who committed a major sin was not a believer, and in the Hereafter he would abide in Hell forever.

The *Murji'ah* said: the texts prove that those who commit major sins, if they die believing in Allah Alone, will ultimately end up in Paradise. Because they believed in the principle mentioned above, which they and the *Khawaarij* were agreed upon — that faith is indivisible and if any part of it is lacking then faith is lacking altogether — they said that the only solution was to limit faith to belief in the heart, and leave actions out of it, because if we include actions in faith, then saying that part of it is lacking would imply that all of it is lacking; so we say what the *Khawaarij* say.

The result was that the *Khawaarij* denounced as a *kaafir* everyone who committed a major sin. For example, they said that unjust rule was a major sin, and that it was ruling by something other than that which Allah has revealed, so it was major *kufr*, even if it was only in a specific case, and even if the one who did that believed that he was disobeying Allah. They said the same of the one who consumed *riba*, or drank wine, or committed adultery — even if he did not regard that as being permissible. Undoubtedly this is misguidance and a serious deviation.

The *Murji'ah* ended up contradicting themselves in a strange manner when they said: everyone who believes in his heart is a believer even if he does what he does. So in their view, no person could become a *kaafir*, regardless of whatever he did, so long as he believed in his heart. When it was said to them, what is your view of one who knowingly insults Allah or prostrates to an idol or stomps with his feet on the *Muṣ-ḥaf* — is this not *kufr* according to the consensus of the Muslims? They say, Yes it is. Then it is said to them, this could be done by one who believes in his heart, but he is stubborn or arrogant, or he thinks that this is a trivial matter; so one who believes in his heart could be guilty of *kufr*. This is the case of *Iblees*, Pharaoh and the Jews, who knew the truth in their hearts, but they were *kaafir* because of their stubbornness and arrogance.

The *Murji'ah* gave an answer which contradicts common sense when they said: everyone who commits *kufr* in word or deed, that is a sign of the lack of belief in his heart or of his ignorance and lack of knowledge.[2]

This is contrary to reality, as indicated above in the case of Pharaoh, who knew of his Lord, but despite that he did not believe and follow the Messenger of Allah Moosa (Moses) (عليه السلام), so he was one of the *kuffaar*. Allah (سبحانه وتعالى) says:

﴿ وَجَحَدُوا۟ بِهَا وَٱسْتَيْقَنَتْهَآ أَنفُسُهُمْ ظُلْمًا وَعُلُوًّا ... ﴿١٤﴾ ﴾

> ﴿And they belied them [those *aayaat*] wrongfully and arrogantly, though their ownselves were convinced thereof...﴾ *(Qur'an 27: 14)*

The same was true of *Iblees*, and of the Jews, who,

﴿ ... يَعْرِفُونَهُۥ كَمَا يَعْرِفُونَ أَبْنَآءَهُمْ ... ﴿١٤٦﴾ ﴾

> ﴿...Recognize him [Muhammad] as they recognize their sons...﴾ *(Qur'an 2: 146; 6: 20)*

We have discussed the views of the *Murji'ah* in detail above, in the chapter on specious arguments.

As for *Ahl as-Sunnah*, Allah has guided them to the truth and the moderate path, whereby they believe that faith is composed of words, belief and action; it increases when one worships and obeys Allah,

---

[2] Some of them said: he may be a *kaafir* outwardly whilst in reality he is a believer.

and it decreases when one disobeys Him and sins. The principle which the *Khawaarij* and *Murji'ah* believed in is a corrupt principle, because the fact that one aspect of faith may be lacking does not mean that the rest of it is also lacking; rather it may or may not be lacking, depending on the degrees and branches of faith. The one who commits a major sin — if he does not regard that as being permissible — is a believer whose faith is lacking, or he is a disobedient believer. In the Hereafter he will be subject to the will of Allah; if He wills, He will punish him and if He wills, He will forgive him. Although the *salaf* were certain of the general warning — as indicated by the texts — no one will abide in Hell forever except the *kuffaar*. People who committed major sins, apart from the *kuffaar*, will — after they have been punished in the Fire — be brought forth from it and admitted to Paradise.

The methodology of the *salaf* in classifying a person as a *kaafir* is based on a number of principles, including:

1 - That everyone who declares his Islam and pronounces the *Shahaadatayn* is a Muslim, with all the rights and duties of any other Muslim. We do not describe any of the people of the *qiblah* (i.e., Muslims) as being beyond the pale of Islam except in very clear-cut cases. Hence the error of some sects and groups, who claim that all the people are *kaafir*, is quite obvious. Those groups claim that all the people are *kaafir*, except those whose Islam is proven in the manner dictated by them, such as joining their groups and the like. This may have been correct in the *jaahili* society of Makkah at the time of the Messenger (ﷺ), before the conquest, and in idolatrous or Christian societies in which the *kuffaar* are prevalent and the Muslims form a minority. Yet and despite that, whoever pronounces the *Shahaadatayn* and does not commit any action that invalidates Islam, is a Muslim.

Those who classify Muslim societies — for whatever reason — as being *kaafir* or apostate societies, and therefore regard each individual member as being a *kaafir* unless he declares his Islam, are extremists who are deviating from the way of the *salaf* (may Allah have mercy on them). Look at the story of Usaamah, when he killed the man who was fighting him after he had uttered the *Shahaadatayn* — what did the Messenger (ﷺ) say to him?[3]

2- That a believer cannot be labeled a *kaafir* for each and every sin, in contrast to the view of the *Khawaarij* and those who agreed with them, and *kufr* may take the form of actions, in contrast to the view of the *Murji'ah* who said that no one can be labeled as a *kaafir* except the one who disbelieves (in his heart), even if he does whatever he does.

The *Ahl as-Sunnah* said that the type of *kufr* and *shirk* which put one beyond the pale of Islam may take the form of words spoken on the tongue, actions of the heart (beliefs in the heart) and deeds of the body. Hence they spoke of matters which nullify Islam, which include different kinds of *kufr* and *shirk*.

The Muslim may be one of those who utter the *Shahaadatayn* and perform the pillars of Islam, and do many kinds of good deeds, yet he may be beyond the pale of Islam when he does something that nullifies Islam. The *Murji'ah* went astray concerning this issue, because they thought that everyone who uttered the *Shahaadatayn* and entered Islam could never leave Islam unless he disbelieved in a manner that showed there was a lack of belief in his heart:

a) For example, the person who worships someone other than Allah, such as a *wali* (saint) or the occupant of a grave. They

---

[3] Muslim, *Kitaab al-Eemaan, Baab Taḥreem Qatl al-Kaafir ba'da qawlihi Laa ilaaha illa-Allah*, hadith no. 96, 97.

said that he cannot be described as a *kaafir* unless he believes that this *wali* or the occupant of this grave had independent powers of creation, because this is the meaning of *Tawḥeed al-Uloohiyah* (the unity of the Divine), according to them; if a person directs his worship to anyone other than Allah, if it is not accompanied by any belief in *shirk*, then this is not *shirk*, in their view. This is mistaken, because the *mushrikeen* who worshipped idols used to believe that the only Creator and Provider was Allah, and that the idols were intermediaries who would bring them closer to Allah; despite that, they were *mushrikeen* and *kuffaar*.

b) Some of them regarded it as permissible to prostrate to the sun, the moon and the heavenly bodies, and to offer sacrifices and make vows to them. Then they said: this is not *shirk*, so long as one does not believe that they are in control; but if one regards them as a means of drawing closer to Allah or as intermediaries, this is not *shirk*.[4]

c) Concerning the topic which we are discussing here, the *Murji'ah* said: whoever rejects the shari'ah of Allah and replaces it with man-made laws which go against the laws of Allah, is not a *kaafir* unless he regards that as being permissible, because *kufr* is the matter of beliefs only. This is a serious mistake, as explained above.

3 - The one who examines the texts that have been narrated concerning the topic of faith and its opposites, namely *kufr* and *shirk*, will inevitably — in order to be consistent — have to say that hypocrisy, *kufr*, *shirk*, wrongdoing and rebellion, etc., include major types which put one beyond the pale of Islam, and lesser types which do not put one beyond the pale of Islam. Therefore a person may

---

[4] *Dar' Ta'aaruḍ al-'Aql wan-Naql* by Ibn Taymiyah, 1/227.

combine obedience and disobedience, *kufr* and faith, Islam and hypocrisy, but this does not put him beyond the pale of Islam. This is unlike the view of the *Murji'ah* who interpret the texts as all meaning the same thing. Every mention of *kufr*, hypocrisy or *shirk* mentioned in the texts, in their view, is a major form which puts a person beyond the pale of Islam. This is misguidance and deviation which involves accepting some texts whilst overlooking others which state that some of those who do these things are still believers, as is well known and well established from the texts.

4 - There is a difference between a general ruling that leads to classifying some actions or some matters which constitute *kufr*, and applying that in a specific case.

Two groups erred concerning this matter:

The first group thought that an individual can never be labeled as a *kaafir*, so they closed the door to apostasy by saying that it is too difficult to apply the ruling to an individual, because none of the conditions for classifying him as a *kaafir* is present, or because there is an impediment which prevents us from doing so. We referred to this briefly above, when discussing the view of the *Murji'ah* that no one can be classified as a *kaafir* except the one who disbelieves in his heart. What this means is that we cannot judge any individual to be a *kaafir* for any words or deeds - no matter how much they contradict Islam — because he may be a believer by virtue of belief in his heart.

The other group thought that if there is a general ruling which describes some actions as being *kufr*, this is applicable to all individuals who do this action, so they will all be classified as *kaafir* individually, without any need to examine each individual case on its own merits, to see whether the conditions of classifying a person as a *kaafir* apply in this case, or whether any impediment which prevents us from doing so is present. The *Ahl as-Sunnah*, however, do not say that a specific individual can never be classified as a *kaafir*, and they do not apply the label of *kaafir* to every person who commits an evil action without seeing whether this case is qualified to be judged as *kufr*.

If we examine what the *salaf* (may Allah have mercy on them) did, we will see that they often applied the label of *kufr* to some actions, innovations, opinions and the like. Whenever they wanted to apply this label to an individual, they were very strict in applying it, because sometimes the one who does such things may be ignorant, or it may be a case of excusable misunderstanding, or the person may be new in Islam, or there may be some other reason why he should not be judged to be a *kaafir*.

Shaykh al-Islam Ibn Taymiyah said: "The ideas or actions which are described as *kufr* in the Qur'an, Sunnah and scholarly consensus should be regarded as such in general terms, as is indicated by the *shar'i* evidence. For the matter of judging whether a person has faith or not is subject to the rulings received from Allah and His Messenger, it is not something that is for people to judge based on speculation or on their whims and desires. We should not judge every person who says such things to be a *kaafir* unless it is proven that he meets the conditions of *kufr* and the impediments to classifying him as such are shown to be absent. An example is the case of one who says that alcohol and *riba* are permitted, because he is new in Islam, or because he grew up in a remote desert, or he heard words which he denied and did not believe that they were from the Qur'an or from the *aḥaadeeth* of the Messenger (ﷺ).

Similarly, some of the *salaf* rejected things until it was proven to them that the Prophet (ﷺ) had said that. And the *ṣaḥaabah* (Companions) doubted some things, such as seeing Allah (in the Hereafter), etc., until they asked the Messenger of Allah (ﷺ) about that. For example, the one who said, "When I die, turn me into dust and scatter me in the sea, so that I am lost from the grip of Allah (and not resurrected and punished)," and so on. Such people cannot be classified as *kaafir* until proof is established against them, as Allah (ﷻ) says:

﴿ ... لِئَلَّا يَكُونَ لِلنَّاسِ عَلَى ٱللَّهِ حُجَّةٌۢ بَعْدَ ٱلرُّسُلِ ... ﴿١٦٥﴾ ﴾

﴾...In order that mankind should have no plea against Allah after the [coming of] Messengers...﴿

(Qur'an 4: 165)

Allah has forgiven this ummah for its mistakes and for what they forget."[5]

Imam Aḥmad and others applied the label of *kufr* to ideas of *Jahamiyah*, denial of the attributes of Allah, saying that the Qur'an was created, denying that we will see Allah (in the Hereafter) and denying the Divine will and decree, but they did not label any individual as a *kaafir* except in a few cases, where the person's *kufr* was proven by the conditions being met and the absence of any impediments. Only then did they carry out the rulings of apostasy such as executions etc.

5- When a group is fought, that does not necessarily mean that they are believed to be *kaafir*. This is another issue concerning which some people err, and think that everyone whom we are obliged to fight or whom it is permissible to fight is a *kaafir* and an apostate. This is obviously incorrect. It is well known from the rulings of Islam that execution or fighting may involve people who are not apostates, such as executing a murderer or fighting rebels, just as fighting may be directed against oppressors or rebels, without classifying them as *kaafir*. Indeed, the *ṣaḥaabah* were unanimously agreed that they

[5] *Majmoo' al-Fataawa*, 35/165-166.

should fight some people — such as the *Khawaarij* — but there was some dispute among the scholars as to whether they were *kaafir*; the most likely view is that they are not *kaafir*, even though they committed some innovations such as denouncing the people as *kaafir* and fighting them.[6] On the other hand, the *Ahl adh-Dhimmah* such as the Jews and Christians are *kaafir* beyond doubt, but they are not to be fought except when they break the treaty... and so on.

From the above — and we are discussing the issue of ruling by something other than that which Allah has revealed — we may say that this book is aimed at explaining the ruling of Islam and what the scholars said concerning this issue. This is a theoretical study which explains the ruling of shari'ah through the texts and words of the scholars on this matter. With regard to applying it in an appropriate manner — in a particular country, this is something which we need to study very carefully, then apply the ruling, whilst paying attention to the conditions and impediments of classifying a person as a *kaafir* — as stated above. And Allah knows best.

---

[6] *Majmoo' al-Fataawa*, 3/282, 7/217-218, 28/500, 518.

CONCLUSION

It becomes clear that the issue of ruling by something other than that which Allah has revealed is one of the most serious issues that have arisen in recent times, and is a calamity which the Muslims are going through. It has become widespread and prevalent, and it is one of the reasons for the sorry state of the Muslim ummah, which grieves every Muslim who feels protective jealousy towards his religion.

It is essential for the scholars, seekers of knowledge and *du'aat* (Muslim missionaries) who call people to Allah to undertake their obligations towards this serious matter and explain to the people — rulers and subjects alike — the importance of ruling by that which Allah has revealed and of referring for judgement to the shari'ah in all matters. They should point out that this is obligatory, and the Muslim has no choice in this matter at all, and they should tell them of the danger of turning away from the ruling of Allah and referring for judgement to something else among the systems, laws and legislation of *jaahiliyah*. I hope that this study will form a humble contribution towards explaining the truth of this matter. I ask Allah to grant me sincerity and purity of intention, and to make this work beneficial to others.

We have established — in this study — a number of important points which may be summed up as follows:

1- The status of ruling by that which Allah has revealed in Islamic *'aqeedah*. This is connected to *'aqeedah* in a number of ways, such as belief in Allah, the obligation to obey Him, affirmation of His names and attributes, the testimony that Muhammad is the Messenger of Allah, and what is implied by the twin testimony of faith, the testimony that there is no god but Allah and the testimony that Muhammad is the Messenger of Allah (ﷺ).

2 - The texts which indicate that it is obligatory to refer for judgement to the laws of Allah are many and varied. They describe those who turn away from that sometimes as *mushrikeen*, sometimes as *kuffaar* and sometimes as hypocrites. The variety of the evidence is an indication of how important and serious the matter is, for both individuals and the ummah, when they turn away from the laws of Allah and from obeying Him and His Messenger (ﷺ).

3 - Ruling by something other than that which Allah has revealed may take two forms:

(i) It may constitute major *kufr* which puts one beyond the pale of Islam. This may vary, but it is not restricted to cases of regarding it as being permitted or of denying that which Allah has revealed, as some people claim. Rather it includes denial and believing it to be permitted, but it also includes promulgating legislation that goes against the laws of Allah and imposing *jaahili* laws and making them binding.

(ii) It may constitute lesser *kufr* which does not put one beyond the pale of Islam. This is when there is injustice and oppression in individual cases, provided that the judge believes that he is a sinner and that the ruling of Allah is true. This is still a major sin, and is worse than many other major sins.

The condition in this case — as in the case of the major sins of adultery, theft and *riba* — is that it should not be regarded as being permissible. If it is regarded as being permissible, then the one who is doing that is a *kaafir*, because regarding what is forbidden as being permissible, in and of itself, nullifies Islam, as is well known.

4 - Discussion of the comment of Ibn 'Abbaas on the *aayah*:

﴿ ... وَمَن لَّمْ يَحْكُم بِمَآ أَنزَلَ ٱللَّهُ فَأُولَٰٓئِكَ هُمُ ٱلْكَٰفِرُونَ ﴿٤٤﴾ ﴾

﴾...And whosoever does not judge by what Allah has

revealed, such are the *kaafiroon* [i.e. disbelievers].﴾
(Qur'an 5: 44),

that it is a lesser form of *kufr*, and explaining the truth of the matter.

Refuting those who quote this report and ignore the many other texts on this topic, by which I mean the texts of the Qur'an and Sunnah, and the words of the *ṣaḥaabah*, and even that which is narrated from Ibn 'Abbaas himself concerning this matter.

5- There have been various attempts to change the shari'ah of Allah, which the scholars of Islam confronted. Several examples have been given in this book, which are of interest to those who study the history of the Muslim ummah and related ideological issues.

6- Those who hold opposing views quote many specious arguments, which they try to promote and try to prove that this serious issue does not really matter. This book is an attempt to respond to them from a number of angles.

I have also discussed the specious arguments of those who go to extremes with regard to this topic and label people as *kaafir* even in specific cases.

7- Finally, discussion of these topics requires a cautious approach to its results and implications. We should not confuse the legislative system with the purely administrative system, or hasten to label people as *kaafir*. We should be careful when examining specific cases to make sure that the conditions for classifying an individual as a *kaafir* have been fulfilled and to ensure that there are no impediments to doing so. The book ends with a discussion of these matters.

Finally, I say that this is my effort, in which I have relied upon Allah, and then upon the evidence. I have based this work on the views of the *aimmah* (the leading Muslim jurists and theologians) — the Imams of *Ahl as-Sunnah wal-Jamaa'ah*, classical and modern. I ask

Allah to benefit the Muslim ummah by this book, and to make my intention purely and sincerely for His sake. I ask him not to deprive me, my parents, my *shaykhs* and my Muslim brothers of the reward.

May Allah bless our Prophet Muhammad and his family and Companions, and grant them abundant peace. Praise be to Allah, the Lord of the Worlds.

REFERENCES

* The Noble Qur'an

Aḥkaam Ahl adh-Dhimmah: Ibn al-Qayyim, edited by Ṣubḥi aṣ-Ṣaaliḥ, 2nd ed. 1401 H, Daar al-'Ilm lil-Malaayieen, Beirut.

Aḥkaam al-Qur'an: Ibn al-'Arabi al-Maaliki, edited by 'Ali Muḥammad al-Bajaawi, 2nd ed. Ḥalabi, Egypt 1387 H.

Aḥkaam al-Qur'an: Jaṣṣaaṣ, Daar al-Fikr, Beirut.

Irshaad as-Saari: Qasṭalaani, 2nd Bolaq edition.

Izaalat al-Wa'atha' 'An-Ittibaa' Abi Sha'atha': Saalim ibn Ḥamoud as-Samaa'eeli, edited by Syed Ismaa'eel Kaashif, Cairo 1399 H, Published by Ministry of National Heritage and Cultural, Sulṭanate of 'Oman.

Asbaab an-Nuzool : Abul Ḥasan 'Ali bin Aḥmad al-Waaḥidi, edited by 'Iṣaam ibn 'Abdul Muḥsin al-Ḥameedaan, 1st edition 1411 H, Daar al-Islaaḥ, Dammam.

Aḍwaa' al-Bayaan : Shinqeeṭi, Maṭb'ah al-Madani, 1386 H.

Al-'Itiṣaam : Shaaṭibi, Maktabah at-Tijaaria al-Kubra, Egypt. Another publication, second part, edited by Hisham aṣ-Ṣeeni, computerized publication.

'Iraab al-Qur'an : Zajjaaj, Beirut Print.

Al-'Ilaam : Zarkali, 6th publication, Daar al-'Ilm lil-Malaayieen Beirut.

'Ilaam as-Sunnah al-Manshoorah : Shaykh Ḥaafiẓ Ḥukmi, edited by Aḥmad 'Aloosh Madkhali, Maktbah ar-Rushd, Riyadh 1st edition. 1414 H.

'Ilaam al-Mooqi'een 'An Rabbil 'Aalameen : Ibn Qayyim al-Jawzia, edited by 'Abdur Raḥman al-Wakeel, Daar al-Kutub al-Ḥadeethah, Cairo. Also by Idaarah aṭ-Ṭabaa'ah al-Muneeriyah. Egypt.

Iqtiḍaa' aṣ-Ṣiraaṭ al-Mustaqeem : *Shaykh al-Islam* Ibn Taymiyah, edited by Dr. Naaṣir al-'Aql, 1st edition. 1404 H.

Al-Iqnaa' Fi Fiqh al-Imaam Aḥmad ibn Ḥanbal : Sharfuddin Musa al-Ḥajaavi, edited and annotated by Abdullaṭeef Muḥammad Moosa as-Subki, Maktabah at-Tijaariah al-Kubra, Egypt, Al-Maṭba'ah al-Miṣria al-Azhar.

Anṣaab al-Ashraaf : Biladhuri, al-Qism ath-Thaalith, edited by 'Abdul 'Azeez ad-Doozi, Beirut 1398 H.

Al-Eemaan : *Shaykh al-Islam* Ibn Taymiya, 3rd ed. 1392 H, Al-Maktab al-Islami. Second print under *Majmoo' al-Fataawa* compiled by Ibn Qasim. Another edition, edited by Maḥmood Ḥasan Abu Naaji ash-Shaybaani, published by Al-'Abaykaan, Riyadh.

Al-Eemaan al-Awsaṭ : *Shaykh al-Islam* Ibn Taymiya, published under *Majmoo' al-Fataawa* vol. VII compiled by Ibn Qasim.

Al-Bidaayah wan Nihaayah : Ibn Katheer, 1st edition. Maṭba'ah as-Sa'adah. photocopy, Maktabah al-Ma'aarif, Beirut and Maktabah an-Naṣr al-Ḥadithah, Riyadh 1386 H.

Al-Badr aṭ-Ṭaali' bi Maḥaasin min ba'd al-Qarn as-Saabe' : Shawkaani, Muḥammad bin 'Ali 1st edition. 1348 H, Maṭba'ah as-Sa'adah, Cairo.

Taaj al-'Uroos : Sharaḥ al-Qaamoos, Zubaydi, Al-Maṭba'ah al-Khayriah, Egypt 1307 H.

Taareekh Baghdaad : Khaṭeeb al-Baghdadi, 1st edition 1349 H, Maktabah al-Khanji, Cairo, Maktaba al-'Arabia, Baghdad. And Maṭba'ah as-Sa'adah, Cairo.

Taareekh Damishq : Ibn 'Asaakir, MS, Maktabah ad-Daar, Madeenah an-Nabawiyah.

Taareekh Faatiḥ al-'Aalam Jahaankushaey [*Taareekh 'Aṭa Malik al-Juwayni*] : 'Aṭa Malik al-Juwayni, edited by Muḥammad at-Tonji, 1st edition 1405 H, Daar al-Mallaaḥ lit-Ṭaba'ah wan Nashr.

At-Taareekh al-Kabeer : Imam Bukhari, printed under the supervision of Muḥammad 'Abdul Mu'eed Khan, India.

Toḥfat al-Aḥwadhi Sharaḥ Jaame' at-Tirmidhi : Ṣafi ur-Raḥman Mubarakpuri, Letho Printing, India.

Toḥfat al-Baari Sharḥ Ṣaḥeeḥ al-Bukhari : *Shaykh* Zakariya al-Anṣari, Al-Maymania in Egypt along with Irshaad as-Saari: Qasṭalaani.

Taḥkeem ash-Shari'ah wa Da'awi al-'Ilmaania : Dr. Ṣalaaḥ aṣ-Ṣaawi, 1st edition Daar Ṭeebah, Riyadh 1412 H.

Taḥkeem al-Qawaaneen : *Shaykh* Muḥammad bin Ibraheem, 1st edition.

At-Tadmuriyah : *Shaykh al-Islam* Ibn Taymiyah, edited by Muḥammad bin 'Awdah as-Sa'awi, 1st edition 1405 H.

Ta'ẓeem Qadr aṣ-Ṣalaat : Imam Muḥammad bin Naṣr al-Muruzi, edited by Dr. 'Abdur Raḥman bin 'Abdul Jabbar al-Fareew'aee, 1st edition 1406 H, Maktabah ad-Daar, Madeenah al-Munawwarh.

Tafseer Ibn Abi Ḥaatim vol. 1 : Edited by Aḥmad 'Abdullah al-'Imari az-Zahrani. Part 1 from *Aal-'Imraan*, edited by Ḥikmat Basheer Yaseen, 1st edition 1408 H, Maktaba ad-Daar, Madeenah.

Tafseer al-Baghawi : *Ma'alim at-Tanzeel* edited by An-Namr, Jumu'ah, Al-Ḥarsh, Daar Ṭeebah, 1st edition 1409 H, Riyadh.

Tafseer aṭ-Ṭabari : Edited by Maḥmood Muḥammad Shaakir, Daar al-Ma'aarif, Egypt.

Tafseer Ibn Sa'di : Edited by Muḥammad Zahri an-Najjaar, Al-Muassasah as-Sa'eediyah.

Tafseer al-Qur'an : 'Abdur Razzaaq aṣ-Ṣan'aani, edited by Muṣṭafa Muslim Muḥammad, 1st edition 1410 H, Maktaba ar-Rushd, Riyadh.

Tafseer al-Qur'an al-'Aẓeem : Ibn Katheer, edited by Ghunaym, 'Aashoor, Al-Banna. Printed by Ash-Sh'ab, Cairo. Another printing, Maṭba'ah al-Istiqaamah, 3rd edition, Cairo, 1376 H.

Tafseer al-Qurṭubi, al-Jaame' al-Aḥkaam al-Qur'an : Abu 'Abdullah al-Qurṭubi, 2nd edition 1382 H, Daar al-Kutub, Cairo.

Tafseer Mujaahid : Edited by 'Abdur Raḥman aṭ-Ṭaahir ibn Muḥammad as-Soorti, Maṭba'ah ad-Doha al-Ḥadeethah, Qatar. Photographic printing in two volumes: Al-Manshooraat al-'Ilmiyah, Beirut.

Tahdheeb al-Aathaar : Aṭ-Ṭabari, edited by Naaṣir Rasheed, 'Abdul Qayyum 'Abd Rabb an-Nabi, 1402 H, Maṭba'ah aṣ-Ṣafa, Makkah al-Mukarramah.

Tahdheeb al-Kamaal : Mazi, MS in three volumes, Daar al-Maa'moon lit-Toraath; Another copy edited by Bashaar 'Awaad and published by Muassasah ar-Risaalah, Beirut.

Tayseer al-'Azeez al-Ḥameed fi Sharḥ Kitaab at-Tawḥeed : *Shaykh* Sulayman ibn 'Abdullah ibn Muḥammad ibn 'Abdul Wahhab, 4th edition 1400 H, Al-Maktab al-Islam, Beirut, Damascus.

Ath-Thiqaat : Abu Ḥaatim Muḥammad ibn Ḥibaan al-Bastee, 1st ed., Daa'irat al-Ma'aarif al-'Uthmaania, Ḥyderabad, India, 1402 H.

Jaame' Bayaan al-'Ilm wa Faḍlihi : Ibn 'Abdul Barr, edited by 'Abdul Kareem al-Khaṭeeb, Egypt. Other copy published by Idaarah aṭ-Ṭaba'ah al-Muneeriyah, Cairo.

Jaame' al-'Uloom wal-Ḥikam li ibn Rajab al-Ḥanbali : Edited by Shu'ayb al-Arna'ooṭ, Ibraheem Baajis, 1st printing 1411 H. Muassasah ar-Risaalah, Beirut.

Al-Jarḥ wat-Ta'deel : Ibn Abi Ḥaatim, 1st printing 1371 H, Daa'irat al-Ma'aarif al-'Uthmaania, Ḥyderabad, India.

Al-Jaame' Bayna's Ṣaḥeeḥayn - Bukhari wa Muslim: Imam al-Ḥumaydi, edited by 'Ali Ḥusayn al-Bawwaab, 1st printing 1419 H, Daar Ibn Ḥazm, Beirut, Distribution Daar aṣ-Ṣami'ee, Riyadh.

Al-Ḥadd al-Faaṣil Baynal Eemaan wal Kufr : 'Abdur Raḥman 'Abdul Khaliq, 2nd edition 1404 H, Ad-Daar as-Salafiyah, Kuwait.

Ḥaqeeqat al-Bid'ah wa Aḥkaamuha : Sa'eed ibn Naaṣir al-Ghamidi, 1st edition 1412 H, Maktabah ar-Rushd, Riyadh.

Ḥawl Taṭbeeq ash-Shari'ah : Muḥammad Quṭb, 1st printing 1411 H, Maktaba as-Sunnah, Cairo.

Al-Khuṭaṭ al-Maqreeziyah [*al-Mawa'ez wal I'tibaar*] : Al-Maqrizi, Bolaq edition.

Daar' Ta'arruḍ al-'Aql wan Naql : Ibn Taymiyah, edited by Muḥammad Rishaad Saalim, published by Jame'ah al-Imam Muḥammad ibn Sa'ood al-Islamia, Riyadh, 1400 H.

Ad-Durar as-Sunniah fil 'Ajoobah an-Najdiyah : Compiled by 'Abdur Raḥman ibn Muḥammad ibn Qaasim, 1st edition, 1356 H, Ummul Qura', reprinted by Daar al-Ifta' 1388H.

Ad-Durr al-Manthoor : Suyooṭi, Daar al-Fikr, Beirut, 1403 H.

Da'awi al-Manaw'een li Da'wat ash-Shaykh Muḥammad ibn 'Abdul Wahhab : 'Abdul 'Azeez ibn Muḥammad ibn Abdullaṭeef, Daar al-Waṭan, 1st edition 1412 H.

Daawlah al-Isma'eeliyah fi Iran : Muḥammad as-Sa'eed Jamaaluddin, Muassasah Sijil al-'Arab, Cairo, 1395 H.

Ad-Dawa' al-'Aajil fi Daf'i al-'Uduw aṣ-Ṣaai'l : Shawkaani, published under *Ar-Rasaa'il as-Salafiyah lish-Shawkaani*, photoprinting from the 1st print 1348 H, Daar al-Kutub al-'Ilmiyah, Beirut.

Rooḥ al-Ma'aani lil-Aaloosi : 2nd edition, Idaarah aṭ-Ṭaba'ah al-Muneeriyah, Cairo.

Ar-Rawayataan wal Wajhaan lil Qaaḍi Abi Ya'ala : Edited by 'Abdul Kareem al-Laaḥim, 1st printing 1405 H, Maktabah al-Ma'aarif, Riyadh.

Sabeel an-Najaat wal Fikaak : Ḥamad ibn 'Ateeq, edited by Al-Waleed ibn 'Abdur Raḥman al-Fariyaan, 1409 H.

60. *Sunan Abi Dawood* : Edited by 'Izzat ad-Du'aas, 1st edition 1388H. Muḥammad 'Ali as-Sayyid, Ḥimṣ.

Sunan at-Tirmidhi : Edited by 'Abdul Wahhaab Abdullaṭeef, 1st printing 1384 H. Other editions, vol 1-2 edited by Aḥmad Shaakir, vol. 3 edited by Muḥammad Fuw'ad 'Abdul Baaqi, vol. 4-5 edited by Ibraheem 'Uṭwah 'Awaḍ, printed by Muṣṭafa al-Baabi al-Ḥalbi.

As-Sunan al-Kubra : Bayhaqi 1st edition Daa'irat al-Ma'aarif al-'Uthmaniya, Ḥyderabad, India. photocopy printed by Daar al-Ma'aarifah, Beirut.

Siyar 'Aalaam an-Nubala : Dhahabi, edited by a number of researchers and supervised by Shu'aib al-Arana'ooṭ, Muassasah ar-Risalah, Beirut.

Shaa'n ad-Dua'a : Abu Sulayman al-Khaṭṭabi, edited by Aḥmad Yusuf ad-Daqqaaq, 1st edition 1404 H. Daar al-Ma'moon lit-Torath, Damascus and Beirut.

Shubhaat Ḥawl as-Sunnah, war Risaalah al-Ḥukm bighayr maa anzalallah : *Shaykh* 'Abdur Razzaq 'Afeefi, 1st edition Daar al-Faḍeelah, Riyadh, 1417 H.

Sharḥ Uṣool 'Itiqaad Ahl as-Sunnah wal Jama'ah : Laalkaee edited by Aḥmad Sa'ad Ḥamadaan, Daar Ṭeebah, Riyadh.

Sharḥ as-Sunnah: Barbahari, edited by Dr. Muḥammad bin Sa'eed al-Qaḥṭaani.

Sharḥ al-'Aqeedah aṭ-Ṭaḥaawiyah : Ibn Abil 'Izz al-Ḥanafi, Al-Maktab al-Islami. Another edition, edited by At-Turki and Arnaa'ooṭ, published by Muassasah ar-Risaalah.

Sharḥ al-Kawkab al-Muneer : Muḥammad ibn Aḥmad al-Futooḥi [Ibn an-Najjar], edited by Muḥammad az-Zaḥeeli and Nazeeh Ḥamaad. 1400 H, Kulliat ash-Shari'ah, Makkah, Markaz Iḥya' at-Torath al-Islami.

Sharḥ an-Nawawi 'Ala Ṣaḥeeḥ Muslim : 1st edition 1347 H, Muḥammad 'Abdullaṭeef, Al-Maṭba'ah al-Miṣriyah at Al-Azhar.

Ash-Shari'ah al-Islamia laa al-Qawaaneen al-Waḍa'iyah : Dr. 'Umar al-Ashqar, Daar ad-Da'wah, Kuwait 1404 H.

Shari'ah al-Kamaal Tashku min al-Ihmaal : Abdul Wahhab Rashid Ṣaliḥ, Daar 'Ammaar, Jordan 1404 H.

Ash-Shari'ah : Aajri, edited by Dr. 'Abdullah ad-Damiji, Daar al-Waṭan, Riyadh.

Sh'ab al-Eemaan : Bayhaqi, Ad-Daar as-Salafiya, India, 1st edition.

Ash-Shifa' : Qaḍi 'Ayaḍ, edited by 'Ali Muḥammad al-Bajawi, Al-Ḥalabi, Cairo.

Shifa' al-'Aleel : Ibn al-Qayyim, edited by Moḥammad Badruddin an-N'asaani al-Ḥalabi, 1st edition. Al-Maṭba'ah al-Ḥusaynia al-Miṣriya 1323 H.

Aṣ-Ṣaarim al-Maslool 'Ala Shaatim ar-Rasool : Ibn Taymiyah, edited by Muḥammad Muḥiuddin 'Abdul Ḥameed 1st edition. 1379 H / 1960C, Maṭba'ah as-S'aadah in Egypt, publisher Maktaba Taaj, Ṭanṭa. Another copy edited by Muḥammad al-Ḥalwaani and Muḥammad Kabeer Choudhry, 1417 H, Rimaada lin-Nashr and Daar Ibn Ḥazm.

Ṣaḥeeḥ al Bukhari : Muḥammad Fuw'ad 'Abdul Baqi, printed along with *Fatḥ al-Baari*, Al-Maṭba'ah as-Salafiyah, Cairo.

Ṣaḥeeḥ at-Targheeb wat-Tarheeb : Naaṣiruddin al-Albaani, 1st edition 1402 H, Al-Maktabah al-Islami, Beirut.

Ṣaḥeeḥ Sunan Abi Dawood : *Shaykh* Naaṣiruddin al-Albaani, Maktabah at-Tarbiyah li-Duwal al-Khaleej al-'Arabi, supervision, Zaheer ash-Shaaweesh.

Ṣaḥeeḥ Sunan at-Tirmidhi : Naaṣiruddin al-Albaani, Maktabah at-Tarbiyah li-Duwal al-Khaleej al-'Arabi, Riyadh.

Ṣaḥeeḥ Sunan an-Nasaai' : Naaṣiruddin al-Albaani, Maktabah at-Tarbiyah li-Duwal al-Khaleej al-'Arabi, Riyadh.

Ṣaḥeeḥ Muslim : Edited by Muḥammad Fuw'ad 'Abdul Baaqi, 1st edition 1374 H. Daar Iḥya al-Kutub al-'Arabiya, 'Eesa al-Baabi al-Ḥalabi.

Aṣ-Ṣalaat : Ibn al-Qayyim, printed under Majmmoo' al-Ḥadeeth an-Najdiyah, Al-Maṭba'ah as-Salafiyah, Cairo.

Aḍ-Ḍaw' al-Lamey'li-Ahli'l Qiran at-Taasey': Shamsuddin as-Sakhawi, printed by Al-Qudsi, Cairo, photocopy published by Daar Maktabah al-Ḥayaat, Beirut.

Aṭ-Ṭabaqaat al-Kubra : Ibn Sa'ad, Daar Ṣaadir 1380 H, Beirut.

'Umdah at-Tafseer 'an al-Ḥaafiẓ Ibn Katheer : Summary and edited by Aḥmad Muḥammad Shaakir, Daar al-Ma'aarif, Egypt 1376 H.

Ghaayah al-Maraam fi Takhreej Aḥaadeeth al-Ḥalaal wal Ḥaraam : *Shaykh* Naaṣiruddin al-Albaani 1st edition 1400 H / 1980 CE. Al-Maktab al-Islami.

Al-Ghayathi [*Ghayath al-Umam fi't Tayath aẓ-Ẓulm*] : Abul Ma'aali al-Juwayni, edited by 'Abdul 'Aẓeem ad-Deeb, 1st edition 1400 H, Shu'oon ad-Deeniyah, State of Qatar.

Fataawa Muḥammad Rasheed Raḍa : Compiled by Salaḥuddin al-Munajjid, Daar al-Kitaab al-Jadeed. 1st edition.

Fataawa wa Rasaa'il Muḥammad ibn Ibraheem : Compiled by Muḥammad ibn 'Abdur Raḥman ibn Qaasim, 1st edition. 1399 H. Maṭba'ah al-Ḥukoomah, Makkah.

Fatḥ al-Baari : Ibn Ḥajar al-'Asqalaani, al-Maṭba'ah as-Salafiyah, Cairo 1st edition.

Fatḥ al-Baari Sharḥ Ṣaḥeeḥ al-Bukhari: Ibn Rajab al-Ḥanbali, in an anthology 1st edition 1417 H, Maktabah al-Ghuraba' al-Athariyah, Madeenah an-Nabawiyyah.

Fatḥ al-Majeed Sharḥ Kitaab at-Tawḥeed : 'Abdur Raḥman ibn Ḥasan Aal-Shaykh, edited by Muḥammad Ḥaamid al-Faqee. Another edition edited by Al-Waleed ibn 'Abdur Raḥman al-Faryaan, Daar aṣ-Ṣamee', Riyadh.

Al-Furooq : Imam al-Qaraafi, 1st edition 1346 H, Daar Iḥya' al-Kutub al-'Arabia, Cairo.

Al-Faṣl fil Milal wal Aḥwaa wan Naḥl : Ibn Ḥazm, edited by Muḥammad Ibraheem Naṣr, 'Abdur Raḥman 'Umayra 1st edition 1402 H, Shirkah Maktabaat 'Ukaaẓ, Jeddah, Riyadh, Dammam.

Faḍaa'iḥ al-Baaṭiniyah : Abu Ḥaamid al-Ghazali, edited by 'Abdur Raḥman Badawi, Ad-Daar al-Qawmiyah lit-Ṭaba'ah wan Nashr, Cairo 1383 H, Ministry of Culture.

Al-Faqeeh wal Mutafaqqih : Khaṭeeb al-Baghdadi, edited by Isma'eel al-Anṣaari, Daar Iḥya' as-Sunnah an-Nabawiyah, 1395 H.

Qawaa'id al-Aḥkaam fi Maṣaaliḥ al-Anaam : 'Izz bin 'Abdus Salam, edited by Ṭaha 'Abdur Ra'oof Sa'ad 2nd edition 1400 H, Daar al-Jaleel, Beirut.

Al-Qawl al-Ma'moon fi Takhreej Maa Warada 'An Ibn 'Abbaas fi Tafseer: Wa man lam Yaḥkum Bima Anzalallah... : 'Ali Ḥasan 'Abdul Ḥameed al-Ḥalabi, 1st edition 1410 H, Daar al-Hijrah, Dammam.

Al-Kaamil fit Taareekh : Ibn Atheer, edited by Iḥsan 'Abbaas 1385 H, Daar Ṣaadir, Daar Beirut, Beirut.

Mu'aalifaat ash-Shaykh Muḥammad ibn Abdul Wahhab : Edited by a number of researchers, supervision and printing by Jame'ah al-Imam Muḥammad ibn Sa'ud al-Islamia.

Mujamma' az-Zawaa'id wa Manba' al-Fawaa'id : Noorudding 'Ali bin Abi Bakr al-Haythami, Maktabah al-Qudsi, Cairo 1352 H.

Al-Majmoo' ath-Thameen min Fataawa Ibn 'Uthaymeen : Compiled by Fahd Naaṣir as-Salmaan, Daar al-Waṭan, Riyadh 1410 H.

Majmoo' al-Fataawa Shaykh al-Islam Ibn Taymiya : Compiled by 'Abdur Raḥman ibn Muḥammad ibn Qaasim and Muḥammad, Maṭab'ey ar-Riyadh 1381 H.

Majmoo' al-Fataawa wa Maqaalaat Mutanaww'ah li Samaaḥat ash-Shaykh 'Abdul 'Azeez ibn Baaz : Compiled by Muḥammad ash-Shuway'er Daar al-Ifta' Riyadh.

Maḥaasin at-Taa'weel : Muḥammad Jamaludding al-Qaasmi, printed by 'Eesa al-Baabi al-Ḥalabi and Co. Cairo, 1376 H.

Al-Muḥarrir al-Wajeez fi Tafseer al-Kitaab al-'Azeez : Ibn 'Aṭiyah al-Undulusi, edited by Al-Majlis al-'Ilmi, Faas, Ministry of Awqaaf and Islamic Affairs, Kingdom of Morocco. 1395 H.

Mukhtaṣar aṣ-Ṣawaa'iq al-Mursalah li Ibn Qayyim: Summary by Muḥammad al-Mooṣali, 1st photo printing with correction by Muḥammad 'Abdur Razzaaq Ḥamzah, Distributed by Presidency of Iftaa' - Riyadh.

Madaarij as-Saalikeen : Ibn Qayyim al-Jawziyah, edited by Muḥammad Ḥaamid al-Faqee, Maṭba'ah as-Sunnah al-Muḥammadiya Cairo, 1375 H.

Masaa'il al-Eemaan : Qaḍi Abi Ya'ala, edited by Sa'ud 'Abdul 'Azeez al-Khalaf, Daar al-'Aaṣima, Riyadh 1410 H.

Al-Mustadrak 'Ala aṣ-Ṣaḥeeḥayn : Ḥaakim and along with it summary of Dhahabi, 1st photo printing in India, Al-Maṭboo'aat al-Islamia, Ḥalb, Muḥammad Ameen Damaj, Beirut, Distributed by Daar al-Baaz, Makkah.

Al-Musṭasfa : Abi Ḥaamid al-Ghazaali, Bolaq printing.

Musnad al-Imam Aḥmad : 1st Photo printing along with Al-Albaani's contents, Al-Maktab al-Islami, Daar Ṣaadir, Beirut.

Al-Muṣannaf fil Aḥadeeth wal Aathaar : Ibn Abi Shaybah, edited by 'Aamir al-'Umari al-Aa'ẓami, Ad-Daar as-Salafiyah, India.

Al-Muṣannaf li 'Abdur Razzaaq aṣ-Ṣan'ani : Edited by Ḥabibur Raḥman al-Aa'ẓami, 1st edition 1390 H, published by Academy of Letters (Al-Majlis-al-'Ilmi), South Africa and Pakistan, Distributed by Al-Maktab al-Islami, Beirut.

Ma'aani al-Qur'an wa I'rabihi liz-Zajjaaj : Printed by 'Aalam al-Kutub, Beirut 1408 H.

Al-M'ujam al-Kabeer : aṭ-Ṭabarani, edited by Ḥamdi 'Abdul Majeed as-Salafi, 1st edition 1399 H, ad-Daar al-'Arabia, Baghdaad.

Al-Ma'aarifa wa't-Taareekh : Abu Ya'qoob Yusuf bin Sulayman al-Fasawi, edited by Akram al-'Umazi, 2nd edition. Maktabah ad-Daar, Madeenah an-Nabawiyyah.

Al-Mughni li Ibn Qudaama al-Ḥanbali : Edited by At-Turky, Al-Ḥuluw, printed by Daar Hijr, Cairo.

Al-Maghol fi't Taareekh : Fuw'ad 'Abdul Mu'ṭee aṣ-Ṣayyaad, Daar an-Nahḍah al-'Arabia, Beirut 1400 H.

Al-Muntaqa, Sharḥ Mua'ṭṭa al-Imam Maalik : 'Abdul Waleed al-Baaji, printed by the Sulṭaan al-Maghrib al-Aqṣa 'Abdul Ḥafeeẓ 1st edition 1331 H, Maṭba'aah as-Sa'adah, Egypt.

Minhaaj as-Sunnah an-Nabawiyah : Ibn Taymiyah, edited by Muḥammad Rishaad Saalim, printed by Imam Muḥammad bin Sa'ud Islamic University.

Al-Muwaafiqaat fi Uṣool ash-Shari'ah : Abu Isḥaaq ash-Shaaṭibi edited by 'Abdullah Daraaz, al-Maktaba at-Tijaariah li-Muṣṭafa Muḥammad, Egypt. Another edition edited by Mashhoor Ḥasan Salman, Daar Ibn 'Affaan, al-Khobar, 1417 H.

Al-Mu'jaz Abi 'Imaar 'Abdul Kaafi al-'Ibaaḍi : Edited by 'Imaar Ṭaalibi, as part of Aara' al-Khawaarij al-Kalaamia, printed at al-Jaza'ir.

Meezaan al-'Itidaal fi Naqd ar-Rijaal lidh-Dhahabi : Edited by 'Ali Muḥammad al-Bajaawi, 1st edition. 1382 H. Daar Iḥya al-Kutub al-'Arabia, 'Eesa al-Baabi al-Ḥalabi, Cairo.

Nihaayah al-Muḥtaaj fi Sharḥ al-Minhaaj lir-Ramali : Muṣṭafa al-Baabi al-Ḥalabi and Co., Egypt, 1357 H.

Al-Manhaj al Asmaa' fi Sharḥ Asmaa' Allah al-Ḥusna : Muḥammad ibn Ḥamad al-Ḥamood, 1st edition 1406 H. Maktaba al-Mu'allah, Kuwait.

Hady as-Saari, Muqaddimah Fatḥ al-Baari : Ibn Ḥajar al-'Asqalaani, 1st printing by Salafiya al-Oola, Cairo.

Waq'ena al-Ma'aaṣir : Muḥammad Quṭb, 1st edition. 1407 H, Muassasah al-Madeenah lis-Ṣaḥafa, Jeddah.

Wathaa'iq al-Ḥuroob aṣ-Ṣaleebiyah wal Ghuzu al-Magholi : Muḥammad Maahir Ḥamadah, 1st edition.

Wujoob Taḥkeem Shar' Allah lish-Shaykh Ibn Baaz : 4th edition 1401 H, Daar al-Iftaa', Riyadh.

SYMBOLS' DIRECTORY

(سُبْحَانَهُ وَتَعَالَى) : *Subḥaanahu wa Ta'aala* - "The Exalted."

(ﷺ) : *Ṣalla-Allahu 'Alayhi wa Sallam* - "Blessings and Peace be upon him."

(عَلَيْهِ السَّلَام) : *'Alayhis-Salaam* - "May Peace be upon him."

(رَضِيَ اللهُ عَنْهُ) : *Raḍi-Allahu 'Anhu* - "May Allah be pleased with him."

GLOSSARY

A'immah	أئمة :	Sing. Imam; Leading Islamic jurists and scholars
Aayaat	آيات :	Sing. *Aayah*; Signs, Proofs, Verses of the Qur'an
'Aalameen	عالمين :	The worlds, the universe. Mankind, jinn and all that exists
Aḥkam al-Ḥaakimeen	أحكم الحاكمين :	The Most just of the Judges, an attribute of Allah
Kufr al-'amal	كفر العمل :	*Kufr* (disbelief) of action; disbelief manifested in action
Kufr al-I'tiqaad	كفر الاعتقاد :	*Kufr* of belief; disbelief
Al-Maṣaaliḥ al-Mursalah	المصالح المرسلة :	Matters which serve the common interests of the Muslims and which do not go against the basic principles of Islam, one of the major principles of ijtihaad in *Maaliki* and *Ḥanbali* school of *fiqh*
Al-Qadar	القدر :	Divine Decree
Al-Meezaan	الميزان :	The balance
Al-Maytah	الميتة :	A dead (animal)
Ar-Rabee'	الربيع :	The season of spring
Ahl al-Kalaam	أهل الكلام :	Scholastics, Islamic philosophers dealing with divinity
Ahl al-Ḥadeeth	أهل الحديث :	Hadith scholars, group strictly adhering to hadith

Ahl as-Sunnah wal Jamaa'ah	أهل السنة والجماعة :	The Sunnis, the people strictly adhering to the Sunnah of the Prophet, the *Khulafaa' ar-Rashidoon* and the early generation of the Muslims
Asbaab an-Nuzool	أسباب النزول :	Reasons for the revelation
Awliya'	أولياء :	Sing. *Wali*; Supporters, guardians, friends
Bid'ah	بدعة :	Reprenhensible innovation in religion, heresy
Baaṭini	باطني :	Esoteric, a group of the shi'ites, Isma'eelis
Daleel	دليل :	Proof, Evidence
Deen	دين :	Religion
Deeni	ديني :	Religious
Diyah	دية :	Blood money
Ḍa'eef	ضعيف :	Weak
Daar al-Islaam	دار الإسلام :	Muslim land
Eemaan	إيمان :	Faith
Fitan	فتن :	Sing. *Fitna*; Tribulations, trials, tests
Fiqh	فقه :	Islamic jurisprudence
Fisq	فسق :	Pl. *Fusooq*; A sin, disobedience to Allah, rebellion
Faasiqoon	فاسقون :	Sing. *Faasiq*; The rebellious, disobedients
Fuqahaa'	فقهاء :	Sing. *Faqeeh*; Scholars of Islamic

		jurisprudence, the Jurists
Fatwa	فتوى :	Religious verdict on particular issue/s
Ḥaraam	حرام :	Forbidden in Islamic Shari'ah
Ḥaraj	حرج :	Impediment, prohibitions, sin, guilt
Ḥasanah	حسنة :	Good deed
Ḥaajib	حاجب :	Chamberlain
Ḥalaal	حلال :	Permissible in Islamic Shari'ah
Iblees	إبليس :	Satan, devil
Iḥraam	إحرام :	The ritual garments for 'Umrah and Ḥajj
Istislaam	استسلام :	Submission, total surrender
Istiḥsaan	استحسان :	Application of discretion in legal matters, juristic preference
Ijmaa'	إجماع :	Consensus, agreement of Muslim jurists over certain issue/s, a source of Islamic jurisprudence
Jizyah	جزية :	Poll tax realized from non-Muslim subjects in an Islamic state, protection tax
Kufr	كفر :	Disbelief
Khawaarij	خوارج :	Lit. the secessionists; a group of people who seceded the camp of 'Ali, the fourth caliph of Islam and later emerged as a sect with specific dogmas. Committing sin is *kufr* to them
Kaafiroon	كافرون :	Sing. *Kaafir*; Disbelievers,

		arrogants
Khayr al-Ḥakimeen	خير الحاكمين :	The best of judges, an attribute of Allah
Kaaffatan	كافّة :	All Perfectly
Khulood	خلود :	Abiding
Kawnee	كوني :	Universal
Kaffaarah	كفّارة :	Expiation
Murji'ah	مرجئة :	A sect in Islam with the dogma that belief and action are not interrelated, belief is not affected by sin
Mu'tazilah	معتزلة :	A deviating sect in Islam adhering to the belief that sin puts a believer in the middle between *kufr* and Islam i.e., he is neither a disbeliever nor a Muslim. This sect is said to be founded by Waaṣil ibn 'Aṭaa'
Muṣ-ḥaf	مصحف :	The Divine Scripture
Murtad	مرتد :	Apostate
Mufassireen	مفسرين :	Sing. *Mufassir*; Exegetes - the commentators specially of the Qur'an
Muḥsin	محسن :	Good-doer, pious
Mushrikoon	مشركون :	Sing. *Mushrik*; Polytheists, associating deities besides Allah, believing in deities (more than one)
Muttaqoon	متقون :	Sing. *Muttaqi*; The pious, God-fearing

Munaafiqoon	منافقون :	Sing. *Munaafiq*; Hypocrites
Mujtahid	مجتهد :	Lit. Diligent; In Islamic terminology a legist formulating independent decisions in legal or theological matters, based on the interpretation and application of the four *Uṣool* as opposed to *muqallid* (imitator)
Muhaymin	مهيمن :	Overseer, overwhelming, the preserver of safety, an attribute of Allah
Minbar	منبر :	Pulpit
Muadh-dhin	مؤذن :	Caller of prayer
Mujrimoon	مجرمون :	Sing. *Mujrim*; Polytheists, sinners, criminals
Nidd	نِدّ :	Rivals, parallels, equals
Qiyaas	قياس :	Analogy, a principle source of Islamic jurisprudence
Qaḥṭ	قحط :	Famine
Qiṣaaṣ	قصاص :	Retaliation, Law of equality, punishment
Qaaḍi	قاضي :	Judge of Islamic shari'ah court
Ruboobiyah	ربوبية :	Lordship
Riba	ربا :	Usury, interest
Riddah	ردة :	Apostasy
Shari'ah	شريعة :	Islamic law

Salaf	سلف :	The pious predecessors
Siḥr	سحر :	Magic or witchcraft
Shirk	شرك :	Polytheism, associating deity with Allah
Ash-Shirk al-Akbar	الشرك الأكبر :	Major polytheism
Ash-Shirk al-Aṣghar	الشرك الأصغر :	Minor polytheism
Ṣaḥaabah	صحابة :	Sing. *Ṣaḥaabi*; The Companions of the last Prophet
Shahadatayn	شهادتين :	The twin testimony of faith. i.e witnessing that there is no deity save and except Allah, and Muhammad is His Messenger
Shayaṭeen	شياطين :	Sing. *Shayṭaan*; Devils
Ṣiddeeq	صديق :	True believer, title of Abu Bakr, the first caliph
Shar'i	شرعي :	Legislative, legal, Islamic
Shai'	شيء :	Anything
Sayi'ah	سيئة :	Bad, bad deed
Ṣadaqah	صدقة :	Charity
Ṣalaat	صلاة :	The prayer (obligatory / optional)
Tawḥeed al-'Ibaadah	توحيد العبادة :	The unity of Worship
Tawḥeed ar-Ruboobiyah	توحيد الربوبية :	The unity of Lordship
Tawḥeed al-Asma' waṣ-Ṣifaat	توحيد الأسماء والصفات :	The unity of the Divine names and Attributes

Ṭaghoot	طاغوت :	Lit. one who exceeds legitimate limits; In the Qur'an it refers to a creature who exceeds limits of his creatureliness and arrogates to himself godhead and lordship. First stage of man's error is *fisq*, second stage is that of *kufr* and the last stage where man not only rebels against Allah but also imposes his rebellious will on others. False gods. Leaders calling to establish non Islamic orders etc.
Ta'ṭeel	تعطيل :	Denying Allah's Attributes
Tamtheel	تمثيل :	Anthropomorphism
Taḥkeem al-Qawaaneen	تحكيم القوانين :	Referring (to man-made laws) for judgement
Ṭayyibaat	طيبات :	Sing. *Ṭayyib*; All that is good as regards foods, things, deeds, beliefs, persons
Ṭahaarah	طهارة :	The ritual purity
Ṭaalib al-'Ilm	طالب العلم :	A seeker of knowledge, student
Uloohiyah	ألوهية :	Divinity
Uṣool ad-Deen	أصول الدين :	The basic principles of religion (Islam)
'Uboodiyah	عبودية :	Servitude, total submission to Allah, bondage
Wali	ولي :	Protector, helper, saint
Zina	زنا :	Unlawful sexual relations, adultery, fornication
Ẓulm	ظلم :	Wrongdoing, disbelief.

INDEX OF THE QUR'AN

***Soorah* No./Name** — ***Aayah* No.** / Page No.

2 - Al-Baqarah	**256**/24,64, **112**/36, **128**/36, **208**/38, **213**/41,63,157, **165**/60, **166**/61, **159**/150, **85**/200, **275**/217, **278-279**/240, **34**/293, **146**/344
3 - Aal-'Imraan	**102**/13, **19-20**/30, **85**/31, **31-32**/32,65, **19**/37, **31**/54,60, **128**/69, **154**/70, **23**/79, **23-24**/80, **64**/108, **97**/163
4 - An-Nisaa'	**1**/13, **59**/28,155, **60-65**/28, **125**/30, **65**/32,48,53,94,156, **60**/50,90, **51**/65,84, **14**/67, **105**/68, **59-65**/86, **150-151**/200, **115**/218, **35**/226, **165**/350
5 - Al-Maa'idah	**44**/16,59,83,199,355, **50**/33,180,192,199, **13**/99, **41-50**/119, **93**/164, **87**/175, **103**/177, **95**/225, **17**/294, **73**/294, **41-44**/333
6 - Al-Ana'am	**114**/26,39,70, **57**/27,54, **121**/33,111,189, **136**/44,176, **1**/63,221, **62**/73, **57**/73,225, **139**/177
7 - Al-A'raaf	**54**/25,35,70, **87**/27
8 - Al-Anfaal	**39**/239
9 - At-Taubah	**31**/25,45,50,105, **19**/147, **111**/162, **37**/174, **103**/237, **66**/290, **65-66**/292
10 - Yunus	**59-60**/77
11 - Hud	**45**/27
12 - Yusuf	**40**/24,74, **39-40**/42, **67**/74
13 - Ar-Ra'd	**41**/27,74, **31**/73, **37**/73
16 - An-Naḥl	**89**/31, **116**/176

18 - Al-Kahf	**26**/33,72,74,188, **54**/150
21 - Al-Anbiyaa	**112**/71
24 - An-Noor	**51**/29, **46-52**/74, **63**/75,100
26 - Ash-Shu'araa'	**97-98**/62
27 - An-Naml	**14**/286,344
28 - Al-Qaṣaaṣ	**68**/26, **88**/39, **68-70**/76, **87-88**/76, **70**/179
31 - Luqmaan	**22**/31
33 - Al-Aḥzaab	**70-71**/14, **45-46**/45, **36**/77
34 - Saba'	**28**/170
36 - Yaa-seen	**60-61**/190
37 - Aṣ-Ṣaaffaat	**35**/113
39 - Az-Zumar	**46**/39, **29**/46, **65**/224
40 - Ghaafir/Al-Mumin	**60**/47, **12**/54
42 - Ash-Shoora	**10**/41,54,78,88,190, **21**/44, **17**/78, **11**/167
45 - Al-Jaathiyah	**18-19**/78
46 - Al-Aḥqaaf	**20**/148
47 - Muhammad	**26-28**/199, **9**/206
48 - Al-Fatḥ	**28**/179
49 - Al-Ḥujuraat	**1**/78
59 - Al-Ḥashr	**7**/32
60 - Al-Mumtaḥanah	**10**/27,72,79

INDEX OF HADITH

BOOK	CHAPTER / *BAAB*	NO.	PAGE NO.
Bukhari	*Kitaab al-Eemaan*	46	17, 286
	Kitaab al-Masafaah	2187	95
	Kitaab al-Manaaqib	3363	123
	Kitaab al-'Itiṣaam....	6801	149, 234
	Kitaab al-'Ilm	115	150
	Kitaab al-Fitan	6570	151
	Kitaab az-Zakaat	1312	231
Muslim	*Kitaab al-Eemaan*	49	40
	Kitaab al-Aqḍiya	3243	66
	Kitaab al-Ḥudood	3212	124
	Kitaab al-Imaarah	3491	148
Aḥmad	*Musnad Bani Hashim*	2102	127
Tirmidhi	*Kitaab al-Eemaan*	2544	236

Note: The above given reference nos. of hadith are from the CD programme "Hadith Encyclopedia" by Harf Information Technology.

TRANSLITERATION CHART

أ	a
آ . ى	aa
ب	b
ت	t
ة	h or t (when followed by another Arabic word)
ث	th
ج	j
ح	ḥ
خ	kh
د	d
ذ	dh
ر	r
ز	z
س	s
ش	sh
ص	ṣ
ض	ḍ
ط	ṭ

ظ	ẓ
ع	‘
غ	gh
ف	f
ق	q
ك	k
ل	l
م	m
ن	n
هـ – ه – ـه	h
و	w
و (as vowel)	oo
ي	y
ي (as vowel)	ee
ء	’ (Omitted in initial position)

َ	Fatḥah	a
ِ	Kasra	i
ُ	Ḍammah	u
ّ	Shaddah	Double letter
ْ	Sukoon	Absence of vowel